The Wars Within

The Wars Within

Peoples and States in Conflict

Robin M. Williams, Jr.

Cornell University Press

Ithaca and London

First published 2003 by Cornell University Press

Printed in the United States of America

Library of Congress Cataloging-in-Publication Data

Williams, Robin Murphy.
    The wars within : peoples and states in conflict / Robin M. Williams Jr.
        p.   cm
    Includes bibliographical references and index.
    ISBN 0-8014-4133-1 (cloth : alk. paper)
        1. Ethnic conflict.   2. Political violence.   3. Civil war.
    4. Genocide.   5. Ethnic relations.   I. Title.
    HM1121.W55   2003
    305.8—dc21

                                            2002156468

Cornell University Press strives to use environmentally responsible suppliers and materials to the fullest extent possible in the publishing of its books. Such materials include vegetable-based, low-VOC inks and acid-free papers that are recycled, totally chlorine-free, or partly composed of nonwood fibers. For further information, visit our website at www.cornellpress.cornell.edu.

Cloth printing   10 9 8 7 6 5 4 3 2 1

To Marguerite,
and to our daughters,
Nancy E. O'Connor and Susan Y. Williams,
and to the grandchildren,
Julia, Tara, Tyler, and Robin O'Connor,
and to the memory of Robin M. Williams, III

Contents

Contents

Acknowledgments

My debts to those who helped bring this book to completion are so many that not all can be noted appropriately here. But all who have been involved in this lengthy process will know that I deeply appreciate their contributions.

I do want to send special thanks to Judith Reppy, associate director of the Peace Studies Program at Cornell University, and to Sandra Kisner of that program for indispensable support, encouragement, and editorial assistance, without which this work never would have seen the light of day.

Similarly, I am grateful for the helpfulness of Cornell's Department of Sociology, to Victor Nee, its chairperson, and especially to Susan Meyer and her associates on the staff.

At the University of California, Irvine, vital support was provided by the Department of Sociology, by its successive chairpersons, Judith Treas, Francesca Cancian, and Judith Stephan-Norris, and by the unfailing and very special aid of Linda Cleland and Janice Meza. Remarkable also at UCI was the superb assistance of Vicki Ronaldson and Reneé Martin of the School of Social Sciences. I owe a separate vote of thanks to Paula Garb of the Global Peace and Conflict Studies program.

As numerous citations attest, the book profited greatly from the studies of Paul Brass, Milton Esman, Ted Robert Gurr, Donald L. Horowitz, Charles Tilly, and Pierre van den Berghe. Further mentions would make this short list even more invidious than it unavoidably may seem, but the other valuable contributors will be evident in the text to follow.

I greatly appreciate the wisdom of those who patiently read and critically commented on the successive drafts of a difficult manuscript. Thus a place of honor is reserved for Frank Bean, Donald P. Hayes, Phyllis Moen, Judith Reppy, and an anonymous reviewer. For major editing and revisions I am happy to thank our daughter, Nancy E. O'Connor of the College of Santa Fe. Her sister, Susan Y. Williams, likewise provided crucial assistance in the course of several revisions.

I want to emphasize the usual disclaimer that none of the persons mentioned bears the slightest responsibility for the remaining defects herein.

Finally, and not lesser, I appreciate the extraordinary editorial aid and counsel of Frances Benson, editor, and Melissa Oravec of Cornell University Press, who deserve much credit for whatever merit the reader finds here.

ROBIN M. WILLIAMS, JR.

Ithaca, New York

Preface

This will be a personal preface. I have been studying social conflict, especially ethnic and "racial," for more than fifty years—fascinated by it as an intellectual puzzle, as a crucial problem for public policy, as a moral challenge, as a source of incalculable human suffering.

My purpose in writing this book is to make the world more interesting, more complex, and more understandable. Beneath the obvious surface chaos of riots, pogroms, civil wars, and state-inflicted democides and genocides are recurrent patterns of correlation and sequence. Vast storehouses of historical and comparative data have provided grist for thousands of scholarly mills of description and causal analysis. We do not wholly lack the needed facts, nor are we bereft of essential concepts and theories. What is needed is a sifting of the evidence, a critical reexamination of the concepts, a clearing away of some erroneous interpretations, and a concise rendering of what appears to be the most reliable and valid knowledge we have.

A reviewer of this work has called upon the author to state clearly his own "position" or "stance" in arriving at conclusions and evaluating policies.

As I believe the whole book suggests, my personal value-position is that I abhor cruelty in all its forms, reject extreme ethnocentrism and unilateral ethnic dominations, support representative and responsive democratic political forms, and favor negotiation and consensus-building procedures. At the same time, I recognize the prevalence of warfare and oppression and their deep and widespread sources.

My stance concerning a commitment to a single disciplinary or theoretical "school" is that I find it unnecessary and misleading to thus constrict the attempt to explain ethnic conflict. Accordingly, this book draws freely on concepts, hypotheses, data, and explanatory schemes from several academic disciplines. The practical methodological motto is: use what works best for the problem at hand. By "works best" I mean those concepts and procedures that most clearly produce reliable knowledge that can be checked and refined by criticism, replication, and new data.

The twentieth century was the bloodiest century in history. The statistics numb the mind. Although estimates vary widely, the tale of death and destruction is monumental: since 1900 some 115 million persons killed in battles—plus perhaps an equal number of civilian fatalities (Tilly 1992, 67). These were mass killings in organized wars, but, as we note in the introduction, the slaughter was not confined to wars between states, for governments have savaged their own people—possibly as many as 170 million killed in democides within states (Rummel 1994).

Even since World War II, the basic facts are stark. The vast majority of deaths from collective violence since 1945 have been within national states rather than between states; credible estimates say some 80 percent. The percentage of all battle deaths that were deaths in civil wars has risen from about 7 percent in the 1930s to around 90 in the 1990s. The world total of refugees may be close to 40 million. Since World War I genocides and other mass killings greatly increased, and states are now the greatest killers of their own people. In the closing decade of the twentieth century the number of wars per year continued to fluctuate between 25 and 35, rain or shine, Cold War or not.

In all this, the good news is that by the end of the 1990s substantial numbers of violent ethnopolitical conflicts were deescalating (23 of 59), and the number of new ethnic rebellions was rapidly declining (Gurr 2000, 164, 180).

The long-term rise in ethnopolitical violence extended from the 1950s to about 1993. Since 1994, however, there has been a moderate decrease in the number of ethnic rebellions. Few new armed ethnonational conflicts began after 1994, and violent secessionist outbreaks have sharply declined (Gurr 2000, 275–77). Gurr suggests that a global shift is underway from warfare to a politics of accommodation. Whether or not these changes foretell a long-term trend remains to be seen, but at least more conflicts are being settled and fewer are now emerging (see the epilogue in this book).

The vaunted territorial integrity and sovereignty of states, enshrined in the charter of the United Nations, increasingly confronts the doctrine of the self-determination of peoples—often carried to the extremes of secessionist rebellions. (Self-determination, of course, need not imply secession. More about this later.) Self-conscious ethnies, proud of a distinctive culture and history, demand political voice, economic access, and cultural autonomy in state after state around the world. National states, at the same time or earlier, seek to impose a common identity upon resisting peoples (Kurds in Turkey, Turks in Bulgaria, the Islamic government in Sudan, Tibet in China).

Assimilation and mutual accommodation have helped to reduce ethnic conflicts in Western democracies, even as power sharing and cultural pluralism have become favored policies in countries as different as Canada, Belgium, and South Africa. Efforts to manage or resolve dangerous cleavages have included changes in electoral systems, federalism, and devolution of authority, and many other "structural" devices. The various approaches to conflict reduction, containment, resolution, and transformation will be explored in Chapters 10 and 11.

We can be sure that ethnicity is not about to be abolished, nor are complex national states likely to wither away in any foreseeable future. As Donald Horowitz has persuasively argued, a moderate degree of ethnic solidarity is a positive factor in building a sense of community, but there is a great need to reduce and redirect its extreme exclusionary forms (Horowitz 1985, xii–xiii).

The chapters of this work move through four main concerns. First, what are the actual characteristics of ethnies and states in the present world—the realities that set the conditions for conflict or cooperation, for peaceful coexistence or struggle and dominance? In other words, the first task is to describe the situations that are to be explained. Second, the difficult question "Why" emerges: what are the necessary and sufficient conditions for the remarkably divergent outcomes of different forms of ethnicity and political authority that we can observe in the real world? Third, going beyond static or structural factors, what processes constitute the continually changing movements through time of ethnic identities, mobilization, confrontation, conflict, negotiation, and reestablishment of collective relationships? Finally, what actions and policies of relevant individuals and collective actors have shown themselves to be effective in "managing" or "transforming" conflicts to avoid undesired negative outcomes?

In a task of this scope, no quick answers or final dicta are possible. The hope is only to construct a partial synthesis of available theories and empirical research sufficient to make a sound basis for future advances.

The Wars Within

World System and Global Disorder?

- One world—or many?
- Civic nationalism—or ethnic purity?
- Mutual accommodation—or genocidal fury?

We confront at the dawn of the twenty-first century a "globalized" world of economic interdependence, of mass media and extensive networks of nearly instantaneous point-to-point communication, of numerous governmental and nongovernmental organizations that criss-cross state borders. At the same time we observe fierce nationalisms, fragmented and collapsed states, warlordism, "ethnic cleansing," and attempted genocides. Hence our initial questions. Will the future bring reality to the vision of One World? Can we anticipate the growth of democratic states that rely upon a shared sense of civic consensus—or do we face instead the threat of spreading anarchy and the violent destruction of whole peoples? Surely these are questions that deserve a determined search for better understanding.

Let us be candid at the start about the basis of our interest. This book aims to focus upon ethnic conflicts because their effects are, so often, terrible by any defensible ethical standards. In the last decade of the twentieth century, in country after country, men, women, and children by the millions were tortured and slaughtered, their homes burned, their lives totally disrupted. Millions of individuals today are refugees from state terror and communal fighting; they live in camps and in flimsy shelters; they trudge through snowy hills carrying a few meager possessions. Today's civil wars and state-sponsored mass killings are "*dirty*" wars." It has been well said

globalism v/a nationalism

that "they are deep rooted, highly internationalized, fought ruthlessly with enormous human suffering, and difficult to resolve" (Ganguly and Taras 1998, 184).

These armed conflicts are not just far away, local events that we can conveniently ignore and shunt aside. They often spill across lines on the map. Waves of refugees tax the resources of receiving areas and may profoundly destabilize governments. Civil wars threaten whole regions—as witness Bosnia and Kosovo and Kashmir and Afghanistan—and mass murders cannot rest lightly upon the human sensibilities of bystanders who are aware of the genocide in Rwanda or the agonies of the South in the Sudan.

It would be a serious mistake to take the national state as the basic social unit for analysis in studying (or dealing with) such massive violent conflicts. Neither separate individual persons nor the large-scale superstructures of national states are the proper units for understanding many of the world's most severe conflicts since the end of the Cold War. In the period 1989–96, for example, there were 101 instances of collective armed conflict—but only six were conflicts between states (Wallensteen and Sollenberg 1999). The "wars within" really are *within*—nearly all now wreak their havoc within the nominal boundaries of territorial states.

Since the Peace of Westphalia in 1648, wars have been of three main kinds. First are the relatively limited wars between well-organized states over rights of succession, control of territory and resources, and relations with allies. These may be called institutionalized wars, with defined objectives, agreed-upon "rules of war," and expectable means of termination. The second type—total wars—are conflicts of nationalisms and ideologies, of mass mobilization and unlimited or undefined means. The Napoleonic wars provide one illustration, and World Wars I and II raised warfare to new heights (or depths) of ferocity and destruction. The third kind are intrastate conflicts—civil wars, communal fighting, state democides, guerrilla wars. Wars of this third kind (Holsti 1996) now comprise nearly all large-scale killing. They often involve relations among states, but are more a matter of relationships within states, especially in newly independent, economically stressed, multi-ethnic states.

By our advisedly vague title, we refer to violent collective conflicts occurring within the boundaries of national states. Our primary interest here is in substantial wars—those resulting in 1000 or more battle deaths per year—but we will also pay attention to some conflicts of lesser lethal magnitude—military coups, massacres, pogroms, riots, persisting terrorism.

The "wars within" include, first, civil wars in which organized rebels fight government forces for autonomy or for control of the state. Second, there are violent struggles of states with separatist movements, in which an ethnic or regional segment seeks to break away from the central polity. Third is diffuse but massive interethnic violence involving widespread killing; such cases include the civil wars in which several armed groupings fight each other within a "failed" or "collapsed" state, as in Liberia, Somalia, and the former Zaire in the 1990s.

Finally, there are the enormously deadly actions of states toward their own populations in political mass murders (democides) and attempted genocides. These are assaults inflicted upon civilians without weapons in their hands (see Rummel 1994). The list of such events is long—the Stalinist Soviet Union, Maoist China, Hitlerian Germany, Uganda under Idi Amin, the Khmer Rouge in Cambodia, the Rwandan genocide . . . and many others.

As a recent research review (Williams 1994) has noted,

> The current significance of this topic is not in doubt. First, the world-wide prevalence of ethnic diversity is indicated by the presence of about 6000 languages (Grimes 1988) and around 1600 (Levinson 1991–93) major cultural groupings. . . . Second, of the over 180 states in the United Nations, only a handful are ethnically homogeneous; multiethnicity is the rule. Third, in a warring world (Brogan 1990), ethnic-related conflict is frequent and deadly. One half of the world's states have experienced significant ethnic conflict since World War II. About 80% of deaths in warfare during that period have been internal to national states (Russett and Starr 1989, 171), and much of that total has come from collective ethnic violence. Estimates of the number of deaths attributable to ethnic violence since 1945 vary widely . . . but an upper figure of 20 million fatalities does not appear to be an excessive guess. In the ultimate case of genocide, as Leo Kuper (1985, 161) has noted, the majority of deaths in domestic genocides result from struggles for power by ethnic, racial, or religious groups.

For example, in the year 1993 every one of the thirty-four major armed conflicts then under way were *within*, not between, states. There were struggles between the military, paramilitary, and police forces of governments, and rebel insurgents, or among the fighting forces of cultural, religious, or so-called "tribal" groupings (Klare 1995, 52). Interstate wars have been rare in the years since 1990, but what are now called "small wars" within territorial states have become one of the two dominant forms of human carnage—the other being the mass killings inflicted by states on their own people. Between 1900 and 1987, according to data compiled by Rummel (1994, 1–4), about 170 million persons were killed by states in democides and genocides—about four times the total deaths in battles. This grim finding may be surprising—but the estimates have been carefully and conservatively done. States are the greatest killers.

Our subject is unavoidably complex. We have to deal with different types of "communal groups" (Gurr 1993b), "ethnies" (A. D. Smith 1986; van

3

den Berghe 1987), or "ethnic groups." Six types have been singled out by Gurr (1993b): ethnonationalists, ethnoclasses, indigenous peoples, militant sects, and advantaged and disadvantaged communal contenders. Esman (1990) deals with diaspora, irredenta, nonstate nations, and transnational ethnic networks. There are several other useful classifications. These diverse ethnies are situated in different kinds of political orders—democratic, authoritarian, totalitarian; the encompassing states may be weak or strong, centralized or not, repressive or open. Mobilized ethnies may be subject to economic, political, social, and cultural discrimination. They may seek the collective goals of exit (secession), voice (access), loyalty (accommodation), control (rebellion). They may use nonviolent protest, violent protest (turmoil), or armed rebellion. Processes of accommodation and conflict may lead to mutual acceptance and peaceful cooperation, to cooptation, to suppression, to rebel or state victory, or to protracted warfare. Any reasonably comprehensive treatment of ethnicity must have something to say about all these intimidating complexities.

Further, many instances of intrastate warfare that are called "ethnic" by the protagonists or outsider observers may actually stem primarily from class struggles, regional claims and demands, or antagonisms among kin-based and locality groupings. As we have said elsewhere (Williams 1994, 65), ethnicity often coincides with class, but neither is reducible to the other. Further,

> Increased scholarly attention to ethnic conflict does not lessen the importance of class and economic sectorial bases for other forms of collective rebellion, e.g., peasant-based revolts and revolutions (cf. Paige 1975, Jenkins 1982). Yet an emphasis on class struggle can lead to a neglect or downplaying of ethnic cleavages as a factor in peasant uprisings. Detailed studies of particular cases, not surprisingly, show complex interactions of class, state, ethnicity, and local social structures (e.g., on southern Peru: Orlove 1990).

Of course not all civil wars or intrastate outbreaks of collective violence are ethnic—although about two-thirds are. Let us note a few recent instances.

In Uganda, otherwise peaceful, the press reports that the Lord's Resistance Army, led by a former Roman Catholic altar boy, has killed between five and ten thousand civilians since 1993; most of the "soldiers" are teenagers. Both attackers and victims are members of the same ethnic grouping.

In Tajikistan, a four-year civil war has pitted government forces against rebel coalitions and breakaway military commanders.

In Liberia—a classic case of a collapsed state—a multiparty civil war has raged since 1989. Deep ethnic divisions have combined with factional fighting to create an intractable chaos and to contribute to the conspicuous failure of multinational peace-keeping efforts.

In El Salvador, severe class and regional conflicts, coupled with external aid that supported the war, led to the loss of more than 75,000 lives before the recent peace accords.

In Algeria, the so-called "terrorist insurgency" since 1993 has resulted in some 50,000 deaths. The conflict involves ethnonationalism, international influences, power-transition struggles, and massive religious-secular conflicts (St. John 1996).

These few cases out of many suggest a simple but basic initial lesson: most major intrastate wars involve multiple identities and interests—ethnic, class, regional, religious, even gender and generational—power struggles for control of states, and external interventions. Accordingly, it is no surprise to find that simple explanations fall short and that quite complex analyses are required. Likewise, we may anticipate that successful conflict resolution will depend upon both generalized understanding and detailed knowledge of particular cases.

Violent conflicts in which ethnic identities are the primary lines of cleavage have the appearance of unusual ferocity and resistance to termination. A prototypical example is the attempted genocide in Rwanda. Yet, overall, the ethnic and non-ethnic civil wars have similar casualty patterns, do not differ greatly in duration, and seem about equally open to negotiated settlements (Licklider 1995, 1997). These counterintuitive findings are difficult to interpret, but a major clue lies in the central fact of civil war: once under way, sheer survival becomes salient for all parties; the process of conflict itself creates fear of extinction, desires for revenge, and deep distrust of any negotiated settlement. Hence, the initial character of the conflict may not predict well the nature of its ending. As we will see later, it may be the intensity of the security dilemma—who disarms first—that blocks negotiated settlement and helps to account for the fact that most civil wars are ended only by the military victory of one side (Licklider 1995; Walter 1997). This deep puzzle is another example of why our topic warrants close and serious attention.

Given the circumstances just sketched, our next task, in Chapter 1, must be to examine ethnicity itself. In so doing we will avoid the cumbersome and potentially misleading term "ethnic group," employing instead the more accurate "ethny" and "ethnies" as advocated by Pierre van den Berghe (1981). Ethnies are culturally distinctive collectivities of substantial size that define membership by birth (real or fictive descent). They are not "groups" in any usual meaning of the term.

The distinctiveness of ethnic violence is twofold—in the meaning of "ethnic" and of "violence." Neither term has an obvious, clearly defined

5

referent. As Chapter 1 shows, "ethnicity" can refer to a wide range of diverse characteristics; hence the meaning of this, and related, terms requires specification. The same necessity applies to other central concepts in our discussion, such as the definition of conflict, as over against competition and rivalry. We have said elsewhere, for example, that competition consists of striving for scarce valuables under conditions that regulate the means used and restrict the damage competitors are allowed to inflict upon each other (Williams 1947, 43; 1994, 54). "Violence" has a core meaning of actions causing bodily harm, but can carry multiple additional connotations. And ethnic violence is usefully specified as "violence perpetrated across ethnic lines, in which at least one party is not a state . . . and in which the violence is coded as having been meaningfully oriented in some way to the different ethnicity of the target" (Brubaker and Laitin 1998, 428).

The processes that drive the apparently diverse cases of ethnonationalism, communal warfare, religiously sanctioned conflict, and the struggles of indigenous peoples have obvious differences—lost independence or political autonomy, wars in the service of a religious faith, deadly struggles to gain control of a state, or defense against encroachments upon vital resources and homelands. Nevertheless, as we shall see, there are common features of domination and discrimination, of collective identity and mobilization, of the dynamics of conflict itself.

In a period of history so studded with protracted civil wars, failed and collapsed states, democidal regimes, and social movements advocating and practicing militant dominance through violence, it seems that a vigorous social science would do well to try hard to understand the sources of these recurrent and, may we say, well-nigh awesome events.

Thus, in spite of its intimidating appearance of chaotic complexity, the study of ethnic conflict—of the "wars within" of our sloganized title—does disclose understandable patterns and recurrent sequences. Underneath the chaotic surface there are discernible regularities. The actors out there on the stage of history do have their entrances and their exits. They do play their parts, even if imperfectly scripted. There are surprises aplenty, and the regularities rarely are obvious and often are deeply hidden. But reliable knowledge does exist and the unanswered questions are, indeed, why we need to study the matter at all. There are literally hundreds of empirical generalizations well supported by extant research. Many more wait upon our insights, skills, and persistent search.

The following chapters aim both to describe some of the specific, concrete, historical features of today's states and ethnic formations, and to uncover regularities and uniformities in the processes that create and maintain them. This two-fold task requires that we first see the collectivities we examine in all their socially constructed and contingent character—

as varied, changing, complex, multiform human creations. This will be the primary aim of Chapters 1, 2, and 3. But the search for repeatable and understandable patterns leads us in Chapters 4, 5, and 6 to treat states and ethnies for some purposes of analysis as if they were relatively unitary actors, having interests and collective goals. The two approaches are complementary, not contradictory; both help us to make sense of the real world we hope to better comprehend; nevertheless, the two emphases are different. Let the reader be warned.

PART I

THE COLLECTIVE ACTORS

CHAPTER ONE

The Multiple Realities of Ethnicity

"Ethnicity is one of those forces that is community-building in moderation, community-destroying in excess."

Donald L. Horowitz, *Ethnic Groups in Conflict* (1985)

The sheer number of the world's distinguishable and publicly recognized "cultural groupings," "minorities," and "languages" is impressively documented: over 6,000 languages (Grimes 1988); some 1,600 "major" cultural groupings (Levinson 1991–93); a worldwide encyclopedia notes minorities in 200 states and dependent territories (Minority Rights Group International 1997); and there are over 200 politicized communal groups in 92 countries (Gurr 1993b). Smaller and localized, but named and acknowledged, ethnies undoubtedly number in the thousands. The finer distinctions of difference and identity are passed over in inventories of the more politically significant groupings, but the broad lesson is clear: ethnicity is pervasive.

Thus, ethnic identities and ethnicities, if not universal, are nearly so. Certainly solidary ethnies—distinctive, historical-cultural "communities"— have been prominent and consequential around the world and throughout recorded history.

Here are a few of the questions, covered in this chapter, that are suggested by ethnic phenomena.

1. What is ethnicity? What are its sources? What are the prior conditions that predict its emergence?
2. What makes ethnic distinctions *salient?* What circumstances and events render them prominent or cause them to recede into the background?
3. What causes ethnic social *boundaries* to become rigid or impermeable? Do the same factors account for increased flexibility or openness?
4. What internal and external conditions accentuate or diminish in-group *solidarity?*

What Is Ethnicity?

There is a strong and easily observable tendency for people within any bounded social space to categorize themselves and to form dense clusters of interaction. The signs or "tags" that form the lines or divisions are extremely varied, and initial differences do not have to be objectively great—indeed, artificial markers that are externally imposed can serve to create real identities. But the most important and enduring social categories have developed out of the basic biological and social exigencies of group living. Ethnic collectivities belong among these basic structures.

Social differences will occur in any interacting population over time, even if there are no initial differences among the interacting individuals. This conclusion is supported by formal models as well as by empirical research. Internal differentiation of roles and status evaluations rapidly develop in small experimental groups (Bales 1999). Simple categorization of individuals produces marked group distinctions in laboratory experiments (Tajfel 1970), and in classroom settings (Bremer 1999, 71–74). Small and random initial advantages can cumulate over time into large status differences (Merton 1968, on the "Matthew Effect"). In naturally forming communities, the restrictions upon interaction generated by distance and the necessary distribution of time and effort inevitably lead to collective boundaries, and such discontinuities in interaction eventually will create cultural differences.

It appears, therefore, that no special explanation is needed for the emergence of culturally distinctive collectivities. Perpetuated through reproduction and contingent kinship relations, localized ethnies predictably emerged. Ethnicity is, first of all, a special form of universal processes of differentiation and categorization.

Because these collectivities are not really "groups" in any strict sociological sense of the term, we will avoid the awkward and possibly misleading term "ethnic group," but rather use the better word "ethny," as proposed by van den Berghe (1981, 22; cf. Dutter 1990) and used routinely by A. D. Smith (1989).

Many of the disputes concerning ethnicity pose polarized conceptions as mutually exclusive: ethnicity is either primordial or instrumental, either structural or situational and changeable, either based on "race" or language/culture. Careful reviews of existing data, in contrast, show that actual examples of ethnic collectivities typically combine the alleged opposites. Some ethnies are deeply rooted in family and extended kinship groups, in networks of fellow participants who share emotionally charged historical memory and sacred symbols of identity. Some ethnies are ancient, while others are recent social inventions, led by entrepreneurs, and primarily focused upon economic and political advantages. Some have ambiguous and fluid boundaries, others are endogamous and closed to social interaction by outsiders. Most large ethnies are simultaneously primordial and instrumental, changing but retaining boundaries, their leaders alert to situational advantages but mindful of history, continuity, and tradition.

An obvious but often overlooked perspective in our efforts to understand ethnicity is that different aspects of the phenomena require different explanations. One problem is to account for the origins of ethnic distinctions, and their ubiquity and persistence in time and space. For this task, we cannot afford to neglect sociobiological considerations centered upon kinship and human capabilities for socialization (Trivers 1985; van den Berghe 1987; Diamond 1992; Wright 1994). What helps us to understand the origins and strength of ethnic ties, however, may be much less useful in explaining fluidity and change in ethnic boundaries and allegiances; here economic interests, rivalries for social status, and struggles for political advantage may come to occupy center stage. Ethnic politics, in turn, inescapably draws attention to the part played by elites—intellectuals, agitators, ethnic entrepreneurs—and their strategies and tactics.

Although scholarly definition of "ethnic" or "ethnicity" are numerous and sometimes quite divergent, a common core of identifying markers does exist and is recognized. However, a comprehensive understanding of ethnicity requires an integration of perspectives from sociobiology, cultural studies, sociological analyses of relationships and groups, and social psychology. So, for example, without kinship and the associated capabilities for symbolic generalization of kin-recognition, there would not be ethnicity as we know it.

Most, perhaps all, serious definitions of ethnicity are *range definitions*: they specify a number of characteristics that identify, in combination, the referent. The more of these items, the more "ethnic" the collectivity of reference. Thus the three most central characteristics include

1. cultural distinctiveness (a "range" itself, including language, food preferences and taboos, songs, dances, literature, games, and so on);
2. membership by birth (descent), endogamy (in-group marriage);
3. a population larger than small kinship units or face-to-face groups.

Once given these three defining criteria, ethnies may be further specified by any one or a combination of the following:

4. geographic concentration, segregation;
5. historic homeland—fatherland, motherland;
6. distinctive occupations;
7. differential treatment by other ethnies;

8. historical memories of a common past;
9. strong sentiments of mutual obligation (solidarity);
10. claims for autonomy, resistance to outsiders;
11. demonstrated capability for concerted action to defend or advance common interests.

Further, to understand the extent and character of ethnic conflict today requires close and detailed analysis of the internal social structure and dynamics of ethnies, the relationship between different ethnies within a particular territorial polity, and the relations between ethnies and the states that attempt to encompass and rule them.

Many of the scholarly discussions, as well as popular commentaries, simply take for granted the existence of ethnic distinctions. This historical perspective lacks comparative depth; the result is a foreshortened and narrow conception of ethnicity and its implications, often mistaking as universal that which is local and transitory. The remedy is to start from basic questions rather than topical descriptions.

Ethnic identity grows out of the same conditions that favor the development of other kinds of "community," such as repeated interactions with significant others sharing a similar culture under conditions of interdependence. Ethnicity then *varies*—in prominence or salience, solidarity, sharpness, and rigidity of boundaries. It is highly dependent upon the existence of differences and contrasts, and is rendered salient and central by interethnic conflict. It is, indeed, a sociocultural emergent; in one formulation: "Rather than a constant ascribed trait that is inherited from the past[,] ethnicity is the result of a process that continues to unfold" (Yancey, Ericksen, and Juliani 1976, 400). To this it must be added that to the extent that ethnic identity is carried in kinship groups, the *process* is one of ascription, although the *outcome* is not an eternally fixed attribution.

What conditions will maximize the extent and intensity of ethnic awareness and salience especially of a sense of collective identity? The list is long with historically observed conditions that have been important in one or many societies (cf. Dutter 1990). A widely shared sense of ethnic identity is more likely when

• An ethny preceded the territorial state into which it has been incorporated, and the basis of incorporation emphasized ethnicity.
• There are only a few large ethnies within the claimed jurisdiction of the state.
• The population of the ethny is geographically concentrated.
• The ethny's members are concentrated in a few salient occupations.
• There is a history of recent ethnic conflict.
• There are many cultural differences with other nearby ethnies.

• Social closure, including in-group marriages, is strong.
• Discrimination is prevalent.

Wherever we find all these conditions, ethnic distinctions will be prominent and individuals will have a strong sense of ethnic membership.

In evolutionary terms, as van den Berghe has convincingly argued, ethnicity is an extension of kin-based solidarity: "The prototypical ethny is thus a descent group bounded socially by inbreeding and spatially by territory" (van den Berghe 1987, 24). Such small, endogamous localized groupings are very far from the huge, ethnically labeled populations of today's complex societies, but the sociobiological bases remain essential. During the several million years of biological evolution since hominids and chimpanzees diverged, there was ample time and circumstance for selective processes to shape human social behavior according to the principles of *inclusive fitness* and *reciprocal altruism* (Trivers 1985; Diamond 1992; van den Berghe 1987; Wright 1994). Evolutionary theories center upon natural selection: any characteristics that enhance survival and reproduction will be passed on in the gene pool. "Inclusive fitness" posits the selection of the genes of those individuals who help to ensure survival and reproduction of close relatives—those with a similar genetic heritage. Much solid evidence supports this supposition. This line of explanation provides a plausible account of the emergence of cooperative, survival-enhancing behavior in small groups of kin, although it fails to adequately account for large groups formed by cooperative behavior among individuals who are not close relatives. "Symbolic" extensions of kinship undoubtedly exist, but seem a weak basis for the solidarity of very large collectivities.

A partial further explanation is provided by the concept of reciprocal altruism. In the evolutionary history of human groups, the reciprocation of advantage-conferring behavior toward others (cooperation) could lead to stable patterns of recurrent helpfulness. Such conditions must have existed in the small hunter-gatherer groupings that were the dominant societal forms until a few thousand years ago.

Thus, taken together, the two processes of (1) natural selection through inclusive fitness and (2) the elaboration of cooperation through reciprocal altruism give a persuasive account of the bases for group formation, identification, and solidarity. The resulting tendencies to form durable, emotionally significant relations with immediate family and extended kin are not likely to disappear. Similar relations of identification and reciprocity are impressively recurrent in villages, clans, work groups, military units, and religious collectivities. The whole body of evolutionary evidence thus suggests that there are deep-seated and powerful sociobiological bases for the observable persistent dispositions to form group attachments, to define membership boundaries (inclusion/exclusion), and to define

15

many specific patterns of trust and cooperation in terms of such attachments and boundaries (Goetz 1996).

To call attention to the importance of kinship in ethnicity is often seen incorrectly as overly "biologistic," but such an imputation is misplaced. The main point is, simply, that kinship is the core of social networks within which ethnic identities are assigned and acquired. So, for example, in today's huge extended ethnic categories, with millions of members, each individual will have no more than a few co-ethnics who are kin, but most of each individual's immediate circle of friends and relatives will be within the ethnic category. This result is inevitable to the extent that there is preferential ethnic in-group marriage and territorial clustering. Ethnicity persists even with high social mobility and interethnic marriage so long as there are even modest preferences for in-group marriages and having a co-ethnic as a neighbor.

The central importance in genuine ethnicity of myths of common descent and of familial images has been stressed by Walker Connor (1992, 53): "It is the intuitive conviction of common descent that causes ethnonational identity to be more deeply rooted and potent than are nonkinship group-identities, class, common religion, common locale (or region), or common citizenship." Any of the latter conditions can reinforce ethnonational identity, as Connor indeed recognizes.

Most socialized members of human societies have an ethnic identity—they are members of "a collectivity within a larger society having real or putative common ancestry, memories of a shared historical past, and a cultural focus on one or more symbolic elements defined as the epitome of their peoplehood" (Schermerhorn 1970,12). And further, Gurr (1993b, 3) speaks of "communal groups" (ethnies) as "those whose core members share a distinctive and enduring collective identity based on cultural traits and lifeways that matter to them and to others with whom they interact." Our own definition will be given shortly.

Ethnicity is one among several kinds of collective identities; ethnies are one among many kinds of social formations. All collective identities have so-called objective and subjective aspects, such as boundary markers vs. we-feelings. Collectives may be defined in cultural, social, or psychological terms. So in social terms, under the inclusive rubric "collectivity," ethnies take their place along with families, villages, religious groupings, unions, firms, states, military brotherhoods, voluntary associations, and so on and on.

But ethnies have crucial characteristics that set them off from other types of social formations. True, their boundary markers may be highly diverse—language, religion, dress, food taboos and preferences, or physical appearance. The essential characteristic is that the shared items are taken, both within the ethny and by outsiders, as markers of a distinctive boundary. Thus the first defining characteristic is a recognized *cultural signal of membership*. Obviously, however, this alone does not differentiate ethnies from other collectivities. What does become decisive is that those sharing a distinctive culture do so by *reason of birth in a group self-identified as having a common "ancestry or origin,"* no matter how tenuous or how far in the past. Such symbolic kinship can be, and often is, extended to very large populations. As it is extended from traceable lines of descent, the ascribed status becomes more and more fictive, of course, until it can fade away entirely. What is clear, however, is that the idea of a common origin, implying a common history, is not wholly arbitrary—not "socially constructed" without any reference to underlying social reality. The "Yamato race," or descent from the Yellow Emperor, is fictive but not arbitrary—Japanese or Chinese do not trace descent from George Washington, and Ugandans would hardly regard Queen Victoria as a plausible ancestor (cf. van den Berghe 1987, 1990; Horowitz 1985).

Finally, ethnies are distinguished from families or villages by extensive interaction, going beyond face-to-face groups. So ethnies, for present purposes, are *relatively large, culturally distinctive groupings in which membership is conferred by birth in a group claiming a common origin*. While ethnies thus look backward into history, they also look sidewise to persons who share in communal distinctiveness, and forward into a future of shared fate.

A Gallery of Identities: Ethnicity, Religion, Nationality

People identify themselves in many ways: by gender and age, by occupation, by ethnic origin, by religion, by citizenship, by "national" origin, by "race." Individuals are placed in such varied categories by other people, often with life-long consequences. How are these several bases of identity related to one another? It is easy to think of a fusion of religion and ethnicity: Orthodox Jews, Irish Catholics, Greek Orthodox. But in a society such as the United States that is experiencing both extensive erosion of national-origin ethnicity and considerable shifting of religious affiliations, what actually is the relationship between ethnic identity and religious affiliation? Is ethnicity a different phenomenon from religious identification? Are the two essentially the same? Does the distinction, if any, rest upon the extent to which identity is ascribed by birth? Very often in both scholarly and popular discourse one reads of "ethnic and religious" groupings—implying separable bases of collective identity. But one can speak also of "ethnoreligious" or "religioethnic" alignments, and whole civilizations may be identified by religious labels—Hindu, Islamic, Confucian, Western Christian, and so on.

Religious allegiance certainly can change radically in the long run: large populations convert to Islam or Christianity, or world religions displace local cults and animistic belief systems. But in the short run, of one generation or a few, religious identity typically is fixed at birth and is difficult to change. To the extent that this situation prevails, "religion" *is* ethnic, another cultural marker of the boundary between members and nonmembers, along with language, family patterns, and other beliefs and practices. As Demerath (2002, 9) has insisted, ethnicity and religion are not the same: there can be ethnicity without religion and vice versa. Ethnies can be subdivided by religious allegiances, and religious collectivities often contain multiple ethnies. The differences are many. Nevertheless, religious affiliations can be ethnic in their cultural distinctiveness, ascribed membership, rigid boundaries, and intense commitments.

In modern industrialized and urbanized societies, having high rates of geographic and social mobility and multiple religious faiths, individuals are relatively free to change religious membership, and many do so. In the exceptional setting of the United States, the association between religious affiliation and ethnic origin has declined, as ethnic identity has weakened and become more complex (Alba 1990, 303–5), and as religious identification has become less salient (Hammond and Warner 1993). But rates of conversion within a single generation typically remain low, and substantial erosion seems to require high rates of interfaith marriage over several generations. To the extent that voluntary changes do occur, religion ceases to be an ascribed status and thus, by definition, ceases to be ethnic and then becomes instead an "ideological" affiliation.

Of course, religion is not merely a boundary marker. Different religions indeed do have very different beliefs, rituals, normative demands, and forms of organization and leadership. They answer to deep and persisting human needs and hopes and fears. For devout adherents, a specific religious system has ultimate significance and value. Accordingly, when religious groupings become politicized and seek incompatible goals, they take on all the characteristics of mobilized ethnies, for example, of Gurr's (1993b) "militant sects" and "communal contenders." On the other hand, when identities that have been bound up with national ("country of origin") differences fade, religious affiliation can become separated from other bases of cultural distinctiveness. In that case, the persistence of religious identity is greatly aided by the elaborate structure of doctrines and of institutional supports in organized faith-groupings.

For many legal purposes and for public policies, states find it expedient to distinguish between religious affiliations and ethnic memberships (Poulter 1998). Members of religious collectivities often make special political claims, such as a special system of domestic law, exemption from military service, rights to private schooling for children, or exemption from certain health and sanitation regulations. Religious collectivities usually have an organizational structure and representatives accountable to a constituency—features not so universal in large and diffuse ethnies. Religious membership in some societies may be freely chosen; by definition, the initial ethnic status of individuals is conferred by descent.

Yet all these distinctions are variable and subject to blurred criteria in practice. Persons who at one time identify themselves and are categorized by others in religious terms may at other times invoke language as a primary basis of collective identity, as suggested by the familiar case of Catholic Francophones in Quebec. In another well-described instance, some of the so-called "Muslims" in Jammu and Kashmir differ from the main body of other Kashmiri Muslims in language, occupations, areas of residence or activity, access to particular resources, relations to state authorities, and, indeed, in political definitions (access to government jobs, rights to buy land). Such agro-pastoral people as the Bakkarwal and Gujar have been successively redefined by changes in economic and political circumstances: whether they were "ethnic" or "religious" (Muslim) depended greatly upon political struggles. Even the religious identity was diverse: people known as Gujar who are found in areas from central Afghanistan across Pakistan and extensively in northern India may be Muslim, Hindu, or Sikh. The realistic consequences of such "floating identities" are so dependent upon political events that, in the opinion of a knowledgeable observer, "one cannot talk of group identity without also talking of politics" (Rao 1999, 82).

When religious collectivities become adversaries in severe conflicts, each contender is likely to claim absolute and exclusive virtue, to hold the one and only true faith. The conviction of absolute rightness lends fervor to the struggle, as opponents are stigmatized as infidels or heathens. Absolute convictions can be deadly. Holy wars have a long record of merciless destruction.

Thus, ethnoreligious groupings do have special characteristics. A further question is important in today's world: What distinguishes an ethny from a "nation" or "nationality"? A. D. Smith (1992, 73) has proposed that we mean by the term "nation" "a large, territorially bounded group sharing a common culture and division of labour, and a common code of legal rights and duties." This restrictive definition would exclude most ethnies, including many that are large and culturally distinctive. What seems to be implied by Smith's characterization is that as an ethny takes on more and more the status of "nation," the more nearly it can be seen as capable of forming a viable state of its own. This implication would be consistent with van den Berghe's definition (1987, 61). "A nation is a politically conscious ethny, that is, an ethny that claims the right to statehood by virtue of being an ethny." Otherwise said, a nation is a definite people claiming a state by reason of its cultural identity. An ideology in support of such a claim is nationalism.

When the population ruled by a state is overwhelmingly of one ethnic group, we have a nation-state and its members have sentiments of ethnonationalism (Smith 1981). A self-conscious ethny that actively seeks political autonomy or control of a state may be termed a "nation" (or "nationality") and thus a political ethny (Yun 1990, 531). Very few nation-states now exist, but "nations" in the sense of nationalities are numerous. Nationalism, then, may be regarded as an ideology and as an accompanying social movement in support of a nation. It must be quickly added that this *ethnic* nationalism is radically different from *civic* nationalism, which entails identification with loyalty to a state-society regardless of the ethnic composition of its population.

Especially significant is the degree to which an individual's total set of interactions rigidly excludes those who are not co-ethnies. At the extreme, a person's social world from one day to another and from birth to death is exclusively an "in-group world." Thus, many ethnies are not only thus culturally distinctive, but also socially closed. The crucial closure is obligatory endogamy, which creates ascribed membership and dense networks of kinship ties. Even short of the total prohibition of exogamous marriage, effective closure can be attained by restriction of intergroup dining and informal social interaction. Residential segregation powerfully aids all forms of closure, reinforcing ethnic boundaries. Occupational specialization increases ethnic visibility, enhances common in-group interests and values, and encourages intensive in-group relationships.

After having operated for several generations, the forces of homogeneity and internal interdependence thus engendered, and expressed in socialization and pressures for conformity, lead to a strongly bounded social formation. Perpetuated by descent, it remains only for processes of rivalry, domination, and ranking to create a caste—in other words, an endogamous, ranked ethny.

To the extent that ethnic distinctiveness is transmitted through socialization in families, it will be best preserved through endogamy. In-group marriage is not a perfect defense against erosion of cultural identity in an assimilationist society; indeed, the evidence is that religious and ethnic endogamy in the United States and some European countries has decreased in recent decades. Nevertheless, nearly all members of ethnies marry within the boundaries more often than would be the case under random mating, and the extent of closure is still high for recent immigrants and many ethnoracial categories.

Spatial concentration increases the likelihood of ethnic salience. Geographic region and cultural distinctions can combine to reinforce visibility and to encourage social distance between groupings. Residential segregation itself is a powerful generator of ethnic self-consciousness and potential solidarity. Ethnicity is similarly reinforced by occupational concentration, as in the classic instances of "middleman minorities"—Phoenicians and Greeks in the ancient Middle East, Jews in medieval Europe, Chinese in Southeast Asia, Lebanese in West Africa, East Indians in East Africa, and other distinctive trading peoples.

Ethnic distinctions are reinforced also by inequalities in wealth and income; and the conditions that maximize salience overlap with those that tend to create ideologies that support ethnic domination. So it is that actual ethnic dominance creates the conditions that favor ideologies of superiority and vested privilege. For example, a historical study of Detroit shows that restrictive covenants in the 1940s effectively excluded Blacks in every subdivision that was developed from 1940 to 1947; real estate deeds specified the exclusion of Blacks. Similarly, Blacks were excluded from certain occupations. Housing segregation resulted in occupational exclusion, and lack of occupational opportunities resulted in a casual labor market that reinforced stereotypes of Blacks. Mutually reinforcing residential barriers, hiring practices, union policies, and local politics forged the conditions that created and maintained whites' belief that they had a vested right to racial exclusion.

To the extent that the members of an ethny do not occupy identical social statuses or niches, there will be internal differences in interests. Similarly, to the extent that subsegments of the ethny differ culturally (e.g., in religion or political ideology), the encompassing larger ethny will not have unitary interests. Therefore, if the ethny is to have a commonality of interest (or to present a united political claim), its members must center their attention and commitment upon ethnicity as such: we are all brothers/sisters/comrades because of our *common identity*—derived from out common history, our shared fate, our shared aspirations, our common enemies. For this convergence and centering to occur, ethnicity must somehow have a greater appeal than class, occupation, region, and other cross-cutting lines of allegiance and interest. India has the fourth- largest Muslim population in the world, following Indonesia, Pakistan, and Bangladesh. Muslims are substantially disadvantaged politically and economically, but have not built a united political program, partly because of ideological and socioeconomic cleavages within the population (Kahn and Gurr in Gurr 2000, 266–73).

Situational interpretations of ethnicity come in many different versions. All stress the importance of differences within (nominal) ethnies, as well as the constraints and opportunities of the immediate economic, political, and sociocultural environments. A common ground may lie in the suggestion of Yancey, Ericksen, and Juliani (1976, 392) that ethnicity is "crystallized under conditions that reinforce the maintenance of kinship and friendship networks." Such conditions include stable residential clustering, common economic positions and occupations, participation in common institutions, and reliance on shared services. These basic conditions, in turn, vary over time with changes in technology (e.g., transportation, factory organization), availability of housing, urban concentration or dispersal, levels of economic well-being, and economic opportunities in particular occupations. The "portable heritage" of ethnies is thus in continuous interaction with the specific contexts of time and place.

Instrumental (or more broadly situational, or circumstantial) interpretations of ethnicity and of nationalism often seem to imply that ethnies and nations are temporary social constructs that are viable solely or primarily because of the invention or dramatization by elites, whose interests are thereby served. There is no doubt that elites do seek to create myths of collective origins and interests. But first, such "myth-making" is a property of all social collectivities, from families to international religions—not just ethnic formations. Second, efforts to create and mobilize ethnies do not succeed unless there is some common core of identity and loyalty to which appeal can be made—witness the failure of an attempt to mobilize a region of "Occitania" in France (Tiryakian and Rogowski 1985). Third, manipulated "identities of convenience" are like political coalitions of interest in their temporary and fragile character. They are unable to elicit the strong emotions and solidarities typically manifest in ethnonationalist movements (cf. A. D. Smith 1981, 1989; Douglas 1988, 147, 204).

In summary, the primary conditions that most strongly favor the creation and maintenance of strongly bounded ethnies include the following:

1. a set of cultural traits that differ from those characteristic of other collectivities with whom interaction occurs;
2. distinctive phenotypical characteristics;
3. common occupational positions;
4. residential concentration including perhaps enforced segregation;
5. shared participation in common institutions and services (e.g., religious organizations, schools, local business, civic associations).

Give these circumstances, there will develop a dense network of kinship relations, friendships, and interactions among neighbors. The result of these processes will be a perceptually salient collectivity. Its boundary markers will be accentuated by interaction with other different ethnies, especially in competitive relationships and in direct conflict.

Evidently ethnicity is powerfully strengthened not just by a "portable cultural heritage," but by the specific relationships of an ethny to others, within the constraints and opportunities of an environing polity and economy.

Ethnicity as a Variable

Ethnic distinctions are rarely as clear as lines on a map; only in extreme conditions of conflict are the boundaries completely impermeable and allegiances total. Boundaries often are vague and fluid, in the first place because variations in language and other cultural characteristics usually are continuous rather than discrete. At the same time, distinctions are mixed and blurred by mobility, migration, trading relationships, conquests, political separations, annexations, and merging. Over the long run there may also develop cross-ethnic ties, ranging from political affinities to intermarriage. For all these reasons people often are uncertain or disagree about what boundaries exist and what they signify. Finally, a great variety of social changes (war, depression, changes in technology, rise and decline of industries) can lead to changes in cultural characteristics and in ethnic identities (see Levine and Campbell 1972, chap. 7).

As a general rule, the more closely one observes an ethny, the more internal diversity, change, and uncertainty of identity will be found. Absent conditions of extreme polarization in conflict, few ethnies are internally homogenous and sharply bounded. The exceptions are relatively small, localized ethnies and tightly organized ethnoreligious groupings. Nevertheless, many of the most important large ethnies do maintain substantial internal cohesion and firm boundaries, primarily in response to the interaction of the high *internal rewards* of membership with *external pressures* (discrimination, state impositions, ethnic rivalries and conflicts).

Because of the varying mixtures of internal and external forces, the several different characteristics of social boundaries and cultural commonalities can change at different rates and in different ways. For example, a high rate of ethnic intermarriage need not mean a low level of involvement in an ethnic community, as strikingly illustrated in the case of Japanese Americans (Fugita and O'Brien 1991). A sense of community of intensive, in-group interaction can persist even with massive cultural and social assimilation to an environing society.

It is important in judging the rigidity and stability of ethnic boundaries to distinguish between long-run and short-term views. Over the very long run there is much movement across nominal boundaries; some ethnies disappear entirely, mergers occur, divisions fade, subethnies develop, entire systems of classification change (e.g., from linguistic to religious, from cultural to racial). Indeed, in countries of immigration in which diverse populations are intermingled over substantial periods of time, processes of assimilation and the interdependent accommodations of daily coexistence can erode boundaries and integrate cultures to such an extent that ethnicity becomes largely symbolic and loses its strongly ascribed character (Gans 1979).

Weak forms of ethnic identity are commonly recognized as such when advanced assimilation has greatly reduced cultural distinctiveness. People then speak of "Passover Jews" or "Saturday Italians" and the like. Distinctive ethnic behavior becomes episodic and ritualistic or confined to minor matters of food preferences, celebrations of holidays, and fragments of language and history. Long after extensive erosion of an original culture has occurred, such "symbolic" or "ghost" ethnicity can manifest itself in political party preferences and special sensitivities to certain issues—thus an "ethnic public."

We regard "race" as a special case of ethnicity. In this we agree with both Horowitz (1985) and van den Berghe (1987) that race is a marker—a sign—rather than a substantive ethnic characteristic. It signifies no necessary connection with any particular cultural content. The argument that racial relations are especially likely to generate in-group/out-group distinctions and hostility is not supported by comparative and historical evidence (Horowitz 1985, 43). In seventeenth-century North America, for instance, the original distinctions were between Christians and heathens, only later "Indians," Africans, or "Blacks." In ancient Greece a main distinction was between Greek speakers and "barbarians"—those who "babbled." Persons of the same so-called racial category often align with other races and fight each other. Racial ("color") differences often are not present in the most extreme cases of ranking and conflict. Racism either as an ideology or practice is not universal.

Bartlett (1993) has concluded that early in the expansion of Latin Christendom (to the north, east, and south) ethnic distinctions were based on language and customs, and individuals often changed their ethnic identities. But after several centuries of conquest and colonization, ethnic identities came to be defined by ancestry rather than by cultural differences. The subtle shift to the "racial" criterion of descent foreshadowed the later European emphasis in its overseas expansion after the voyages of discovery.

Phenotypical characteristics such as skin color can serve as racial markers primarily when long-distance migrations have juxtaposed substantial populations that differ in easily observable, reliable physical traits. Cultural markers tend to develop between nearby populations that, in the nature of the case, less often have such physical markers. Thus, an implied prediction is that the racism that appears after long-distance migration will persist only so long "as social barriers to exogamy prevent intermixtures, and thus the recreation of a more typical situation where intragroup genetic diversity exceeds intergroup differences" (van den Berghe 1993, 8).

In the United States in the nineteenth century, popular conceptions often merged ideas of "race" and "nationality" or ethnic origins. (This conflating still occurs.) In a prototypical example, Irish immigrants often were regarded not merely as Irish or Catholic, but as a separate "race" distinct from the established "white" population of earlier European origins. Over time, as the Irish were more and more culturally assimilated and rose in socioeconomic status, the racial designation receded into the background and finally disappeared. The Irish became "white" (Ignatiev 1995)—partly, it must be added, by taking on the racist conceptions, attitudes, and behavior that were prevalent in the environing population. This experience contrasts with the long-continued discrimination inflicted on African Americans.

Ethnicity is a variable: this correct statement is open to serious misinterpretation. It does not mean that ascribed status is non-essential or that a common culture is irrelevant. What it does mean is that the extent to which a common culture or a common origin defines the boundaries of an ethny varies over time and from one social setting to another. *Ethnicity is a process* that varies greatly in time and space, and both responds to and influences its social context. The strength of ethnic boundaries (and of cohesion) and their persistence or change are empirical matters, not to be specified by fiat or by the plausibility of arguments. As Horowitz (1985) has put it, ethnies are "neither stone nor putty." What is needed for advancing an understanding is greater specificity concerning the several aspects of ethnicity, as well as concerning the surrounding conditions. For example, in any particular case we need some inventory of cultural distinctiveness, such as religious beliefs and practices, language (including dialects and accents), dress, body ornamentation or style, holidays, historical events and figures, and rituals and ceremonies. So a first criterion of ethnicity is cultural distinctiveness.

But many culturally distinctive populations are not ethnies—they are adherents to a political ideology, followers of a fashion in dress, devotees of a new style in popular music, networks of writers, and the like. So a second useful criterion will be the *openness or closure of social interaction* among members as distinct from nonmembers. Relative closure is clearly apparent in endogamy, followed by restrictions on intimate sociability, as in informal visiting and inter-dining, but also in work relations, membership in voluntary associations, and separation in education and in residential areas. The scope of ethnic-related activities provides other indicators of the practical significance of ethnicity—the percentage of free time spent with ethnic fellows, the extent to which ethnic solidarity is invoked in politics, and the extent to which economic dealings are ethnic-mediated.

Sources of Ethnic Cohesion and Salience

Without some social boundaries, ethnicity does not endure. But the mere existence of ethnic boundaries does not explain the mobilization of vast populations around symbols of common identity. As Simon (1990) has shown, sociopsychological processes of socialization ("docility" in learning) and conformity are crucial in the development of extended altruism. Ethnic loyalties rest upon exceedingly complex processes of identification and hierarchy formation, as well as upon processes of cultural differentiation and change. At the level of social structures, ethnies can be seen to develop out of networks or relationships that extend from small-group formation to classes, political movements, and states and interstate relationships.

In the widest perspective, as suggested above, the sources of ethnicity are sociobiological and evolutionary—resulting in capabilities for symbol-mediated behavior that include kin-recognition and emotional bonding. On these foundations there develop pervasive tendencies for categorizing other persons, for extending the boundaries of in-groups, and for identifications such that people can come to feel passionately about large-scale social entities that extend far beyond direct personal experience.

Sociopsychological processes thus mediate and modify primordial solidarities. A striking example, well specified by research, is the finding that when for any reason persons are categorized (given labels or tags) and when the probability of encounter across the categories is unequal, social cleavages will result. Even a small difference in the size of the assigned categories will produce some fragmentation (Orbell, Zeng, and Mulford 1996, 1019). From such elementary processes differentiated social structures can grow.

So it is that one often observes a hidden set of relationships "beneath" large ethnic categories—networks of interdependence, commonality of interests, and sentiments of solidarity derived from intertwined structure of kinship and locality. For example, geographic concentrations of kinship groupings create networks that overlap with and interpenetrate neighborhood networks of co-workers, co-religionists, and co-participants in local economic and sociability relationships. Such special densities of interaction, it is true, can create factions and feuds, but they can also constitute a basis for mobilization against outside threats. Thus a recent study documents the important role of neighborhood solidarities in organizing conflict formations in the Paris Commune of 1871 (Gould 1995). From apparently commonplace relations such great events can develop.

In the long sweep of human development, the first well-bounded societies must have been quite small, kinship-based, and for the most part territorially restricted. "Original" ethnicity could develop when the more extended groupings encountered culturally different ascribed entities in relations of trade and/or rivalry for resources. Such relatively closed, small endogamous groupings still exist, but are almost wholly overshadowed by the very large territorially extended networks that now carry ethnic names. That is, the units of identity and loyalty have become symbolically generalized and extended to populations in which descent myths have only a remote connection with past realities. Nevertheless, the core myths of common origins and histories, of membership by birth, and of similarities of culture and aspirations continue to bind together many millions of individuals into categorical collectivities.

The vast extent of many ethnic collectivities—spread over diverse environments and far removed from a common-descent grouping—is inexplicable without analysis of cultural affinities, the role of common symbols, and the processes of socialization and mass indoctrination. Pan-human capabilities for responding to "markers" that elicit something akin to "clan-recognition" probably exist, but are not sufficient to explain the enormous variability in size, cohesion, durability, and collective action among modern ethnies.

What are the directly observable indicators of ethnic membership? Such symbols of identity are highly variable. They may be arbitrarily imposed, as in Nazi Germany's use of armbands and the Star of David to publicly stereotype persons as "Jews." They may be as minimal as slight differences in pronunciation of certain words or as minimal as minor dietary habits. But when ethnic characteristics are most fully developed, there will be a panoply of cues: distinctive language, distinctive dress, distinctive alphabet (e.g., Cyrillic or Roman), separate and obligatory religious beliefs and rituals, prohibited foods and methods of food preparation, marriage customs, residence patterns, legal systems and norms of justice, continuously recreated history and mythology, remembered heroes and villains. From dawn to dusk, around the yearly cycle, from birth to death, in every major experience of daily life, the "total" ethny encompasses the individual and defines the meaning and direction of life.

The enormous variation among named "cultural groups," "communal groups," or ethnic collectivities ranges from "categorical ethnies" (populations having little more concrete existence than a name and a vague sense of a common history) to the exclusionistic, culturally homogenous, endogamous peoples claiming common ancestry, occupying a contiguous homeland and tightly linked by dense networks of interaction and interdependence. Evidently, the degree of ethnic salience and of boundary closure depends greatly upon the character of relationships of any given ethny with other collectivities, especially the degree of conflict and threat.

Ethnic boundaries arise from contrasts. Adjacent populations that do not differ in cultural or social organization are unlikely to conceive of

27

themselves as different "peoples"—although they may, indeed, come into conflict as kin-groupings (e.g., clans) or territorial collectivities (e.g., village communities). But ethnic considerations emerge only when there is a contrast between two or more groupings of people that interact in a particular social setting, and when that contrast can be defined in cultural terms as identities derived in each case from real or fictive descent from common ancestors or origins (see Francis 1976, 382).

Part of the processes leading to ethnic salience are those of reference-group reinforcements. In general, perceptions of any social units are strongly influenced by the groups that individuals take as points of reference. So an individual's sense of ethnic membership is supported by the words and deeds of family members, neighbors, work associates, and fellow participants in religious groups. A consequence is that when political conflict is centered on issues related to ethnicity (including religion), the main reference-group processes of support and conformity will reinforce conflict—because of the homogeneity of the ethnic reference group. Conversely, when political conflict primarily concerns ideological difference or political factions, the individual's closest referents are more likely to be heterogeneous. In this way, reference groups then moderate the conflict. These contrasting outcomes well illustrate why ethnic affiliations so often accentuate identity-related conflicts (cf. Kelley and Evans 1995, 161).

The greater the stake that individuals have in their ethnic membership, the clearer or harder will be the ethnic boundaries, including the emphasis upon descent as the criterion of membership. When ethnic identity is not challenged, boundaries tend to become more permeable and changeable. The criteria of cultural distinctiveness then will be salient, and individuals can change membership by changing language, customs, or even religious affiliations. But when an ethny, particularly when politicized, continually confronts rivals, hostile resistors, and assimilationist threats, boundary markers become more rigid and ancestry becomes more crucial. In a word, *opposition reinforces identity*.

The self-reinforcing effects are accelerated by threats. Any social segmentation arising from the mere fact of differential size of categorical groupings and from "benign" processes of in-category preferences will be accentuated to the extent that any "other" category is seen as threatening or hostile. And the more the members of a particular group feel themselves to be collectively oppressed and unfairly treated, the more likely it is that they will come to regard the members of other categories as threatening (Bobo and Hutchings 1996, 951).

Ethnicity is as politically potent as it clearly is because its inclusive-as-cribed qualities render ethnies readily mobilizable on a large scale—"especially under external threat from an enemy who is himself defined in ethnic or racial terms" (van den Berghe 1993, 7). The political boundaries of large and complex modern states typically include diverse populations, so that ethnic pluralism becomes a dominant reality. That condition, in turn, creates ethnic politics "that range from civic to violent" (Esman 1994, 2). In the United States the long history of ethnic dominance and subordination—of slavery and racialism—has shown the multiple and often contradictory meanings of "pluralism." Even for European migrants, acculturation and assimilation were slow and uneven processes; racial-ethnic relations were often hostile and more than occasionally violent. Over the long course, however, European-origin ethnies did largely move into mainstream American life. But "racial" divisions, especially in white resistance to African Americans' claims to equality, remained deep, and the new immigration after 1965, although peaceful, was met with the anti-minority politics of the 1980s and 1990s (see Rose 1993).

The effects of external threats, including economic and political pressures, upon ethnic cohesion are quite varied, depending upon such contextual factors as initial homogeneity of culture and intra-ethny class relations. But given some substantial initial level of shared identity and solidarity, "external pressures on a group usually intensify the sense of group identity. Ethnogenesis also can occur in the course of protracted conflict, as has happened in revolutionary Ethiopia" (Gurr 1993b, 89). For example, the thirty years of warfare by secessionist Eritrea against the Ethiopian state developed a strong enough sense of a common Eritrean identity to override the initial tribal, linguistic, and Christian-Muslim divisions and to enable the formation of the independent state of Eritrea.

Ethnic salience starts with perceived differences of high social visibility—the familiar list of language and speech patterns, religious practices and symbols, phenotypical physical markers, dress, marriage and kin relationships, or even shared food preferences and avoidances. In local interactions what may appear to outside observers as quite small differences can become the starting point for contrasting collective identities. A favored food in one ethny is a forbidden evil in a neighboring community. And when such symbols of separate identities coincide with differences in income, wealth, prestige, and power and authority, ethnies and classes can begin to fuse. Reinforcing ethnic stratification typically will be economic and political discrimination by agents of state authority.

Numerous empirical studies show how specific policies and practices of states can create, increase, diminish, or destroy the boundaries of salience of ethnic categories (e.g., Karpat 1985; Young 1985). The most widely cited case is that of the former Soviet Union, but other examples are numerous. So it was that in the prolonged civil war in Guatemala, class-based and linguistic identities developed that cut across prior localized identities (Wilson 1995). State repression created ethnicity from the top down, while common experience at the local level built ethnicity from the bottom up. In still another example of state/ethny interaction, Catalan-speaking villages in a region divided between France and Spain tended to seek a national identity that held out the promise of greater practical gains. A "sense of place" seemed to go along with particular economic and political interests that were not necessarily dependent upon linguistic or cultural affinities (Sahlins 1989).

Thus ethnic salience will be favored by any or all of the conditions and processes reviewed here, but the potential consequences will be heightened whenever two or more contrasting ethnies are rivals for power and control in a multi-ethnic national state. Such collective contestations are likely to simultaneously increase the perceived importance of particular ethnic issues, each of which may become a symbol of relative power and prestige.

The Continuing Significance of Ethnicity: Persistence and Change

By picking and choosing, one can show instances of rapid change or instances of ethnic persistence over centuries. In general, it is difficult to say which is the more remarkable—the ceaseless change in ethnic identities and boundaries, or the centuries-long persistence of such identities or boundaries. The current line or zone between "East" and "West" in Eastern Europe, for example, corresponds roughly to the line between Roman and Greek Christianity, which was also the boundary of Mongol and later Russian political control. Eastern Europe's present ethnic/nationality conflicts represent in part the consequence of the breakup of empires—Ottoman, Habsburg, and Soviet. Indistinct and drastically changing political frontiers and vast intermingling of ethnic peoples have not prevented the enduring cleavages of ethnic "nations."

As Esman (1994, 47) eloquently reminds us, "ethnic collective identity and politicized solidarity are free-standing societal phenomena. They are not myths, fantasies, or surrogates for manipulations, or psychological malaise." Ethnies do not melt away easily even under the impact of economic interdependence, high rates of geographic mobility, extensive ethnic intermingling, and numerous pressures toward assimilation to host cultures in multi-ethnic societies. Because of large-scale migration, industrialized societies now increasingly find that ethnic diversity becomes an important issue of public policy.

Long-distance migration of ethnically diverse populations might seem a likely solvent of former identifications. But attentuation of identities does not inevitably follow from contemporary interstate migrations that are large, volatile, complex, and often highly politicized. Modern transportation and communication make possible global diasporas that can retain strong economic and cultural ties across diverse national settings. With long-distance telephone service, television, fax, and e-mail, along with relatively cheap air transport, migrating people no longer feel that they are severing kinship, ethnic, or national ties. Thus, modern diasporas (dispersed ethnic migrants) usually can maintain sentimental affective ties and political and economic linkages with their place of origin (Sheffer 1986). They exist in many countries, and their numbers and prominence are increasing (Armstrong 1982).

Diasporas frequently develop stable and influential interstate networks of trade, remittances, credit, information, and political influence. Their members may and do petition and lobby host countries on behalf of the sending country. Rival diasporas dispute and agitate over contrary historical claims, as witness the continuing Turkish denial of genocide against Armenians, the opposing claims of Israel's supporters and opponents, or the political factions within numerous other migrant peoples.

Given the strength and ubiquity of ethnicity, how could ethnic solidarities and cleavages be abolished or at least rendered peripheral and politically inconsequential? A liberal or modern answer could be that the liberating effects of individualistic values—nurtured by urbanization, commercialization, education, and social and geographic mobility—will gradually dissolve particularistic structures, emancipating cosmopolitan, rational individuals to freely participate in voluntary associations and personal relationships. A neo-Marxist prediction might be that class interests and solidarities in the long run will override the false consciousness and mystifications that permit ethnic divisions to mask the real structure of social dominance. And a democratic utopian could hope that fraternal solidarities among enlightened citizens would lead to progressive, consensual social orders.

Whatever their particular form, however, all interpretations that dismiss ethnicity as a major factor in societal functioning are overlooking the centrality of kinship in human affairs. We can abolish ethnicity—just as soon as we can abolish the family. So long as there are solidary kinship units, parents will talk to children, relatives will share culture, generations will have continuity, and historical memories will be shared. It is true kinship that has a radically diminished structural importance in modern westernized societies. But some form of kinship unit remains as a primary source of identity and meaning in individual lives. So long as this is the case, children will acquire an ethnic identity along with all other results of familial socialization.

Many specific aspects of ethnicity are open to fairly rapid change—details of public behavior in an assimilationist society, use of a second language, loss of "traditional" occupations, or other criteria for group boundaries. But an ethnic identity that commands loyalty and is transmitted from parents to children can last for centuries, while its overt markers shift radically. The markers change; the boundary remains. The case is similar for cultural "content": specific beliefs may change, values may be reordered, and rituals and ceremonies may be altered, while a sense of historical identity is maintained. Long-persisting religious collectivities provide major examples—Jews, Roman Catholics, Hutterites. Continuity is like a rope, in which separate strands overlap and end, but the rope is continuous.

Evidence continues to accumulate that ethnic identifications can be multiple and overlapping or hierarchical, and can be strengthened by group competition and by threats to boundary maintenance (cf. Constable 1996). None of these conditions, however, negates the actual importance of ethnic solidarities where they do exist. And in the world today, thousands of self-identified ethnies exist and hundreds of them are involved in severe political struggles. Ethnic networks and linkages, from trade and tourism, are redefining state boundaries and interstate relations.

Yet in the future, ethnicity may be less closely linked with territory or physical proximity of individuals than in the past. The widespread and increasing availability of relatively inexpensive transportation and means of communication already has linked together dispersed populations. Newer technologies facilitate targeted or "addressable" communication through satellites with many channels, including e-mail, the World Wide Web, and other emerging devices. Thus possibilities exist for reinforcing separate cultures and languages across existing political boundaries and for reconstituting or even creating new ethnic identities (Elkins 1997). "Possibility" need not mean actuality, of course: the technology is permissive, not directive, and non-ethnic uses may dominate, or unforeseen restrictions may develop. Certainly, however, expanded opportunities exist for diffusion and contagion of ethnic movements and appeals.

There has been much discussion, both scholarly and popular, since the 1960s concerning a "revival" or "resurgence" of ethnicity. But ethnicity never really went away. What has taken place, indeed, has been the *politicizing* and *historicizing* of ethnies—some very old and some quite new. The phenomena of ethnogenesis—of the creation of new ethnic identities—have been produced in several different ways, including the development of an over-arching identity resulting from partial assimilation and a sense of common fate among former sub-ethnies. But primary importance must be attributed to the behavior of national states and to ethnic entrepreneurs.

Perhaps the most salient processes have been those of state formation and state expansion—the first apparent in new states formed by decolonization and the breakup of multi-ethnic states. These vast changes produced new state boundaries and created a hundred or more newly independent national-territorial political entities.

With this observation, we turn to Chapter 2, "The Reality of States and Nationalism," in which the interaction of "peoples" and "states" takes center stage.

CHAPTER TWO

The Reality of States and Nationalism

What Are States?

The creations we call states, nations, nationalities, and nationalism—what are they and how did they come to be? We can easily speak of states as if they were permanent facts of nature. Not so. States did not always exist in the past, and there may someday be a future in which they no longer exist, at least in their present forms. Not only that, but for most of human existence the very idea of "state" or "nation" was unknown.

To read the present into the past is the "sin of presentism," and we must divest ourselves of the notion that present-day realities are unproblematic and permanent. We must try to see the strangeness of the great collectivities called states that display flags, anthems, monuments, and myths—and make wars and commit mass killings. Like all other social structures, states are social creations. Not all societies have states. When states emerged, they have appeared in many different forms: tribal states, city-states, leagues of city-states, theocratic centers, empires, and national states. The present world is uniquely marked by the total partitioning of populations into named, geographically bounded national states, each with its own myths of origin, continuities, unitary character, and historical trajectory or "destiny." But this whole system is changing and the present forms will not always endure.

A long scholarly tradition has emphasized that states are coercion-using organizations that claim priority in the exercise of physical force over a population. Formal definitions are diverse, but most agree on this characteristic. A useful formulation says that states are "coercion-wielding organizations that are distinct from households and kinship groups and exercise clear priority in some respects over all other organizations within substantial territories" (Tilly 1992, 1). At one extreme, states are highly centralized organizations that successfully monopolize coercion over the people of a sharply bounded territory and that successfully claim absolute sovereignty, both internally and externally. ("The sovereign is obeyed and does not obey.") At the other pole, a state may be little more that a military band extracting revenue from a subjected population.

Statehood is, of course, a matter of degree—of the degree of monopolization of force, of the degree of centralization of rule-making and rule-enforcement, of the extent of control of institutions of socialization (family, school, "church"), of commonality of culture (e.g., language, religion, arts, science). There have been state-like structures such as the Hanseatic League that constituted themselves as "transnational politico-commercial" complexes (Balibar 1990, 342). There are countries with extremely porous borders and a low degree of centralized state control or of effective penetration into local populations, as for example in Somalia, Afghanistan, and many regions of South Asia and Africa. Even as modern national states claim a right to a monopoly of the legitimate use of violent physical force within a bounded territory and in relation to the population therein, such states rarely have an actual monopoly. Individual subjects may possess arms, often in significant amounts. Subsidiary forces—police, local militias, paramilitary groups, gangs, terrorists—may resist central control or may carry out covert operations on behalf of the state. And arms flow in large quantities across state boundaries. It is not quite literally correct but it is usefully evocative to say with Verdery (1993, 44), "The international weapons trade had made a mockery of the state's supposed monopoly on the means of violence." The ability of small groups to disrupt a state's functioning is now enhanced by the increased availability of relatively cheap, easily transportable, and quite lethal weaponry, ranging from shoulder-held missile launchers to automatic rifles, to car bombs, to nerve gas.

And, of course, national states are not the only territorial political units recognized by existing states and international law. Short of official recognition as a state, for example, there may be the status of a belligerent power "which requires a government and military organization, a real war as context and a large area under the control of the belligerent" (Frankland and Noble 1996, 409). Other examples are protectorates, trusteeships, safe havens, and territories. But the system of sovereign, territorial national states eventually spread around the world, and by the beginning of the twenty-first century the standard form of the sovereign unitary state had been adopted even by the numerous mini-states that do not meet the criteria of Tilly's definition. Modern national states not only claim a monopoly of legitimate violence, they also seek a monopoly "of the legitimate means of movements" by establishing controls over individuals' movements and identification; the passport is the epitome of such controls (Torpey 2000).

At the same time, processes of globalization in trade, investment, communication, and many other sectors are rendering states less strongly bounded than in the recent past. To many observers, the national state-form now is seen as being weakened by no less than six great processes: the development of supranational institutions (e.g., the European Union), regional and ethnic movements for autonomy and separation, immigration, transnational economic relationships, the growth of consumerism, and increasing inequality and alienation (Schnapper 1997, 199–201). Nevertheless, states regularly invoke the doctrines of sovereignty and territorial integrity, and vigorously condemn and reject "interference in domestic affairs."

States and governments are not the same, although the two terms are often used interchangeably. States are both actual social organizations (regularized systems of interaction), and the standing sets of cultural norms, values, and beliefs that define the organization and can be used to legitimize its authority to make binding decisions for an entire population. A government, on the other hand, consists of the persons who occupy the state structure and control its actions at a particular time. Governments may come and go, while the state remains. Citizens may detest the incumbent personnel and their policies, but revere the state and its laws. So it is that strong and enduring states not only successfully claim a dominant right of legitimate coercion within a territory or "sphere of influence," but also embody a consensual set of defining values and beliefs. Successful states are able to extract resources, maintain order, provide services, allocate benefits, resolve internal conflicts, and defend against external threats. Weak or failed states cannot do well at any of the things that are expected of strong states.

State and nation need not be the same. A "nation" or "nationality" is a more or less distinctive people sharing a common culture; it may or may not have its own state or even aspire to statehood. Indeed, the modern national state as a recent creation is typically not the result of a gradual outgrowth of a primordial ethny, but represents both the extension of state control over territories that contain several distinct ethnic populations and the incorporation of immigrants. Thus, the modern European-style state is "national" in the sense of centralized control and bureaucratic penetration, but is not a unitary nation. If "nation" refers to a population characterized by high levels of common culture and clear boundary closures, then very few national states meet the criteria. Multi-ethnicity is the rule (Connor 1981).

It is no new insight that "nation" (or "nationalism") and "state" are different terms, referring to different social realities. But the monstrous hybrid term "nation-state" continues to be used in spite of repeated demolitions, by Connor (1981), van den Berghe (1987), A. D. Smith (1989), Ra'anan (1980, 1990), Esman (1994), Lawson (1995), Williams (1994), and others. The entire academic field of "*international* relations," indeed, is mislabeled, for its primary focus, at least until the 1990s, was *interstate* relations. If cultural homogeneity and common ancestry are the marks of a pure nation-state, few cases exist today. And, indeed, the development of a national unity typically has been a varying and uncertain process. To establish a common language, to develop a substantial commonality of beliefs and values, to create and sustain a patriotic ideology—these have been and are extremely complex tasks. Out of many examples of state-building, it is generally recognized by today's historians that "Germany" and "Italy," for example, were late historical constructions out of great initial diversity of local and regional political entities. In popular usage France is often, if not universally, regarded as a unitary nation-state: its complex centralized state is supposed to exert effective authority over a relatively homogeneous native French people. But quite aside from the actual regional diversities (Brittany, Provence, and so on) and recent immigrants, the cultural unity that now exists is a rather recent social construction. For it was not until the early years of the twentieth century that there were finally established within the territory of France "universal schooling and the unification of customs and beliefs by interregional labor migration and military services and the subordination of political and religious conflicts to patriotic ideology" (Balibar 1990, 344, citing Weber 1976).

Internal and external processes in state formation and expansion have interacted continually. States do form systems as they interact with one another, and the resulting interstate systems create, shape, and erase individual states. Over and above both the specific domestic and interstate forces that drive the system, there are pervasive cultural structures that define and endorse sovereignty, regulate jurisdictions, adjudicate boundaries, legitimize independence, and influence in numerous ways the working definitions of appropriate state behaviors. Much of the cultural context is diffuse—spread out across local structures and through time, and not located in central organizations. On the other hand, there are worldwide organizations that focus and implement cultural beliefs, values, and norms, as in the United Nations complex, the World Bank, regional interstate organizations, and numerous nongovernmental bodies. States are not free-standing monoliths, but rather permeable entities that acquire sovereignty and reciprocal legitimacy within wider systems of shared culture and organized interactions (Thomas and Meyer 1984).

How Did States Come to Be?

Over many thousands of years, humans lived in stateless societies. Although the origins are still debated, plausible hypotheses link the development of states to the rise of an agricultural surplus in areas subject to geographic and/or social constraints upon expanding populations and to the resulting warfare. Agricultural surplus created possibility, constraints created rivalries, and wars created states—which in turn waged wars. Thus it is fair to say that the essential state characteristic is effective coercion over a territory and its population (Carneiro 1970, 1988).

It is sometimes said that selective processes among large human collectivities are difficult to discern because few whole societies disappear. Upon inspection, this appears to be an unsupportable assumption. Over the very long periods of state-construction, many societies were engulfed and many destroyed. At a time of the first real cities (Jericho, Çatal Hüyük) around 6000 B.C., there must have been as many as 100,000 "societies"—the basic social units of small bands and collections of them. The smaller, technologically weak groupings were vulnerable to natural disasters as well as to military force exerted by the larger, resource-rich, more centralized groupings. With the development of agriculture, surpluses emerged that could be appropriated by centers of coercive powers, thus setting into motion the processes of conquest and consolidation that led to states, to empires, and eventually to centralized complex "nation" states (cf. Lenski 1994, 78; Tilly 1992).

Highly organized social formations, especially those that are centralized and hierarchical, evidently gain effectiveness as fighting machines. After all, it is the modern national state that has created the most deadly wars of all time and has been the greatest killer of its own subjects (van den Berghe 1992; Rummel 1994). For most of the last millennium, military forces have been the largest component of states, and the largest part of state expenditures have been devoted to the armed forces. Thus, taxation and other forms of the extraction of resources from the people—always problematic—and the accompanying "struggle over the means of war created the central organizational structures of states" (Tilly 1992, 57). State-making always involved the expansion and consolidation of authority (primarily, but not exclusively, through war), the establishment of internal order (e.g., control of class and ethnic conflict), and the extraction of resources. Long before the rise of modern sovereign territorial states, large autonomous centralized political units had developed, as in the great historical empires.

But it was the development of capitalism and of the system of national states in Europe that eventually spread to most of the rest of the world. That history has been characterized as one in which states were consolidated by wars and the emerging states in turn waged other wars. Tilly's general thesis has been summarized by Hall (1993, 5–6) as follows:

> Wars make states quite as much as states make war. Continual competition between states leads to an arms race requiring ever greater funding. Kings are thereby forced not just to sit on top of the various cultural segments within their territories, but rather to interact with them more closely in order to extract greater funds. . . . Over time, those states able to consolidate their territories into a single unit subject to bureaucratic rules fared best in warfare.

This result occurred in a system of mutual threats of invasion and conquest, in which over several centuries those states that were able to combine economic and military strength dominated and absorbed lesser states.

Thus the basic argument is that the centralized, complex, territorial state dominated because it was able to combine concentration of capital, a powerful economy, and control of internal struggles, and therewith deploy large, well-armed military forces. Consistent with this formulation is Small and Singer's massive review of historical data (1982), showing that the states most likely to fight interstate wars have been those near the top in ranking based on military-industrial capabilities, wealth, and diplomatic status. These are the states that fought wars often over long periods to attain and hold their high power rank. Indeed, in the European case, prior to the eighteenth century states were primarily war-making machines (Mann 1993a, 1993b), and they shared political authority with other entities (churches, empires, local lords). The great eighteenth-century expansion of states has been documented (by Mann 1993b, 116–17) in the rise of state finances as a percent of GNP—from around 5 percent in peacetime and 10 percent in wartime in 1700, to 15 percent and 25 percent in 1760, and to 25 percent and 35 percent by 1810.

When the emerging European states broke out from their continental confines—after centuries of militarized pressure from the East and South—they embarked upon a career of imperialist expansion. In that process, the small kinship-based local social units that had been the primary form of human existence for many thousands of years were subjected to relentless pressure through military conquest and economic domination. Whole ethnic peoples were subject to systematic killing, new diseases, alcohol, loss of hunting grounds and access to fishing areas, loss of lands and forests, and destruction of cultural integrity. The roll call is long: the Indians of the Americas, the Tasmanians, some of the "tribals" of India, the hill people of Bangladesh, the San of Botswana, the Marquesas (once 100,000 people, by 1980 perhaps 5,000) (Ashworth 1980, 101, 140–44).

Thus, the historical record shows how the partitioning of the world into territorially distinct and nominally sovereign states originated with their initial establishment in Europe. In the fifteenth century, the European populations of some eighty million people were more or less ruled by about five hundred political entities—states, aspirant states, and statelets, and state-like organizations: bishoprics, duchies, principalities, free cities, fortified villages, commercial-military leagues, ecclesiastical territories, manors, free-booting crusaders, armed bands, and others. It was a world of overlapping authorities, shifting allegiances, and numerous violent conflicts. From this chaotic multiplicity of diverse units, a lengthy and complex set of struggles finally led to the emergence of national states (Tilly 1992, 43). It is worth recalling that almost up to the twentieth century much organized violence, although sponsored by states, was carried out by trading companies, pirates, privateers, and mercenary forces. Eventually, the beginnings of universal interstate jurisdiction appeared in the doctrines that pirates were the "enemies of mankind" and could be apprehended, tried, and sanctioned anywhere by any state. Only slowly were such actors delegitimized, as interstate relations became more dense and recurrent, and as states increasingly could support their own military arms (cf. Thomson 1994). But by the culmination of the process in the late twentieth century, Europe's some 600 million people lived within the borders of no more than twenty-eight states. Most of the political units of the earlier times had not survived—they had been conquered and their identities erased, or they had been incorporated as parts of the larger states. And as the scale of the states had expanded, so had the size and organization of ethnic subnations.

The relation of the states to ethnies has differed radically among types of states. The great historical empires did not seek to build a culturally homogenous realm. They demanded resources and obedience, and often were ruthless in their impositions, but ethnic uniformity was not envisioned. Thus, the territories controlled by empires have been a patchwork of peoples differing in language, religion, and other cultural traits—witness the long history of the Ottoman and Czarist realms or the eighteenth-century roster of people ruled by the Habsburg system, including Germans, Hungarians, Poles, Croats, Czechs, Slovaks, Ruthenes, Flemings, Romanians, Italians, and Serbs. When empires break up, the fault lines frequently are ethnoregional.

So it was that the world has experienced four great waves of state-building, with massive ethnic consequences, attendant upon the collapse of empires. These waves were in Latin America, with the nineteenth-century dissolution of the Spanish Empire; in Europe after World War I, with the end of the Czarist Russian, Austria-Hungarian, and Ottoman rules; in Asia and Africa after World War II, with the end of colonial rule by Britain,

France, Belgium, Portugal, and the Netherlands; and in Eurasia and Eastern Europe after 1989, with the breakup of the Soviet Union. In each period, many of the newly independent states immediately encountered ethnic issues. The newly independent countries were strongly shaped by colonial powers, by interstate relations, and by the interventions of other states. They usually did not have a unitary communal base, but rather were multi-ethnic; they attempted to exercise authority over diverse peoples assembled within "arbitrary" boundaries and lacking in civic traditions. In terms of ethnic relations, it was crucial that interstate recognition of the independent statehood of former colonies in the post–World War II dismantling of empires did not require that political arrangements be established for citizenship, popular sovereignty, or protection of minorities. Lack of provisions for "self-determination of peoples" or for protection of subordinated ethnies was no barrier: former colonial status alone was enough to earn United Nations membership.

Partly as a consequence, the great majority of wars since 1945 have been ignited by the efforts to create new states, to maintain borders, to repress separatism, and to dominate ethnic and religious contenders for political power and cultural autonomy. As Holsti says, "The problem of war in international politics has thus been reduced primarily to the problem of state-maintenance and state failures" (1996, 79). In Holsti's terms (1996, chap. 5), such states lacked a strong base in either horizontal legitimacy (consensual support by an "affective community") or vertical legitimacy (the principle on which the right to rule is based). Small wonder, then, that many were soon beset by ethnic contention, separatism, and civil war—or that some became so much the creatures of self-interested factions as to earn the label of kleptocracies. Their legitimacy, such as it was, came primarily from "international" (i.e., interstate) recognition and from de facto control of territory and people, rather than from popular sovereignty and internal consensus on political institutions and ideologies.

In view of the prominent facts that very few territorial states are actually nation-states, containing only a single ethny or uniform culture, and that they remain multi-ethnic in spite of vigorous efforts by state authorities to create a common culture, it may seem surprising that since World War II there has been a remarkably widespread interstate commitment to the inviolability of state boundaries, invoking the dogma of nonintervention in the domestic affair of nominally sovereign states. The norms of sovereignty and nonintervention appeared for decades to have created a genuine taboo against forced boundary changes, possibly helping to account for the extraordinary rarity of interstate wars in the 1980s and 1990s (the Persian Gulf War being a salient exception) (cf. Hall 1993, 21). (Recent challenges to the non-intervention dogma will be discussed later.)

Even if a state's borders are arbitrary, in the sense of cutting across ethnic lines, state leaders typically resist any efforts to change such boundaries. Multi-ethnic states with weak central control have reason to fear that the very anticipation of boundary change could set in motion a cascade of secessionistic and irredentist claims and threats. Africa provides a large-scale demonstration. Leaders of states that attempt to govern diverse and often competitive and hostile ethnics may well be reluctant to risk exacerbating internal cleavages through irredentist ventures—although some (e.g., Somalia) may take the risk (Jackson and Rosberg 1982).

States are made "real" by recognition from already-existing states. The criteria are evidently vague and flexible, but the idea of legitimacy through interstate acknowledgment is central (McNeely 1995). The standard recipe of statehood has become nearly universal. Everyone must be a member of a state or else a refugee existing on sufferance of a state. The modern passport is a universal necessity for travel across the boundaries of these exclusionistic political entities, although this requirement has been waived in the European Union. The standard definition and format of sovereign states has been enshrined in the Charter of the United Nations. These cultural specifications are "standard recipes" (Strang 1996) that serve as blueprints or templates, and thus imply the reality and legitimacy of states as actual social organizations.

Within this general format, then, nominally sovereign states attempt to create cultural unification through a formidable set of social mechanisms—a favorite is a system of universal education with compulsory elementary schooling. Compulsory national service and unplanned social processes—as in interregional labor migrations and in upward social mobility that is controlled by national elites—also serve. One common state-unity argument is that there is some necessary and primordial affinity between statehood and a single language. Of course, this very modern notion does not fit either the great historical empires or modern multi-ethnic states, from India to Canada or the United States. On the other hand, it is clear that a standard language (or languages, as in the three-language system in India) is an important base for cultural unity, national identity, and the consolidation of authority in complex national states (see Thórarinsdóttir 1994).

The so-called social construction of states includes a grab bag of very diverse processes. The slow growth of some states over centuries contrasts sharply with states established by great powers or by interstate fiat. A few twentieth-century cases of state formation constitute the rare species of successful secession—violent in Bangladesh, peaceful in Slovakia's separation from the Czech Republic. And then there are the new states hammered out on the anvil of protracted separatist rebellion. The amalgamation of small ethnies into a large, national unity is well illustrated by the outcome of the thirty-one-year civil war in which Eritrea won independence from Ethiopia. At the beginning of the insurgency, of the some two million people of the region, one-half were Muslim and one-half were Christian (including Coptic Christians and some Protestants), speaking nine languages and belonging to nine ethnies. The long armed struggle against the powerful Ethiopian military campaigns, in which Eritrean rebels received no help from either the United States or the Soviet Union, solidified a sense of nationhood and common purpose. Although subject to strain, the new "Eritrean" identity survived the early years of independence and of renewed warfare with Ethiopia (Iyob 1995).

National states wishing to integrate a diverse populace typically try to remove regional, ethnic, and local barriers to mobility, communication, and social interaction and to promote the free movement of goods, persons, and ideas throughout the national territory. Often, such states adopt an official language and a unified educational system. At the same time the state clarifies and strengthens its external boundaries by controlling immigrants, interstate travel, trade, and communication, and by inculcating a patriotic/nationalistic ideology (Francis 1976, 396). But an assimilationist state can nevertheless protect diverse ethnies with a federal polity, asking only that primary loyalties be afforded to the central state.

During the twentieth century the combination of popular sovereignty, state centralization, and politicized ethnicity (as "nationalism") lent itself to wars of secession, irredentism, "ethnic cleansing," and genocide. The notion that ethnic identity should be the basis for statehood has led directly to the idea of the homogeneous nation-state. States now claimed to be nations and nations claimed the right to statehood, "whether 'captive' in multinational states or fragmented into a multiplicity of states" (van den Berghe 1996, 64). Recognition of these processes and of their drastic and often deadly consequences has led many observers to focus their attention upon the alternative of civic nationalism.

The Varieties of Nationalism

Many current definitions of nation, nationalism, ethnicity, and allied concepts are backward-looking: they refer to ancestry, culture, descent, history, shared experience. Thus, "The existence of a nation entails the conscious recognition by a group of people of a sense of belonging to a community on the basis of a perceived shared culture, language, history, race, religion, or political experience" (Frankland and Noble 1996, 402). This formulation is reasonable enough but it is incomplete in its failure to include another form of collective identity—the sense of sharing common aspirations and hopes and fears for the future, a better life for our children, a "more perfect union," a shared fate. American nationalism seems to provide a prototypical example of such a non-ethnic basis of identity, but even there continuing tensions exist between ethnoreligious demands and secular/democratic claims.

The idea that there is a civic nationalism—in which otherwise diverse people share a sense of common membership in a political community—has found strong support among scholars, especially those who see great danger in ethnic/religious nationalism. Yet civic nationalism is itself complex. It can mean that there is national solidarity based on the widespread acceptance of shared values and beliefs, including legal-political principles. The state, in this view, can elicit loyalty insofar as political practice exemplifies democracy, individual freedom, the rule of law, and so on. Thus Habermas (1984, 1987) has emphasized "constitutional patriotism." On the other hand, agreement upon broad cultural values or principles may be seen as too thin and abstract to generate a strong and resilient civic nationalism. For example, Schnapper (1998) advances the claim that particular historical experiences and distinctive political projects define the civic integration of people in democratic states. Clearly, civic nationalism can contain both some sharing of "universalizing" political values and beliefs as well as the particular histories of individual countries.

Nationalism in well-established multi-ethnic states, then, is not the same as ethnicity, or as ethnic self-consciousness, or as ethnic claims to autonomy or statehood. The nationalism of the Western national state is a constructed collective identity, not necessarily identical with a subnational or even a core-dominant ethny. It includes both identification with a common culture and the common citizenship of individual persons. This conception rejects the idea of the mono-ethnic state as well as the idea that "subnationalities" have priority over the "civic nation" (cf. Tiryakian 1997). The strong version of such nationalism is "a political doctrine extolling the nation as a supreme value and representing it as a dominant principle of societal organization" (Francis 1976, 387). Obviously, the intensity of such integral nationalism varies widely.

The struggle between secular/democratic and ethnoreligious political forces has taken on major world significance in the remarkable case of India since its independence after World War II. A vast population there represents dozens of major languages, hundreds of ethnies, and numerous religious adherents who are Hindu, Muslim, Christian, Sikh, Buddhist, Jain, and others. An ancient, complex, diverse civilization has a long history of intercultural contact, merging, and change (for a nuanced historical account, see Larson 1995). A major challenge to the secular state has developed in the form of Hindutva ("Hindu-ness") advocated by a leading political party, the Bharatiya Janata Party (BJP), which urges teaching Hindi as the official language and inculcating a strong sense of cultural unity and patriotism. This program aims at a religio-ethnic national state.

In contrast, Turkey has strongly emphasized its secular state, resisting all attempts to change to a theocratic Islamic state. Meanwhile, revolutionary movements have established Islamic forms in Iran, Afghanistan, Pakistan, and elsewhere. The tensions and struggles continue.

Despite the great variation in content, form, and historical contexts we can identify a common core in many of the particular modern nationalisms. As formulated by Hall (1993, 2), the core of nationalism is "the belief in the primacy of a particular nation, real or constructed; the logic of this position tends to move nationalism from cultural to political forms and entail popular mobilization." As we examine present day societies, three main forms of such nationalism dominate the international system.

The first is the inclusive civic variety in which loyalty is owed to a national state that represents such generalized principles as the rule of law, inclusive citizenship, and individual rights. In contrast, the second variety is particularistic and exclusionary: membership and participation in the polity are based on ascriptive criteria—essentially birth or descent—within a collectivity defined by language, shared history, and common beliefs and values. Overlapping with these types is ethnoreligious nationalism, which differs from a narrower ethnic nationalism primarily in its more universalistic emphasis: all adherents to an inclusive religious "community of faith" are defined as potential members and others may join by conversion—but the state itself is an integral part of the religious order (as in Islamic states). Militant ethnoreligious movements within secular states have demonstrated impressive political strength.

Nationalism of the civic kind (Smith 1989) in the West has been secular and ethnically pluralistic and inclusive (e.g., citizenship by birth within the country or by relatively easy tests of residence and commitment). Such nationalism does not depend upon ancestry, and in the case of the United States has been compatible with a "country of immigration" par excellence. Although the contrast must not be overemphasized, this orientation differs sharply from nationalism based on ethnic and religious communities. "Nationality" (e.g., American, French, Spanish) in many modern industrialized societies is political and cultural, not primordial-ethnic, and "nationalism" is oriented to assimilation, not exclusion. Very different are those nationalisms that base themselves upon ethnic membership, a membership that is overwhelmingly conferred by birth. The distinction, accordingly, is one of civic versus ethnic identity.

The apparent simplicity of this distinction may obscure the phenomenon of "fictive ethnicity" as created by states aspiring to become nation-states. In those cases, the putative "national community" is an institutionalized creation: as originally separate social formations are brought into a nationalizing state, these populations are "ethnicized, that is, represented . . . *as if* they formed a natural community, possessing of itself an identity of origins, culture, and interests which transcend individuals and social conditions" (Balibar 1990, 349). In this ideal form, each individual in the population over which the state claims control would have one and only one ethnic identity: French, German, Russian, Indian, Ugandan, and so on. The so-called ideal form is seldom achieved.

Stable national identity can emerge in three basic ways. In the one case, the sense of common identity builds upon an earlier ethnic core of shared culture and historical continuity. In a second form, mutual accommodation creates a multicultural state. In the third case, the contemporary identity has been gradually constructed by the envelopment (by conquest, or annexation, or incremental state-building) of segmented identities that are eroded and/or merged through processes of acculturation and structural assimilation. Lacking either of these conditions, emergent national states are likely to seek to expel, suppress, or exterminate ethnic minorities and to impose cultural requirements, ostensibly "national" but representing a politically dominant ethny within a multi-ethnic state. Such suppressions and impositions often, perhaps usually, arouse feelings of humiliation and resentment (Horowitz 1985; Greenfield 1993; Scheff 1994; Tavuchis 1991), and increase the likelihood of severe ethnic conflict, as we shall see in Chapter 6. The great wave of ethnic nationalistic conflicts that emerged after World War II has extended through the last decade of the twentieth century and into the twenty-first century. It is an era of ethnic peoples against peoples, and peoples against states, and states against peoples—that is, of *The Wars Within*.

Variations among States

As over against the abstract purity of ideal state forms, the real world "out there" is a lumpy place, inhabited by strong and weak states, failed and collapsed states, predator or kleptocratic states, welfare states, and fragmented quasi-states. The watchword is heterogeneity, not uniformity. Dozens of the members of the United Nations have fewer than a million people; China and India each have over a billion. Some states occupy tiny bits of territory—small islands such as St. Kitts-Nevis or the Seychelles, or enclaves encompassed by larger states. Population density (persons per square kilometer) varies from 5,534 in Hong Kong or 4,457 in Singapore to 2 in Mauritania and 1.4 in Mongolia, (1993 data from Kidron and Segal 1995, World Table). There are extremes of wealth and poverty, and of income inequality. Governing regimes range from highly repressive dictatorships to relatively egalitarian democracies. And, cross-cutting the distinctions of political forms, states vary from strong to weak in their capabilities for governance.

What does it mean to say that a state is "strong" or "weak"? This is an extremely difficult question to answer in any simple way. The most obvious answer is that a state is strong to the extent that the existing government controls the military and police force on the basis of strong support by the politically relevant public. A second aspect of strength is the state's ability to extract large revenues from a flourishing economy. A third form of strength is that a state enjoys such political support as to permit it to have wide latitude in the allocations of resources and of rights and privileges among various segments of the population. Still another interpretation equates strength with the degree and kind of legitimacy possessed by the state.

In a major formulation, Holsti (1996, 144–45) has noted that today "strong states" and "democracies" are nearly overlapping categories, but he prefers to refer to strong states "because the critical criterion of state strength is the degree of vertical and horizontal legitimacy, and not particular political institutions and practices" (1996, 144). This formulation seems to equate strength with legitimacy—a potentially confusing procedure. In common usage, many strong states are those that maintain centralized coercive control within their borders and command large military forces; such states are Great Powers. What Holsti contends is that states based primarily on coercion, lacking legitimacy of both normative principles and of popular consent, are not basically strong. Obviously, this is a matter of definition, but we have to remember that long-lived empires—such as the Chinese, Roman, and Ottoman—did not rely upon popular sovereignty, although they undoubtedly claimed various "principles of the right to rule," ranging from divine right to hereditary claims. And up until the end of the nineteenth century, states regularly recognized a "right of conquest" to justify control of territory and peoples (Bilder, Korman, and Kennedy 1997). Relatively small elites often are successful in the use of force to subjugate and control large populations. Numerous autocratic states have been stable over long periods. Might may not ensure right, but it often prevails with a minimum of legitimacy.

All this is to say that "strength" need not be equated with legitimacy nor with democracy. This is not a trivial point. Deadly conflict is high in very weak states and stateless societies, but even higher in highly centralized and autocratic states (Cooney 1997). Wars in the last decade of the twentieth century were almost entirely civil wars, concentrated in weak or failed states. State failure or state collapse invites warlordism, rule by gangs, communal massacres, "ethnic cleansing," waves of refugees, and economic chaos.

"Failed" states are those that do not carry out essential domestic functions—to maintain order, to prevent police and military forces from harassing civilians, to protect peaceful economic activities, to provide education and health care, or to maintain and improve infrastructures (roads, canals, air transport, communications). By such criteria, failed states in Africa in the early 1990s included Zaire, Chad, Sierra Leone, and Equatorial Guinea. "Collapsed" states were those in which governments were under siege or in which civil war had erupted, such as Colombia, Afghanistan, Angola, Liberia, Burundi, Somalia, Rwanda, and the Sudan (Widner 1995, 137). The lists change from time to time, but the distinction between failed and collapsed states remains: poor performance does not always lead to collapse, and some "effective" governments have collapsed into civil warfare.

But highly centralized, despotic, militarized governments, even when not warring with other nondemocratic states, are even more deadly in total effect. So it was that during the twentieth century, the mass slaughter of unarmed peoples by governments accounted for about four times the total of deaths in battle. Most of the democides (over 80 percent) were committed by centralized and dictatorial regimes—for example, in the Soviet Union, China, Nazi Germany, Yugoslavia, Japan, Vietnam, and the Khmer Rouge in Cambodia (Rummel 1994, 4–5). Within the modern state system, these facts suggest, "the less freedom people have the greater the violence; the more freedom, the less the violence. I offer this principle here as The Power Principle: power kills, and absolute power kills absolutely" (Rummel 1994, xvi). This refers to "power" as sheer coercion—the ability to compel by the use or threat of injury or deprivation. Raw coercion contrasts with legitimate authority, the ability to secure obedience through coercion that is supported by the consensus of an effective community. As the full range of types of societies shows, beneficent freedom does not include total license or anarchy. The least lethal forms of statehood in modern times have been those we call democracies.

Democracies and Other State-Forms

Democracy as a form of statehood represents a range within a scale extending from rule-governed, fully participatory decision making to totalitarian dictatorship. For example, Rummel (1995, 11–14) has used factor analysis to identify no fewer than five main patterns of political regimes: democracy, totalitarian, centralized-autocratic, total power, and elite power. Democracies survive only under particular conditions, and the growth of democracy over the last several centuries was slow, spasmodic, and painful as changing constellations of people bargained with rulers for voice and influence. Although war sometimes provided opportunities for enlarged political participation, in the longer run frequent wars tended to produce centralized and autocratic regimes. In general, not only do democracies not fight democracies, but reduction in the threat of war is a condition favorable to the growth of stable democracies. In general, threatening environments inhibit the development of democratic states and favor the emergence of militarized autocracies (Midlarsky 1995).

In its fullest form democracy provides for relative freedom of speech and assembly, for citizens who have juridical rights (e.g., to vote, to hold office, to enjoy minority protection), and for legislatures elected in competitive elections. It entails widespread suffrage and a representative state that is internally sovereign, especially over the armed forces and the conduct of foreign affairs. It provides for an independent judiciary, and more broadly for separation of powers and checks and balances among legislative, executive, and judicial agencies. There is general adherence to the "rule of law," that is, restraint of decision makers by laws not of their own making (cf. Kober 1994). It provides protection for political, ethnic, religious, and other "minorities"; without such guarantees, democracy is likely to quickly turn into the tyranny of the majority.

The more these features a state has, the more democratic it is at any given time. Obviously a particular state may be democratic in one period, and autocratic at another. Indeed, of 28 European states in 1920, 26 were at least nominally democratic, but by 1938 only 12 remained; similar reversals occurred in Latin America and Africa in the decades after World War II. But a new wave of democracies emerged after the 1970s, and by 1993, 107 countries out of 186 had competitive elections and some nominal guarantees of political and individual rights. By 1996, over 60 percent of the world's independent countries were formally democratic, although many of these were partial or "facade" democracies (Schwartzman 1998).

Western democratic states exert authority, and resort to coercive power, in interaction with various ethnic "communities" and with a civic sphere consisting of numerous free-standing networks and voluntary associations. In the ideal-typical case, then, popular nationalism is civic nationalism, not ethnically or religiously exclusionist, but inclusive of all individual elements of the total society. Individuals are the basic social units. Loyalty and commitment are to the values, beliefs, and aspirations that support the civic order. Inevitably, genuinely democratic societies are contentious and disorderly, but—in the long-lasting cases—within the limits generated by commitment to democratic values and procedures (Jowitt 1992).

Within such limits, the prospects for a democratic political order increase with increasing economic development and social differentiation. Initial stages of economic growth typically increase income inequality, but continued growth (coupled with social differentiation) increases the likelihood of countervailing economic forces. Social differentiation—occupational, regional, religious, ethnic (again, up to some limit of fragmentation)—reduces the likelihood of a single dominant ruling social formation. In contrast, the more extreme mass poverty and the sharper the inequalities of wealth and income, the lower the likelihood of stable democracy. Similarly, there is much other historical and comparative data suggesting that democracy is favored by the presence of countervailing power centers (e.g., free cities and merchants and financiers) that can restrain absolutist rulers, or organized labor against employers, or regions and ethnies against increased taxation and military conscription, or urban militias against the claims of central rulers.

On the other hand, many of the limited democracies in early city-states failed by being conquered by more powerful states, and over long periods war and the threat of war favored centralized and hierarchical political systems that were unfavorable to democratic development. Thus some historical analyses suggest that "minimization of the threat of war is an important condition for the emergence of a durable democracy, as indicated by the evidence pertaining to four ancient societies and the systematic analysis of the modern period" (Midlarsky 1995, 254).

And in present-day societies, serious threats to democracy can be seen to develop from intrastate conflicts; in general, the higher the level of communal conflict, the greater the likelihood of autocratic, especially militarized, governments and state structures. Similarly, over substantial periods organizations that oppose one another in important ways (trade, arms transfers, voting in the United Nations) tend to become more like their rivals in organizational structure (e.g., more hierarchical) and in tactics and strategies (e.g., greater use of threats). Both internally and externally, therefore, the relation between violent conflict and the structure of the political system of states are reciprocal. As formulated by Carmet and James (1995, 89), "States involved in recurring episodes of violent ethnic conflict tend to develop elite political cultures that sanction the use of violence and maintain institutions specialized in the exercise of coercion. . . . By contrast, frequent success in the use of reforms and concessions to manage internal challenges leads to the development of institutions and norms of democratic rule."

Democratic state structures, to the extent that they are effective in practice rather than merely nominal, minimize or reduce government arbitrariness. The rule of law over freely elected officials, together with an independent judiciary and civilian control of the police and armed forces—all these tend to reduce caprice in relations with those ruled. It is in this context that advocates of democracy can assert that "political arbitrariness creates much more anger than does social inequality. People prefer reform to revolution, the possibility of peaceful changes to the dangers of the barricades. Liberalism thus diffuses conflict through society whereas authoritarianism concentrates it" (Hall 1993, 17).

But of course, "liberalism" is not self-standing. It is unlikely to be effective unless supported by sustaining social structures and cultures consisting of pluralistic interest groupings, civic associations, crosscutting social allegiances, and multiple oppositions. Such conditions are products of gradual long-term processes that have been most evident in the societies of northwest European origin. Although cultural factors undoubtedly are influential, such as doctrines of theocratic rule in some Islamic countries, the precise weight and nature of their influence are not clear. What is abundantly clear is that "democracy" in its many particular forms is a complex historical outcome of many diverse processes that have converged upon similar political bargains that created elaborate institutionalized arrangements of authority and consent.

Some of these processes may be discerned by examination of the contrasting conditions that have been associated with authoritarian states. On the whole, the weight of historical and comparative evidence supports the following generalizations concerning the conditions that favor authoritarian regimes.

1. Frequent and severe wars, creating centralization and suppression of dissent. More generally, frequent and severe external threats, including environmental stresses.
2. Severe internal conflicts, producing highly insecure state elites—for example, by sudden economic collapse or ethnic polarization.
3. Great economic inequality, such that democratization would raise the possibility of strong redistribution policies.
4. Substantial state/regime income derived from sources outside of domestic popular control, for example, exports of state-controlled mineral wealth (*rentier* states).
5. Low levels of social differentiation in occupations, civic associations, freestanding local government.
6. Concentration of material resources under the control of a small proportion of the populations, so that a narrow ruling group can dominate the state (Vanhanen 1997).

The more centralized a national state and the greater its powers of allocation of scarce valuables, the greater the stakes in control of the government. The scarce valuables include jobs in state service; credit; access to education; contracts; health, pension, and welfare benefits; and the protection of political and civil rights (including religion and language rights). When the society in which the state is embedded is economically "underdeveloped," political office, governmental employment, and military service become rare and highly valued opportunities. Partly for these reasons, struggles for control of centralized states in such circumstances acquire special intensity.

It is important to note in this connection that "centralization" has two major dimensions, which may be termed "authoritarianism" and "totalitarianism." The first dimension is the contrast between autocracy and democracy, the degree of centralization and closure of decision making, from dictatorship to town-meeting democracy. The second dimension, ranging from totalitarian to libertarian, represents the extent of state penetration and attempted controls of the whole society. The most deadly states are those that combine the two dimensions—prime examples are Maoist China, Stalinist Soviet Union, and Hitlerian Germany.

Authoritarian regimes, often although not always, engender or perpetuate economic inefficiencies in the societies they attempt to control (Sutter 1998). They extract high rents through taxes and other means. They may use foreign aid, intended to foster economic development, for military support and political patronage. They impose restrictions on the allocations of capital and labor. Thus, the continuation of authoritarian rule (except possibly in tightly controlled "export platform" societies à la Singapore) is costly to the subject population. The costs, however, may not be generally known, whereas the anticipated costs of rebellion may be very high indeed.

Many autocratic states do not manage to establish "deep" control of substate formations, but do have central control of vital resources. Among such states a prominent type is that of *rentier* states—those in which a high percentage of the central government's revenue comes from sources other than direct taxation of the domestic population, such as high-value exports of narcotics, oil, diamonds, or other minerals; income of state-operated corporations; duties on imports; and grants and loans from external agencies. Ruling groups in such states have little incentive to stimulate and guide economic development, and their relative independence from popular support encourages centralized authoritarian rule with repressive policies concerning political rights and civil liberties. In short, the more the state subsists on rent, the less the development of the private sector and of democratic polity. If such states rule a multi-ethnic society, the dominant ethnies will be intolerant of ethnic and regional claims for greater rights or autonomy.

These rentier states can ignore internal demands for democracy as they maintain domestic coercive control through military and paramilitary forces. Examples in the 1990s included Zaire, Nigeria, Myanmar (Burma), Angola, Indonesia, and many more. Furthermore, when rulers have resources not dependent upon consent of those ruled, they have considerable opportunity to make unpopular decisions. Thus Kiser, Drass, and Brustein (1995) showed that in early modern Western Europe, the more autonomous the rulers, the more often they initiated wars. And in the world today a society composed of mutually exclusive ethnies contending for control of a centralized repressive state is likely to experience military or one-party rule. If at the same time the ruling elites have access to non-tax revenues, the temptations will be great for private enrichment at the expense of the public sector. The list of such predator regimes, or klep-tocracies, is a long one. When other effective countervailing power is absent, ethnic as well as other intrastate conflicts can be expected to occur over and over.

We have now briefly examined the characteristics of democracies and the conditions likely to lead to authoritarian or democratic regimes. The next obvious consideration is, what difference does it make? What are the consequences of democracy or autocracy?

Although there are problems of definitions, the general conclusion is that democracies do not initiate major warfare against one another, and on the whole they fight less deadly wars than nondemocracies (Bremer 1993; Kegley and Hermann 1995; Maoz 1997). The controversial but well-supported generalization is that democracies only rarely fight each other, even at low levels of deadly violence (Ember, Ember, and Russett 1992, 573). What has long been unclear is why the infrequency of interdemoc-racy war should exist. Several major hypotheses have been advanced: al-liances, common ties in a network of institutions, historical rarity of physical proximity of democratic states, shared interests in defense against a common threat, unattractiveness of war to leaders of democracies, which tend to be politically stable and economically advanced. But even when sta-tistical controls are applied for proximity, alliances, wealth, economic growth, and political stability, democracy retains independent explanatory power (Ember, Ember, and Russett 1992, 575). Other studies have sup-ported this finding (Mintz and Geva 1993; Maoz and Russett 1992).

An extensive scholarly literature has endorsed the idea of a "democratic peace," entailing three separate propositions: (1) that democracies do not wage war against one another; (2) that democracies engage in wars, over-all, less frequently than nondemocracies; (3) that democracies are much less likely than other states to kill large numbers of their own citizens or subjects.

In turn, a vast body of skeptical commentary criticizes, qualifies, or at-tempts to refute the thesis of a democratic peace. What are we to believe? The controversies involve disagreements about the empirical evidence. What are the relevant facts?

First, it clearly is true that well-established democracies do not slaugh-ter large numbers of their own citizens or sojourners (Horowitz 2001, 514; Fein 1993). Centralized, autocratic, and especially totalitarian states do engage in such massive killing of the populations they rule—thus, Maoist China, Nazi Germany, the Soviet Union under Stalin, Pol Pot's Cambodia.

53

But, second, settler-democracies in the great overseas European expansion did kill enormous numbers of indigenous peoples.

Third, some democracies have supported, given financial aid, and supplied arms to dictatorial regimes engaged in deadly repression or civil warfare against rebel movements. These so-called "proxy wars" were not interstate wars under the standard definition, but they certainly caused vast destruction and loss of life.

Fourth, societies moving rapidly from autocratic to democratic regimes do experience much deadly ethnic conflict. In the years since the end of the Cold War, however, transitional regimes actually have had less ethnopolitical conflict than autocracies and only slightly more than democracies (Gurr 2000, 154–55).

Indeed, the inconsistent effects of attempted democratic transitions show that ethno-rebellions in these cases have primary causes other than democratization. The essential conclusion is that "*the formation of new states in heterogenous societies is the primary risk factor for serious ethnopolitical conflict, not the formation of new democracies per se*" (Gurr 2000, 163; italics in original). Also, ethnopolitical groupings in democratic societies tend to engage in protests rather than violent rebellions. The movement toward democracy has aided peaceful accommodations in societies as different as South Africa, Lebanon, and Guatemala.

Fifth, since the end of World War I there have been no actual wars between pairs of democratic states. None. And an outstanding critic of the "democratic peace" does note that across the entire period 1816–1980, "members of pairs of democratic states are significantly less likely to engage each other in war and other militarized disputes then are members of other country pairs" (Gowa 1999, 61). Critics of the democratic peace usually rely upon data on the *incidence* or frequency of wars between states, neglecting the *magnitude* (deadliness) of wars. When the number of people killed is taken into account, the wars that democracies fight are less deadly than wars between nondemocratic states (Rummel 1995, 1994).

Sixth, the democratic peace hypothesis is held to be refuted because of the problematic record before 1914, such as the Spanish-American War of 1898.[1] This conclusion rests on the stringent and debatable assumption that peace among democracies should hold uniformly across historical periods.

Seventh, critics of the hypothesis dismiss it on the grounds that peace between democracies derives from *common interests* rather than *type of political system*. More specifically, it is argued that the Cold War created a com-

---

[1] But see Gowa 1999, 82: "before 1914, the character of major-power interactions makes it difficult to distinguish democratic from other country dyads."

mon interest among democracies in military security. This is a straightforward realist position—that the interests of states are independent from the type of internal regime they have, and that the primary interest is survival in an anarchic interstate system.

There is no foreseeable end to debates over this radical thesis, and we do not have to settle the issue here. For our purposes it is enough to note the long peace among democracies, and particularly the weighty evidence showing that modern democracies tend to use negotiations and peaceful accommodations to deal with ethnopolitical demands (Gurr 2000, 84–85, 154ff., 211).

Finally, some supporters of the democratic peace have endorsed the idea that democracy is a sovereign remedy for genocides and democides. The critics are profoundly correct in holding that the attempts to "export democracy," often dubious at best, can be extremely dangerous if done abruptly and without regard to the particular circumstances in receiving countries.

The weight of the evidence, then, is that democracies are less violent than nondemocracies. This is clearly so for the *severity* of violence (the number of persons killed in wars and in democides and genocides), and generally so for frequencies of war, for the initiation of violence in crises, and for the escalation of violence in crises (Rummel 1995, 473). The relationship between state authority and deadly conflict, however, is not linear. The most complete evidence is that death rates in lethal conflicts (wars, rebellion, executions, homicides) are high when state authority is weak or absent but much higher when the state is extremely strong and highly centralized. The most deadly situations are those in which decision making is concentrated in a centralized power structure and when the centralized state deeply penetrates into many areas of social life, with detailed regulations, censorship, secret police and informers, and so on. The most lethal states, thus, are autocratic and totalitarian (Cooney 1997). This means that the actual relationship between degree of authoritarianism and deadliness of conflict is U-shaped—high levels of killings at both extremes, but greatest when Leviathan dominates.

The most complete evidence on this crucial matter has been assembled and analyzed by R. J. Rummel (1984, 1994, 1995, 1995b). Drawing data from 218 regimes (141 states and 77 stateless societies or quasi-states), these studies focus upon democides—the mass killings of people "without arms in their hands." Such deaths inflicted by the governments upon their own populations were nearly four times as great as all fatalities in combat in the years between 1900 and 1987. Rummel estimates the grim total of deaths so inflicted by governments as an astonishing 170 million (Rummel 1994, 1995). The two variables that best predict the number of deaths are (1) the degree of democracy in the state regime, and (2) the extent of the state's involvement in war or rebellion. In democracies during war, central-ization of decision making occurs and "pockets" of secrecy and unchecked authority develop. In nondemocracies, these features are chronic, not sit-uational. So a central research finding is that democracies are far less likely than nondemocracies to use deadly violence against the people over whom they hold sovereign power.

Although well-established democracies are more peaceable than autoc-racies, the likelihood of *interstate* wars is greater in *rapidly democratizing* re-gimes than in those that are stable or moving toward autocracy (Mansfield and Snyder 2001). It is the transition from autocracy to democracy that is likely to make states more nationalistic and belligerent, as the process leads to "weak central authority, unstable domestic coalitions, and high-energy mass politics" (Mansfield and Snyder 2001, 120). Diverse internal interest groupings, including ethnies and elites from former governing strata, make incompatible political demands and render nationalism and war as escape options for internally threatened governments.

As always with such complex aggregated historical phenomena, some cautions must be recorded. First of all, the findings are gathered from a particular historical period (although they appear to be valid as well for prior decades in the nineteenth century), and there is no guarantee that they can be generalized to other times and places. In part this qualifica-tion is necessary because of the rarity of earlier democracies. (Athenian "democracy" did not refrain from merciless attacks on other peoples: see the chilling account by Thucydides in "The Melian Dialogue.") A second reservation is that although democracies avoid full-scale wars with other democracies, they do frequently engage in incursions and other limited miliary actions against democratic states (Kegley and Hermann 1995). Third, the data on fatalities are very imprecise and subject to wide varia-tions in estimates made by different students of the same events. Fourth, democracies have inflicted great violence upon stateless and tribal peo-ples, and have supported dictatorships that were waging war against sub-jected peoples.

Nevertheless, when all the evident sources of unreliability and all major difficulties of interpretation have been taken into account, the main point remains: democracies are less deadly political entities than nondemocra-cies. This impressive conclusion is not negated by the fact that the wars of the late twentieth century have been primarily civil wars within weak states—for such wars lie on the weak side of the U-shaped distribution of deadly violence described above. For example, the democides and at-tempted genocides in the weak states of sub-Saharan Africa and southeast Asia represent "ethnic cleansing," warlordism, rule by gangs, state-spon-sored communal massacres, and the destruction of local solidarities. But in no case could we attribute such violence to an excess of democracy.

Accepting this central conclusion, how can we account for the relative peacefulness of democratic states? The question implies another: why are nondemocracies more deadly?

First, the lesser deadliness of democracies may be due in part to the effectiveness of democratic participation in expressing the reluctance of the citizenry to incur the costs of war—the deaths, injuries, destruction of property, disruption of life-courses. Through the checks and balances of the polity, warlike leaders and interest groups may be prevented from provoking war or from escalating nonlethal controversies. (This is the Kantian explanation.) Second, the practice of democratic norms of negotiation, compromise, and the ethic of live-and-let-live may carry over into the conduct of leaders in foreign affairs. Third, democratic leaders, in dealing with their counterparts in other democracies, may expect reciprocal restraints and understandings.

Conversely, the greater belligerence of autocracies arguably derives from the greater capability of leaders for decisive and quick action that escalates disputes into violent conflict, or permits preventive or preemptive war. Dictators have less assurance of popular support (because of repression and secrecy) and hence may be inclined to create foreign diversions. Leaders of autocratic regimes probably are aware of the temptations for war that other leaders like themselves will have—Stalin and Hitler were well advised to distrust one another. And the autocrat, unrestrained by the populace, may simply resort to war in the hope and expectation of gaining territory, resources, and prestige from victories. The gains to ruling elites from victories in war are real and can be enormous, even if suppressed elements of the people endure great hardships.

The Complex Relations of States and Ethnies

The place of ethnicity in the twenty-first century can not be understood without charting its intersections with states. As we have reviewed, modern "national" states have emerged from the earlier chaos of numerous small, diverse, loosely connected states, leagues, feudal domains, military orders, and religious jurisdictions. From such origins, the main states of Western Europe were created by wars, alliances, and rivalries in which ruling dynasties conquered and bargained successive forms of states (Tilly 1992)—with little regard for ethnicity. These states were creatures of "dynastic hazard" (Pfaff 1992, 60), not of ethnic solidarity. Nevertheless, as such states expanded their territorial control they also spread locally reproducible cultural forms—a standard language, law codes, town charters, forms of religious organizations (Bartlett 1993). Today, however, "the world is transforming itself, with a strong movement to small culturally homogeneous units, often characterized by intense intolerance, downright hatred of foreigners, especially foreigners within the gates, mitigated by some movement toward freer trade and more weakly toward international political community" (Keyfitz 1995, 226).

In the face of these separatist tendencies, the entire world, as noted, is currently partitioned among over 190 nominally sovereign territorial states—those jealous claimants for primary coercive authority through the use and threat of force over a population within a geographic boundary. Asserting rights to control land, the air space above, and the sea zones around the land, these sovereign entities also attempt to regulate immigration and emigration, and to exert primary authority over ethnic peoples within. Yet by any practical criterion less than one in ten of such states represent an ethnic unity.

Ethnic pluralism and intermingling is the rule. The sources of today's mixtures lie in conquests, political changes in boundaries, in forced population expulsions and transfers, in enslavement, and in large-scale voluntary immigration. The great historical empires expanded by conquest, and the peoples that they did not kill or enslave remained as mosaics of diverse cultures within a system of political domination. In later times of colonization, large derivative ethnies were created by enslavement, as in the Americas. Modern colonization likewise extended political control over indigenous peoples, juxtaposing different and often antagonistic collectivities. When such colonies later became independent countries, their boundaries usually perpetuated the former administrative areas that crisscrossed ethnic lines. Forced population transfers, as in the Soviet Union, relocated and changed many ethnies. Voluntary migration created great ethnic diversity, as in the United States. And the construction of new national states, such as India or Yugoslavia, incorporated large and politically salient ethnies under a nominally unitary national state.

In all their motley profusion, both states and ethnies exhibit enormous diversity—in degree of central authority and control, in homogeneity of culture, in closure of networks of interactions, in sharpness of boundaries, in clarity of lines of leadership, and in control over material resources. Some states are little more than congeries of patronage networks and armed gangs. Some ethnies develop substantial military and paramilitary forces and exercise authoritative control over sizeable territories and their people. Nevertheless, in the "ideal" case states as compared with ethnies have more definite boundaries and tests of membership, more centralized authority and definiteness of leadership, more resources, and greater capability to mobilize resources and act as a unit for some purposes. Ethnies, on the whole and with few exceptions, are more likely to be characterized by fragmentation of allegiances, by rivalry among factions and their leaders, and by inability to make firm and enforceable agreements with other collectivities. Neither ethnies nor states are unitary actors, but ethnies typically are more fluid, more amorphous, less clearly bounded.

Ethnic diversity by itself need not lead to politicized conflict. The often-cited examples include the "mosaic" societies of historical empires in which the concentrated coercive power at the center was used to extract tribute, taxes, and military forces but otherwise rarely penetrated deeply into the internal functioning of religious and cultural communities. Sovereignty was often brutal, but in times of relative peace was a sort of film over the surface of local communities and other particularistic formations, notably ethnies. Rent-seeking imperial states were ruthless in their extractive behavior but typically had little interest in or were opposed to homogenization of the peoples they ruled. Indeed, divide-and-rule policies depended upon preserving and accentuating various cleavages among subject populations. Subversion and rebellion were likely to be met with extreme harshness, but there was little need to make ethnicity itself politically salient.

Because of conquest, slave transfers, colonialism, and annexation during the several centuries of European expansion, "the great bulk of ethnic group formations attain subordinate or minority status as the result of coercive subjugation by dominant groups. . . . The overriding relationship has been one of force and compulsion" (Schermerhorn 1970, 156). Indeed, European states and ethnies were themselves products of a long history of creating, destroying, absorbing, and transforming successive collective forms. "Europe" of the late Middle Ages was a congeries of societies with a long experience of conquest, state-building, colonization—and of ethnic conflict and accommodation and assimilation. As Bartlett summarizes the case, "Europe, the initiator of one of the world's major processes of conquest, colonization and culture transformation, was also the product of one" (1993, 314).

A great step toward a radically different situation was the emergence of the national state—a centralized and differentiated structure ruling over multiple contiguous regions and claiming priority, if not always strict monopoly, over the legitimate use of physical force within a territory (Tilly 1992, 1–3). Originally organized primarily for extraction, warfare, and territorial defense and expansion, such "national" entities over time broadened their scope and deepened their penetration of the social structure. As they did so, they began to press for standardization of rules and uniformity of culture. Under specific historical circumstances, then, they developed doctrines of nationalism that could easily undergird demands for cultural uniformity and the submergence of substate ethnies. From the French revolution onward, European nationalism became a major force. From World War I onward, increasing salience was given to the principle of self-determination of peoples. The collision of state sovereignty with ethnic self-determination became all the more explosive to the extent that multi-ethnic national states claimed to be nation-states. At the extreme, self-determination in the face of absolute state sovereignty could be a recipe for collective conflict, extending to democide and genocide.

After 1945, the United Nations aided in state creation by setting forth the basic terms of independence, of decolonization. The UN Charter had established the *principle* of "self-determination," but the General Assembly in its 1960 Resolution raised it to a *right*. The "peoples" to whom self-determination applied were those within the antecedent colonial boundaries—not peoples defined by ethnicity, religion, historical autonomy, or other collective identities. There was no sign of a right to secession for ethnonational separatists within the new, ex-colonial states. Former "artificial" administrative boundaries—no matter what diversity they encompassed—were to be treated as inviolate, as sacrosanct (Holsti 1996, 75). Thus the UN joined with all the established Westphalian states in insisting upon and supporting the sovereignty of the unitary territorial state—and thus ensuring a future of domination and resistance in many of the newly enshrined, but weak and repressive, Third World states.

Given the sudden creation of multi-ethnic new states without well-established civic structures, political instability frequently occurred. Many post-colonial regimes were highly dependent upon the support of local elites (e.g., landed aristocrats, urban business classes) and multinational corporations. The combination of upper-class and foreign dominance thrived on the political passivity of urban masses, who could be kept subservient by a mixture of patronage and appeals to ethnic pride and loyalties (cf. Hintzen 1989). Precarious elites often find that ethnoracial appeals may be a quick and cheap route to mobilize support and silence in-group dissent—a tactic intensely used from Sri Lanka to Bosnia to Zaire (also known as the Democratic Republic of the Congo, in which the newly installed president, under attack from rebels in 1998, issued racial-categorical calls against "Tutsis" and attempted to unify ethnically diverse Congolese as "Bantu").

The claimed sovereignty of national states in actual practice has almost always meant the political supremacy of one ethny, or of a small coalition, that pressed for cultural as well as economic and political unity. Give this circumstance, an additional—and explosive—component of the modern condition was the doctrine of the "self-determination of peoples." For in the doctrine of popular sovereignty, the sovereignty of the state rests on the will of the people it claims to govern. If this is the case, that legitimacy can be challenged by any restive "nationality" that claims to speak of a "people," and "if at the same time it is claimed that sovereignty is absolute, so that states treat as illegitimate all external humanitarian efforts or human rights interventions, then ethnic issues can become crucial not only for regime and government stability but also for state autonomy and international relations" (Williams 1994, 60–61). What we are now seeing is a worldwide trend toward smaller and more homogeneous states, even as economic "globalization" proceeds. The processes of ethnic fission, once begun, have few obvious stopping places—as Keyfitz says, "an infinite regress is in prospect if all claims of every group are to be satisfied" (1995, 214).

Since states typically strongly resist secession or even boundary changes, the stage is set for ethnonational conflicts (Shtromas 1990, 39). Ethnies thus affect states, often decisively. Not surprisingly, states affect ethnies. State policies and practices can, in fact, create, destroy, suppress, increase, or reduce the rigidity of boundaries, and generally intensify or diminish ethnic salience (cf. Karpat 1985, Young 1985). In a remarkable instance, the former Soviet Union linked ethnicity to territorial divisions and their administrative structures and required ethnic identification of all citizens. The effect, contrary to the policy of creating Soviet unity, was to make ethnicity salient, to create incentives for autonomy claims, and to increase separatist attitudes.

The pressures for state unification and state expansion have thus come into headlong collision with the multiple forces making for claims to autonomy and separation. When state dominance ceased to be overwhelming, disaffected ethnies often sought political access ("voice"), greater autonomy or secession ("exit"), or outright rebellion. In Gurr's summary (1993b, 132), "the net effect of state building in most parts of the world has been to substantially increase grievances of the majority of ethnic and communal groups that have not been able to either protect their autonomy or to participate meaningfully in governing coalitions."

States do not merely deal with a legacy of historical nonstate identities. "In fact virtually all states are deeply implicated in the perpetual reinvention of categories that organize, hierarchize, and divide their populations" (Boyarin 1991, 387). Such actions include the classifications used in censuses and in numerous administrative actions, legislation specifying ethnic rights, laws and regulations concerning discrimination and segregation, and litigation and judicial decisions. The role of state agencies in defining ethnic/racial categories is well illustrated by the elaborate (if somewhat incoherent) classifications used in the U.S. Census of 1980. The categories were defined in terms of origins, that is, of ancestry or descent (not language). The apparent inconsistencies were initially passed over in the interests of amplification of criteria for "minority status." Thus the common element in the various distinctions has been a "rule of descent"—of group (category) membership on the basis of birth. The use of "hereditary groups membership," as Killian (1981) has termed it, enshrines ethnicity in the official statistics of the country. Objections to the rigidity of the census categories increased over the years, and the 2000 census permitted the use of multiple ancestry responses.

Through conferral of rights and privileges, and of restrictions, exclusions, obligations, and disabilities (in thousands of state jurisdictions around the world), the agents of state authority define and shape ethnies. Through these processes, states create and attempt to destroy particular ethnic identities. Nor are states themselves immune to processes of identity formation and change.

By itself, ethnic classification by the state seems innocuous enough. But in the European history of our day, we have seen how a series of state actions led from invidious classification to discrimination, to persecution, to "ethnic cleansing," and to the Final Solution in the Nazi genocide. As Arne Ruth reminds us, "The Holocaust was only the climax of a policy whereby a state set out to exclude a casually classified group of citizens, positioning them as enemies of the 'real,' ethnically-defined citizens, then making large segments of the population state accomplices by allowing them to profit from the elimination of the so-called enemy" (Ruth 1997, 270).

So, as van den Berghe (1981, 1990) has long insisted, the national state has been the greatest killer of our times. And we now have to recognize that the safeguarding of minority rights cannot be made secure under unlimited sovereignty of national states. The tyranny of the majority is never clearer than in ethnocracies. States cannot be left to their own devices, if minorities are to be protected from gross violations of rights.

In analyzing many of these cases, it is useful to think of the ethnopolitical struggles as constituted by a set of triangular relationships—among (1) a national (mobilizing ethny) minority, (2) a nationalizing state within which the "minority" lives, and (3) an external national homeland (Brubaker 1995, 107–32). Each of the three entities is actually a dynamic field of diverse forces. Examples are numerous. In the former Yugoslavia, the Serbian minority within the newly nationalizing state of Croatia interacted strongly with the renationalizing "homeland" of Serbia, even as the two states pressed their incompatible claims. In Sri Lanka, the triad consisted of a Tamil minority, a nationalizing Buddhist-Sinhalese state, and an external homeland of Tamil Nadu in India. These instances remind us that ethnic relations only rarely are two-sided. For additional complexity, we have only to look at the Grand Experiment of the Soviet Union. The experience of the Soviet Union suggests that to maximize political and coherent ethnic nationalism, a complex set of conditions can act as contributory causes. These include (1) central state policies encouraging cultural retentionism and political leadership by local persons; (2) territorial ethnic concentration coupled with territorial administrative units based on ethnicity; (3) subordination of such units to a dominant center; (4) shifting and contradictory ethnic policies from the center; (5) persistence of local "traditional" cultures (segmented, autonomous niches); (6) uneven, patchy economic development and uneven cultural assimilation; (7) urbanization (creating new social formations), industrialization, and secular education; and finally, (8) weakening of the political control of the central state. The cumulative effects in the Soviet Union were to accentuate ethnic identities, to make life-chances highly dependent upon ethnicity, to create or reinforce localistic elites, and thus to ensure the persistence of ethnic nationalism and to increase the likelihood of secessionistic movements (cf. Suny 1991).

States that base their legitimacy upon ethnic or religious affiliations typically discriminate against and/or attempt to assimilate minorities or to force cultural uniformity. In short, the nation-state policy is one that puts minorities at risk and sharply raises the likelihood of internal conflict. In contrast, the civic, secular state bases its legitimacy upon popular sovereignty and the rule of law, granting citizenship without stipulation as to ethnicity, "race," or religion. Thus a major form of the social integration of national states is the creation of universal citizenship that is not conditioned upon ethnicity, property ownership, or other special social statuses. In its fully developed form, this citizenship treats individuals as members of the state, endowed with such rights as voting, office-holding, the bearing of arms, trial by jury, due process of law, freedom of religion, freedom of movement, and so on. Such citizenship rights (and applicable duties) create a "domain of the people" that transcends subnationalities and ethnies. In democratic polities, this domain creates the ground for common values, access to opportunity, and numerous specific integrative public policies.

CHAPTER THREE

Ethnies

Contenders and Rulers

Ethnies can create states, and destroy them. States can create and destroy ethnies. The state can be an arena in which ethnic formations struggle for influence and control. Ethnies can seek to escape from state control. Relations between states and ethnies can deeply affect relations among states.

Let us examine these diverse assertions.

The State as Creator and Shaper of Ethnicity

States create ethnicity by categorizing people according to ancestry, origins, or cultural background, and by differential treatment of those so categorized. For example, a crucial distinction exists between states with inclusive citizenship that can be acquired by residence or various legal tests, as over against exclusive citizenship based on descent. So the rule of *jus sanguinis* ("blood" origins) creates an ethnic state: citizenship is based on ancestry. Among Western countries, the policies of Germany that in the past granted citizenship only to persons of German ancestry have provided a conspicuous example. Around the world there are numerous other cases. For example, in Fiji the 1990 constitution guaranteed "native" Fijians a majority of seats in the legislature and a dominant voice in choosing the prime minister and the president. These provisions relegated the Fijians of Indian descent, who were slightly over half the population, to what the Indian-origin people regarded as a permanently subordinated political position (Nanda 1992). The attempted dominance, however, proved unstable. Subsequent events included the election of an Indian-origin prime minister, followed by a military coup aimed at reasserting "native Fijian" control, followed then by court decisions returning civilian rule. This volatile complexity reflected the continuing tension between the homeland people and the later settlers—exacerbated by rivalry over material resources (Lall 1999; Grofman and Stockwell 2001).

Some of the most striking cases of state influence upon ethnic distinctions come from areas of former colonial domination. In Rwanda under German and then Belgian colonization, the Tutsis had been favored over the peasant Hutus in education and job opportunities. The Tutsi-Hutu distinction in pre-colonial times had been based on a relatively mild form of traditional rule (Newbury 1988)—the Tutsis were primarily defined by ownership of cattle, intermarriage was common, Tutsi membership could be gained by accumulation of cattle, and the physical characteristics (especially height) of the two populations greatly overlapped. Under Belgian administration, however, the Tutsis were treated as a clearly separate and privileged population, thereby making ethnicity categorical and increasingly rigid. Diverse subgroupings were merged under the political label of "Hutu" (see Newbury 1988). The earlier interdependence of client-patron relations between Tutsi and Hutu changed into individualized economic activities (e.g., coffee cultivation) promoted by centralized state policies; newly competitive economic relations thus were joined with state ascription to accentuate ethnic distinctions and status rivalries. These conditions, then, were further politicized and intensified after Rwanda's independence in 1959. Beginning at that time, politicized elements of the Hutu and Tutsi struggled for power over the state. Violent clashes escalated until large numbers of Tutsis were driven out of the country—only to regroup and, a generation later, to mount a military campaign against the Hutu-dominated government. That government itself had actively organized the mass slaughter of at least 800,000 Tutsis and moderate Hutus in 1994 (for descriptions of the horrors and their origins, see Prunier 1995 and Gourevitch 1998).

This unchecked genocide had complex causes, including partisan foreign intervention and international failure to prevent or stop the killing. But it was the initial politicization of ethnic distinctions that later could move power contests toward ethnic extermination.

In many other newly independent states that were formerly ruled by colonial powers, present-day ethnies grew out of administrative rulings. In an illustrative case, Cote d'Ivoire spent more than seventy years as a French colony, acquiring independent status in 1960. Many of the more than sixty ethnies now recognized did not exist as such prior to the 1890s; in earlier times the identities of individuals were variously tied to clans, lineages, villages, or occasionally to kingdoms. The French colonial authorities subsequently assigned people to administratively defined "tribal" units from which the modern ethnies have been derived. Since independence, the state has made systematic efforts to create a "national" identity but, unsurprisingly, multiple and overlapping affiliations persist (Vogel 1991).

As we have already noted repeatedly, the ethnic markers—the signs or labels of membership—are diverse: languages, religion, physical appearance, location of residence, homeland, dress and ornamentation, food taboos and preferences, marriage and family values and practices, and a great variety of other beliefs, norms, and values. The definiteness of ethnic boundaries increases as these distinctions become overlapping and cumulative. Ethnic boundaries are affected accordingly by the ways in which states classify and count their populations, and by the policies of states in allocating resources and establishing differential treatment. As Chapter 5 will describe, to the extent that a central state is a major source of differential ethnic benefits, it is likely that political rivalry will be accentuated. And the sheer fact of ethnic categorization by state agencies encourages ethnic self-awareness and creates incentives for mobilization.

Whenever the state becomes a central distributor of resources—of social goods and bads—its interventions carry the possibility of accentuating cleavages of class and ethnicity—processes prominently displayed, for example, in many sub-Saharan African states (Chazan 1986, 149) and dramatically illustrated in the former Soviet Union and the former Yugoslavia (see the Spring 1992 issue of *Daedalus*). To the extent that the state recognizes ethnicity as the legitimate basis for political participation and for social rewards and deprivations, it increases the salience of ethnic divisions, renders them more permanent, and encourages the mobilization of previously unrecognized ethnies (Nagel and Olzak 1982).

The growth in scale of national states increases the possibilities for merger and expansion of smaller ethnic groupings into larger ethnies—possibilities that are enhanced by state-generated pressures for categorization, as well as by interethnic rivalries. These tendencies are strengthened as facilities for transportation and communication become extensive and accessible, especially if ethnies are large relative to class-based organizations.

The worldwide distribution of ethnic intermingling and the development of ethnic mosaics within bounded (territorial) states is the result of several main historical processes (Levine and Campbell 1972). Of these, the most prominent is the establishment of large multi-ethnic states by conquest and territorial annexation, in which indigenous peoples are overrun and subjugated, as in the United States or the Soviet Union. Similarly, ethnic residues are left from former empires that intermingled peoples through trade, internal migration, forced population movement, and the spread of dominant languages and other cultural patterns. Such "remnants of empire" are conspicuous in Africa, as also are areas containing successive waves of refugee populations (notably in Ghana and other parts of West Africa). Still another source of within-state diversity is the presence of economically specialized ethnies, often living in enclaves, such as traders, guest workers, and nomads. Other "enclave peoples" are distinct ethnoreligious groupings encapsulated in state-societies, such as the Hutterites, Old Order Amish, Hasidic Jews, or Druze.

The extent to which states and ethnies coincide obviously depends upon the criteria used to define ethnic homogeneity. By the stringent criterion that 95 percent of the population speaks the same language, about 73 percent of the world's national states is multi-ethnic, whereas 42 percent of large ethnies is spread across one or more state boundaries (Neilsson 1985). Even in the states that most closely approximate national homogeneity, some internal diversity is found, as for example in Japan. And interstate linkages of ethnies are extensive: nearly two-thirds of the 233 communal entities included in Gurr's global survey (1993b, 133) have members in one or more adjacent countries.

If the unfortunate term "nation-state" is taken to mean that state and nationality (ethny) are coterminous, only a handful of cases exist. Multinationality is the rule. Colored lines on maps do not make nation-states. Even in the Japanese case, conceptions of the nation-state did not arise spontaneously out of a sense of cultural identity, but were developed out of the Meiji leaders' efforts to build a modern state capable of resisting Western encroachment. In these efforts, the national polity was pictured as an extended family with the emperor as the father. As Tamamoto says (1995, 13):

> All Japanese families, if traced far back enough in time supposedly were related by blood to the imperial family. . . . To work and sacrifice for the state was to work and sacrifice for the family. The two Japanese ideograms for state/country and family/household—expressed the idea of the unity of the state, the emperor, and the family.

A better example could hardly be hoped for to show the merging of kinship, ethnicity, and national state. And the major impetus for this construction was the external threat of Western imperialism. Although the imperial myth no longer prevails, the conception of a timeless ethny (the "Japanese race") has continued into the present.

Since World War II, in much of Asia, Africa, and Latin America centralized states have vastly expanded their territorial control through improved transportation and communication facilities, state educational systems, expanded military forces and centralized bureaucracies, and state-operated or state-regulated economic firms and markets. Such state expansion inevitably brings—along with its advantages to many people—clashes of interests and values with local communities and ethnic groupings. In Europe, the emergence of states, ruling over diverse ethnies, preceded the development of nationalism in support of states. In this complex process, states were not neutral arenas for ethnic rivalry, nor were they autonomous from their main ethnic support. *Both* states and their subsumed ethnies were internally complex entities in which elites typically were struggling for control (Brass 1991, 268–71).

State-building itself is a major source of intrastate conflict. Rebels against the state (including ethnic rebels as well as others) have often arisen to contest political centralization and the accompanying coercive extraction of resources (e.g., taxes, forced labor, and conscription). As Gould (1996) has shown, the use of patronage in early stages of state-building often has been a means to pacify and co-opt substate elite members who are potential leaders of violent resistance. Such co-optation, however, sometimes produces the very result it aims to avoid: this backlash or negative side effect occurs when factions of the elites are in disadvantaged positions in local patronage networks. Benefits from the state thus divide elite groupings into advantaged supporters and those excluded from central political connections. The latter—the victims of partial co-optation—tend to join with popular insurgency against state expansion (read "intrusion"). Although Gould's monograph on the Whiskey Rebellion of 1794 in the United States convincingly specifies this pattern, similar studies of present-day ethnic conflicts are scarce. The importance, nevertheless, of patron-client networks in conflict-ridden, multi-ethnic societies suggests that mobilizations may be strongly influenced by partial co-optation of ethnic elites.

Of course, we must continually recall that the incorporation of ethnically distinct peoples within the claimed boundaries of empires and national states often has been forcible and violent. The long process of European conquest and domination in the Americas is too well known to require more than a reminder. The Soviet Union's reestablishment of Czarist Russia's boundaries in Eastern Europe after World War II met with armed resistance in Estonia, Latvia, Lithuania, the Western Ukraine, and Moldova (Marshall in Gurr 1993b, 189). (After the Russian Revolution of 1917, the state of Georgia was not brought back into the Soviet Union until 1922.)

One way in which states have reacted to ethnic minorities thus incorporated has been the refusal to recognize ethnic identity. This refusal is a recurrent phenomenon. For many years the successive governments of Turkey denied the existence of the Kurdish people—characterizing them instead as "mountain Turks." In Bulgaria, in turn, Turkish people were denied a separate identity by a prohibition against using Turkish family

68

names. In the mid-1990s the Greek state refused to admit the existence of ethnic minorities or to recognize demands for cultural autonomy. Self-identified Slavo-Macedonians were called "Slavophone Greeks," and an application for a permit to establish a cultural center for the cultivation of Macedonian language and culture was denied; instances were reported of arrests of persons who identified themselves as Macedonians (Pollis 1994).

From the French Revolution of 1789, the Jacobin conception of one central cultural identity fostered the assimilationist state, as did the American tradition of *E Pluribus Unum*—out of many, one. Both societies pressed for rapid acculturation of individuals, not for the maintenance of separate cultures. Indeed, the ruling groups of centralized national states usually have regarded "minority" ethnicity either as outmoded, vestigial, and reactionary, or as dangerously divisive. To the extent that such rulers have sought to establish maximal central authority, they have deployed an impressive array of policies and practices aimed at cultural "integration." Some of these policies have been concisely formulated as follows. States attempt to create a national culture

(1) by removing traditional . . . barriers to statewide mobility, communication and social interaction; (2) by adapting an official lingua franca; (3) by promoting the free movements of goods, persons, and ideas throughout the state territory; (4) by heightening the barriers against other states through the control of immigration, travel, the traffic of goods, and the flow of ideas across international boundary levels; and (5) by propagating patriotism. (Francis 1976, 386)

And as territorial European states became more centralized and firmly bounded, their rulers typically sought to make ethnicity coincide with statehood. To the extent that this tendency prevailed, membership in the dominant ethny was increasingly institutionalized and, by the same token, lesser or dissident ethnic factions were politicized. These two interacting processes were prominent where expanding states encountered resistance from culturally alien populations—Muslims, "pagans," and various recalcitrant ethnic groupings (Bartlett 1993). Several centuries of such "frontier" interactions hardened conceptions of ethnicity, verging upon racial categorization. In contrast, in many pre-national states, central political decisions could transfer whole populations from one empire to another with minimal effects upon peasants to whom ethnicity was not salient nor politicized (Schermerhorn 1970, 194). Efforts by states to create ethnic homogeneity (whatever other aims this may serve) have led to "ethnic cleaning" (mass killings and expulsions) in Bosnia, to the Final Solution in Nazi Germany, to vast population transfers in Greece and Turkey after World War I, to the enormous waves of refugees in country after country in the 1990s (culminating as the decade closed in the mass expulsion by Serbian Yugoslavia of the people of Kosovo).

National states centered upon a core ethny or coalition of ethnies often seek to induce or force mass assimilation. Attempts to force assimilation— banning use of "minority" languages, changing place names, obliterating symbols, and so on—create deep resentments and can create conformity only when the state has overwhelming coercive power. Induced assimilation, on the other hand, can occur through the long-term provision of economic opportunities, mass public education and military service, health and welfare benefits, and political rights. The latter approach has had some notable successes in modern industrialized societies.

Further Consequences of State Actions

States often seek ethnic homogeneity in the service of the nation-state ideology. To do this, they may exterminate or expel whole peoples, or they may follow the opposite policy of assimilation. But assimilation may be induced and voluntary, or coercive. In the coercive cases, the refusal of states to acknowledge the very existence of an ethny is a recurrent phenomenon.

Political dominance often shows itself in linguistic dominance. Thus it was in the Middle Ages in Europe, when ethnies were primarily defined by language and the language of the courts represented a crucial exercise of ethnic preeminence. In this way ethnic identities could be decisively shaped by state power as embodied in the laws (Bartlett 1993, 214).

The principles of rule, varying drastically over the centuries, have gone from divine mandates to rights of conquest and dynastic succession, to natural law, popular sovereignty, universal citizenship, and "human rights." The Great Divide in the last decades of the twentieth century was between states claiming political legitimacy on the basis of the consent of a civic community, in contrast to those claiming rulership by ideological mission or religious investiture (theocracies, as in Iran, or the Taliban in Afghanistan, or the aspiring Hindu militants in the Bharatiya Janata Party in India), or by reason of ethnic descent. (We leave aside traditional, kin-based regimes.) The deadly implication of rule based on ethnicity or on hegemonic religion is *exclusion*—those not in the brotherhood are denied legitimacy, and at the extreme they may be annihilated (cf. Holsti 1996, 88).

In relation to the ethnic "minorities" within their borders and under their rule, states can develop and use four main types of policies and practices: (1) containment, (2) assimilation, (3) pluralism, and (4) power-sharing (Gurr 1993b, 306). Striking historical contrasts illustrate the implications of different choices.

The typical structure of empires is that of centralized military and administrative organizations ruling over diverse territorial units, each of which is likely to have a separate ethnic identity or identities. Subordinate administrators or traditional territorial rulers therefore constitute heterogeneous political elites, subject to fission when for any reason central dominance is weakened. Thus it is a recurrent historical pattern that the opposition of regional authorities to the central polity "tends to be expressed and mobilized in ethnic terms. Whenever territorial lords or other power groups seek a greater independence from the paramount ruler and imperial institution, they are likely to activate latent ethnic divisions which are apt to legitimize their claim to freedom and to mobilize wider support for their political designs" (Francis 1976, 385).

The breakup of empires and of other conglomerate states through secessionistic movements is most likely when internal "peoples" lack effective political access. As Hall formulates the point, "When it is possible to have voice within a system, exit loses its attraction. Differently put, the nature of a political regime matters: nationalism has historically involved separation from authoritarian polities" (1993, 11).

Many students of ethnicity and politics have agreed with the main thrust of this argument. Some qualifications, however, are in order. The empirical evidence does indicate that "voice"—effective access to political decision-making—generally does reduce incentives for separatism or rebellion. But separatism in Québec has continued long after most of the province's original demands had been met through full representation in the central polity. No single formula suits all cases. Nevertheless, with only minor exceptions, societies that have institutionalized democratic political systems have facilitated nonviolent communal protest rather than violent rebellion. Nonviolent protests and rebellions are largely separate phenomena: in Gurr's (1993b) worldwide study, there is only a weak correlation of ~.14. A similar finding is reported by Beissinger (1991, 2002) for events in the former Soviet Union.

A prototypical case of the complexities of institutionalized ethnicity had been provided by the former Soviet Union—a multi-ethnic federation held together by a centralized one-party polity. In spite of a class-centered ideology that held out the ideal of a unitary society that would transcend all ethnic and local particularisms, the actual situation had the paradoxical effect of solidifying ethnic identities. This outcome was favored, in the first place, by obligatory individual ethnic identity ("nationality"); each time a person had to show his/her ID card, the distinction was reinforced. Second, the administrative structure of the Soviet Union divided the country into layers of territorial units: the fifteen Union Republics and successive tiers of sub-units. Each territorial division, in turn, was identified with a "titular nationality" that was granted some special privileges; each favored nationality was protected in its own distinctive culture, its own national language and customs. So "national" cultures coexisted in a complex way with territorial political units; for example, some republics were internally diverse. The mixture was potentially unstable. Final break-ups hinged also on the circumstance that the leaders of administrative units developed strong vested interests in the status of the region they governed. With the collapse of central Communist party control, such local elites rapidly moved to seek political autonomy. (On all this, see Amalrik 1969; Carrère d'Encausse 1979; Brubaker 1995, 1994; Slocum 1995). Thus the titular elites most favored under the old regime turned out to be strong advocates of autonomy and, soon after, of separatism. The very structure of the Soviet system had favored "the long-term cultivation and consolidation of national administrative cadres and national intelligentsia" (Brubaker 1994, 53) and of "local networks of corruption and influence" (Slocum 1995, 8). Both in the Soviet Union and in Yugoslavia, the institutions of titular nationality provided a basis for national-state claims after the disintegration of the federated systems.

A core ethny that controls a multi-ethnic national state may either seek to assimilate its peoples to a common culture and (national) identity, or it may accept ethnic pluralism (including varying degrees and kinds of autonomy), or it may expel, discriminate against, massacre, and suppress its "minorities." In the cases of the latter, most drastic measures, the agents of dominant states act as if the target ethnies had no rights at all that the state was legally or morally bound to respect or even to acknowledge.

Thus a prominent pattern in the modern world is the denial of civil rights to whole categories of people. The familiar examples need not be (again) reviewed at this point. Short of the most extreme instances, however, there are prominent examples of attempted denial of ethnicity. Thus the Japanese state leaders have been notably reluctant to acknowledge the presence of ethnic minorities. When their existence could no longer be denied, the state resorted to euphemisms or to a reluctant acceptance of the category of "resident alien."

Indeed, the Japanese case illuminates several more general patterns (see Esman 1994, 207). Faced with an urgent need for cheap labor but committed to a doctrine of racial exclusiveness, the government has accepted immigration of ethnic Japanese from Brazil, under the concept of *jus sanguinis*—the criterion of ancestry. Meanwhile, ethnic Koreans, Filipinos, and others are either defined as resident aliens or covertly tolerated as illegal immigrants. Because the immigration of foreign workers is not officially recognized, a thriving trade in illegal immigrants has developed. But because what can be seen as racial exclusiveness is not internationally acceptable, the illegals cannot be condemned and expelled without harmful consequences for a country aspiring to international leadership. Nevertheless, leaders periodically have made public statements having a stereotypic "racial" flavor, and the continued presence of illegal immigrants means that problems of "rights" are systematically ignored or denied. Indeed, highly visible immigrant diasporas easily become targets of blame for social ills of crime, welfare dependency, drugs, unemployment, and public disorder.

Late-twentieth-century political controversies in the United States concerning immigration pointed to similar patterns—notably the acceptance of immigrants when needs for labor or special skills are uppermost, and demands for exclusion and/or proposed denial of welfare benefits for immigrants who are not United States citizens. The United States, however, does make the attainment of citizenship by legal immigrants relatively simple, and of course children born in the United States are automatically citizens. In contrast, societies that deny citizenship to resident aliens can have large numbers of second-, third-, or later generation residents who are partially assimilated culturally, but segregated and marginalized socially and politically, as in the instance of "guest workers" in Germany. (By the year 2000, however, the German government had finally granted that Turkish guest workers could become German citizens.) In several other European countries, such as Switzerland, immigrating workers have been treated as sojourners with minimal rights—a kind of "proletariat on loan."

Clearly the meaning of civil rights will differ between relatively homogenous societies and those that are highly segmented by ethnies, especially when each ethny seeks substantial cultural and political autonomy. A central issue in the multi-ethnic cases is the question of the rights of *individual persons* as over against the rights of *collectivities* as such. For example, in divided societies in which the primary political parties are ethnic parties, majority or plurality rule more often than not results in denial of rights to ethnic outsiders. Thus individual rights often depend crucially upon "group" (collectivity, ethny) membership. In such situations, a right to self-determination in various forms raises difficult questions of balancing "equal treatment" with group integrity and protection (cf. Van Dyke 1985, 3–16). Totally homogenous societies, now almost never found in the real world, could ignore any notion of group (communal) rights; but this is not so in pluralistic countries, where simple majority rule easily leads to ethnic tyranny. This is especially the case when visible and marginalized ethnoclasses evoke working-class hostility as competition arises for jobs, housing, public benefits, and use of public facilities.

State policies concerning language have massive and complex consequences. As an unavoidable medium of daily life, language is *useful*—it has intrinsic instrumental value, affecting work, business transactions, education, interactions with governmental officials, and basic relations of sociability. Simultaneously, language is a central symbol of communal *identity* and of the prestige or disesteem attached to one's membership. Political domination and subordination are starkly signaled by the preeminence or equal recognition, or disfavor and restriction or suppression, of one's primary language. Demands for language hegemony are a potent source of ethnic discord in such diverse settings as Sri Lanka, Quebec, Malaysia, Spain, and the United States.

There appears to be a growing tendency for large and compact ethnic minorities (immigrants, diaspora, guest workers) to demand autonomy not only in language use, but also in family relations, control of property, and control of police and legal institutions. If made effective, these claims constitute a strong form of political multiculturalism. Although often confused with more informal policies of toleration or neutrality, this type of multicultural coexistence contrasts sharply with societal assimilation. In Esman's pithy formulation, "Group incorporation with minority privileges is the polar opposite of individual assimilation" (1994, 213).

Brass (1991, chap. 7) has argued strongly for the importance of the internal differentiations and internal processes of interaction, controversy, and change found in any large ethny, including controversies over concrete issues and among competing intra-ethnic elites. Examples of divisive intra-ethnic issues are numerous: affirmative action, separation or integration, electoral policies, direct action and use of violence, cooperation with or opposition to other ethnies, and assimilation or cultural interethnic distinctiveness. Evidently ethny-state and interethnic relations can depend heavily upon the internal dynamics of each of the interacting collective bodies. Furthermore, a fragmentation of loyalties, policies, and tactics is typical of many subordinated ethnic and political minorities under repressive state rule. Thus in the Syria of the 1970s and 1980s, an Alawite faction led by Hafez el-Assad governed a country containing the Muslim Brotherhood, Christians, Kurds, Druze, Jews, Sunni, Shi'ia, and others. Expatriates from Syria were divided into several ideological factions. States that may create ethnies may also seek to destroy them by fragmentation.

Differing patterns of ethnic conflict and accommodation have been shown in detailed case studies of relationships between homeland nationalists and immigrants in, for example, Catalonia, the Basque country, Latvia, and Estonia (Shafir 1995). All four cases share the characteristics of being economically developed regions in comparison with their encompassing state-society, while at the same time having distinctive cultures and relatively strong nationalistic social movements. Yet there are sharp contrasts in the relations of immigrants and homeland nationalists, even though each of these "developed" regions did attract immigrants and did experience substantial degrees of assimilation. Catalonia was relatively open to immigration, Latvia and Estonia less so; the Basque region showed intermediate levels of opposition to immigration. A key factor in Catalonia's acceptance was that Catalan elites were secure in their leadership of a prosperous and prestigious society, whereas in the other three cases there were competitive relations between host and immigrant elites. Particularly acute were the tensions where immigrant and homeland peoples were separated into different economic sectors, forming "a society within a society" (Shafir 1995, 210). The opposition between culturally dissimilar and competing elites hinged on a sense of threat to locals' privileges and particular way of life. Even with widespread willingness of the immigrants to assimilate, such social segmentation and rivalry served to maintain hostility toward immigrants. And in the newly independent Baltic states, the recent experience of Russian "colonialism" had embittered discourse on citizenship and language rights for ethnic Russians (for a nuanced description of the situation in Estonia see Taagepera 1993, 216–25).

The State as an Arena for Conflict

States not only encompass and act upon ethnies in internal affairs. They also act domestically as a consequence of their external relations. Numerous historical cases show how interstate struggles can have major effects upon the intrastate status of ethnic and religious minorities. Great Power conflicts have recurrently affected intra-ethnic relations within other states. Domestic ethnic conflicts can be reduced or, more commonly, exacerbated and prolonged by external influence, including aid and active intervention. Interstate rivalry often has been decisive in the fate of ethnic minorities, as in the conspicuous instances of the Armenians, the Palestinians, and the much-betrayed Kurds. In a detailed historical review of some lesser-known cases, Clark (1998) has stressed the importance of international competition for the treatment of four seventeenth-century religio-ethnic minorities, and has formulated five sets of general propositions predictive of outcomes.

In Clark's propositions (1998, 1291–99), minorities living in a region of high strategic importance to contending states will not be left alone, especially when there is a fusion of local and interstate struggles. External powers will be more likely to extend favorable treatment to such ethnic collectives when there is a similarity of culture and when the minorities are useful in interstate rivalries (e.g., for weakening the bargaining potential of an adversary). Negative treatment can be expected when visible and vulnerable minorities are caught "in between" interstate struggles, especially in warfare.

Since the state is also a political prize and an arena for intrastate rivalry and conflict, when a society has a deep preexisting ethnic cleavage the emergence of ethnic political parties will intensify ethnic opposition and conflict. As Horowitz (1985, 291) has proposed, "By appealing to electorates in ethnic terms, by making ethnic demands on governments, and by bolstering the influence of ethnically chauvinist elements within each group, parties that begin by merely mirroring ethnic divisions help to deepen and extend them."

The greater the internal cohesion and solidarity of the ethny, the more easily political entrepreneurs can develop an ethnic party. And the greater the ethnic rivalry for power and influence in the polity, the more likely the formation of explicitly ethnic parties to seek votes and offices.

The modern centralized state is the primary arena in which ethnies *as collectivities* become rivals for scarce and distributive values. Ethnicity is a strong basis for the collective mobilization that allows effective rivalry in struggles for control of the resources that the state can disperse (cf. Esman 1990, 58). Wherever national states have extensive authority to redistribute resources, to allocate opportunities, and to regulate individuals and organizations, it is evident that influence upon and control of the state is a central prize in any rivalry of regions, classes, ethnies, and other major interest groupings. Therefore, the more intense the ethnic rivalry among individuals and local groupings, the more likely it is that the struggles not only will become politicized, but also will escalate to the higher levels of the political structure. Given these tendencies, it is not wholly surprising that of 233 politicized communal groups in Gurr's 1993 work, 79 had engaged in guerrilla and civil wars since 1945; 34 of these violent conflicts were protracted and extremely deadly (Gurr 1993b, 98–99).

These wars were concentrated in weak but repressive states in the Third World and in the peripheries of industrialized countries. Because of this concentration, it is instructive to examine the sequels to the sudden emergence of new independent national states in the 1960s. In a great many instances, independence from colonial rule was quickly followed either by governmental discrimination against certain ethnic groupings, by expulsion, by violent conflict, or by all of these. Among other conspicuous examples, the experiences of East Indians in the former British colonies of Kenya, Tanzania, and Uganda are prototypical. After independence in the first two cases, the East Indians were gradually squeezed out of their primary niche in trade, as well as in clerical, technical, and administrative jobs. In Uganda, after the accession to power of Idi Amin, the Indians were summarily expelled en masse within a very short period, being forced to leave their possessions behind (van den Berghe 1981, 147–56). As early as 1970 Melson and Wolpe (1970, 1113) were reminding their readers that so-called modernization was not automatically producing national integration, but was creating conditions favoring the creation of new communal groups.

The geographic dispersion of many small ethnies within the territory of a national state renders unlikely an autonomy or secession movement, and thus would seem to lower the likelihood of ethnic conflict. But enclaves or readily identifiable clustering of ethnic "outsiders" are convenient targets for violent attacks (cf. Gurr 1993b, 205). This kind of communal strife is especially likely if the homeland ethny is experiencing economic distress, for example in the form of massive unemployment of young males.

Nevertheless, minority ethnies in relatively democratic polities sometimes can advance their collective interests if there is considerable apathy among majority voters. That is to say, when the mass of the electorate is largely indifferent to issues that matter a great deal to some numerically small ethnic populations, the latter may be able to make gains through mobilization and concerted voting, lobbying, and other interest-group tactics. A crucial factor is majority tolerance for organized effort on "minority issues."

The smaller a dissatisfied ethny and the less drastic its claims, the easier it is for a resource-rich state to make concessions, including allocations of resources. But what is implied if a state defines a major proportion of its population as having special legal rights by virtue of group identity? A striking case is India, where the constitution provided "reserved seats" in legislative bodies for the scheduled castes and tribes in proportion to population (Larson 1995, 285). The Anthropological Survey of India has reported about 325 languages and dialects, in 12 distinct language families, and as many as 4,599 distinct "communities" (possibly "cultural groupings"). The original provision was to terminate in ten years, but had been regularly renewed up through 1990. In 1980 the Mandal Report (of the Backward Classes Commission) recommended a job reservation quota in central government service of 22.5 percent for scheduled castes and tribes, and 27 percent for Other Backward Classes. (Although the commission estimated that the latter category actually could comprise 52 percent of the population, it kept its recommendation to 27 percent in order to avoid having the total reservations exceed 50 percent [Larson 1995, 261–62].) In 1991 a government order raised the total percentage to 60, including another 10 percent for "economically backward" upper castes and classes. As a final rough estimate, the report proposed a need for some "compensatory discrimination" for the remarkable total of 72 percent of the total population. Frustration and anger among the "forward" caste populations that were thus excluded has been a predictable response (Larson 1995, 266).

As we have seen, the interactions between states and their subsumed ethnic components can increase or decrease ethnic salience, can sharpen or blur ethnic boundaries, and can strengthen or weaken ethnic cohesion or solidarity. Let us be clear about these interactions. Ethnicity is a dependent variable when we deal with how it emerges and changes. But it is an independent variable when we find it already in existence as a real social formation that has tangible consequences, as when initial ethnic mobilization leads to later mobilization, and violent conflict predicts later conflict. As a general rule, increased political centralization of a multi-ethnic territorial state will sharpen ethnic boundaries, if for no other reason than the likely enhancement of rivalries for advantages at the center. But also to the extent that centralization involves redistributive processes (as it typically does), it is likely that rewards will favor some ethnies over others. To the extent that rewards are perceptibly distributed on the basis of ethnic membership, ethnic boundaries will be rendered more salient, and ethnocentrism will increase. Within a political unit or region where interethnic comparisons are made, the ethnies most likely to be highly ethnocentric will be those that have an internal hierarchy of power and authority, are wealthier, have higher occupational rank, and are more successful in warfare (cf. Levine and Campbell 1972, 70). It follows that ethnies so characterized are likely candidates for control of the state; when they succeed, the outcome is an ethnocracy. But stable dominance will be threatened whenever several powerful ethnic formations are rivals for central control—a situation of communal contention such as Afghanistan.

There is no such thing as a single, unitary kind of violent ethnic conflict. Instead, there are at least three main types, which differ radically in origins and consequences.

First, there are ethny-to-ethny conflicts—those often called "communal"—that consist of mob attacks, street brawls, gang fights, and larger-scale riots. The smaller scattered confrontations may be chronic and widely diffused; the more massive incursions and riots tend to occur in waves. Arson, vandalism, and other property damage usually accompany both the chronic low-level violence and the larger episodes.

Second, there are ethny-to-state conflicts ranging from continuing turmoil to local and regional attacks upon state facilities and personnel, and to rebellion and guerrilla warfare. Only rarely, however, do ethnic rebellions escalate into full political revolutions (see Enloe 1980).

Third, there are state-to-ethny conflicts in which governments direct armed force against resident peoples to establish and maintain domination. The ethnic target at first need not be an actual military threat or even a realistic challenger to the state. The central power holders often incite and organize democides against relatively harmless populations—as a means to keep power, to express an overriding ideology, to seize resources, or to seek an interstate advantage.

This third kind of ethnic/state conflict is by far the most deadly and the most far-reaching in its consequences; it is by far the most highly organized and centralized; it typically involves the manipulation of diffuse ethnic prejudices to mobilize and "justify" mass expulsions and killings.

Violent intra-ethnic struggles are common in confrontations with ruling states. In Sri Lanka, the rebellion of the Tamils against the dominant Sinhalese state was plagued by deadly internal conflicts. In the Eritrean fight for independence from Ethiopia, severe and lengthy warfare was waged between the Eritrean Liberation Front and the Eritrean People's Liberation Front. Fratricidal cleavages in Kosovo marked the conflict between the militant separatists in the Kosovo Liberation Army and the "moderates" who possibly would have accepted negotiated autonomy within the remaining Yugoslav state. Similar fragmentation has been endemic among the Kurds in conflicts with the governments of Turkey, Iraq, Iran, and Syria.

Mobilized ethnies often splinter along ideological lines, as among the Sinhalese in Sri Lanka. Ethnic homogeneity does not necessarily stop conflicts based on regional and kinship divisions, as in Somalia or Afghanistan. An "umbrella" ethnicity (Ibos in Nigeria) that unites several sub-ethnies against an external threat may fall apart under adversity. Independence movements routinely experience divisions between outright secessionists and those who favor the status quo or some compromise, as in East Timor in the 1990s.

Ethnies against States, States against Ethnies

The accumulated research findings show not only how state structures affect and are affected by ethnic formations, but also how political changes react upon ethnies. In general, for instance, successful ethnic challenges to central states are more likely to follow a state crisis than to succeed because they produced a state crisis (Waller 1992, 43). And the politicization of ethnicity has been a prominent feature since the 1970s of transitions from authoritarian rule to some degree of democracy in some twenty-five countries. Such periods of change relax suppression and open new opportunities for ethnic entrepreneurs. In the recent experience of Europe and the Soviet Union, ethnies or ethnoregional groupings with advanced economics and great cultural differences vis-à-vis the dominant political groups are those most likely to seek autonomy or national sovereignty (Frye 1992, 623; but cf. Horowitz 1985 on "advanced" and "backward" groups). Examples are Basques and Catalans in Spain; Estonia, Lithuania, Latvia, Moldavia, Armenia, and Georgia in the former Soviet Union; and Slovenia and Croatia in the former Yugoslavia. Of twelve early seekers after autonomy, ten were in advanced regions (the exceptions being Slovakia and Kosovo).

Recall the striking facts concerning the prevalence of collective violence within states. For instance, all but five of the twenty-three wars being fought in 1994 were based on communal rivalries and ethnic challenges to states

79

(Gurr 1994, 3). In the year 1993, every one of the thirty-four major armed conflicts then underway were within, not between, states. They represented deadly struggles between the military, paramilitary, and police forces of governments and rebel insurgents, or among fighting forces of ethnies (cultural, religious, or tribal) (Klare 1995, 52). Interstate wars have been rare in the years since 1990, but the so-called "small" wars carried out within the boundaries of territorial states have become one of the two dominant forms of human carnage—the other being the mass killings inflicted by states on unarmed civilians.

In terms of ethnic characteristics and relationships, is there a world system? Yes, insofar as everywhere there are ethnies and states. But no, in the fact that interethnic and ethnic-state relations differ radically in different regions of the world. Thus Gurr (1993a, 1993b) has classified some 233 "communal groups" in 92 countries into five main types. There are 81 *ethnonationalist* groupings, marked by large size, regional concentration, cultural distinctiveness, and loss of historical autonomy. These are rare in Latin America, but salient in some regions of Asia and Africa and in the former Soviet Union. Very different are *ethnoclasses* (45 cases), which are communal groupings that occupy disadvantaged positions, often in specialized economic roles, such as African Americans in the United States and many populations in Latin America. A third type, *militant sects* (49 cases, primarily Muslim), is concentrated in the Middle East, North Africa, south and southeast Asia, and in the former Soviet Union. The fourth category consists of some 82 *indigenous peoples* (24 of which are also ethnonationalists). These are culturally distinct groupings, often living in peripheral areas where they have been conquered or segregated by encroaching national states. Familiar examples are Native Americans, Australian Aborigines, native peoples in Central and South America, Masai and San in Africa, and Nagas and Santals in India. Finally, there are the 66 *communal contenders* (41 disadvantaged, 25 advantaged) that struggle for power in states ruled by interethnic coalitions or by a dominant ethny. Most frequent by far in Africa, some also are present in the Middle East and Asia (Gurr 1993b, 15, 23).

It may not be too much to say that the world since the end of World War II has come to be divided into peace or domesticated zones and warring or feral zones—what Lash and Urry (1994, 324) have called "wild zones of disorganized capitalism." So Gurr's data show that severe protracted communal wars have occurred almost entirely in Asia, the Middle East, and Africa (Gurr 1993b, 98–115). In Asia such conflicts were found in Burma, China, India, and Indonesia. In the Middle East, the major rebellions have been carried out by Kurds, Palestinians, and Shi'ite Muslims. In sub-Saharan Africa some twenty-five short- and long-term guerrilla and civil wars occurred between 1945 and 1989 (Gurr 1993b, 99). Authoritarian regimes in poor countries are especially likely to encounter or instigate such communal rebellions. During the twentieth century the combination of popular sovereignty, state centralization, and politicized ethnicity (as "nationalism") lent itself to wars of secession, irredentism, "ethnic cleansing," and genocide. The notion that ethnic identity should be the basis for statehood leads directly to the idea of the homogeneous nation-state. "States now claimed to be nations, whether they were or not. Ethnicities become nations, and nations claimed statehood, whether 'captive' in multinational states or fragmented into a multiplicity of states" (van den Berghe 1996, 64).

At the same time, the large increase in violent rebellions by communal contenders can be explained in part by the fact that

> in poor authoritarian regimes there are few resources to satisfy disadvantaged claimants, and those in power are disposed to think in zero-sum terms and to respond with force rather than compromise. Since few of these states have overwhelming military capacity, the use of force against communal contenders usually engenders greater resistance. The typical result is escalation of protracted communal conflict. (Gurr 1993b, 116)

Claims or demands of ethnonationalism are a threat to governing elites of many states. Leaders of multi-ethnic states that contain restive ethnies typically fear and resist international endorsement and support for rights of autonomy, and vigorously reject any claim to a "right of secession." States act as if their citizens and subjects were possessions to be jealously guarded. More generally, the imperatives of domestic politics always affect the actions of states in dealing with ethnic conflicts—as is starkly clear in the breakup of Yugoslavia and in the efforts in Sri Lanka and India to deal with Tamil insurgency (for the latter, see Ganguly and Taras 1998, chap. 7).

Conflicts against a ruling state can actually create not only new ethnic allegiances, but also new ethnic identities. So the successful secession of Eritrea from Ethiopia through a thirty-year war marked the development and consolidation of a new sense of nationality out of an unlikely combination of Muslim, Christian, and multiple-ethnic identities. The protracted fight for independence did not simply free an already-established ethnic "nation" from foreign domination; rather, the struggle itself created a new cultural identity and its associated social solidarity. The fight against Ethiopia was at the same time a struggle against entrenched social forms, exemplified in the rebellion's so-called "liberation of women" (Frankland and Noble 1996).

The processes of state fission along ethnic lines can result in a cascade of separatism, as dramatized in the fragmentation of the former Soviet Union. Yet even then there was not infinite splintering. For example, in the new country of Kazakhstan, named for the titular nationality, only 43 percent of its population were Kazakhs in 1993, while 36 percent were Russians, and there were over a hundred other ethnically distinguishable populations (Kendirbaeva 1997, 746–47). Ethnic diversity in territorial states is the name of the game in the foreseeable future in most parts of the world.

The overwhelming historic facts are that whatever ethnic appeals have opposed class appeals in political struggles, it has almost always been ethnicity that dominated. Very often the most intense conflicts have been between ethnies that were fractions of the same class. Ethnies can act against their own class interests, and class conflicts can occur within ethnies. The two systems, of ethnicity and of class, can criss-cross, sometimes reinforcing one another, sometimes acting in opposition. Ethnic collectivities and accompanying sociopolitical cleavages exist across a vast variety of economic situations, and do not disappear under "socialism," as in the former Soviet Union, Yugoslavia, or China.

Contrary to many expectations, Marxist or not, ethnic divisions have regularly proved stronger than class solidarities as a basis for polarization and violent conflict. This regularity may be surprising, calling for a specific explanation. Several plausible hypotheses are available.

Ethnic challenges to state authority may be less threatening to political elites than class struggles. Class appeals are potentially universal across an entire society, whereas ethnic appeals are more likely to be self-limiting.

Owners and managers of economic enterprises may use ethnic cleavages to reduce solidarity among workers and to hamper class-based organization.

In their turn, political elites often use ethnic appeals to demobilize opposition to their rule and to build their dominant position by inciting ethnic violence (for evidence, see chaps. 5–7).

Further, when ethnic discrimination blocks the upward social mobility of aspiring members of disadvantaged minorities, those so frustrated may be thrown back upon their ethny of origin. Such individuals then find ethnic politics a useful road to achievement, and violent protest as an option for gaining power and influence. Thus discrimination can fuel ethnicity.

And, as Chapters 1 and 2 have noted, ethnic identification is learned early in life, is closely linked to family and kinship loyalties, and usually entails both strong emotional ties and realistic interdependence.

Particular social mechanisms may reinforce ethnicity more strongly than class. When an ethnic population is highly concentrated in a single geographic area or is segregated in urban ghettos, a typical result is the development of dense networks of intra-ethnic relationships that facilitate potentials for mobilization and collective action.

Cultural similarity within ethnies encourages commitment to cultural goals, such as language use, religious freedom (or dominance), and general respect and recognition. If a multi-ethnic state is controlled by a particular ethny, those excluded or subordinated will struggle against its dominance (Esman 1994, chap. 8). No doubt other factors are involved, but further discussion of this complex puzzle had best be deferred to Chapter 5.

Numerous studies have examined the proposition that collective protests and/or rebellions are greatest at intermediate levels of political opportunities, and lowest under full access or extreme repression (Jenkins and Schock 1992, 172–75). Conditions favoring collective action have been variously identified as including moderate political freedom, moderate repression, extreme but incomplete repression over an extended period, elite divisions, and political instability. Several of these circumstances are likely to be found in weakly institutionalized ethnocracies in multiethnic societies (cf. Horowitz 1985). There is considerable evidence that the type of political system does strongly affect the frequency and intensity of protest behavior; that is, protests are more intense in elitist and autocratic than in democratic states (Zimmerman 1980, 173; Tiryakian and Rogowski 1985; Beissinger 1991, 2002; Gurr 1993b, 184–85). In general, democracies have more extensive but less deadly protests.

"Protest" refers to overt activities by dissidents against a state regime: rallies, parades, demonstrations, strikes, petitions, mock trials, and a variety of other specific actions. State coercion includes arrests, imprisonment, taking hostages, harassment, arson, withholding of employment and credit, and "disappearances" and killings, among others (cf. Francisco 1995, 209–11). The cases examined by Francisco (1995) were Czechoslovakia, East Germany (German Democratic Republic), and the Intifada in Israel. Each case had unique features, of course, but the results showed low levels of protest in the Warsaw Pact states under close and continuous surveillance and punishment, up until loss of party control in the late 1980s (as a consequence of external events). In contrast, the Intifada rebellions in Israel flourished under harsh repression that failed to impose effective control upon a highly mobilized population. Clearly, dissident protest and regime coercion are interactive processes that can drastically change magnitude and form over time.

It has been commonly held that the relationship between protest and state coercion is most likely to take the form of an inverted U: low protest under extremely tolerant and extremely repressive regimes, heightened frequency of protest under intermediate levels of coercion. Although the posited relationship has been inferred from cross-sectional data, a further plausible inference is that the maximum likelihood of protest would arise when a regime moves from either extreme to the middle. (The relationship is different for interstate wars: democratization increases the probability of international conflicts.) The inverted U has been found by several studies, but exceptions exist, and measurement problems confound the conclusions. As the studies have multiplied, additional possibilities have emerged, notably that severe repression may have opposite effects at different points in a sequence of events (Tsebelis and Sprague 1989; Mason and Krane 1989; Khawaja 1993); for example, they may be effective when severe in early signs of insurgency, but counterproductive against later phases of higher mobilization.

It is immediately plausible to think that the "strength" or "weakness" of states would be a highly important condition affecting internal conflict. For example, economic distress may be expected to increase popular discontent while reducing the resources of the state. Thus weakened states with reduced resources facing increased internal turmoil are especially likely to react with intensified repression (White and White 1995, 333). The attempted repression in these circumstances is rarely successful, and often counterproductive. The end of the line in such societies, as in Somalia, Liberia, and Sierra Leone, has been a collapsed state. And some of the most deadly intrastate conflicts occur in collapsed states—those in which the central political authorities have lost control over contenders for power and in which multiple armed groupings are in conflict. Such situations have been found in *la violencia* and later civil warfare in Colombia, Lebanon, Somalia, Zaire, and Liberia, to mention only a few.

Holsti (1996, chap. 5) has identified as essential elements of statehood (1) the idea of the state (history, tradition, culture, ideology), (2) the physical basis (territory, population, resources), and (3) institutional bases of laws, norms, governmental structures, and regimes. To these, Holsti adds the characteristics of horizontal and vertical legitimacy: the first refers to the basis of the "community" over which the state rules (ethnic, religious, civic), and the second to the principles that justify authority—a "right to rule." Vertical legitimacy comes in many forms—kinship, religion, conquest, past and present performance, ethnicity, ideology, and others. Horizontal legitimacy is attained when there is some workable consensus as to which groups, communities, and other social entities "belong" to the state-society. Mutual accommodations and acceptance define the inclusive community. Weak and failed states exhibit low levels of one or both of these types of legitimacy.

It turns out that Holsti's "strong states" have many specific characteristics that go beyond a generalized right to rule. Many of today's war-torn states lack authority, popular trust, and accountability. And when states fail to provide either external or internal physical security (lost wars, civil warfare, rampaging crime), are unable to deliver workable infrastructures and essential services, and preside over economic collapse—in short, when they are both ineffective and inefficient—it is hardly necessary to invoke

84

"loss of legitimacy" to account for loss of state power or popular consent. In minimal terms, strong states may be thought of as those that have a large per capita economic base, the ability to raise substantial revenues, the allocative authority to distribute benefits, and substantial resources for enforcing order. Strong states may also be defined as those that can claim legitimate authority, based both upon consensual domestic support, persuasive claims to legitimizing principles, and external recognition. Such states have the allocative authority to distribute and withhold benefits; they have great powers to influence intrastate ethnic relations.

How State-Ethny Relations Can Affect Interstate Relations

We know that ethnic relations affect interstate relations in many, even if imperfectly understood, ways. An incomplete list drawn from the literature follows.

(1) Domestic suppression by one state of a transnational ethny threatens stability of another state, e.g., Kurds in Iraq, Iran, and Turkey.

(2) Ethnic insurgency elicits foreign aid and intervention on behalf of the rebels or of the threatened state, e.g., Afghanistan, Vietnam, Angola, Guatemala.

(3) Ethnic conflict in a client state elicits intervention by a patron state, e.g., France in Chad.

(4) Ethnic turmoil stimulates the disturbed state to embark upon foreign interventions, including war. (Unquestionably, however, a much overrated pattern.)

(5) Alleged mistreatment of fellow ethnies in another state evokes interstate conflict.

(6) Domestic ethnic conflict produces large numbers of political refugees, creating political tensions within states of destination, e.g., Haitians in the United States, Eastern Europeans in Germany, Hutus from Rwanda in Zaire and Uganda, Chechens in Dagestan, Afghans in Pakistan.

(7) Ethnic turmoil reduces clarity and predictability among states and interstate organizations; witness the former Soviet Union and the former Yugoslavia.

(8) Domestic ethnopolitics affects foreign policies, e.g., in the United States, policies toward Ireland, Israel, Poland, Turkey, Russia, and many others.

(9) Ethnic solidaries and cleavages contribute to militant nationalism in many times and places, e.g., Basques in Spain, Sinhalese in Sri Lanka, or the political movement for Hindu nationalism (Hindutva) in India.

(10) Ethnic rivalries lead to coups d'état that produce internationally aggressive regimes, e.g., Iraq and Syria.
(11) Military options in foreign policies may be affected by ethnic composition of armed forces.
(12) Interstate relationships affect domestic ethnic policies and politics.
(13) Ethnic cleavages directly transform states through protests, turmoil, rebellion, and revolution.
(14) Domestic ethnic concepts compel regimes to resort to widespread coercion, subvert governmental programs on a societal basis, and overload the state's capabilities to protect and facilitate normal activities.
(15) Ethnic mobilization in one country may be encouraged and shaped by examples in other countries—the demonstration effect.

A few examples of some of these processes will be enough to suggest their pervasive importance. Disadvantaged ethnies within national states manifest four main orientations toward the states that encompass them: (1) exit, (2) autonomy, (3) access, and (4) control (cf. Gurr 1993b, 292 ff.). Those that want "exit" seek to break away from a state regarded both as oppressive and as holding little promise of future beneficial change. At the extreme, the militant secessionists turn to armed struggle in the drive for total political independence, rejecting any compromise. In many instances, such drastic conflict grows out of the failure to achieve lesser forms of autonomy, as in the Tamil insurgency in Sri Lanka, or the protracted civil war in Sudan. In contrast, many ethnoclasses (composed of immigrants, former slaves, or indigenes) focus their organized efforts upon securing access to economic, political, and educational opportunities, and to civic and cultural rights and privileges. Finally, in the case of the collectivities called "communal contenders," the organized and politically mobilized portions of distinctive ethnies strive for dominance in the polity/society of which they are members. When a territorially concentrated ethny lives in proximity to co-ethnics across the boundary of national state, there is always the possibility of irredentist claims from one or the other state seeking to "redeem" its fellows. Thus, Somalia tried to "reclaim" Somalis in the Ogaden region from Ethiopia, but lost the war. Hitler used the presence of Sudeten Germans in Czechoslovakia as a vehicle for territorial expansion. Militant minorities seeking separation may try to induce a neighboring state to wrest their region from its host state. Irredentist claims arouse strong emotions, creating conditions favorable to zealotry and appealing to ambitious politicians. Irredenta, therefore, are not only likely sources of domestic discord, but are also potential foci for interstate conflict.

Extensive and complex networks of ethnic relations obviously extend across the boundaries of national states. Ethnic influences are pervasive in interstate relations, although only recently so recognized in the scholarly literature. The tendency of many analysts has been to regard "international" relations as interstate relations and to focus upon states as if they were closed systems. In particular, cross-state influences upon domestic ethnic conflict have rarely received systematic analysis. In a pioneering article, Esman (1990) proposed that ethnic influences upon interstate and transnational relations be conceptualized under six major categories: irredenta, diaspora, nonstate nations, strategic uses of ethnicity, ethnic economic networks, and the internationalization of minority rights.

Illustrative of such influences are the actions of ethnic populations across the boundaries of national states. Thus, immigrant populations, retaining loyalty or affinity to their home country, may be mobilized to support the national state of origin in its conflicts with another state, as in the case of Greek-American efforts to block U.S. aid to Turkey. Such diaspora, on the other hand, may actively influence political processes in the home country, as Italian Americans sought to influence elections in Italy immediately after World War II, and Irish Americans have given tangible aid to the Irish Republican Army. In numerous cases, the diaspora send money, information, moral support, or even military assistance to groups within the country of origin. Self-conscious ethnic formations with a particular state often exert organized political pressures to influence foreign policies. In the United States during the Cold War, major groupings of people of Eastern European backgrounds provided clear examples in their support of strong anti-Soviet policies—sometimes in opposition to *realpolitik* considerations.

The internationalization of "internal" conflict is no new thing. Major collective violence within the claimed jurisdiction of a state almost always attracts some form of aid, support, or intervention from external sources. Often the outside influences operate on more than one of the communal groupings. The effects, more often than not, include the prolonging of the violent conflict. Yet in recent times the unprecedented growth of networks of transportation, communication, and trade has linked together some previously insulated localities and ethnic segments. If at the same time the central state extends its visible control into important areas of daily life, the stakes of political control increase. And if the central state is perceived as disproportionately representing the interests of a particular ethny or ethnic coalition, the excluded or subordinated ethnies are likely to be attracted by militant opposition or separatism. This sequence is particularly favored if upwardly mobile "minority" persons attempting assimilation are blocked in their aspirations (Fishman 1981, 236). "Internal" and "external" processes thus continually interact.

The preceding chapters have shown the many variations and nuances in the collective actors we are calling "states" and "ethnies." It is abundantly clear that simplified models of such internally complex and often amorphous entities may seem to unduly reify and homogenize them. When we say that "states do so-and-so," we understand that particular governing groups make the decisions. When we say an ethny "seeks autonomy," we understand that certain leaders and their followers act on behalf of and in the name of the ethny. Yet these social constructions represent standing waves of behavior and persisting cultural patterns that are sufficiently coherent to be treated as real structures at particular times and places. This does not mean that the collective actors are homogenous, coherent, rational decision makers. It does mean that such collective actors can behave as units in highly important ways that have significant real-world consequences.

These considerations are a necessary background for Chapter 4, which examines what is at stake in ethnic-based contestations.

Part II

SOURCES OF CONFLICT

CHAPTER FOUR

The Stakes

Interests and Claims

When ethnic formations clash with one another or with an encompassing state, what is at stake in their struggle? For what do they fight? To what do they lay claim and on what basis do they attempt to legitimate their demands? In Chapters 1–3 we saw the collective actors. Now we seek to understand what those actors want, demand, and claim as their right.

The Stakes of Contention: General Considerations

In terms of its significance for ethnic conflict, the most important characteristic of an "object of contention" may appear to be "how valuable it is" to the protagonists. Yet it is no obvious or simple matter to determine how much is at stake. One aspect of the magnitude of the stakes certainly is the *size of the immediate allocations of scarce values*, e.g., which ethny gets how much of wages, profits, oil, land, water, social honors, political offices, and so on. A second major consideration is the *reversible or irreversible character of such allocations.* Some outcomes may transfer consumable valuables (oil, timber, endangered species) which are then irrevocably transformed or used up; others may allocate fixed loci of value (land, buildings) that can be reallocated later. In the third place, how much is at stake in an ethnic conflict may depend in part upon whether the current allocations have important *implications for future advantages,* e.g., they may represent strategic military capabilities, productive capital, access to channels of mass persuasion, and the like. Fourth, the size of the stake depends upon implications of the outcomes for the *relative power* of the parties in the future.

Finally, the stakes may be increased or decreased by the effect of the struggle upon *rules or norms* for anticipated future occasions of cooperation, competition, or conflict. (Are the rules of the game to be changed?)

A particularly important issue is the defense of positions that represent heavy investments, not only of money and material resources, but of time, effort, concern, emotional significance, endurance of risk and suffering, and so on. The importance and the actual character of vested interests will be badly misjudged unless we take into account the so-called symbolic investments. Historicized accounts of an ethnic past that vividly present collective sacrifices and heroic defenses encourage such investments. Established interests typically come to be thought of as *rights* in the view of those who have established them. Accordingly, immediate and severe threat of an attack upon such vested interests is a prime incitement for conflict. And in violent collective conflicts, the intensity of the struggle typically is increased by the fear of a permanent loss.

Similarly, the size of the stakes will have differing effects depending on whether the participants enjoy a continuing relationship that is guided by established norms. So, a small monetary claim may be amicably settled between friends in their own neighborhood, but result in a violent fight between strangers in a foreign city. Well-defined and limited stakes reduce the likelihood of severe and protracted conflict, even in warfare. An incursion to gain control of a small territory contrasts with an undeclared war with no explicit demands or a war waged with the declared demand for unconditional surrender.

In general, we may speculate that the intensity of a conflict will increase as the issues at stake move from one to seven below:

(1) specific allocations of low-value resources;
(2) specific allocations of high-value resources;
(3) opposition over norms—the "rules of the game";
(4) contest for power and authority;
(5) opposition over values—the basic standards of desirability, of "good" and "bad";
(6) struggle for collective prestige or self-esteem;
(7) unconditional domination.

This ordering is quite crude, and does not allow for the great variations in importance within each of the categories. It is reasonable, however, to suppose that any given opposition at levels one to three will be made more intense, and less open to compromise or other cooperative solution, by the addition of any or all of levels four to seven.

In studies of collective conflict there has been a long, generally inconclusive debate over the relative importance of broad categories of causal factors—"economic factors," "population pressure," "power positions," "ideologies," and so on. Thus there are often outright contradictions between claims that ideological or symbolic issues are more important than economic or political issues, and opposing contentions that emphasize "material factors" or changes in coercive power. These excessively broad generalizations are not really open to decisive empirical test. Both interstate and intrastate conflicts typically involve relative power, ideologies, symbols, economic interests, internal political processes, and other factors. To untangle the specific effects of these conditions would require new research that does not yet exist.

Pending such analyses, appraisal remains a matter of informed judgment rather than crucial evidence. Thus it is plausible that the magnitude of conflict would be greater when both "interests" and "ideology" are at issue than when only one basis of conflict is present. For example, it may be assumed that the desire to protect, maintain, or extend a belief, value, or ideology against resistance will be more likely to lead to violent conflict when it is joined together with more specific kinds of economic and political collective self-interest. When interests and "rightness" are so linked, ideological justifications can give individuals a sense of conforming to group standards and reduce inhibitions against the use of drastic means; hence the development of such supporting and channeling ideologies tends to increase the likelihood of intense and violent conflicts. The intellectual work of "objectifying conflicts," transforming opposition of interests into incompatibilities of ideas and providing public justifications, may increase the stakes by generalizing the issue beyond the immediate objects of contention: a struggle over "ideas" or "principles" rather than territory, trade, and so on. Furthermore, the generalization and justification may make the conflict seem inevitable and impersonal. At the same time, this objectification often seems to lead to de-humanization of the opposition—apparently an effective means of reducing empathy and increasing willingness to employ drastic means.

"Stakes" are the objects of contention in social competition, rivalry, or conflict—the "goods" that are sought and the "bads" that are to be imposed or avoided. Anything that one party desires can be a stake as soon as another aspirant seeks to attain it. Many of the objects of contention are *distributive goods*—those that can be divided up and parceled out to various social actors. Distributive goods include money, credit, jobs, contracts, votes, promotions, parking rights, tickets for recreational events, weapons, copyrights, patents, and claims to property. *Nondistributive (collective)* goods are shared: they are indivisible, participated in rather than divided up, as in collective honor, respect, prestige (ethnic pride, national prestige), collective security, language use, religious participation, communal rituals, and festivals.

It is a commonplace assumption that a zero-sum contest is likely to be more intense than a positive-sum game. In a rapidly expanding economy as compared to a stagnant one, for example, struggles over politicized ethnic allocations are likely to produce less intense psychological involvement, less intransigent bargaining strategies, and less drastic means of conflict. Also, qualitative differences in the stakes may give rise to different *patterns* or *types* of conflict. For instance, imbalance or ambiguity of power between rival ethnies may be expected to exacerbate oppositions based on more *specific* interests. And because leaders and representatives are typically more sensitive to power relations than are the other members of their collectivities, and because such spokesmen and decision makers are especially likely to have their personal interests directly affected by the collectivity's power relationships, they are especially likely to escalate conflict over such particular issues. Given a clear and "balanced" power relationship, on the other hand, conflict can more easily be restricted to more specific oppositions of interests and concrete objectives. For example, if threats are used in a situation of opposing interests, the likelihood of a cooperative resolution is reduced. One factor that appears to be important in this result is that the introduction of threat extends the struggle from an *allocative* problem to an *ascendancy* contest—from a question of relative gains to one of power—who wins.

A related factor is the degree of emphasis on cooperative or competitive orientation. Whether the situation at hand is socially defined—for example, by state authorities or ethnic leaders as regulated by norms of cooperation or competition —will greatly affect the likelihood of conflict. It has been demonstrated that even experimentally induced definitions of interpersonal relationships as cooperative, individualistic, or competitive can be strong enough to substantially alter the behavior of subjects playing the same standardized game for money. Instructions for cooperation in such experiments resulted in mutual trustworthy behavior, which led to mutual gain. Instructions for competition produced nontrusting behavior and mutual loss, and "individualistic" definitions led to similar results.

Whether rule-abiding competition (or rivalry) will dominate or whether it will be transformed into direct conflict depends not only on the existence and strength of regulatory agents, and not only on the acceptance (or rejection) by the parties of rules of peaceable competition, but also upon the "mutual deterrent" balance in the relationship of the parties. Competition rather than overt conflict probably is especially favored by relationships of low and approximately equal coercive power.

In a zero-sum struggle between two parties, each claiming more than the other is willing to grant, the fewer the alternative possibilities of *both* the parties (who are in opposition over the particular issue) for satisfactory or acceptable outcomes in relationships with still *other* parties in the same area of interest, the more likely it is that the opposition will lead to overt conflict. Since under these conditions one party (or both) has to reduce a claim in order to permit compromise, the apparent stake is likely to be augmented by a sense that power and collective esteem/prestige are also involved. The resulting increase in psychological salience and intensity tends, in turn, to widen the scope of disagreement, and to increase the probability that threats will be made. If threats are made, the negative cycle tends to be repeated. Up to some limit of extremely high cost, then, conflict for high stakes tends to elicit a preference for high-payoff strategies even if the probability of success is low; since both parties are subject to this effect, the process often leads to escalation of scale and severity of means.

The higher the stakes, the more likely it is that rules and restraints against extreme violence will be violated; an old proverb says that all is fair in love and war. Aside from the restraints of mutual deterrence, it is difficult to maintain limits in warfare. The eighteenth-century notion of wars of "sedate hostility" between European states was occasionally enacted when war was primarily the sport of kings, but any restraints of that kind quickly disappeared in colonial wars, and were ignored in the total wars of the twentieth century. In today's fratricidal civil wars in which the opponents see the stakes as domination or extermination, the violence is unrestrained by rules of war.

Short of the most extreme wars of extermination, economic stakes enter strongly into the initiation and continuation of intrastate collective violence. More specifically, civil wars can represent an alternative to peaceful governance by creating a system of "profit, power and protection" (Berdal and Malone, 2000). Governing elites and rebel warlords can gain enormous wealth from the conditions that prevail in failed and collapsed states, particularly from trade in narcotics, oil, diamonds, and other high-value goods that state regimes want to tax or expropriate, and that rebel groups can seize and use to carry on civil war. Obviously, rebels against state regimes need material resources to maintain armed struggle. Indeed, it is argued by Collier (2001) that grievances or ideologies are *not* the causes of civil war. Instead, "the motivation of conflict is unimportant; what matters is whether the [rebel] organization can sustain itself financially. It is this, rather than any objective grounds for grievance that determines whether a country will experience civil war" (Collier 2001, 145).

The extreme claim for the dominance of economic resources contains a partial truth, but cannot be sustained as an adequate account, for reasons that we will now explore. Two central questions must be disentangled. First, why do people use violence rather than peaceable means of exchange, persuasion, and political influence? Second, why do so many violent conflicts occur along ethnic lines? The first question will occupy several later chapters, but the second requires immediate attention.

95

Culture, Symbols, and Collective Identity

What is "ethnic" in ethnic conflict? How can we decide what part ethnicity has in struggles involving labor unions, regions, classes, business firms, clans, and other social formations? These struggles often have the appearance of confusing mixtures of structures and interests that approach chaos. A first step toward increased clarity is the elementary distinction between *ethnies as social groups* and *ethnic issues* (values, beliefs, symbols). Thus, for example, there are many military coups in which the stakes simply are control of a central state and its resources—no ethnic content is involved. But if the contending parties are identified by ethnic allegiances (in Nigeria, Hausa-Fulani vs. Yoruba or Ibo), we would have an ethnic coup, as distinct from a similar event in which the antagonists have the same communal identity. To show that in a civil war the parties have different class interests need not be to deny that the lines of cleavage are primarily or also ethnic allegiances.

The second type of ethnic conflict is one in which focal issues are themselves ethnic: for example, language use, religious practices, marriage and family norms, observation of holidays, exhibiting symbols of identity (flags, icons, distinctive dress or ornamentation), and content of school instruction. In many cases, conflicts are ethnic in both dimensions.

Over and over again, states attempt to impose or prohibit manifestations of ethnic identity. Ethnic Russians in Moldavia are forced to learn the Romanian language. Turks in Bulgaria formerly were forbidden to use the Turkish language, even in their family names. Business firms in Québec must use French. In one country after another street names are changed, statues are demolished, photographs of religious leaders are forbidden in public, and textbooks are rewritten. At the extreme, the attempt is made to destroy a cultural identity. A recurrent pattern in ethnic conflicts is the targeting of symbols of identity: the desecration of cemeteries, the destruction of the Babri Masjid (mosque) at Ayodhya in India, the burning of Black churches in the American South, the public burning of the national flag, graffiti on religious buildings. Symbols do matter. In the year 2000, a major controversy erupted in the United States over the display of the Confederate flag in public buildings in South Carolina—to African Americans a symbol of ethnic domination. The examples are endless.

How much does the content of an ethnic culture matter in relations of ethnies to other ethnies and to states? The answer has to be context-specific. Content matters greatly if a politically dominant ethnic grouping attempts to impose religious or linguistic restrictions and requirements upon those who resist. Content may matter little if the question is the economic consequences of ethnic trading and credit networks or the availability of a culturally distinct labor pool (e.g., Collins 1994, 303). So ethnies often are moved to demand greater economic and political opportunities when they have suffered political and economic discrimination and disadvantages, but they are most likely to attempt secession when they have a history of political autonomy (Gurr 1993b, 86). In general, cultural differences are more likely to lead to social and cultural claims than to political and economic demands.

A priori it would seem that religious differences would be an especially potent source of violent collective conflict, as claims to the One True Faith collide in practice. Nevertheless, the most comprehensive available survey of communal groups concludes that "religious cleavages are at best a contributing factor in communal conflict and seldom the root cause" (Gurr 1993b, 317). This conclusion, however, is drawn from a set of data that expressly excludes terrorism, political murders, and massacres and military violence by states against helpless or unresisting people. And in any case there are enormous differences among religious groupings: some practice quietistic withdrawal from the secular world, others vigorously seek converts, and others seek to impose the one true faith by the sword. The range is from absolute pacifism to the advocacy of Holy War, from Gandhian nonviolence to violent imposition of religious law and the extermination of heretics and infidels. In this field, the particulars are crucial.

Nevertheless, conflict-ridden intransigence surely is often traceable to the fact that the stakes are not the divisible and transferable goods—the so-called tangible or material resources of land and physical capital, or of trade advantages—but rather the indivisible "communal" values of identity, of historicized symbols, of prestige and collective respect, and of distinctive cultural patterns and life ways. As Gurr (1994, 11) also points out, economic inequalities and discrimination are not, in fact, strongly correlated with *ethnonationalist* grievances and rebellions.

Yet common observation tells us that "economic conditions" or the level of "material welfare" are important factors affecting conflict and harmony. The exact relationships between levels of real income—and changes in them—and the expectations and normative claims of the recipients have not been adequately studied. Nevertheless, certain empirical generalizations are reasonably well supported and help us to locate ethnic conflicts in understandable contexts. For example, "Conflict among ethnic, racial, and religious groupings is most likely in periods of rapid change in levels of living" (Williams 1947, 58). If, however, the differentials between ethnies are not extreme and such differentials are not increased by general prosperity, conflicts that do occur are likely to be less intense in a society of stable affluence than in a society with a low level of economic welfare. With these qualifications, "The higher the level of prosperity, the less intense the conflict between ethnic and racial majorities and minorities" (Mack and Snyder 1957, 237).

97

There are some circumstances in which additional interfering variables will falsify this proposition, but it holds as a "statistical" rule of thumb. Its dependability rests upon two mediating regularities: (1) with high prosperity, the average level of frustration tends to be lowered (provided that extremely rapid and large increases in rewards have not pushed expectations to unrealistically high levels); and (2) at high levels of total real income the marginal utility of a given unit added or subtracted is lower than at low levels of income. From these propositions it follows that aggressive instigations will be lower, and that the allocative struggles that do occur generally will be for stakes that are less crucial: one is likely to fight less fiercely for caviar than for bread.

It is when change is very rapid and of quite uneven impact on different subcollectivities that it is likely to increase the likelihood of *new* oppositions and conflicts—by two main socio-psychological mechanisms: (1) changes in expectations of reward and in aspirations; and (2) shifts in the relative positions of individuals and collectivities in the scales of distribution of scarce values. Among changes having these effects, especially important are major changes in availability of consumer goods and services, and in control of economic resources and facilities. For the first case, "Conflict is especially likely in periods of rapid change in levels of living. The probability of conflict is increased insofar as the changes have a differential impact on various groups" (Williams 1947, 58). As a special example of shifts in the relative positions of collectivities, whenever subordinated ethnic strata acquire substantial means to challenge the status quo (through increased income, education, control of communications, or rising political influence), the likelihood increases that their demands will go beyond increased individual opportunity to claims for collective advantages, such as African Americans in the United States or lower castes in India (cf. Larson 1995, 261–66).

We must emphasize the basic distinction, often ignored, between two kinds of ethnic oppositions (rivalries, conflicts). In the one case, the *objects of contention* are non-ethnic but the *contenders* are ethnies. The most obvious examples are "communal" contenders for political office and patronage: ascriptive ethnic identities *define the parties* in the struggles, but the *direct stakes* are the mundane rewards of power and pelf. In such cases the contenders obviously could be non-ethnic—they could be trade unions, regional organizations, non-ethnic political parties, industrial associations, professional groups, and the like. In the extreme or pure type of ethnic struggles for non-ethnic stakes, ethnicity resides only in the boundary markers that define the collective entity. Quite different are the struggles in which both the contenders and the stakes are ethnic. In such cases, not only are collectivities defined by ascriptive-cultural boundaries, but the stakes are themselves cultural.

Just as in interstate relations, the overt public issues in ethnic struggles may not be the actual operative issues. A struggle between class or caste groupings that starts as an ordinary political contest may rapidly acquire an ethnic identity. A similar trajectory often marks the transformation of limited economic rivalry into deadly ethnic opposition. And interactions that are initially couched in ethnic terms almost always admit a mixture of economic and political interests.

Many of today's ethnic civil wars strike external observers as bizarre, irrational, or inexplicable because it appears that the parties do not have clearly defined economic, political, or ideological stakes. The violence often seems spontaneous, a "senseless slaughter"; the *wars within* have the appearance of being "wars about nothing at all" (Enzensberger 1994, 30). But in fact ethnic purity is itself a deadly ideology, and the stakes often are nothing less than survival vs. genocide (cf. Meštrović 1995, 768–69).

It is difficult to overemphasize that there are real and important differences among identified cultural groupings in their shared beliefs, values, and social practices. Not all of such practices, values, and beliefs are easily accepted under a doctrine of state neutrality and cultural pluralism. Examples are prominent and numerous, including parental punishment of children, legal punishment of norm violators (e.g., amputation of hands of thieves, castration of rapists), forms of marriage (e.g., polygamy), circumcision of males, clitoridectomy and infibulation of females, arranged vs. free-choice marriages, ritual sacrifice of animals, education in a "minority" language, religious garb in public schools, use of drugs in religious ceremonies (e.g., peyote), or refusal to accept secular medical treatment (cf. Shweder et al. 1997).

Increases in ethnic salience lead to increased attention by ethnic members and their leaders to collective goods—especially group status—and to discrimination. Relevant collective goods include language use, recognition by outsiders of cultural distinctiveness, political rights, economic opportunity and parity with other ethnies, and regional/ethnic autonomy in various economic and political realms. The focus upon collective goods means that competition will increasingly come to be seen as *rivalry:* not individualized, interpersonal competition, but collective or categorical contention between known (named) groupings as such.

The possibility of overt conflict is likely, then, to be high if collectivized competition leads to group inequality when there is low positive interdependence of ethnies within the same society. Especially potent in such situations is a sense of *victimization*—of perceived unfairness occasioned by discrimination or other violations of prior norms, for example, encroachment upon established rights and privileges (see Bélanger and Pinard 1991).

The remarkable importance of symbolic goods in ethnic relations is evident in many crucial instances of conflict. Two salient cases in the 1990s were (1) the status of Jerusalem and its religious sites, and (2) the destruction of the Babri Masjid (mosque) in Ayodhya, India. It is not possible to explain these foci of conflict without taking into full account the beliefs and values embodied in symbolic expressions of collective identities (Friedland and Hecht 1996). Similarly, in Sri Lanka, as in South Asia more generally, ethnic leaders and intellectuals tend to define ethnic claims as historical rights: long-ago events and ancient grievances can thus become a large part of present-day controversies and opposing claims and demands. Specifically, in Sri Lanka, Sinhala media have emphasized an exclusionary view of ethnic membership, claims to historically based rights, and the idea of a "chosen people" (the defenders of a pure Buddhism and a glorious past) (Coomaraswamy 1994, 140).

Thus once again the "real world out there" demonstrates that there need be nothing intangible in cultural content as a stake in social struggles. In the very obvious fact that the culture at stake includes language and other basic forms of communication and understanding (body language, dress, many other identity codes), culture represents an omnipresent, encompassing, everyday medium for relating individuals and groups to one another. It is an immediate, tangible social resource. At the same time, it is a treasure of historical memory, a sign of the continuity of personal and collective identity.

Language itself has both important practical implications and symbolic significance. From a practical standpoint, as Esman says, "those who attend school, take examinations, compete for employment and transact with government in their native tongue enjoy a considerable advantage over those who must function in a second language. Thus language policy can be a subject of bitter controversy and a weapon in ethnic conflicts, but it can also be a sign of respect, recognition, and accommodation" (1994, 219).

To the extent that ethnic membership is salient in daily life in any society, it will matter whether one's ethnic identity is treated by nonmembers with respect or contempt. To the extent that ethnic solidarity exists, affronts to individuals by reason of their ethnic identity become a collective concern. To the extent that ethnic mobilization occurs, ethnic leaders will press for public recognition and symbols of respect, and for acknowledgment of valued qualities and achievements. This crucial aspect of interethnic relations has been repeatedly noted by many studies (see, e.g., Horowitz 1985; Williams 1994; Esman, 1994). Individuals who strongly identify with an ethny often respond to threat or injury to the collectivity and its symbols as if they themselves were being personally attacked. In these cases, one can observe that "members of a group involved in serious conflict with other groups display very high levels of emotionality, especially hate-filled rage with destructive intent" (Wedge 1986, 56). Disputes over beliefs and values are just as real as disputes over wealth and power, and ideological conflicts can be as violently ferocious as conflicts over so-called material interests (see Friedland in Howard 1992, 84–85). Indeed, many of the opposing stands on particular issues in the conflicts of ethnies and states are so incompatible as to defy compromise in the here and now. Thus the claims for a Palestinian state and the commitment to a Greater Israel in the same territories were the basis for decades of protracted and bitter conflict. Similarly, the conflict between the Tamils and the Sri Lankan state, and between the Southern Sudanese and Sudan's Islamic government (set off by the imposition of Shari'a), involved basic contradictions of values and interests. This is not to say that such deep incompatibilities cannot be overcome, only that reframing the issues and changing the context will be necessary for compromise or resolution.

Claims for favored-group position frequently invoke priority or origin or possession of and residence in a territory: "*We* were here first." The search for priority of origins and territorial occupation was made highly visible, controversial, and politically consequential by archeological discoveries in the Americas in the late twentieth century. Skeletal remains and artifacts attested to earlier occupation and more diverse origins than previously envisioned. The sociopolitical results included demands by Native Americans to custody of the relics, under provisions of the Native American Graves Protection and Repatriation Act. Possession of the past emerged, once again, as a passionate ethnic issue (*New York Times, Science Times,* November 9, 1999). Concurrently, in acrimonious confrontations between militant Muslims and Christians in Nazareth, contrary to all expectations, the State of Israel supported the Islamists, and the Palestinians took the part of the Christians who opposed the building of a mosque adjacent to the Church of the Annunciation. The unusual political alliances were seen as strategic preludes to later negotiations over control of Jerusalem and its sacred sites.

Our review thus far suggests that cultural differences can enter as a factor in intrastate conflicts in three major ways: first, as boundary markers that define membership in separable collectivities; second, as the substantive content of the issues at stake in collective rivalries and contentions; third, as deep assumptions or beliefs, for example, about human nature, morality, the nature of the state and of the good society. *Who* is Serb or Croat, Tamil or Sinhalese, Ibo or Fulani-Hausa, Sikh or Hindu, Breton or French, Czech or Slovak, and so on? *What* aspect of culture is being threatened or suppressed—language use, religious observances, domestic law and customs, identity (songs, flags, monuments, street names)? Do identified collectivities have different beliefs about the value of individualism, the possibility of a secular state, or justifications for violence?

Of course, ethnicity is not everything. People have multiple identities and statuses. Everywhere there are men and women, old and young, employers and employees, politicians and officials and citizens or clients, unions and professions, capitalists and proletariat, neighbors and distant people, natives and newcomers, recreational associates and co-workers, friends and strangers, and ideological comrades and opponents. In all this profusion, it is remarkable how often and how widely ethnic identities and loyalties prevail over other alignments in everyday behavior and in contention over public issues.

Issues of Identity, Priority, and Possession: Land, Rule, and Legitimacy

With impressive regularity, ethnic rivalries and conflicts are accompanied by historicized claims to priority of origins or of occupation of territory. Mythic representations of the past are created and elaborated as a basis for current demands and claims. Thus in Sri Lanka Sinhalese intellectuals and spokesmen claim a (disputed) priority over Tamils in control of territory, even though Tamil settlement admittedly is many centuries old. In the Georgian-Abhazian conflicts in the Caucasus region, the contending parties seek to establish priorities in several interrelated areas: the origin of the state; which early "tribes" were first in the territory; which ethny founded historic kingdoms; whose language was dominant; and even which ethnies were the original source of ancient Christianization. These historic-ideological claims are stakes in the struggle for legitimacy of territorial and other political claims (Shnirelman 1995). In the former Yugoslavia, Serbian claims to Kosovo utilized elaborate historical narratives to support precedence in religion, culture, and military prowess (including the "glorious" defeat of Serbian forces by the Ottomans in 1389). And a particular history does not have to be lengthy in order for myth-making to flourish and for claims of homeland priority to be contested. Even in the United States, there is the cult of the Mayflower, the Daughters of the American Revolution, and the United Daughters of the Confederacy.

Recurrently, these rival claims to indigenous status are aspects of the ethnic search for legitimate priority in current struggles. Always the basic questions are, whose country is this? Who has the right to superior status and political control? So, in a Hutu refugee camp in Tanzania, the refugees who had been displaced from Burundi after the 1972–73 massacres justified their claims to Burundi on priority of possession, as opposed to the dominant Tutsi, who were said to have been invaders from the north (Malkki 1995).

Whose land is this? What is a "homeland"? Why is *ours* the sacred soil?

What establishes territorial sovereignty? Contrary to the views of some students of international relations (e.g., Ullman 1991), the control of territory has not lost its place as a major focus of interstate and interethnic conflict—as witness, among other cases, Israel-Syria or Serbia-Albania in Kosovo. Opposing claims, border wars, and border changes have not disappeared from the earth. Geography still matters.

The long history of conflicts over control of territory raises the question of how, if at all, possession and use of territory can be legitimized by socially validated claims. A starting observation is that *claims* are not just wants or demands. To make a claim is to invoke some criterion of legitimacy of rightful action, some principle accepted by a moral community. What criteria or principles could conceivably provide a resting place or touchstone for controversy over possession or rule?

Territorial claims, in the first place, represent claims to valuable resources—land for agriculture, forests, fishing grounds, oil, diamonds, other mineral resources. Further, "land" often is a military strategic resource: an otherwise worthless area may have commanding military advantages. And boundaries may be fought over in tests of military strength and tactics, or as a surrogate for other interests of states. And territory (location) frequently has high symbolic value, as a homeland or site of crucial historic events, such as Kosovo as the location of the great defeat of Serbia in 1389 by Ottoman forces, or the site of religious structures (as in Jerusalem or Ayodhya). The intensity of feelings of possession of "sacred" territories must not be underrated.

In the symbolism of territorial claims there often is a merging of land and kinship: Fatherland or Motherland, "land where our fathers died." Special poignancy is evoked by the claims to sacred shrines and holy places—Jerusalem, Mecca, the birthplace of Lord Ram or Buddha, a sacred mountain, or the burial ground of ancestors.

"Homelands" may be very large: China, Russia, India. As a perceived marker of identity, a homeland may even be defined as a whole continent, as when ethnic spokespersons refer to "Africa" or "Asia," in contrast to "Europe." But the behaviors and psychological processes that thus define a place of origin or of current identification seem remarkably similar to those involved in the defense of a local "turf," whether it is the territory claimed by a juvenile gang or the resistance of a homogenous urban ethnic neighborhood to an influx of outsiders. So, for example, a study of racially motivated crime finds high rates in white neighborhoods in New York City that had experienced immigration of Blacks, Asians, or Latinos (Green, Strolovitch, and Wong 1998).

Over time, claims to possession of territory and of a right to rule have been invoked on many disparate bases. Still invoked in today's civil wars is the ancient assertion of right of conquest—which was an accepted interstate principle even in the nineteenth century. This form of "might makes right" comes in many versions: our sacred dead have consecrated this land for us, we fought and won our right, or, in a cynical vein, as was said of the United States' possession of the territory of the Panama Canal, "We stole it, fair and square." A second justification is priority of possession: we were here first, we have always lived here, this is our ancestral home. Then, third, there is interstate legality: essentially, recognition by other states and international organizations. Fourth is the usually ignored claim of need: our people are starving; we must have these fishing grounds/these grasslands for our cattle. Fifth is the claim of sacrifice or investment: generations have toiled to build these terraces and irrigation works; our parents spent their lives to clear these forests. Sixth, there is the classic imperial-colonial claim to possession or rule on the basis of effective use of resources: the indigenous people could not or would not cultivate the land. Seventh, ours is a higher civilization, of greater achievements, a superior morality; the others are pagans, barbarians, savages—outside the bounds of law. Eighth (not in order of priority), our claims come from God. Ninth, our holy places are located there. Tenth, it was transferred to us by a higher authority: by an international mandate, the edict of the emperor, or a court decision. This list, no doubt, is incomplete, but it may serve to illustrate the range of claims as well as the presence of acute contradictions and incompatibilities.

When mobilized ethnies seek voice, exit, autonomy, or control, their representatives and spokespersons only rarely present demands devoid of justifications. Raw *demands* are couched as *claims*—that is, as legitimated by something other than sheer expediency or coercive force. Actual cases of intrastate ethnic contention exhibit an extensive set of such "justified demands" or legitimized claims.

Especially prominent in the claims of indigenous peoples and ethnonationalists is the appeal to prior occupation of a homeland territory: our present demand is justified because we were here first—no matter how uncertain or ambiguous may be the asserted priority. The claim of Native Americans to prior occupation of the lands of North and South America can be supported by archaeological evidence (although the meaning of "occupation" or "possession" can be in dispute). But most historical societies of Europe, the Middle East, and Asia have been repeatedly swept over by the surge and ebb of empires and vast migrations of peoples over many centuries. When is first? Palestinians and Israelis can claim priority in the same territories in endless inconclusive arguments. Yet the homeland claim appears to have a powerful appeal even in populations such as Anglo-Americans, whose residency in the United States is very short.

The importance of territory is sharply emphasized in cities inhabited by antagonistic ethnies, especially when the city contains sites of high symbolic value, such as temples, mosques, churches, monuments, or locales of historic events. Recurrent conflicts often occur within such confined spaces, as in Jerusalem, with holy sites of three world religions; in Belfast in Northern Ireland, where violent clashes have led to fortress-like hyper-segregation; in Sarajevo; and others.

In sum, when ethnic mythology lays claim to sacred homelands, and two or more ethnies have such claims to the same area, the likelihood grows of ethnic violence and nationalistic wars. So it is that the closer the association of rival ethnies to a particular place, the more likely is intense conflict (Smith 1992, 450).

In many of the newly independent states emerging in the decades immediately after World War II from prior colonial status, the early phases of independence brought claims to legitimacy by reason of succession from prior authority, either of the colonial power or of traditional leadership. A partially competing and partially overlapping claim was made in the name of the ethny's role in achieving state independence.

Especially prominent are separatist movements and ethnoregional mobilizations aimed at autonomy of a homeland. During the decades since World War II the roster of such occasions includes Biafra in Nigeria, Scotland in Great Britain, Québec in Canada, Eritrea in Ethiopia, Tamil Eelam in Sri Lanka, the southern region in the Sudan, Kosovo in Yugoslavia, Sikh Khalistan in India, and numerous breakaway regions in the former Soviet Union. At the same time, still other conflicts emerge when rival ethnies, especially recent immigrants, take land and other economic opportunities, and come to be seen as threatening to reduce the indigenous people to a minority that may lose control of the homeland state, as with Malays in Malaysia, Assamese in India, or Fijians in Fiji. Such situations typically raise fears of being displaced, subordinated, and overwhelmed—economically, politically, and culturally.

Political Power and Authority

The greater the scope of the central state and the more pervasive its influence on daily life activities, the greater is the stake of individuals and collectivities in control of the state apparatus. The modern multifunctional state supports education and medical care, builds highways and ports, regulates commerce, subsidizes economic enterprises, enforces rules for political participation, redistributes income, levies taxes, raises military forces, and so on through a remarkable range of important activities. Therefore, the life chances of persons are decisively affected by the policies of the state. To the extent that those policies differentially affect ethnic collectivities, ethnic activation and rivalry are readily politicized. The greater the stakes, the greater the likelihood of politicization. Given opportunity, the greater the political activation, the greater the collective mobilization. What then happens with high levels of mobilization depends upon complex constellations of other factors, to be discussed in Chapter 5. At any rate, political rivalries within territorial states clearly contribute to ethnic salience and collective mobilization.

An important distinction has been proposed between *spatial* as over against structural or *positional* rivalries among national states. The distinction is likewise significant for ethnies: "For instance, separatist ethnic and regional movements may involve spatial rivalries, whereas structural rivalries can be found in political systems in which two or more groups vie for control of the whole system" (Thompson 1995, 203). The suggested distinction immediately recalls Gurr's (1993b) proposed types of ethnonationalists and communal contenders, and the finding that the latter lead to more deadly conflicts. Thompson argues that among states the spatial rivalries tend to be more frequent and less deadly than positional rivalries. It is relatively easy to have boundary disputes, but the claimants often lack the resources to force a decisive termination. On the whole, with exceptions, spatial contests are more likely to be quickly settled when capacities are markedly unequal, and to be enduring when the parties are roughly equal in coercive power. In contrast, intrastate positional rivalries in which ethnic contenders have substantial resources and roughly equivalent capabilities tend to be prolonged. In addition, struggle over position in a particular geopolitical hierarchy is inherently a zero-sum game in which one party loses what the other gains. Thus positional rivalries involve strong actors and high stakes; hence their potentially severe character.

Within states, "spatial" contests regularly turn out to involve claims for autonomy or separation that states are reluctant to accept—so, even if less threatening than communal contests for state control, they have been potent sources of internal warfare.

Further, in many less-industrialized countries state employees are a substantial and privileged portion of the non-agricultural work force. The military establishment is an especially important case, both because of its central place in the power structure and because its organizational cohesion renders it a powerful political player and source of economic advantages. In addition, employment and contracting in the private sector often are strongly dependent upon state regulation and state subsidies. Patronage is endemic in these situations. Given the lack of alternative opportunities, the struggle for state employment and support is likely to be intense, so that control of the state by one ethny rather than another is a crucial prize.

Ethnies that are interacting with one another over a period of time typically come to be unequal in resources and, partly in consequence, in prestige and respect. To the extent that initial nominal distinctions exist (boundary-markers of culture or physical phenotypes), differences in "material" advantages tend to create status inequalities (cf. Ridgeway, Boyle, Kuipers, and Robinson 1998). In fact, ethnic inequalities are what we almost always observe—genuinely unranked ethnies are at most rare ephemeral cases. Ethnies differ in income and wealth, political power and authority, educational levels, and typical occupations. To the extent that there are geographic concentrations of ethnic populations, they will differ in control of material resources, access to urban areas and political centers, and contact with other ethnies. It is a lumpy world out there.

To the extent that ethnic membership is indeed acquired at birth, and hence passed on to a next generation, it differs basically from any of the voluntary and renounceable identities individuals may have. If ethnic membership has important consequences (economic, political, cultural, social), the ethnic identity itself represents very high stakes, for the consequences are unavoidable and are experienced over a lifetime and carry over to one's children. Strongly bounded and persisting ethnic differentials therefore become psychologically salient and evoke strong emotions.

Because of their ascribed nature, politically dominant ethnies are perceived by rival contenders for power as permanently dominant, with the subordinates doomed to continuing oppression. The counter-mobilization of the now-threatened subordinates, unacceptable in the rigid state system, increases tension and repression. Fear of losing elite control instigates violence, to be met by counter-violence. Mutual fears and hostilities can then escalate conflict over extended periods.

In this way the stakes in ethnic contest can come to focus primarily upon political power and authority. Thus many separate issues become unified in the great question of identity politics—who is in charge. The ferocity so often observed in ethnic politics comes in part because one identity among many is singled out as the crucial division between we and they across a range of otherwise separable issues. When all issues become one, the possibilities for compromise are narrowed and the grounds for moderation are eroded. So ethnic politics are not likely to be the gentlest of the kind.

Data about ethnopolitical conflicts that were ongoing in 1993–94 permit comparisons among those focused on (1) contention for power, (2) indigenous rights, and (3) ethnonationalism. Power-contention conflicts beginning after 1987 were more severe than the others, having more than ten times the deaths of new conflicts over indigenous rights (Gurr 1994, 7–8).

In general the greater the centralization of power in the state and the greater the penetration of the state into the lives of its people (through, e.g., taxation, conscription, policing, regulation, and licensing), the greater the importance of central political control. In other words, the more intrusive the state, the higher the political stakes. When the state is controlled by one dominant ethny or ethnic coalition, the tendency is to turn contests over particular allocations or impositions into ethnic-coded global struggles. To the extent that individuals are ethnically identified, everyone has a stake in the outcomes—all are participants. As Chipman says, "This fact . . . is what makes the resolution of ethnic conflict different from other types of conflict resolution" (1993, 240).

Group Position: The Ultimate Collective Good?

Ethnic conflicts are rarely fully settled, as we shall review in Chapters 10 and 11. To the extent that ethnies persist over long periods—and numerous large ethnies do—their relations with states and with other ethnies will be of continuing importance. Ethnies with a distinctive identity and strong boundaries are consequential for their members. And to the extent that ethnies are treated as real entities by states and by the members of other ethnies, they tend to develop a greater sense of identity and common fate, stronger boundaries, and, usually, greater solidarity. Increases in group salience can be evoked not only by disadvantage, discrimination, and conflict, but also by the sensed threat of individual assimilation that is thought to portend a loss of distinctiveness and collective solidarity. In such cases, ethnic leaders often reaffirm ethnic identity and emphasize differences from other ethnies.

Ethnic rivalry can involve any of a large and diverse set of values, distributive and nondistributive, as we have seen. Of obvious importance are rivalries for economic resources, jobs, credit, educational access, political influence, and other scarce valuables open to individualistic competition. But these rivalries can be overshadowed by struggles for the collective goods of cultural autonomy and acknowledged respect and prestige. In many ways, a sense of group position is a central focus of interethnic and intrastate relations.

Why should group position be a concern to individual persons? A primary fact is that the welfare of individuals can be directly due to categorical membership. Because of ethnic identity, individuals are discriminated against, subjected to insults and harassment, physically threatened and attacked. Further, aside from direct personal experience, individuals are repeatedly reminded of collective fate by significant others, peers, parents, teachers, and religious leaders. Finally, and of increasing importance, mass communication can bring vivid impressions of collective inequality, unjust discrimination, atrocities, and other evidences of the noxious behavior of dominant or rivalrous others.

Group position is always relative to comparison groups, and is not confined to such objective criteria as wealth, income, or political office. For ethnies in modern societies are almost never unranked, and a sense of shared relative deprivation is a strong motivation for mobilization and struggle. It is no news that people dislike being treated with contempt, or that being humiliated because of ethnic membership can be felt as especially arbitrary and unjust. Group position, accordingly, is not an ephemeral or illusory phenomenon, but in deep and pervasive ways the ultimate collective good.

CHAPTER FIVE

Sources and Precipitants
of Rivalry and Violent Conflict

So far we have examined the characteristics of ethnies and states as collective actors, and the stakes in their struggles. That review is essential background for this chapter's focus upon the conditions most closely connected with the outbreak of violent ethnic conflicts.

Oppositions and conflicts can and do occur between and among any tangible social formations, such as families and households, labor unions, business firms, local communities, religious groupings, ethnies, states, and classes (and class-and-state fractions, such as military forces versus civilian agencies of governance). If we look only at the four basic social entities of households, ethnic peoples, classes, and states, we find that the internal and external relations of just these four units generates no less than fourteen different "politics"—that is, sets of particular cooperative or oppositional interactions (Taylor 1991, 398). From this complex matrix, we focus here upon ethnies and states.

Two sharply contrasting generalized images, or conceptual models, of societies are found in discussions of intergroup conflict. One model assumes, explicitly or implicitly, that a society (or a set of subgroupings such as a local community) is a stable set of relationships that tends, in the absence of interfering influences, to become self-regulating through exchange, socialization, persuasion, and consensus-based social control. The whole set of relationships is thought to become over time an integrated system, with many feedback sequences that reduce deviance and reinforce conformity to the norms that are constitutive of the total system. To the extent that collective conflict appears in the conceptual scheme, it is primarily a by-product of "strain" or of an inevitable residue of resistance to social control. In contrast, the opposing model assumes that societies and other collectivities are continually falling apart or breaking up—that, in the absence of interfering influence, social systems are highly entropic. Their natural state is either chaos or a precarious condition of continuous conflict. Opposition of interests, contradictions between beliefs, and incompatibilities among values—these are inevitable and universal characteristics. All social relationships tend toward instability. Conflict is normal, peace is an interlude between wars, consensus is rare and fleeting.

Analyses that begin with the assumption that societies tend to develop reciprocally rewarding consensual relationships will be recurrently confronted with the anomalies of frequent and severe conflicts. Analyses that start with the model of opposition, conflict, and instability continually will be faced with the fact that much stability and peace actually can be found. And, indeed, an accumulation of detailed historical and comparative data and analyses shows that actual systems of interaction always and everywhere develop disagreements and conflicts, while also generating consensus and solidarity. The task for empirical analysis is to specify the basic conditions for differing outcomes. Ethnic conflict and cooperation and accommodation are distinctive processes, but they always occur in the context of more extended social systems.

To understand those processes, a first necessity is to be explicit about the meaning of such crucial terms as opposition, competition, rivalry, and conflict. Considerable confusion has been created in the past by failure to clearly distinguish among these concepts.

First, not all competition is opposition. *Opposition* consists of interaction in which one actor seeks to obstruct, block, or turn aside the efforts of another, against resistance. It is found in debates, contests, and games. *Competition* is the more specific process in which actors seek scarce distributive values such as money within a framework of limits on the use of drastic means. It may be totally impersonal and diffuse, as in large-scale markets. When competitors are few and well identified, we may speak of *rivalries*, as among athletic teams or large corporations, or cities seeking governmental grants. So, competition for jobs among individuals in an open labor market differs from the rivalry of two persons for the same position in a corporate hierarchy.

Further, it is essential to emphasize that not all competitions or oppositions should be called *conflict*. As we have said elsewhere, "It is crucially important to distinguish between peaceful individual competition and regularized collective opposition ... and overt conflict. ... An essential difference exists between rule-constrained individualized striving for scarce values and collective actions aimed at displacing, neutralizing, injuring, or destroying opponents" (Williams 1994, 54). Within the general category of conflict, in turn, it is useful to distinguish between violent and nonviolent forms. Violence represents a phase-shift, as when water turns to superheated steam, and it has distinctive dynamics and consequences. "Violence is not a quantitative degree of conflict but a qualitative form of conflict, with its own dynamics" (Brubaker and Laitin 1998, 426). In the narrowest sense, violence is the intentional inflicting of physical harm upon individuals (or coercing others to inflict such damage). Hutu death squads in the 1994 genocide in Rwanda hacked off the legs of Tutsis "to shorten them"; rebels in Sierra Leone in 1999 amputated hands to induce terror. Severe physical attacks are irreversible, and death is the ultimate irreversible outcome. Physical violence is a world apart from other forms of conflict.

These distinctions must be emphasized because they refer to real-world events that must be kept separate in analysis. So, contrary to some interpretations, competition is not the sole or primary source of violent conflict. Ethnies engage in violent political struggles, even when their members rarely compete on an individual basis. Extensive individual competition for scarce valuables (jobs, credit, housing, educational opportunities) can occur without communal conflict. Indeed, competition among individuals often occurs without involving ethnic identities at all. Rivalry among identified ethnic collectives can occur without overt conflict. Competition or rivalry over scarce and distributive goods—income, wealth, land, individualized social status, or power—is not the only source of conflict. Instead, conflict often arises because of incompatibilities in values and beliefs, including incompatible collective goals such as religious commitments or language maintenance (cf. Bélanger and Pinard 1991, 448).

Contrary to the assumption that ethnicity necessarily leads to conflict, well-identified and boundary-maintaining ethnies can coexist and interact within a given state-society with little violent collective conflict. Neither ethnic identity per se nor competition and rivalry over divisible valuables need result in violent conflict. Peaceable exchange, mutual accommodation, and civil tolerance are other viable options; after all, most ethnies, most of the time, do live together without collective violence. This relatively pacific background makes all the more prominent and problematic the "wars within" that disrupt and wreck so many societies today.

Ethnic conflicts are complex historical events. Accordingly, we must expect to find that they have multiple causes and are highly dependent upon particular contexts. They nevertheless do have common characteristics, arise from common causes, and develop in typical sequences. For a useful understanding, we need to pay attention both to generalizable features and to specific settings. What, then, can be identified as the most important sources of belligerent ethnic confrontations? Sheer listings of "factors" are unlikely to be very helpful beyond simply identifying preliminary clues.

More promising will be analyses of the clustering and interaction of main causal conditions.

It has been well said that detailed and exact knowledge of how the world works is the stuff of which valid theories can be made. It is also true that detailed and accurate descriptions can remain jumbled collections of facts unless organized by a coherent theoretical scheme. For the understanding of ethnic conflict we have an enormous body of diverse information, many plausible inventories of putative causes and consequences, and many ingenious classifications and interpretive accounts. What can be validly extracted from this storehouse that will have general theoretical significance and practical implications?

Violent intrastate conflicts—the focus of our present interest—surely are not always "ethnic," but a large portion, arguably a majority, of the cases examined here are ethnic, as defined by both states and rebels, and by other external collective actors. A preliminary characterization of generic characteristics of these conflicts has been given by Schultz (1995). Ethnic conflicts tend to arise in societies of low consensus and low interdependence in which large ethnies see their differences as permanent and regard ethnicity as their principal form of identification. In extreme cases the differences are seen by the contending parties as irreconcilable, as in opposing claims to territory, or in rejection or acceptance of the state and its boundaries. Escalation of claims and threats in such situations leads to and feeds upon a willingness to use violence. The popular views held by the members of each ethny are amplified and promoted by political elites who seek to lead their followers in opposition to other ethnies and/or to the state.

Certainly many ethnic conflicts are generated by the deprivation of deep needs for a distinctive and recognized identity; for security in valued symbols, values, and relationships; and for effective voice in collective decisions that affect vital interests, beliefs, and values. (The overt issues put forward in claims and negotiations often obscure these deeper long-term issues.) So it is that ethnic-related oppositions and conflicts typically involve a shared sense of *disadvantage* and *injustice*—of both deprivation and of wrongs—that is common to many individuals because they share the same identity, which to them means a common fate.

Severely divided societies in modern times often are poor, with a sharp division between elites and masses. Political elites in those societies are typically narrowly based, and their rule is often corrupt and inefficient. In such societies there is little acquaintance with abstract notions of democracy and civic responsibility. Sovereignty is based on particularistic grounds of ethnic or ethnoreligious identity. In such multi-ethnic states, the doctrine of self-determination of peoples is an explosive background idea. Diffuse and multiple grievances are easily defined in ethnic terms. As weak but repressive states (often ethnocracies) deny access and reform to disaffected ethnies, the potential rebels come to see violence not only as necessary, but also as legitimate, and the perceived weakness of the state encourages hope of successful rebellion. Still, ethnic divisions and state weakness by themselves are not enough to ensure internal warfare, for there are instances in which new states have created civic membership and social peace in spite of these conditions, as in Tanzania. Explanation requires context.

We must not forget that conflicts are anchored in place. Geography matters. Even interstate wars, prior to the nuclear age, were usually between geographically adjacent states. Overwhelmingly, this pattern holds for ethnic warfare—it is preeminently "a neighborhood affair" (Gochman 1996/97, 181). Occasions for conflict are most likely when ethnic peoples that are intermingled or that live in adjoining regions are interacting with a state that asserts authority over them. Territorial adjacency makes direct conflict possible; any resulting interdependence will increase both potential cooperation and potential conflict, and geographic closeness, once violence has broken out, increases the difficulty of securing stable peace.

Because the ethnies within multi-ethnic states often are territorially concentrated, many ethnic conflicts are also *regional* conflicts. Because various ethnies are rarely equal in economic position and rewards, ethnic conflicts frequently are also *class* conflicts. Because ethnic struggles almost always occur within sovereign territorial states, such struggles are inherently *political*—concerned with relative power and influence, that is, ability to gain access, autonomy, or control. We would be hard pressed to actually observe "pure" ethnic conflicts, those that would only involve cultural distinctiveness without any tincture of inequality, territoriality, or relative power. All these characteristics repeatedly appear in the newly independent countries established after World War II. Independence often meant that one ethnic group immediately imposed one-party rule or that an ethnically based multiparty system emerged, but both roads often led to military rule (Collier 1982, 95–117, as cited by Tilly 1992, 218). After the independence rallies and calls for national unity came the ethnic protests, riots, and rebellions.

It is often said that conflict with an external adversary strengthens group boundaries and enhances internal cohesion. Like many other unqualified generalizations, this claim is oversimplified, for the collectivity-unifying processes occur only under special conditions. Contrary examples do exist. Thus, external conflict with Turks in Cyprus accentuated discord within the Greek population (Markides 1977, 143). Efforts to form a unified movement for an independent Kurdistan have failed repeatedly, both because of state suppression and interstate maneuvers (Turkey, Iran, Iraq) and because of severe internal cleavages. In 1995 the Kurdish Workers

Party (PKK) in Turkey clashed with the fighters of the Iraq-based Kurdistan Democratic Party (KDP), which in turn was in conflict with the Patriotic Union of Kurdistan (PUK). The conflict in Sri Lanka between Tamils and the Sinhalese government did not prevent violent conflict between the government forces and militant Sinhalese nationalists, or among Tamil factions themselves. There are other examples, notably political dissent in a besieged Israel. Nevertheless, *if* a collectivity already is highly cohesive and *if* the external threats are perceived as affecting all or most members, the unifying effects of external threats typically do occur. So, given a properly specified context, it is still a well-supported proposition of group dynamics that the perception of a common external threat tends to increase in-group cohesion. The generalization fits best those collectivities that already have considerable solidarity.

In interethnic relations, members of a strongly unitary grouping are likely to react to external threat by increased closure, exclusion of outsiders, increased self-awareness, and heightened internal social control and conformity. Members of other interacting ethnies often interpret such defensive mobilizations as signs of increased hostility and of aggressive intentions. To the extent that these reciprocal processes prevail, interethnic linkages and sentiments of shared interests will decrease. If the sense of threat to group position then intensifies, the classic Security Dilemma becomes fully operative. Mutual exclusion and reciprocal threats between two parties can thus create ripple effects through a whole ethnic network, generating either a mosaic of tightly closed groupings or a shifting set of insecure coalitions. Ethnicity and conflict are mutually interactive.

Ethnies and Other Collective Actors

The place of ethnies as potential actors in conflicts within states can be clarified by observing the several different, although overlapping, types. A useful classification is that presented by Gurr (1993b, 18–23). His *ethnoclasses*, which combine a collective identity with economic disadvantage—as immigrants, former slaves, "guest workers," displaced populations, or peoples stranded in economically depressed regions—typically are not centrally mobilized, and they tend to seek better conditions within the polity by nonviolent means rather than by secession or rebellion. *Indigenous* peoples incorporated into (or, better, ruled by) expanded states typically have been forced into peripheral areas, "reservations," or enclaves; their basic orientation tends to be defensive, consisting of efforts to protect land, forests, fishing grounds, or other resources from encroachment and to retain at least some vestige of cultural autonomy. A third type, however, represents a greater potential for violent conflict: the *communal con-*

tenders—that is, ethnies struggling for political control within a sharply divided multi-ethnic state. A fourth variety consists of *ethnonationalists*—distinctive, self-conscious ethnies seeking a state of their own. They are likely to have had a history of autonomy or independent statehood, and then to have been incorporated by conquest or annexation into a larger political entity. They are more likely to seek separation or political autonomy than to emphasize equality of access or nondiscrimination. Finally, *ethnoreligious collectivities* ("militant sects") have an identity focused upon adherence to a particular faith or set of doctrines and traditions. Many collectivities of this kind are strongly committed to distinctive values and norms, and frequently view secular states and particular governments as corrupt and illegitimate. They typically seek full cultural autonomy, or else control of the state. In the more militant cases, they are intolerant of differing views and are willing to risk or initiate violent conflict (cf. Schultz 1995). Worldwide terrorism is one outcome.

Ethnies do not, however, have to have a compact territorial base to retain their identity and cohesion. The large-scale examples are diaspora, created by the scattering of an ethny over diverse countries. Within a host state, the ethny has no effective territorial base, but its members maintain affective loyalties and socioeconomic linkages with co-ethnies in a home country or countries. Large-scale labor migrations have created proletarian diaspora (Armstrong 1976) that can form ethnoclasses (Gurr 1993b). These social formations typically are economically and politically disadvantaged, and have difficulty in mobilizing to affect major policies of the host state. Voluntary immigrants into a host society are more likely to seek nondiscrimination and equal opportunity for individuals rather than cultural preservation and collective political rights (cf. Francis 1976, 392).

In contrast, some diaspora have substantial resources, skills, and organizations sufficient to exert important political influence on foreign policies of the state of their residence, such as Greek Americans' influence on U.S. policy toward Turkey (Esman 1990, 85). And the members of a mobilized diaspora may attempt to affect events in the country of origin, as in the case of Irish Americans' support of the Irish Republican Army or the efforts of Croats living in Germany to support terrorist acts in Yugoslavia (Esman 1990, 86). There are many other examples. In still another manifestation, states may act on behalf of their diaspora—for example, the mainland Chinese governments' interventions to protect interests of overseas Chinese, the Turkish governments' negotiations with Germany concerning treatment of Turkish workers, or U.S.-Mexico relations concerning Mexican immigrants to the United States.

We have concentrated our attention on states and ethnies, with some note taken of classes and regions as other foci of collective action. We have recognized that "below" the level of aggregation of ethnies there are other collective actors: village communities, gangs, paramilitary groups, clans, lineage groupings, and nuclear families. At a level "above," ethnies and states are alliances of states, interstate, and trans-state networks and organizations, and finally entire "civilizations."

Civilizations are the largest and arguably the least clearly bounded aggregations. They are broadly defined by certain shared cultural and social traits, prominent among them language, religion, some conceptions of a common history, and relatively distinctive social patterns, such as forms of kinship and local communities. Clusters of such characteristics mark off the great contemporary civilizations—Chinese, Hindu, Islamic, Western Christian, and others. Huntington (1996) has suggested that beyond today's struggles of states there may emerge conflicts between major civilizations as such. Gurr's data (1994, 9–10), however, show no shift after 1987 in the proportion of serious ethnopolitical conflicts characterized as primarily occurring along religious or civilizational cleavages. Although the most recent conflicts along these lines may turn out eventually to be extraordinarily intense, the experiences so far do not support the hypothesis of impending conflicts of whole civilizations (see also Jürgensmeyer 1993). One of the problems of the civilization thesis is that it blurs crucial lines of conflict within each postulated civilization, thereby shifting attention away from classes, regions, states, and ethnies. Many of the great historical civilizations have not actually had a high degree of cultural coherence, and, of course, there have been numerous severe violent conflicts within postulated civilizations. The complex and amorphous character of these putative entities means that they are not unitary actors in the same sense as specific states, social movements, ethnic organizations, or even international alliances and organizations (cf. Matlock 1999). So, for present purposes we note the civilizational thesis (which may turn out to be a self-fulfilling prophecy), but limit our analysis to more specific social formations.

After the September 11, 2001, attacks on the World Trade Center and the Pentagon in the United States, intensive efforts were made by Osama bin Laden and his supporters to define the conflict as a religious struggle between Islamic peoples and the non-Muslim West, especially the United States. These initial attempts to create polarization tapped into widespread popular resentments in many countries, but at the time of this writing have not become politically decisive.

Characteristics of Violent Intrastate Conflicts

So far this discussion has proceeded as if differences in types of violent conflicts could be ignored. To remedy this deficiency, we turn to the next section of the chapter. Explanations of violent collective conflicts will differ according to type of conflict, type of state, type of ethny, and other features of particular situations. No general formula is available; hence, the rule must be to disaggregate, to subdivide what is to be explained. Nevertheless, a powerful regularity is the activation of solidary groupings in defensive rebellions against state impositions or against other external interferences that threaten in-group autonomy and integrity (for rural rebellions against such encroachments, see Magagna 1991).

The main types of intrastate violent conflict may be identified by three differentiating characteristics: (1) the extent of mass mobilization (from a small clique to an entire people), (2) the degree of centralized organization and control (from scattered rioting to a military dictatorship), and (3) the amount of violence. In rough schematic terms, illustrative types are shown below.

The simplest type is the coup d'état—often a few hundred troops in the capital city takes over the central government and the mass media, in a short time and with little involvement of the civilian population. In contrast, widespread turmoil can involve very large numbers of participants spread over most of the territory nominally ruled by the state. High levels of mobilization and of violence typify "internal warfare" in rebellions, civil wars, and revolutions. And massive slaughter, usually state-sponsored, reaches extremes of mobilization and violence.

At the most localized and diffuse levels, collective violence appears in brawls, street attacks, and relatively unorganized attacks upon property and group symbols. Such low-level turmoil can continue for long periods, expressing class and ethnic tensions, without becoming an important threat to central state authority.

Table 5–1

Type of Conflict	Extent of mass mobilization	Degree of centralized organization	Amount of violence
Turmoil (diffuse rioting, strikes with violence, sabotage, violent demonstrations)	medium	low	low to medium
Coups d'état	low	high	low
Secessionist rebellions	high	varies: medium to low	high
Civil wars	high	state, high; rebels, varies	high
Revolutions	high	high	high
Genocide:			
Communal	high	low	high
State-organized	medium to high	high	high

At a somewhat more lethal and more politically consequential level we find the deadly ethnic riot or mob attack. Such riots have been characterized (Horowitz 2001) as mass violence among civilian populations in which the targeted individuals are attacked on the basis of their ethnic membership. Many riots show evidence of planning, organization, and some degree of focused leadership or governmental collusion, such as the Hutu death-gangs in Rwanda, or the Sinhalese rioters in Colombo, Sri Lanka, in 1983. But generally riots as distinct from pogroms are diffuse, loosely structured, and seemingly spontaneous. They tend to cluster in geographic locales and to come in waves through time. Riots typically attack individuals solely because of group identity—thus giving the appearance of random, arbitrary violence. Rioters show great hostility and are extremely brutal in their assaults, frequently burning and mutilating their victims; sexual mutilations, in particular, are notably frequent (Brubaker and Laitin 1998, 432).

Riots are public events and thus distinct from the predations of death squads, kidnapping, or secretive police or paramilitary group attacks. Ethnic riots, in which the targets of violence are persons or property selected on the basis of categorical membership, follow a stylized, characteristic pattern: typically there has been an extended accumulation of grievances against members of a different ethny, expressed in charges of exploitation of workers or customers, of hostile and disrespectful behavior, and of public violations of norms of proper conduct. The ethnic targets are easily identified: they are both highly visible and accessible. At the same time, the targeted collectivity is seen as vulnerable and unable to effectively retaliate. Tension is increased by general economic insecurity, often combined with rapid changes in residential patterns and relative numbers in local areas. An additional facilitating factor in the outbreak of violence is the presence of large numbers of unemployed young males who have few prospects for socioeconomic advancement or security, and who consequently lack commitment to civil order (cf. Morrison and Lawry 1994). A precipitating incident, often police behavior, adds the immediate stimulus for collective violence (cf. for England, Peach 1986).

Pogroms are a special form of organized assaults upon ethnic minorities. Although often sporadic and seemingly spontaneous, they typically are instigated, supported, or tolerated by state authorities. The classic case or ideal type is represented by the pogroms against Jews in Czarist Russia. Carried to extremes of violence, these movements can be seen as forerunners of 1980s and 1990s "ethnic cleansing."

These examples show how the main forms of collective ethnic conflict differ with regard to (1) the extent of mass mobilization, (2) the extent of centralized organization and control, and (3) the amount and kinds of violence. Diffuse fighting, rioting, "terrorism," and violent protests are low on all three criteria; rebellions, civil wars, and revolutions are high on all three. A distinctive type is the coup d'état—generally a highly centralized, collective action but without mass mobilization or extensive violence.

Military Coups

The setting for ethnic coups usually is a severely divided society under military rule.[1] Military and paramilitary forces have played central parts in Third World countries for several decades, as authoritarian regimes try to maintain their power. Military forces are both resources for, and objects of, ethnic conflict; in state after state ethnically linked military groupings intervene or threaten to intervene in civilian politics. Seldom is the military ethnically neutral—whether because of the legacy of biased recruiting by colonial regimes, a cleavage between the military and political parties and the civilian government, or the interpenetrating of civil and military ethnic fractions (see the comprehensive treatment in Horowitz 1985, chaps. 11–12).

The importance of ethnicity in the recruitment, deployment, and political role of military forces has been well recognized for several decades (cf. Enloe 1980, Kirk-Green 1980, Janowitz 1977, 1981). Military service, sometimes thought to be a homogenizing, even an integrative, process (e.g., in nineteenth-century France) has proven in many cases to be ethnically divisive and a source of major conflicts.

The importance of ethnic divisions as a factor in military rule varies greatly among regions of the world; very great in Africa and South Asia, for example, joint with religious cleavages in the Middle East, less in Latin America (Tilly 1992, 219). Independence in Latin America came primarily through military revolts; in Africa, through peaceful means. But in Africa, colonial forces had been ethnically skewed, either to ensure loyalty to the colonial power or to make them as apolitical as possible, with the consequence of unrepresentative militaries after independence (Welch 1986, 321).

The difficulties of understanding military coups are highlighted in the recent turbulent history of South American countries (Markoff and Baretta 1986). Detailed local studies have shown how intricate processes of combined class/ethnic politics can produce polarization of interethnic fears and suspicions, as in a military coup in Surinam (Kroes 1982). But more generally, few of the many plausible but empirically dubious explanations proffered give any attention to ethnicity. For Africa, however, numerous studies have examined militarized ethnicity in detail (e.g., Jackman 1978).

The frequency of military coups in many "Third World" countries is truly

---

[1] This section has been adapted from Williams 1994, pp. 69–71, by permission of the publishers.

remarkable; for example, in 1997 the violence-torn country of Sierra Leone experienced its third coup within the span of five years. Indeed, of the 45 independent Black states in Africa, from 1960 to 1982 nearly 90 percent had recorded a military coup, attempted coup, or plot (Johnson, Slater, and McGowan 1984, 627). There were 56 successful coups, 56 other attempts, and 102 plots. Political conflicts have made the sub-Saharan states among the most unstable in an unstable world. In the late 1980s the central executive in some 25 of them was a military regime, and military influence was important in most of the others. The most complete analysis of this extraordinary situation has reviewed four major explanations: political development (weak states and heavy demands), military centrality, ethnic cleavages or antagonisms, and economic dependency (Jenkins and Kposowa 1990). Although the results of detailed factor and regression analyses were highly complex—and differ for plots, attempts, and successful coups—the strongest predictor of military coup activity was military centrality, followed by ethnic cleavages and ethnic political competition (Jenkins and Kposowa 1990; Kposowa and Jenkins 1993). Social mobilization (or "modernization") did not fare well as an explanatory condition: it did not affect coup activity through rising levels of political participation or domestic turmoil, although it was associated with greater likelihood of coups, possibly through enhanced communicative or organizational resources. Economic dependence of the country upon external economies was not a strong or consistent factor. The net conclusion is that military centrality and ethnic tensions are the primary sources of irregular military interventions. Ethnic plurality and competition predict military intervention in governance, whereas ethnic dominance lowers the likelihood of coup activity. Ethnic factors have this impact primarily in elite struggles rather than in mass turmoil. Cultural cleavages and rivalry between the two largest ethnies were primary contexts for military coups. The likelihood of coups was greater when there also was a strong military establishment, along with substantial political mobilization.

Of course, coups constitute a limited set of events and are overshadowed in consequences by large-scale communal violence, rebellions, and civil wars. Still, the regularities apparent in such limited events illuminate the continuing significance of ethnies as actors in political arenas. Many societies experience a succession of ethnically based coups and other violent changes in political control. These see-saw and attrition coups (Horowitz 1985, 499) typically result in an authoritarian, narrowly based ethnic regime—or in state breakdown and fractionated warfare. Once in place, however, ethnocracies such as those in Syria, Iraq, and Sudan establish such rigid and pervasive coercive controls as to render the regime practically immune to displacement other than through civil war or external military intervention.

An observation that seems to contradict common sense is that in intrastate ethnic conflicts weaker groups sometimes attack opponents that are clearly stronger in resources, numbers, organization, and in other ways. Striking cases are the frequent attacks by weak groups upon much stronger coercive rulers—in revolutions, peasant revolts, and prison riots (Goldstone and Useem 1999, 989). If relative strength is indeed objectively apparent and marked, is an attack by the weaker an irrational and/or inexplicable action? Although seldom analyzed in depth, such events do have plausible interpretations. In the first place, ethnic leaders may see violent conflict as the only or at least the most effective way to create ingroup solidarity and ethnic mobilization, hoping to induce a closing of ranks against a common threat. Similarly, leaders may have realistic hopes for enlisting the aid of other aggrieved ethnies in a joint effort against an oppressive state. More commonly, the less powerful collectivity will initiate violence in the hope or expectation of attracting external aid and intervention—from fellow ethnies in another state, from a foreign power, or from interstate agencies. Such support, in fact, often is forthcoming.

Aside from these considerations, strategists of the weaker entity may have reason to believe that the opponent's strength—its unity, resources, effectiveness of organization, and will to persevere—has been greatly overestimated. They see their adversary as a paper tiger, and hope to find weakness behind the ferocious facade. They find it plausible to invoke actual historical instances in which the underrated Davids have vanquished the overrated Goliaths. Finally, all tactical and strategic assessments aside, leaders and followers of the challenging ethny often have such strong convictions of moral outrage, of aggrieved group integrity, and of gross injustice suffered that calculations of cost become secondary, and overwhelming hatred of the enemy makes even a noble defeat preferable to craven acquiescence.

Under conditions of civil war in collapsed states, fighting can involve several mutually hostile militarized groupings, along with armed bands of no particular allegiance that prey upon the populace. In situations of this kind, a feature that is so nearly universal as to be taken for granted is that the primary fighters are very young males. In many civil wars in the 1990s the armed fighters and marauders included numerous males in their early teens, as in Somalia and Liberia. A fourteen-year-old with an automatic weapon and a stolen jeep is a formidable candidate for participation in mass killings, rape, arson, and looting. Many such youths have been exposed to violence from early childhood. Uneducated, unemployed, without prospects for economic security or social respect, the vast pools of such individuals in much of the Third World are explosive tinder ready for a spark. From their ranks come many suicide bombers.

In some cases, the youthful killers have been abducted or forcibly recruited and subjected to severe punishments. Numerous commentators in the closing decades of the twentieth century noted the phenomenon of masses of "child soldiers" in civil wars and Third World interstate conflicts—in Cambodia, Afghanistan, Iran/Iraq, Liberia, Lebanon/Israel, Sierra Leone, Uganda, and elsewhere. Age-graded social movements range from youth gangs to political movements and to direct participation in violent political organizations. In these cases, the general principle is that the more likely the participation of individuals in violent activities, the less their prior associations outside the nucleus of the riotous or belligerent groupings and the greater their sense of exclusion from effective access to channels of influence for alleviation of grievances.

As these observations suggest, in the near-chaos of opportunistic violence, original ethnic issues may be lost. To the questions thus raised we now turn.

Objections to Ethnicity as a Cause of Conflict

Even though ethnic polarization may seem an obvious source of numerous deadly conflicts, nevertheless objections to the identification of ethnicity as a cause of such conflicts continue to be voiced (cf. Gagnon 1995, 1994/95; Pieterse 1997). Some of the criticisms claim that the diagnosis of conflicts as based on ethnic cleavages may ignore the fact that ethnic labels may be used to direct attention away from class conflicts or to manipulate people in the interest of gaining and maintaining political power. Thus, it is said "the terminology of ethnicity is part of the conflict and cannot serve as a language of analysis" (Pieterse 1997, 71).

It is easy to reject ethnic cultural differences as *the* unique cause of conflict: obviously many ethnic differences do not lead to conflict, much less to violent conflict, and many conflicts are non-ethnic. But it is a different matter to wholly reject ethnicity as an important cause of conflict, as some scholars now seem to do. Although the claim may not be that ethnicity is invoked merely as a disguise for class interests or as a manipulated distraction from class domination, it is still possible to view ethnic labels as a facade that conceals struggles that essentially derive from "authoritarian institutions and political cultures and the politics of hard sovereignty" (Pieterse 1997, 71). Nevertheless, the possible use of the "language of ethnicity" as a politicized way of defining issues and group alignments does not mean that ethnic boundaries and commitments are merely "fictions" or mass delusions. The question of the political use of ethnic labels is quite separate and different from the question of the causal role of ethnicity in social conflicts.

As Rule (1988, 70) has paraphrased the extreme materialistic view, "Military action apparently stemming from solidarities of ethnicity, religion, national identifications, language, region, or the like is really a 'disguised' manifestation of shared material interest." But this view ignores the socio-biological bases of solidarity that derive from frequent interdependent actions in kinship groupings and the wider networks of relationships based on these. Actual historical sequences show the various ways in which those initial solidarities and identities are transformed by cultural contact and collective struggles, in addition to and in mutual interaction with "material interests." For example, the overly simple thesis that "capitalism produced racism" is supportable only if one attributes European expansionism, colonialism, and slavery to capitalism. But settlers' greed for gold and desires for land were hardly full-grown capitalist products, and the early contacts of Europeans with indigenous peoples generated rivalries and exploitation under noncapitalistic frontier and farming conditions. As the example of South Africa shows, xenophobia and racist ideology antedate industrial and commercial hegemony. Capitalism in fully developed forms no doubt reinforced racial dominance, but ethnic cleavage was already a primary ground for pre-capitalistic early conflicts and conquests (cf. Van Zyl Slabbert and Welsh 1979).

As we already have seen, territorial states imposing disadvantages upon a population that lacks either voice or freedom of exit frequently generate protest and rebellion. But the question remains: Why are the collective boundaries drawn along ethnic lines rather than regional, rural-urban, class, ideological, or even generational cleavages? Just as in interstate relations, it is not surprising to find that the openly declared or generally understood issues may not be the operative issues. As noted in Chapter 4, a struggle between class or regional groupings that starts as an ordinary political contest may rapidly acquire an ethnic identity.

One example among many is the collective violence, causing more than 7,000 deaths in the five years 1978–83, between Hindu residents in Assam and immigrant Muslims from Bangladesh. The Bengali immigration led directly to competition for land, jobs, political appointments, and other scarce and valuable opportunities. Individualized competition became collective rivalry as cultural distinctions, notably religion and language, were increasingly emphasized in political contestation. What had originally been economic competition was thus transformed into opposition defined by the participants as ethnic and religious. In these developments the state and its political parties were not neutral bystanders. Political parties saw the ethnic populations as "vote banks" that could be crucial in the problematic outcomes of elections. State actions thus directly intensified the ethnic character of the local polarization. In sum, these violent and protracted conflicts involved class cleavages (e.g., land ownership), demographic change that led to Assamese fears of being overwhelmed by "invading outsiders," initial ethnoreligious identities, state interventions, and political rivalries. Was the ensuing violence ethnic? Yes, it was, but it was also an outcome of class, political, economic, and demographic conditions in complex interactions over time (see Darnell and Parikh 1988).

Another objection to ethnicity as a cause of conflict is the view that ethnic boundaries are fluid, porous, ill-defined, and subject to rapid change over time. Also, it is held, ethnic collectivities are not unitary or homogeneous; they may be subdivided by distinctions of kinship, class, caste, region, historical political affiliation, dialects, and other boundary markers. Internal heterogeneity undoubtedly characterizes many if not most well-recognized ethnies—as is true of states, regions, religious groupings, and so on. But porosity of boundaries and internal cleavages are empirical matters of degree, not crucial theoretical distinctions. The fact that some ethnies are not really very ethnic does not apply to the numerous cases of the conflicts we are reviewing.

One more criticism of analyses that treat ethnicity as an important conflict-inducing condition is that interethnic conflicts may have been instigated originally not by ethnic differences as such but by intra-ethnic political processes. For example, in the case of the former Yugoslavia, Gagnon (1995) has emphasized the important point that conflict between collectivities publicly defined in ethnic terms may not result primarily from interactions between the groupings, but may arise from processes *internal* to each of the contenders. Just as the behavior of states in the international arena must be analyzed not only in terms of external relations, but also with attention to intrastate political processes—above all, perhaps, the rivalry for power among elites—so must interethnic conflicts be seen as codetermined by in*tra*-ethnic strivings for influence and power.

But when all objections and qualifications have been taken into account, it is still correct to see ethnic divisions as a necessary condition in most of the collective intrastate violence since World War II. Strong ethnic cleavages are in fact closely associated both with intrastate conflict and with state/regime failures. Thus, for some 115 countries classified and analyzed by Roeder (1999), ethnically heterogeneous countries were far more likely than homogenous countries to experience state failure and regime (government) failure, and much less likely to attain a stable democratic state.

States and Peoples as Contexts for Violence

Contrary to some popular interpretations, the resurgence of ethnic conflicts in the second half of the twentieth century was not simply the result of a revival of ancient animosities. Indeed, it owed much to the efforts of intellectuals and publicists to create and intensify a collective identity in which they themselves could have a significant role. State expansion and state-building in which political elites seek to homogenize a multi-ethnic territorial population into a common "national" culture can be seen by resistant ethnies as cultural imperialism and discrimination. Closely related to such reactive or "backlash" ethnicity is the effect of nationalism, first as an ideology in the service of territorial states that try to create national solidarity, and then as a central claim by ethnies seeking states of their own. In a world in which sovereign states insist upon territorial integrity, the demands of separatist or autonomy-seeking ethnies constitute a potent source of conflict (Smith 1986). These "non-state nations" (Bertelsen 1977) occasionally gain international support for their claims to autonomy or secession based on the doctrine of the self-determination of peoples, but more often they fail to find effective external allies. With only rare exceptions (Slovakia and the Czech Republic), states strongly resist separatist movements, and international agencies and bystander countries are reluctant to support any breakup of existing states. The doctrine of internal state sovereignty typically is dominant.

Major background conditions that have contributed to the increase in ethnic violence since the 1950s include, first of all, changes in states and in interstate alignments. As many of the newly independent Third World states became militarized, there was an accompanying rise in coups and attempted coups, and of extensive state violence against subjects and citizens (Tilly 1992, 211–17). Meanwhile, the industrialized countries of both West and East allowed tremendous sales of advanced weaponry and other war-making facilities to unstable countries, especially in the Middle East. The superpowers' confrontations of the Cold War provided support (funds, arms, military forces, diplomatic support) for proxy wars in Africa, Asia, and Latin America. Meanwhile, decolonization produced a vast array of newly independent, poor, and multi-ethnic states that nevertheless contained relatively strong military formations and aimed to create centralized and unitary regimes. Most of these new states were resource poor or had lost resources after independence, and were relatively ineffective in providing services, fostering economic growth, and maintaining internal order. These were the weak states, quasi-states, failed states, or collapsed states that could not or would not do well what modern states are supposed to do.

Yet over the entire period since World War II, many of these same states have sought to expand their activities, to centralize controls, and to penetrate more thoroughly the societies whose people they sought to rule. State expansion multiplied the occasions for confrontations with resistant ethnoregional groupings. So, both state weakness and attempted state expansion worked in their different ways to increase the likelihood of ethnic conflicts.

With the establishment of the United Nations in 1945, the norm of state sovereignty was enshrined as the basic principle of the interstate order; sovereignty was thereafter freely granted to new states, regardless of the nature of their borders or of their prospects for effective functioning. But the UN also endorsed the norm of human rights in its charter, and then in the 1948 Declaration of Human Rights and in two international conventions (finally becoming operative in 1976). The doctrine of human rights, coupled with the doctrine of self-determination of peoples, seemed to encourage the formation of new states out of the former colonial empires. But once the new states confronted separatist and autonomy-seeking demands from their internal ethnies, the incumbent governments immediately asserted state sovereignty and rejected external intervention. Thus the stage was set for the multiple conflicts of peoples versus states that we survey here.

The obvious fact that most of today's national states are multi-ethnic becomes more meaningful and vivid as one surveys particular cases. Example after example reinforces the point. Afghanistan is a dramatic instance. Next door, the province of Balochistan in Pakistan contains no fewer than seventeen ethnies (the so-called "tribes")—the Bugti, Zehri, Brahuis, Makranis, Mengal, Marri, Achakzai, and others (Weaver 1990). In the Caucasus and Transcaucasus regions of the former Soviet Union, secession attempts and deadly combat have affected Abkhazia (in Georgia), North and South Ossetia, Chechnya, Nogorno-Karabakh, and several other areas (Seymore 1994). Especially likely to experience warfare are states with a moderately high percentage of ethnic people ("minorities"), such as 10–50 percent. Given such ethnic diversity, a situation in which a few large entities are contending for political power seems to maximize conflict. Also, the risks of internal war are higher in countries with low levels of prosperity, health, and education, as measured by the UN's Human Development Index (Smith 1997, 30, 48).

There are striking differences among the major world regions in people-state relationships. Thus Third World ethnic separatism—demands for autonomy or exit (secession)—tends to be strongest among ethnies least integrated into the environing state-society. Such ethnies typically are poor and live in poor and peripheral regions; their stance usually is defensive against encroachments upon land and other resources, and for cultural maintenance. In contrast, it is the relatively well-off and well-organized ethnonationalists in the former USSR and in Eastern Europe who seek to protect and advance their interests by breaking away from the central state of former hegemony—thus Slovenia and Croatia out of Yugoslavia, or the Baltic states and Georgia out of the old Soviet empire. Where the old central state can hold out protection, infrastructure, and economic rewards, newly independent regions are more likely to opt for continued association in some form, as with the Tajiks, Turkmens, or Uzbeks (see Marshall in Gurr 1993b, 192ff.).

This is the state side of the coin. The other side is the activation and consolidation of ethnies. The establishment and expansion of territorial states often created new ethnies and merged numerous small amorphous units into larger and more readily mobilized ethnies. Larger political units tended to produce larger ethnies, as the state's activities heightened group awareness. In the common expression, the state became both prize and arena.

Furthermore, ethnic ties do not stop at the boundaries of territorial states: about two-thirds of Gurr's "communal groups" have co-ethnies in another country (1993b, 175). These linkages favor direct diffusion effects, when events in one state spill over across borders. In addition, there are indirect contagion or "demonstration" effects when protests or rebellions in one state furnish examples of issues, strategies, and tactics for emulation by ethnies elsewhere. More tangible evidence of linkages are the multiple interstate networks of communication, of quick and relatively cheap transportation, of flows of funds and material assistance, and of political advice and support.

The boundaries of states are established by conquests, by treaties that terminate interstate wars, and by de facto or negotiated settlements of territorial claims. But because the geographic settlement patterns of ethnies often do not follow state boundaries, many groupings find themselves to be minorities within a state controlled by a different ethny. When such encapsulated ethnies are territorially concentrated in areas adjacent to those within the boundaries of another state controlled by their co-ethnics, they constitute irredenta. These "unredeemed" ethnic fragments typically arouse political tensions within and between the neighboring countries. Within the host state, the ethny may be a restive and rebellious minority. Within the ethnic home country, the status of co-ethnics under foreign rule easily can become a domestic political issue. Accordingly, irredenta often become resources and pawns in interstate conflicts. Thus, as many examples show, irredenta are potentially explosive, and indeed often do lead to interstate wars or to coercive diplomacy. As Esman notes, irredentist claims—as for self-determination and reunion—tend to be emotionally loaded issues that can escape prudential state restraints (1990, 84).

Intrastate ethnic conflicts complicate interstate relations and not infrequently lead to interstate conflicts. About a third of military interventions since 1970 were in Third World countries as responses to internal ethnopolitical conflicts (Gurr 1993b, 91). For example, the presence of the

Kurds in Turkey, Iraq, Iran, and Syria has evoked a complex series of shifting political alignments and military actions. Violent factions often take refuge across state lines—witness the Basques in France and Spain, and the Tamils in Sri Lanka and India.

When strongly bounded ethnies exist as subsocieties—segments of a total society—their political choices tend toward separatism or autonomy. But secession often will be too difficult and costly, and cultural autonomy may be seen as too limited. Under these conditions, the most likely development is contention for control of the central state. A communal contender of this kind often aims at the exclusion of other ethnies from sharing political power, and even at the expulsion or extermination of ethnic adversaries (Horowitz 1985, 31).

Claims, Grievances, and Group Threats: "A Sense of Group Position"

As we have reviewed in Chapter 5, ethnic claims for special status (including priority or hegemony in social and political orders) often are rationalized by claims to be the ancient or first indigenous inhabitants of a territory—the native sons, the pioneers, the sons of the soil, the first people. Among such claimants are the Buddhist Sinhalese in Sri Lanka, the *bumiputera* in Malaysia, the descendants of the *Mayflower* settlers in the United States, the Israelis *and* the Palestinians in Israel, and the "Yamato nation" in Japan. The idea of an ancestral homeland readily lends itself to politicized claims for special status. Such claims are special cases of the more general phenomenon of a sense of group position.

Any social segmentation arising from the simple facts of differential size of categorical groupings and from "benign" processes of in-category preference will be accentuated to the extent that any other category is seen as threatening or hostile. And the more the members of a particular category feel themselves to be collectively oppressed and unfairly treated, the more likely it is that they will come to regard the members of other categories as threatening (Bobo and Hutchings 1996, 951).

When individual persons experience conditions they perceive as deprivations or disadvantages, they may define the conditions as common to others like themselves, as "fraternal deprivation." Individualized experiences of disadvantage do not automatically add up to collective grievance. The mediating factor is a sense of group membership, coupled with the belief that other members are similarly deprived by reason of that group identity. It is then possible to transform diffuse private resentment into a shared sense of outrage. So it is that threat or injury to a collectivity arouses emotions of hurt and rage similar to responses to individual threat or injury. When one's ethny is defamed, humiliated, treated with contempt, or denied recognition, an ethnic member often reacts with rage and the desire to inflict reciprocal hurt (cf. Wedge 1986, 56–57).

There is abundant evidence that economic competition and rivalry among persons identified as ethnic others increases the prevalence of hostile attitudes and the likelihood of overt conflict (Olzak 1992). But two crucial qualifications must be taken into account before we too readily accept economic competition as a sole or primary explanation. In the first place, ethnic opposition often derives from rivalry for non-economic political advantages and opportunities. So we may find economically advantaged minorities seeking political separation, even though their economic returns will be lessened thereby. Second, economic welfare may be sacrificed to considerations of cultural identity and dominance. For example, we believe that Horowitz (1985, 132–35) is correct in holding that Sinhalese opposition to Tamil autonomy demands in Sri Lanka could not be explained on economic grounds. Both Tamils and Sinhalese stood to gain from a federated system, but every attempt to institute even limited Tamil autonomy produced intense opposition, extending to mass violence, from the Sinhalese. At the same time, the Tamil leaders apparently were willing to accept economic disadvantage in the interests of separatism. In the third place, the interests of elites and masses often differ, so that political elites may instigate ethnic conflict that impoverishes a people in their search to get and hold power. (The former Yugoslavia seems to well illustrate the point.) Finally, the intense emotion and ferocity so evident in ethnic conflicts seems inexplicable on the basis of narrow economic interests alone. More immediate and potent are aspirations and (especially) fears having to do with group identities and evaluations thereof. Being treated with contempt and having one's ethnic membership disparaged are extremely aversive experiences, and the threat of loss of a valued group status is a prime source of fear and reactive rage.

No doubt there are many situations within which disadvantage and discrimination are in part in the eye of the beholder. But disadvantage, deprivation, frustration, and pain are not sheer illusions. People usually are capable of valid cognition of these conditions, and they seek to find the source of their ills. The perceived source may be a specific individual or a collective social actor, and the likelihood of collective conflict will be directly affected by the different perceptions. There is a crucial juncture when group identity is defined by real discrimination. The process is well illustrated by the effects of systematic discrimination against African Americans, as in Detroit, where restrictive covenants in the 1940s effectively excluded Blacks from every real estate subdivision that was developed during the years 1940–47. Similarly, Blacks were excluded from certain occupations. Housing segregation itself resulted in occupational exclusion, and the lack of occupational opportunities resulted in Blacks being forced into a casual labor market in which irregular work and unemployment reinforced negative stereotypes of Blacks. Mutually reinforcing residential barriers, hiring practices, and union policies, together with local politics, created the conditions that in turn encouraged beliefs among whites that they had a *vested right* to maintain racial exclusion (Sugrue 1996). This case is one example of a wider pattern, for a substantial body of research in the United States has shown how racial segregation and high rates of poverty among African Americans result in high degrees of neighborhood poverty concentration—a condition that in turn drastically constricts life chances regardless of individual social and economic characteristics (Massey 1993; Massey, Gross, and Eggers 1991, 426). These are conditions that produce common deprivations that can become the basis for a shared sense of collective grievances.

Additional evidence for the importance of collective grievances comes from an analysis of data from twelve European countries for the year 1988 that shows that prejudice against immigrants and "racial" groupings is greatest where economic conditions are poor *and* the percentages of immigrants are high. The apparent effects of the two conditions are positively interactive. These findings are best interpreted as reflecting "group-threat" as an important factor in prejudice. Most of the variation in prejudice across the twelve countries is accounted for by the presumed threat posed by large immigrant populations under relatively poor economic conditions. In contrast, the particular characteristics of individual persons explain almost none of the differences in levels of out-group prejudice (Quillian 1995).

A heightened sense of injustice can be aroused when a rapid loss of collective economic position is perceived as caused by another ethny, as when jobs and economic opportunities are perceived as being lost to non-natives by rapid and large-scale immigration. In these cases, sentiments of homeland possession and vested rights can be channeled into political movements and interethnic conflict.

Grievances clearly are a crucial part of ethnic mobilization and conflict. Grievances are not merely expressions of deprivation or dissatisfaction. People can be deprived, disappointed, frustrated, or dissatisfied without feeling that they have been unjustly or unfairly treated—their unsatisfactory outcome may be "just the way things are," or the result of divine judgment, or a consequence of personal ineptitude. In contrast, a real grievance, regarded as the basis for complaint or redress, rests upon the claim that an *injustice* has been inflicted upon undeserving victims. Grievances are normative protests, claiming violations of rights or rules. Those who are intensely aggrieved may use the language of moral outrage.

In many historical instances, violent reactions occur when governing authorities fail to follow their own standard rules, when they violate their own laws, regulations, and customary practices. Police give false testimony, plant faked evidence, engage in ethnic harassment. Tax collectors single out ethnic targets for special investigation. For centuries, extending into the seventeenth, much of Europe experienced recurrent acute food shortages. In these periods of dire distress, "On the whole rebellions did not occur when people were hungriest, but when people saw that officials were failing to apply the standard controls, tolerating profiteering or, worst of all, authorizing shipments of precious local grain to other places" (Tilly 1992, 118).

On a larger scale, a major source of mass grievances is the loss of political independence or substantial autonomy that had been enjoyed over a considerable time. A sense of collective bereavement and resentment often deeply affects the people of conquered states or regions, as well as those who live in areas forcibly transferred from one ruler to another of a different ethnic identity. Great waves of conquest and interstate border settlements thus leave numerous disaffected peoples, as in the Baltic states and the Caucasus region in the Soviet Union after World War II.

The key to many historical puzzles lies in identifying the sources of collective grievances. Thus the Great Depression of the 1930s in the United States did not create a major increase in *interethnic* conflict—primarily because of the cessation of immigration and of the decreased internal ethnic migration (Higham 1999, 53). The key variable once more is a sense of *collective ethnic threat*; the great threat in the 1930s was the economic disaster, not waves of new immigrants. But when times of economic hardship coincide with a highly visible influx of newcomers, ethnic tensions increase. As Higham (1999, 46) proposes, "A persistent myth of exclusive possession revives in every crisis in which a core population feels threatened by outsiders."

Why do members of even a dominant ethny come to regard another ethny as a threat? The answers to this question are neither simple nor obvious. At least four plausible hypotheses have been invoked from time to time to account for the observed presence of perceptions of interethnic threat (Bobo and Hutchings 1996). First is the intuitively appealing notion that simple self-interest is the crucial factor; that is, a belief that an out-group is threatening one's job, political opportunities, access to housing, real estate values, quality of education, and so on. Second, a perception of threat may come directly from social inculcated stereotypes and negative evaluations. Third, ideologies concerning social stratification (e.g., beliefs in equality of opportunity) may define those who do not accept the status quo as dangerous. Fourth, a complex sense of group position creates the crucial foundation for perception of threat. Components of the sense of group position are (1) a belief that one's collectivity is superior to or is to be preferred above others, (2) a view of the out-group as different or alien, and (3) an assumption that members of one's own collectivity have proper or proprietary claims over certain rights, resources, statuses, and privileges. In short, group advantages and privileges have come to be felt as *rights,* as vested interests that are socially validated possessions. Any challenge to such a group position is a common threat.

To assess the relative importance of the four posited factors, Bobo and Hutchings (1996) analyzed data from a 1992 survey of about 1900 persons in Los Angeles. The pattern of responses indicates that although each set of factors contributes to perceived intergroup threat, it is the sense of group position that most effectively defines the nature and source of threat. To have a sense of group position, members of a collectivity must share an identity, conceive of controlling collective identities, and merge their individual interests with a group fate.

In a classic but now neglected work, Levine and Campbell (1972, chap. 3) specify a series of propositions that link realistic threat to putative effects upon the collectivities sending and receiving threatening behavior. Thus it is hypothesized that "real threat"

1. causes hostility to the source of threat;
2. increases in-group solidarity;
3. increases awareness of in-group identity;
4. increases the tightness of group boundaries (including sentiments of social distance);
5. reduces defection from the collectivity;
6. increase rejection and punishment of defectors;
7. increases ethnocentrism as a total syndrome.

Levine and Campbell (1972, 41–42) go on to note that false perceptions of threat can have the same effect as real threat. It follows that the intragroup rivalry of individuals and subgroups for scarce valuables—above all, for political control—can lead to the creation of a sense of out-group threat. When this manipulative effect within ethny A is observed by ethny B, the response tends to be counter-mobilization. Thus, "furthering this 'arms race effect' are those external words and acts of belligerent intransigency that an insecure leader says and does for the benefit of this internal group audience and his political acceptance by them" (ibid., 42).

In case after case, a central type of threat is the perceived likelihood of domination by another ethny. Because membership is seen as involuntary, there is no escaping the prospect of subjugation. When ethnic dominance means control of the state and therefore of the military and police forces, political defeat raises the specter of physical danger, extending to the fear of literal extermination. When two or more ethnies thus confront one another within the same polity, mutual insecurity intensifies the rivalry for the "indivisible" prize of control of power. To avert the most dreadful of prospects, violence can come to be regarded as inevitable and as a worthy means for the ultimate good of survival.

Isolated communal groups have few occasions and little need to emphasize their boundaries—which, indeed, are concretely present and easily perceived—or their cultural identity, which is taken for granted ("we are the people"). Boundaries are important *in relation to* other collectivities; they thrive upon contact, rivalry, and opposition. Intergroup interactions grow into systematic connections ("genuine relationships") only when particular encounters come to be perceived as likely to be repeated into an indefinite future, through the growth of extended networks of communication and direct interactions—as when what were once many thousands of small, semi-isolated peoples become merged into large, complex societies (cf. Chase-Dunn 1992, 317–19). Out of the interactions of boundary-maintaining ethnies within such societies grow many struggles for group position.

Ever since the first systematic speculations about human behavior, observers have puzzled over the ubiquity and avidity of the search for power. The classic Hobbesian answer is deceptively attractive: power is sought because control over other humans is an effective means for the satisfaction of any wants whatsoever. Yet the general answer is too general to be very helpful when we confront the puzzle of the intensity of struggles for coercive control by ethnies seeking dominance over state societies. Why does it seem too difficult to reach compromises, to work out live-and-let-live arrangements of mutual accommodation? In any search for more specific formulations, a first major clue is offered by observing the remarkable frequency with which ethnic violence is preceded by shared fears of being dominated by ethnic strangers.

Major Processes of Collective Conflict

As among ethnies living under the same state regime, the basic condition underlying fear of domination—especially the fear of being permanently subjugated—is a mutual threat system. Members of distinct, separate, ascribed collectivities, or at least their elites, see the political situation as an anarchy in which the only way to remedy insecurity is to attain dominance. As in the "Realist" model of interstate relations, to the extent that ethnies within a state are mutually suspicious, each fearing that a rival is intent upon exclusive political control, the greater will be the likelihood of violent conflict.

In multi-ethnic societies in which the state either is a partisan ethnocracy or is too weak to provide guarantees of security, the subordinated or disadvantaged ethnies typically fear for their safety and survival. Mutual fears for the future feed on distrust, as interethnic understanding decreases because of lack of credible information as to the motivations and intentions of rivals—a condition likely to be exacerbated by political deceptions and inflammatory claims of leaders. It becomes increasingly difficult for any ethny to make credible commitments to ensure the security of others. If any one party is perceived as verging upon forcible conflict, and the members of a vulnerable ethny anticipate that "there is even a small chance that it may become the target of a genocidal attack, it may choose conflict over compromise and the risk of future destruction" (Lake and Rothchild 1999, 302). And, indeed, such a threatened grouping may have little or no choice in the matter.

Where strongly bounded ethnies act as rival collectivities (rather than mere social categories or unorganized aggregates of individuals), their *relative* positions become salient. Comparisons are inevitable and, hence, so is relative deprivation and relative gratification. Ethnic contention then becomes a zero-sum game—the greater the gains and the higher the social rank of ethny A, the lower the position of ethny B. Different aspects of group position—economic advantage, political authority, cultural eminence, generalized prestige—become central issues under differing conditions. Comparisons of many ethnopolitical conflicts worldwide show that although contention about economic inequality is only a secondary or a latent issue in most cases, nevertheless conflicts do tend to be most numerous and severe in regions and countries of greatest poverty (Gurr 1994, 12). Extreme poverty may intensify political rivalry in ethnically divided societies, especially when there is rapid change in relative positions among ethnic contenders.

Even so, violent conflict is not inevitable. Discontented people who are restive under the rule of their state of residence have several nominal options. Given permission and sufficient resources, they can migrate to another country—"exit." Some limited escape from state control may be achieved in subsistence agriculture and the informal economy, although this path is not promising. But when nonviolent participation, including protest, in its turn fails to redress grievances, violent protest and actual rebellion are the only remaining routes to effect change.

Historical and comparative evidence, as well as detailed local studies, show that there are systematic and dynamic relationships among the main macro conditions affecting ethnicity. Suppose we start with the political ascendancy of a given ethny. That condition will produce state policies and practices that favor the in-group and, correspondingly, will appear to other subordinate ethnies as discrimination. The greater the actual and perceived discrimination, the more prominent and important ethnic identity will be. Given discrimination and ethnic salience, the more likely is ethnic residential and regional segregation—which in turn favors discrimination and ethnic cleavage. All of these processes will accentuate and help to develop economic specialization. The combination of ethnic salience and occupational concentration means that individual competition will become more likely to be defined as ethnic rivalry; this tendency, however, will be reduced to the extent that economic specialization results in noncompetitive niches (Olzak 1992, 1989). The greater the ethnic rivalry, the greater the likelihood of stereotyping and disliking.

Given this combination of conditions, struggles are more likely to develop over relative group position in any graded multi-ethnic system. If major socioeconomic changes (war, depression, major changes in occupational structure) occur, it is unlikely that the effects will be equally favorable or unfavorable to all ethnies. Accordingly, the greater the differences in the relative standing and advantages of different ethnies, the greater the likelihood of interethnic tension and conflict.

Within a multi-ethnic state, violent conflict among ethnies should be most likely when grievances focus upon ethnic rivals that are *visible* and *vulnerable* (cf. Williams 1947, 54). The belief that an ethnic rival threatens harm but can be attacked with impunity raises the likelihood that activists and entrepreneurs will be able to use existing prejudices to incite overt violence. Vulnerability reduces fear of reprisals: attacking the weak not only costs less in the present, but it reduces the prospect of future retaliation. This targeting of the visible and vulnerable ethnic outsiders often occurs in the classic case of middleman minorities. Although these "middlemen" often are welcomed—as peddlers, moneylenders, merchants, export-import traders, and similar functionaries—they are singled out for violence in periods of social and economic distress and/or nationalistic or religious agitation. The "ideal" target is an ethny that is highly distinctive (in religion, language, and lifestyle), endogamous, concentrated in urban areas, occupationally specialized, visibly successful in sensitive trading activities or in political rivalry—and perceived as unable to retaliate for attacks.

Only rarely and in periods of great social upheaval and political change will large diffuse ethnic populations spontaneously engage in mass conflict with another ethnic population. One of the clearest cases was the Hindu-Muslim conflict at the time of the partition of India and Pakistan. Most instances of what appear to be conflicts of "unorganized masses" turn out on close inspection to be instigated and guided by state leaders and agencies, or by ethnic entrepreneurs and the organizations they lead. Obviously, many deadly intrastate conflicts are carried out by small fractions of the ethny: the militant organizations of militias and other paramilitary bodies, whether highly visible or secretive, elusive networks partially hidden within social movements with the public face of educational, medical, and social service activities (e.g., Hamas in Lebanon and Israel).

Furthermore, state incumbents, in response to sensed threats to their hold on power, often orchestrate organized violence between ethnies. Insecure elites in weak and repressive multi-ethnic states undergoing tentative democratization appear especially prone to such provocative mobilizations as in the prototypical cases of Yugoslavia (Gagnon 1994/95) and Rwanda (Prunier 1995; Gourevitch 1998). A dominant ethny that has little to fear may nevertheless use violence to gain advantage and to consolidate its rule.

The useful distinction between remote (distal) and proximal causes overlaps with the distinction between necessary and sufficient conditions, as for example when remote causes such as long-term population growth or centuries-old value-belief systems are seen as necessary but not sufficient to account for ethnic conflict. So among the Sinhalese in Sri Lanka, Buddhism and the Sinhala language were deeply embedded in myths and historical elaborations supporting an ingrained conviction of ethnic superiority. This cultural complex became a basis for assertive nationalism and anti-Tamil policies and actions eventuating in civil violence and warfare (Kapferer 1988; Tambiah 1986). Whatever the immediate circumstances, a substructure of shared beliefs and evaluations seems a necessary condition for the ethnic distinctions that can define boundaries for conflicts and support negative stereotypes, attitudes of social distance and disliking, and processes of dehumanization. Interethnic prejudices, once widely shared, can then lie in wait, as it were, to be energized by competition, relative deprivation, categorical discrimination, and the like. "Realistic" struggles, in turn, typically reinforce and maintain negative prejudices (Pettigrew 1998).

Our discussions thus far have concentrated upon structural conditions (social and cultural) and upon social processes as such, with little attention to psychological processes. Yet implicit in the analyses have been background assumptions about the significance of fear, suspicion, hostility, cognitive processes, identifications, and so on. And it would be an unjustified omission to pass over the massive evidence for the importance of psychological processes in the dynamics of collective conflicts. Although it is not feasible here to undertake any extended treatment, we can at least note a few salient considerations.

Any initial lack of trust between ethnies typically results in some measure of fear and anxiety about the motives and probable behavior of state authorities and of an "alien" ethny. Such alienation, if unchecked, results in insecurity, which in turn encourages incessant rivalry for power—well described as "the scarcest and dearest value" (Hudson 1968, 21–22). And distrust of an ethnically biased governing regime may indeed be well founded. To the extent that those in control of the state apparatus are seen to behave in particularistic modes—favoring kinsmen, locality groupings, and fellow ethnics—the importance of political control is heightened for those thus excluded from central networks of power. Particularly intense struggles are to be expected during times of rapid sociopolitical change when there is the prospect of a basic shift in the political structure. Low confidence in the impartiality of the government intensifies fear of permanent exclusion from political power and its rewards.

Once armed insurgencies against the state meet violent resistance and neither contender can gain decisive victory, widespread killings and other abuses of the civilian people are likely. Massive violations of "human rights" by military and paramilitary forces are typical of protracted civil wars. Resistance to negotiated settlements with rebels is likely to be especially strong when the officer corps holds strong ethnic/racial prejudices, profits from its role in combating the insurgency, and enjoys important political, economic, and social benefits from its position in the incumbent government (Goodwin 1993, 41–43).

Abrupt and large changes in the political system of a country, whether due to internal struggles, revolutionary changes in power, or defeat in war often are followed by increases in the severity of communal conflict. National crises often bring increased ethnic cleavages, which in conspicuous cases have been followed by mass killings. Gurr (1994, 12–15) presents limited but suggestive evidence that power-transition conflicts are much more deadly than other kinds of ethnopolitical conflicts. Major changes in regimes and power holders are likely to raise the stakes of contention—to produce a "winner take all" atmosphere of severe threat. The historical record is that major political upheavals are strongly linked to politicides and genocides (Fein 1979; Harff 1987).

When ethnic violence has occurred, whatever its initial sources may have been, a regular aftermath is mutual suspicion, exacerbated to the extent that the conflicting parties are subject to an inherent Security Dilemma. A crucial issue always is the question of who gives up their weapons after a cease-fire; each fears the other's intentions. The pattern is clearly evident in civil wars, and even in lesser chronic violence—as exemplified in Northern Ireland in a standoff after a 1999 peace agreement, with the Irish Republican Army refusing to accede to demands for disarmament.

A predictable reaction of resentment appears in those ethnies whose members feel that the collectivity as a whole is being unjustly subordinated in a ranking order. Especially sharp resentment is likely when there is an actual reversal in ranking, so that when a previously subordinate ethny acquires a dominant position we then see the familiar resentment of displaced groupings—those pushed aside, overturned, ignored, and treated with disdain by those earlier regarded as inferior. Ethnic entrepreneurs sometimes rise to power upon such feelings of unwarranted status deprivation, inciting violence as the means to redress an intolerable injustice.

Suspicion and fear are not the only emotions at work in collective violence. Reiterated feelings of hostility can crystallize into intense and rigid sentiments of genuine hatred so strong as to incite violence even in the absence of specific provocation. Desires for revenge are extremely powerful components of long-continued violent conflicts. Thus repeated cycles of violence can develop in which violence itself creates a shared set of antipathies and distrust, which in turn instigates new violence. Protracted ethnic warfare grievously illustrates this cycle.

The difficulties of regulation or resolution are intense when any of the parties regards the conflict as a unique occasion in which defeat will be total and irreversible. Many of the ethnic conflicts reviewed by Esman (1994), Gurr (1993b), and Horowitz (1985) develop genocidal fury because one party believes that another seeks total and irreversible domination: "They will enslave our children and our children's children," or "They intend to kill us all." An accumulation of detailed case studies underscores the importance in ethnic confrontations of the fear and defensive mobilization that arise from such perceived threats. In the prolonged conflicts in Northern Ireland and in Lebanon, a "profound fear of extinction" created political rigidities that contributed to collective violence; students of these situations conclude "that fear of extinction is a far more general feature of protracted ethnic conflict than has so far been recognized" (Crighton and MacIver 1991, 139). These intractable conflicts generate strong sociopsychological effects (for Northern Ireland see Stevenson 1996–97)—intense grief, shame, rage, feelings of irreparable loss and outrageous humiliation, and desires for revenge. Formal political agreements by themselves may do little to resolve such deeply human responses.

Violent conflict has sometimes been interpreted as the outcome of group socialization into approved patterns of aggression, particularly in societies that have been successful in past conflicts. Cross-cultural studies repeatedly note that socialization for aggression is emphasized in societies that frequently fight others and in which interpersonal violence is frequent. But, as Ember and Ember (1994) show, it is the frequency of war rather than of personal violence that best predicts socialization for aggression. The most plausible interpretation is that frequent warfare leads to socialization for violence, and this in turn favors interpersonal aggression. We can speculate that successful warring societies thus generate warrior cultures, rather than the other way around.

The implicit social "logic" of the construction of enemies has been described in studies of right-wing authoritarianism (Altemeyer 1988; cf. Scheff 1994) and has been sharply delineated by Aho (1994). Enemies are identified in terms of one's own moral righteousness; those who are not us are evil, and evil must be destroyed. In conflict escalation, the behavior of the out-group heightens feelings of threat and intensifies self-righteousness. This is a social process involving the whole group, not merely an outcome of an individual's "authoritarianism."

Like all other group-patterned emotional orientations, fear is both culturally constructed and socially instigated and constrained. It involves "the rhetorical process, symbolic resources, and representational forms through which a demonized, dehumanized, or otherwise threatening ethnically defined 'other' has been constructed" (Brubaker and Laitin 1998, 442). Given the particular cultural template, the drive toward action depends upon social processes of persuasion, coercion, and reward, set in motion by intellectuals, religious and political leaders, and other elites. (If the cultural background might be likened to a printed circuit, the social pressures generate the electric current to activate the mechanism.) If there is no cultural foundation, elite manipulations will not succeed, but the cultural patterns alone do not account for collective conflict—above all, they do not explain the savagery of ethnic violence.

In many instances, to be sure, fear is not a constructed fantasy or manipulated emotion, but a well-grounded, realistic response to threat. When a state has shown massive violence against an encompassed ethny, the targeted people have every reason to fear, and the same holds for interethnic violence. A different pattern appears when an ethnic political elite (Hutu in Rwanda, Serbian in Yugoslavia) stimulates and focuses mass fears upon ethnic targets, in the interests of suppressing in-group dissent, eliminating rivals, and consolidating control. Particularly likely to incite violence are struggles among rivals within an ethny to mobilize supporters and immobilize opponents. These struggles easily become "gladiator" contests in which extreme militancy may become the recipe for political victory.

A Review of Some Conclusions

In the existing social science literature we find literally hundreds of empirical generalizations concerning the conditions most likely to lead to ethnic conflict. These propositions deal, first, with the factors that increase ethnic *identity*, *salience*, and *interethnic antipathy*. For example:

1. The more severe discrimination has been against an ethny in the past, the greater will be its members' sense of sharing a common fate and identity.
2. The more that ethnic boundaries are rigid and identity is highly visible, the more likely it is that individual competition will be defined as collective ethnic rivalry.

3. The sharper the boundaries and the more salient the identity, the more likely it is that collective struggles will develop over relative group position.

4. The more rapid and intense the social changes that affect the relative advantages and social standing of different ethnies, the more likely will be both antipathies and overt conflict.

5. The greater state-enforced discrimination in a multi-ethnic society against a subordinated ethny, the greater will be the likelihood of interethnic stereotyping, dislike, and disagreements on public policies.

Similar generalizations in profusion deal with how identity and grievances lead to mobilization, and that in turn either to accommodation or conflict.

Several of the great common factors that run through all the diversity of ethnic conflicts are *identity, possession, domination,* and *threat.* No threat, no conflict. But political and economic domination always threaten someone; when the someone has an ethnic identity, the threat is ethnic. And what often is threatened is a claim to possession—to a homeland, to a sense of group position, to economic advantage, to a distinctive culture, to political power and authority, to individual and collective safety.

Domination translates into grievances plus suppression. When grievances lead to mobilization against resistance, rigid imposition of discriminatory practices and refusal of power-holders to grant voice and accommodative policies typically precede the violence. When such intransigence is bolstered by external aid and support, the expectable result is to prolong and intensify intrastate conflicts. The roster of such cases includes El Salvador, where the United States, Cuba, Nicaragua, and the Soviet Union all played a part (Corr 1995).

Against these background considerations, we find that some commonly advanced explanations are not convincing. The recent and current prevalence of intrastate ethnic violence cannot be primarily due to "modernization" in the usual sense of urbanization, industrialization, and commercialization. Some of these developments do facilitate ethnic mobilization, but some of the most destructive recent domestic wars have been in less modernized countries such as Rwanda, Burundi, Sudan, Zaire, and Cambodia. It is a different kind of modernization that has favored intrastate conflicts—that is, state expansion, the creation of new states, and rapid growth in technologies of communication and transportation. The worldwide tide of cheap and highly lethal weaponry—from AK-47s to land mines—certainly has increased killing power, but Rwanda alone shows what clubs, knives, and machetes can do.

The mere existence of ethnies does not explain conflict. Cultural differences by themselves can be tolerated, willingly accepted, admired, even emulated. Many culturally prominent ethnies do not enter into conflict, and even if violent confrontations occur at one time they may disappear at another. Cultural content that has not been a source of antipathy may come to matter greatly if a politically dominant ethny seeks to impose religious or linguistic restrictions and requirements upon those of a resisting people. Content may matter very little if the question at hand is the economic consequences of ethnic trading and credit networks or the availability of a culturally distinct labor pool (Collins 1995).

A long succession of observers have posited that sharp inequalities among identity groupings (in income, wealth, prestige, and political power) constitute a major cause of collective violence, including political rebellions and resolutions. But the historical record is full of large-scale instances of great inequalities that have persisted for long periods without mass protest. Even if such inequalities produced much discontent, it was a discontent diffusely spread through an unorganized population that was subject to massive repression by landlords and state officials.

Evidently, both inequality and the political opportunity structure should be examined simultaneously. There is some evidence that inequality does increase the likelihood of collective political violence. The apparent effect, however, is weaker than that of political regime repression—deadly political violence is highest in those states exerting intermediate levels of repressive control (Muller 1985).

The importance of multi-causation in ethnic conflicts is not merely that there are several or many necessary conditions, but also that strong interactions usually occur. Thus at a very simple level one might suppose that the incidence of conflict would be greater when a challenging group suffers great disadvantages and has many severe grievances. And it would be plausible to think also that the more resources commanded by the dissident collectivity, the greater the likelihood that it would risk protests or even combat. Yet the *interaction* of the two conditions is likely to produce an inverted U-shaped curve—low conflict when a potential challenger has great resources but little disadvantage, and low also when disadvantage is severe but resources are scanty.

Intrastate collective violence is carried out by states against their own people and by substate collectivities fighting one another or seeking control of the central state. The conditions most likely to promote such violence have been summarized as follows (Tilly 1993, 16): "declining democracy, increasing advantage to rulers of states, threats to rulers, autonomous power of the military, increasing armaments, declining international hegemony, major state interventions in minor states, and international compacts ratifying self-determination." All these conditions have been found since World War II in new, multi-ethnic states, having "arbitrary" borders, with militarized and repressive regimes but with insecure elites and weak capabilities for resource extraction and provision of important services. External permissiveness for strongly repressive state control and the international arms trade accentuate the likelihood of state-induced violence (Mandel 1999).

In a major study of ethnocentrism, several important areas of agreement among major theoretical perspectives were identified by Levine and Campbell (1972, 222–23) as follows:

1. The greater the opposition (contradiction or conflict of interests over important and scarce resources), the greater the ethnocentrism.
2. Hostility tends to elicit hostility: for example, intergroup conflict increases hostility; the out-group with whom the most recent conflict has occurred will be the most hated; positive or negative attitudes will tend to be reciprocated.
3. Real differences between ethnies will be exaggerated in stereotypes.
4. Societal complexity and centralization promotes ethnocentrism and warfare and military expansion.

In summary, "Groups with greater complexity have needed to engage in war more . . . and, as larger and more efficient organizations, have been more successful at it, thus spreading ethnocentrism through conquest, extermination, and provoked retaliation" (ibid., 223).

Cumulative evidence clearly shows that no single factor—a claimed antecedent condition—explains the *persistence* of violent insurgencies. In an analysis of six important cases of such intrastate rebellions, Goodwin (1993) found that several factors often thought to be decisive in accounting for protracted collective violence were insufficient to explain the persistence. Factors thus eliminated were the size of the rebel forces, a substantial overlap between ethnicity and class, lack of reform of economic conditions (e.g., land reform), and denial of free elections. The amount of foreign aid given to governments and/or to rebels was associated with persisting violence, but was not a primary factor. In all cases the rebels had major grievances against the state, but their persistence in warfare was most closely associated with the denial of political voice and with the imposition of extreme state repression. Widespread and persisting violations of human rights were crucial in maintaining reactive rebellion. In contrast, where large-scale rebellions were defeated, the governing regime had granted political voice and abstained from severe repression of the aggrieved population.

These findings may seem surprising in view of the historical record of successful repression of restive people, and of violent coercion that blocked reforms and stamped out overt resistance for long periods. But repression is costly, and to be most effective it has to be pervasive, severe, and consistently applied, and even then the results are mixed (see Lichbach 1987).

Indiscriminate state violence often creates protracted insurgencies (Goodwin 1993; Khawaja 1993). The long list of protracted civil wars in itself suggests the frequent failures of state repression (Licklider 1993).

Apparently it has become a widespread belief that the end of the Cold War "unleashed" a wave of previously suppressed intrastate violence. However, the much-noted upsurge of internal violence began not in 1989, but in the 1950s, and increased throughout the Cold War (Gurr 1993b, 190). Many civil wars were by-products of the superpower rivalries; examples include the Congo, Angola, Ethiopia, Vietnam, Nicaragua, El Salvador, Afghanistan, Somalia, Guatemala, Mozambique, Sudan, and many more, directly and indirectly. Even without unilateral external intervention (e.g., France in Chad; India in Sri Lanka; the United States in Grenada, Vietnam, and Panama), aid to warring parties frequently has escalated and prolonged intrastate conflicts.

The rise of ethnic-based warfare is not *primarily* due to the eruption of previously suppressed "ancient hatreds." It is not a matter of some deep Balkan mystery or of centuries-old tribalism. If long past wrongs are active today, it is because of reactivated or recycled grievances and animosities, open to political manipulations, as clearly is the case in the former Yugoslavia (Gagnon 1994/95). True, without *some* base in ethnic identities and stereotypes, political mobilization could not have such vast and deadly effects. But formerly peaceful coexisting and interdependent peoples do not spontaneously start killing one another simply because their ancestors once fought.

In the great majority of severe conflicts, lack of a common civic culture and of positive interdependence, combined with struggles for control of the state, create intense threats and counter-mobilizations. Ethnicity is rendered highly salient and provides an attractive base for political entrepreneurs. A common result is that ethnic rivals come to see each other as rigid groupings and membership as crucial to all life chances. Every move in that direction escalates and polarizes (cf. Schultz 1995; Williams 1994).

In deeply divided multi-ethnic societies, as we have noted, when disaffected ethnies find secession too costly and cultural autonomy without political power insufficient, the blocked rivals turn to contention for control. A "communal contender" (Gurr 1993b) of this kind aims at the exclusion of other ethnies from sharing political power, and may even aim at the expulsion or extermination of ethnic adversaries (Horowitz 1985, 31). In many parts of the so-called developing world, the state is the main source of wealth and prestige. So rivalry for political reasons is intense, while ethnic membership is a major factor in who gets what. Thus economic impoverishment and social pluralism combine with political centrality to create "communal" politics (Welch 1995). Control of the polity is a great prize for the winners—and a corresponding collective threat to those who may lose.

For example, of the 233 politicized communal groups in Gurr's 1993 work, 79 had engaged in guerrilla and civil wars since 1945; 34 of these violent conflicts were protracted and extremely deadly (Gurr 1993b, 98–99). These wars, with rare exceptions, were concentrated in weak but repressive states in the Third World and in the peripheries of industrialized countries. Especially prone to violent uprisings are formerly authoritarian states that are losing central control and/or engaging in rapid "democratization." Partisan external support to governments and rebels typically prolongs these ongoing ethnic-related conflicts.

As Gurr (1993b, 1994) has shown, conflict among communal contenders is more severe than the conflicts involving indigenous peoples and ethnonationalists. Indigenous peoples typically want limited autonomy and control of resources; ethnonationalists want autonomy or separation. Neither directly threatens central government hegemony. But communal contenders by definition do seek central power, and are likely to have the capabilities to mount credible threats, especially when the government is seen as being in the hands of an ethnic elite bent upon self-enrichment.

Conflict arising from state impositions is especially likely in rentier states in which governing elites have sources of income that render them independent of the potential electorate: Nigeria and Zaire are prominent examples.

Some of the most severe intrastate conflicts occur in collapsed states—those in which the central political authorities have lost control over contenders for power and in which multiple armed groupings are in conflict. Such situations have been found in Afghanistan, in Colombia, in Lebanon, in Somalia, in Zaire, and in Liberia, to mention only a few.

In accepting the risk of dangerous oversimplification, let us finally summarize the main factors that increase the likelihood of violent ethnic conflict. Conflict is favored when there is strong identity, inequalities and grievances, opportunity structures allowing mobilization, provocative state policies, and international contagion and diffusion. Our own capsule summary would respond to four questions about intrastate ethnic "wars": *where, when, how,* and *why*.

Where do these conflicts occur? Wherever main concentrations of predisposing conditions exist. These are found in most large regions of the world, but especially in less-industrialized countries in Africa, South and Southeast Asia, the Middle East, and in the former Soviet Union and the former Yugoslavia.

When should we expect greatest likelihood? In periods of major political transitions and of abrupt changes in economic and social positions of large ethnies within national states.

How do the conflicts develop? Mobilization and counter-mobilization are favored by direct rivalry of cohesive ethnies seeking political autonomy or dominance. Old animosities are not highly predictive, but recent violence tends to evoke new violence.

Why are the conflicts so many and so deadly? Multi-ethnic states that are centralized and repressive fail to provide voice or autonomy to aggrieved ethnic and regional dissidents. Sharply bounded and relatively large ethnies seek control in political systems that do not favor compromise and power-sharing. Particularly explosive are (1) situations of lost autonomy in unstable polities, (2) abrupt impositions of cultural and economic deprivations by a dominant ethnic state, and (3) intrastate conflicts attracting partisan external interventions.

The more general question is *why* does the community-building power of ethnic belongingness sometimes lead to destructive conflict? In this chapter, we have reviewed a complex set of factors. Nothing less will pass as a genuine effort to explain. But if we were forced to state a single proposition as most decisive, among many, for explaining the conflicts between states and the peoples they seek to control, and the conflicts among communal groupings seeking political power, we would not cite ancient hatreds, economic competition, cultural differences, or leadership struggles. Instead, we would argue that the most important root source of *The Wars Within* is exploitative (asymmetrical) *domination*: that is, the use of coercion to control and extract gain from an encapsulated population without any corresponding flow of safeguards and benefits from the state or from its dominant ethnies to the subordinated populace. True, totally suppressed people may be ground down for centuries with little overt revolt. But whenever the submerged collectivities see opportunity and are able to amass resources, the prison quiet is likely to explode. Indeed, many military regimes and one-party states might well be characterized as minimum-security prisons.

Part III

THE DYNAMICS OF
MOBILIZATION AND CONFLICT

CHAPTER SIX

From Grievances to Mobilization

This chapter deals with the following topics:

(1) What is mobilization?
(2) Identity and salience as factors in mobilization.
(3) Basic processes: some illustrations.
(4) Opportunities and constraints.
(5) Major interpretations and theories of mobilization.

The central task of this chapter is to account for the emergence of collective action from previously inactive ethnic populations. How can this remarkable fact be understood?

What Is Mobilization?

Many ethnies never engage in any kind of organized collective action; many never take any united political action. Some are too weak: the people are geographically scattered, severely impoverished, without good facilities for communication, uneducated, lacking in articulate and skillful leaders. Some are literally immobilized by pervasive and extremely severe suppression that has created a terrorized, confused, and disunited populace. Still others are unable to act in any unitary way by reason of multiple internal cleavages and contradictory interests. Multi-ethnic work forces often are immobilized by internal divisions that are used by employers' divide-and-rule practices. Many situations in which workers of different ethnic origins coexist in close contact without any collective mobilization have been well documented. For instance, Bourgois (1989) has described a complex multi-ethnic work force on a United Fruit Company banana plantation in which ethnicity/race and class were merged, and management control and ethnic stereotyping created a firm occupational hierarchy. Finally, some ethnies simply lack any important shared collective grievances: if not fully satisfied with their situation, they at least accept the status quo as preferable to any realistic alternative. So a first requirement for mobilization must be some actual or potential shared grievances. Without some sense of grievance, people do not mobilize. The fate of many ethnies over centuries has been that of endurance, of acquiescence, of quietism. Even when they do become moved to action, they may simply seek escape through migration or by retreat into self-contained enclaves.

Yet grievances can be created. Small groupings of the disaffected and rebellious can articulate and spread conceptions of deprivation, discrimination, unjust policies, unrequited wrongs, looming threats. It is unlikely that grievances can simply be imaginary or invented, but the minimum level of discontent necessary for mobilization to start can be surprisingly low. Thus ethnic mobilization may occur when there is no exclusion from political participation—even when members have full access to political parties and state agencies, but feel deprived or frustrated because their policy preferences are not being granted. In such cases, "There is simply not a pre-existing group of people with interests that are being thwarted; their grievances need to be constructed in the process of building the movement" (Jasper and Goodwin 1999, 117). One obvious route to a focused sense of collective grievance is through the articulation of aspirations for high political aims—autonomy, special group rights, even independence—that predictably will be blocked. (In many respects, these processes were evident in the complex history of group interests and aims in the movement for independence in Québec.)

Over the years, students of ethnicity have repeatedly noted that discontent alone is not enough to instigate mobilization: "Unorganized and dispersed masses of discontented people are not in a position to generate effective political pressure. Only through communication and the subsequent emergence of leadership, authority, and division of functions—i.e., organization—can discontent be mobilized and focused into collective dissent, protest, and structured opposition" (Williams 1978, 61–62). Only rarely and in periods of great social upheaval and political change will a large ethnic population spontaneously engage in mass conflict with another ethnic population—a prototypical case being the Hindu-Muslim clashes at the time of the partition of India and Pakistan. Most instances of what appear to be conflicts of "unorganized masses" turn out on close inspection to be instigated and guided by state leaders and agencies, or by ethnic entrepreneurs and the organizations they lead—as notably in the attempted genocide in Rwanda in the 1990s and in the "ethnic cleansing" in the former Yugoslavia. Violent conflict in particular usually is started by a small number of highly committed activists who not only seek to define objectives, but also to define who is and who is not a member of the group.

In those instances in which ethnies are large, with loosely connected internal groupings and informal social networks, and relatively indistinct boundaries, the lack of a nucleated or centralized organization is an obvious barrier to mobilization. Such ethnies share the amorphous structures of socioeconomic classes or the regions of national states. Short of focused mobilization, they act in unitary ways only as diffuse collectivities—as, for example, in bloc voting in national elections. Mobilization means that leaders emerge, ethnic agendas are formulated, resources are assembled, and political actions can now be taken under a definite ethnic label. The ethny acquires political significance through the efforts of entrepreneurs and spokespersons, who emphasize ethnic identity and solidarity, articulate grievances and objectives, point to adversaries, formulate claims and demands, call for loyalty and commitment, and propose collective action.

Many ethnies pursue political aims through conventional means of voting, lobbying, electoral politics, and local or regional control. Beyond these are the politics of direct action. Gurr (2000, 28) distinguishes four levels of political action by ethnies (communal and identity groups) beyond inaction: mobilization, demonstrations and/or rioting, small-scale rebellion, and large-scale rebellion. Mobilization is the most frequent strategy, large-scale rebellion is the least frequent, and protests and small-scale rebellions fall in between.

In the special cases of ethnic revivals or ethnogenesis, a dominant pattern is the early emergence of intellectuals who elaborate myths, reinterpret history, define collective dangers and enemies, and invoke common interests. Most often these pioneers are nontechnical intelligentsia—language experts, historians, religious scholars, school teachers, publicists; only later do other professional and technical groupings join the movement (Smith 1981).

Our first approximation of a definition is that ethnic mobilization consists of joint action by members of an ethny to seek shared goals through claims for common interests. How does such mobilization relate to ethnic solidarity?

Solidarity may appear to be implied by mobilization, since the assertion of collective claims is made on behalf of an ethny, rather than for collectivities based on other distinctions, such as gender, age, occupation, or military veteran status (cf. Nielsen 1985, 136). But although solidarity is correlated with mobilization, the two are not identical; solidarity may be characterized as a combination of conscious ethnic identification, dense in-group interaction, and strong collective institutions (Olzak 1983, 356). Such intra-ethny sentiments and social ties do provide a ready-made base for actual organization in efforts to attain collective goals. Mobilization occurs only when there is organized action to achieve those purposes (Alba 1992, 581). So the prior existence of strong ethnic solidarities can provide crucial initial bases for collective mobilization and the emergence of protest leadership (Oberschall 1973, 120–33). Just as social ties and solidarities facilitate mobilization, so mobilization as it proceeds creates and strengthens such interpersonal and intergroup linkages and collective identities (Gould 1991, 719).

Mobilization for political purposes, then, builds most easily upon existing social networks and relationships of solidarity. This fact helps to explain what might otherwise have been seen as puzzling and paradoxical developments, such as the effects of the development of democratic political institutions in a caste-centered society. With the coming of an independent democratic state in India, should not a primary effect have been the minimization of caste? The answer is that in the short run the logic of democratic politics ensures that caste remains in the center of rivalry for political voice and power because caste associations constitute a ready-made channel for political mobilization (Larson 1995, 263–66).

The most general features of mobilization are not restricted to a particular culture or social setting. Thus, for example, mobilization for military coups typically occurs within relatively small and well-bounded social groupings. Attempted coups are high-risk enterprises. Because of the need for secrecy, coordination, and speed, the initial recruits must be strongly committed and trustworthy—desiderata most likely to be found among kinship groups and co-ethnics (Horowitz 1985; Welch 1986). Similarly, in the initial phases of high-risk social movements, threatened by informers and by hostile surveillance, trust and secrecy will be sought in close social networks of friends, kin, neighbors, co-workers. Where ethnic lines are sharply drawn, such networks will also be made up of fellow ethny members.

Trustworthiness of commitment is strengthened whenever the interacting parties are involved in multiple relationships that they expect will be continued into an indefinitely long future. Partly for this reason, mobilization often begins by recruitment of persons from the same stable residential areas. The informal social networks so constituted provide solidarities that then can be linked into larger and more formal organizations. These processes are well illustrated in the rebellion of the Paris Commune of 1871, in which the informal locality ties interacted with the formal linkages among the insurgents that had been established by membership in the National Guard. The dual networks facilitated mobilization and helped to maintain combat loyalty (Gould 1995).

But while strong local solidarities and shared grievances may be necessary conditions for widespread mobilization, they are not sufficient conditions for large-scale and "sustained challenges to power-holders in the
name of a disadvantaged population living under the jurisdiction or influence of those power-holders" (Tarrow 1998, 874). A historical case in
point was the outbreak of peasant rebellions in the Russian Empire during the years 1905–07. Grievances were abundant, especially because of
increasing economic insecurity. There also was the resource of the social
solidarity of villages with their relatively autonomous local governments
and traditional relations of cooperation. But these features were not
enough to successfully challenge a central government that was resolutely
and strongly repressive, whereas the peasant communities were isolated
rather than linked together by organizational ties such as urban organizers or a revolutionary political party (Jenkins 1982).

Both the internal resources of the local segments of an ethny and the
organizational links among them are necessary for collective action. Mobilization is not just a process of developing a collective ideology and generating a sense of collective identity, and of shared grievances and
aspirations. It also involves such highly specific activities as raising funds,
recruiting allies, disseminating information and propaganda, initiating
lawsuits, organizing electoral campaigns, creating and maintaining internal organizations, assembling weapons, and training special cadres and
leaders. Leaders must contend with the continuous threat of disabling factionalism. They must formulate and enforce norms of inclusion and exclusion of members and allies—that is, the indispensable rules of loyalty
and boundary maintenance.

When all these processes have been well advanced, a formerly diffuse
ethny becomes a *social movement* with a *cohesive center* and *substantial capability for concerted action*. In the early formative stages, most large ethnies will
encompass many different interests and diverse conceptions of strategies
and tactics. The two major tasks are to find formulations and symbols that
will frame a unitary collective interest, and to develop the organization to
focus and guide action.

Identity and Salience: Preconditions and Consequences

Ethnicity thrives on cultural differences and contact. Shared ethnic
awareness is accentuated by contact with people having different cultural
characteristics. Many of today's ethnies have emerged from the merging of
regional and local identities, brought about by external pressures such as
stereotyping and discrimination from other ethnies. Common experiences of being treated alike create a sense of shared fate.

Hardly in doubt is the proposition that mobilizations are favored by a shared sense of collective identity, based in part upon an awareness of commonality of values and interests. What has been called the ethnic enclosure hypothesis holds that ethnic consciousness is favored by segregation into ("most disadvantageous") residential and occupational settings (Portes 1984, 385). In contrast, the "ethnic competition" interpretation (e.g., Olzak 1983) holds that ethnic awareness is heightened by direct competition with "others" outside of ethnic enclaves. Not surprisingly, both processes can be important in particular contexts (Portes 1984)—depending upon the extent of contact, the experience of discrimination, initial solidarity and self-consciousness, and other factors.

Collective emphasis upon cultural origins and distinctiveness has been seen as arising in two forms. When members of an ethny fear that boundaries are eroding as the collectivity is being assimilated into another, leaders often stress a distinctive group history and culture. When they fear that subgroups are drifting apart, they tend to emphasize the idea of a common historical origin or ancestry and a shared historical experience (Horowitz 1985). On the other hand, similar emphases occur when the ethny as a whole is seen as under severe external threat.

Continuing confrontation with categorical discrimination is especially likely to aid political mobilization when (1) a general improvement in economic and social conditions has raised hopes, (2) the majority-group opposition appears divided or weak, and (3) a middle stratum of ethnic leadership has developed. In terms of conventional political participation, the most plausible prediction is that ethnic voting will be strongest only after ethnic members appear as political candidates—usually only after a middle-income, middle-education leadership has appeared. Thus, it is not enough to have cultural similarities and a diffuse sense of common fate and ethnic membership; these become politically salient when a leadership cadre develops that links ethnic interests to political parties and movements.

When ethnic mobilization is so continuous and pervasive that nearly all political struggle is conceived of and actually organized in ethnic terms, one has a plural—rather than a pluralistic—society. The restructuring of politics along ethnic lines has occurred in many post-colonial nations once the common opponent of the metropolitan power has been overthrown or ejected. On the other hand, resurgent ethnic "nationalisms" have appeared in highly industrialized Western democracies: French Canadians in Québec; Walloons and Flemings in Belgium; Scots and Welsh in Great Britain; Blacks, Native Americans, and others in the United States; even in Switzerland, in the Jura dispute in Bern. A notable feature of these cases has been the rising levels of affluence, education, and political potential of the mobilizing minorities. In nearly all cases, the agitation for ethnic mobilization has been led by a cultural elite that emphasizes an ethnic distinctiveness that would redound to the benefit of members of that elite should ethnicity become the basis of political authority or influence. In a newly bilingual society, for example, an elite from the subordinate linguistic group is likely to reap many advantages in education, government, and business. Collective aims and individual self-interests march together.

As emphasized in Chapter 1, many ethnic collectivities are characterized by diffuse and changing boundaries and internal heterogeneity. Both features increase the difficulty of united action and the probability of "unreliability" (instability) in settlements. In a great many politically important cases, ethnic relations thus combine vague boundaries, loose and unstable organization, internal diversity, diffuse relationships, ascribed membership, high stakes, multiple and symbolic issues, and historical embeddedness (including rigid stereotypes). Small wonder that ethnic conflicts are volatile, easily subject to run-away escalation, and difficult to resolve by conventional bargaining and mediation tactics. For the same reasons, formal organization is not a prerequisite for ethnic protest, nor for collective violence, nor even for the success of protest movements (Goldstone and Useem 1999, 996–98).

An example of an incipient social movement that was stalled by its internal diversity is that of Occitania in the south of France—a vaguely delimited region, roughly linked to the regional variant of French, the *langue d'oc*. According to Alain Touraine's account (1985), the so-called Occitanist movement was not so much a fully formed sociopolitical movement as it was a collection of divergent efforts to create a new unitary force. To make effective claims on behalf of the putative ethnoregion required the union of three main sets of interests: (1) those primarily concerned with maintaining *langue d'oc* and associated cultural characteristics, (2) those of political actors seeking greater regional autonomy and/or a greater voice in the central government, and (3) those concerned with the feared economic "decline and fall" of the region who were seeking modernization and economic development. Although it is conceivable that these interests could have been combined in a relatively unified political movement, the difficulties proved insurmountable even after protracted organizational efforts. As Touraine summarizes the internal differences, "The teachers are defending a gravely threatened language, the trade unionists are defending employment or income, and the militants are devising a nationalist program progressing from autonomy to independence—but there is nothing to bring them together" (1985, 159).

In the contrasting cases of successful revivals or ethnogenesis, an initial amorphous identity is redefined and consolidated so that separate fractions come to be seen and felt as parts of an overarching collectivity. Myth creation is a part of this process. Two distinctive types are evident: those that claim identity on the basis of a "common" genealogical ancestry, as over against those that emphasize the persistence of distinctive cultural qualities. Both typically coexist, but are held by different strata and thus generate dynamic tensions, and both have become widely used in nationalistic claims and mobilizations (Smith 1984, 95–100). However, ethnic mobilizations do not necessarily lead to nationalism, as Zaslavsky (1992, 106) shows in the case of the former Soviet Union. Nationalist ethnic movements aim to establish a separate state having sovereignty over a particular territory. In this sense, a "nationality" is a self-conscious ethny that aspires to control its own state, although some may settle for substantial regional autonomy.

The importance of cultural distinctiveness is well illustrated in the case of the ethnic nationalist movement in Catalonia. Under the Spanish dictatorship of Franco (1939–75), forceful repression had been used in an attempt to erase the regional culture in every aspect, including language, songs, literature, dances, and other aspects of expressive culture. Once some limited political opportunity developed, however, a broad-based mobilization eventually succeeded in gaining substantial autonomy (Johnston 1991). When, as in this example, a large ethny occupied a densely settled region of a modern state that itself is primarily representative of a different ethny, the possibility is always open for movements seeking autonomy or separation. Such a territorially based ethny does not have to be economically disadvantaged to develop grievances against the central state. Many nationalistic movements develop in relatively prosperous regions. Nor does a sense of grievance have to exclusively depend upon feelings of cultural inferiority or social exclusion.

Catalonia is a clear case of a culturally distinct, economically advantaged region in a less-developed national economy. The region itself has had a long history of a distinctive culture, including language, and of an orderly social life, including networks of strong corporate groups. It also has a major city, Barcelona, which serves as a focal political, economic, and cultural center. It never had any occasion to develop a sense of being a colony or backwater (Pi-Sunyer 1985, 254–76). Out of this background, then, Catalan "nationalism" took the form of claims for substantial degrees of both cultural and political autonomy. After the disruptions of civil war and the long Franco dictatorship, the development of a more democratic and responsive central state meant that Catalonia could make effective claims from a position of strength that was based on economic productivity, an intact culture, and strong regional social cohesion.

Separatist or secessionist movements do not have a single universal source, but arise from the confluence of several different conditions. Observe the partially contrasting findings of Horowitz (1985, 236) and Gurr (1993b, 86). Horowitz concludes on the basis of cases from Asia and Africa that most secessionists come from disadvantaged ("backward") groupings in backward regions; these peripheral peoples have little stake in the existing state that encompasses them, and they often fear the competition from more advantaged collectivities. This finding contrasts with the fact that in the former Soviet Union and Eastern Europe the early separatists were primarily from the more prosperous "advanced" regions. And Gurr (1993b, 86) observes that most claims for autonomy or separation have come from peoples who once had self-governance that was lost by conquest or annexation. It is a history of former autonomy, rather than economic or political discrimination, that best predicts these active separatist movements.

The diverse social structures of states and ethnic formations help to account for such differences in outcomes. For example, in country after country the world over, there are tensions and social cleavages between the more rural, more traditional segments of national state societies and the more urbanized, educated, and cosmopolitan sectors. Such rifts are evident in Central Asia, Iran, Pakistan, Egypt, and several other Islamic countries, as well as in India. Major struggles that wear the label of "fundamentalism" versus "secular states" reflect, in part, the fault lines between "immobile" or embedded masses and modernizing and centralizing classes and segments.

Politicized forms of ethnicity, along with religious fundamentalism, may be regarded as manifestations of a process of sociocultural de-differentiation. In the case of religious fundamentalisms there is a central effort to reverse the separation of sacred and secular worlds (Hadden 1992). In the case of mobilized ethnicity, the emphasis is upon a total allegiance that transcends differentiations of class. In both instances there is a denial or submergence of multiple loyalties and collective memberships; differentiations by class, gender, region, occupation, or lifestyles are minimized in favor of the great polarization of the faithful versus infidels, of Them versus Us. Snow and Marshal (1984, 145) join other scholars in arguing that "Islamic revivals are shaped both by government responses to popular demands for a rejection of foreign encroachment and a reassertion of indigenous cultural pride as well as elites' own need for external sources of legitimization." Governments are under threat in countries with militant and violent Muslim movements, from Algeria to Egypt, from the Middle East to Indonesia, and on to Central Asia.

If the composite interests of an ethnic collectivity are to be effectively expressed through interest-group politics, there must be some appreciable unity within the collectivity: incompatible aims and a multiplicity of organizations and spokespersons working at cross-purposes are detrimental to political influence. Ethnic leaders, therefore, are likely to have a special concern for internal politics—the compromises and integration of interests and objectives within the ethnic boundaries—if only as a precondition for effective pressure and bargaining.

Of course, the extent to which leaders will emerge to press for *collective* ethnic interests is itself a variable. Extensive upward social mobility of individuals in a relatively open class system can drain off potential militants whose success induces them to "work within the system" (Purcell and Sawyer 1993; Horowitz 1985). Conversely, severe blockage of opportunity can drive aspiring climbers back into their ethnic origins; frustrated in their personal ambitions and seeing their fate irrevocably linked to their ethnic status, they are likely to become advocates and organizers for *group* rights.

Where highly structured conflicts emerge, ethnic clusterings become real social units; i.e., *collectivities* or *organizations* rather than mere *social categories* or *aggregates*. Only when there is enough structure to allow mobilization of resources (McCarthy and Zald 1977) can diffuse aspirations and discontents be transformed into collective grievances, claims, protests, and conflicts. For example, the forms of domestic protest depend upon both the organization of the state and of the partisan contenders. In Europe, as political centralization of states accompanied industrialization, state resources increased and new class formations appeared. As aspiring groups confronted national states, "reactive" protests defending established rights were replaced by "proactive" claims to new rights (Tilly, Tilly, and Tilly 1975). In a different form of the interaction of states and ethnies, small ethnic minorities that are geographically concentrated and well organized have a political advantage in that their demands can be met with minimal effect on the remainder of the national society (Schermerhorn 1978, 129).

Generalizations concerning mobilization always need to be supplemented by local knowledge of particular cases. In general, it is well documented that mobilization is facilitated by *resources* (e.g., money, free time, communication facilities, allies), by *networks and organizations* (e.g., friends, kin, neighborhoods, workplaces, churches, unions), and by *political opportunity structures* (low risk for organizing, free speech and assembly). In addition to networks and political opportunities, however, mobilization can be affected also by *spatial arrangements and local ecologies*—as apparently was important in the 1989 Beijing student movement (Zhao 1998). It has long been observed that mobilization is favored by (1) spatial concentration, such as clustering of workers around factories and clustering of similar organizations (schools, churches, universities, factories), as well as by (2) physical isolation of tightly knit groupings (miners, working-class neighborhoods). Even the spatial arrangement and "steering" of population movement by streets, buildings, or physical obstructions can have tangible effects upon local mobilizations, especially in situations of constricted opportunity and low development of private associations.

Not grievances alone, but also positive hopes, aspirations, and ambitions are bases for collective mobilization. In the scholarly literature on ethnic mobilization, as well as in that dealing more generally with social movements, grievances have been the main focus of attention—perhaps in part because grievances are easier to identify and more obviously consequential than positive incentives and goals. But even if fear of loss may be an incentive more powerful than hope of gain, a mobilizable ethny can perceive possible economic, political, or prestige gains as decisive grounds for collective action. "Grievances" may be just frustrated *aspirations,* not only losses or deprivations. An advantaged ethny may mobilize to seize control of the state, to secure monopolistic economic gains, or to suppress cultural dominance and the social status held by rivals.

Mobilization, however, is not merely a cool cognitive process in which prospective members calculate their individual preexisting interests. Recruitment and participation in protests and social movements involve emotions—often the strong affects of hatred, anger, grief, shame, resentment, blame, moral outrage—or of joy, love, and enthusiasm. To say "grievances" or "aspirations" is to imply that these putative sources of mobilization are not affectively neutral. In Jasper's formulation (1998, 420), "Emotions give ideas, ideologies, identities, and even interests their power to motivate. Just as they must respond to cognitive grids and moral visions, movement organizers and participants appeal to and build upon preexisting emotions such as fear, outrage, even love." And, indeed, the term "grievances" often is another name for frustrated aspirations, even those that approach ambitions for dominance. Over and over, the activists in ethnic mobilizations show what has been called ideological anger: "a sense of outrage against opponents regarded as immoral" (Exum 1985, 14).

Especially prominent in the great majority of cases of intensive ethnic mobilization is the fear aroused by a sense of severe threat. The sensed threat takes many forms, both realistic and imagined. The common form of ethnic fear is expressed in the language of being overwhelmed, swamped, deluged, dominated, becoming helpless and permanently disadvantaged "in our own land," and ultimately being exterminated (see, e.g., Banac 1992; Anderson 1990, 327; Horowitz 1985, 175–81). What is threatened encompasses a wide range of vital concerns. In addition to loss of economic position (of jobs; of access to markets, credit, and education), the perceived dangers may include loss of political voice and autonomy, of religious freedom, or of civic rights. There often is the threat to life and limb of looming collective violence. And always in some measure there is the threat to a basic sense of group worth.

On the plausible assumption that individuals and groups are more likely to be moved to immediate action by severe threat rather than the possibility of future gain (Esman 1994, 244), we would expect ethnic mobilization to be most likely in the face of perceived threat. And, indeed, collective threat precedes many important cases of ethnic mobilization: for example, Malays and Chinese in Malaysia, Tamils and Sinhalese in Sri Lanka, southerners versus those in the north in Sudan, Ibos versus Hausa-Fulani in Nigeria, and the multiple ethnic conflicts in Yugoslavia.

Certainly some ethnic formations pose deadly threats to other ethnies, and, short of that, constitute real and immediate threats to economic, political, and social opportunity (Chapter 5). Nevertheless, the character and magnitude of threats are also matters of perception and social definition. What appears to the outside observer as a slight threat, or none at all, can loom ominously in the eyes of the ethnic insider. How could the Sinhalese, who were 85 percent of the population of Sri Lanka, believe themselves in danger of being submerged and having their culture demolished by the Tamils, who were less than 15 percent? To many Sinhalese intellectuals, religious leaders, and politicians, the Tamil minority was seen as a foreign intrusion—an extension of the 55 million people in India's Tamil Nadu, a few miles away across a narrow strait. To define the local Tamil population as a threat, such leaders and agitators could also draw on history and myth to dramatize past invasions and dominance, and to exalt the antiquity and value of that Sinhalese culture that now allegedly was vulnerable to being overwhelmed in an alien Tamil sea.

A general rule—no less important for being thought obvious—is that persons dislike being treated with contempt, being subjected to humiliation, or having their ethnic membership denigrated. In ethnic contests, accordingly, collective esteem, respect, or prestige has an important place. Although "materialistic" or narrowly economic theories may attempt to dismiss collective respect as "merely symbolic," the record is unambiguous that group respect is a high-value public good. Indeed, it is often the case that being accepted as a serious participant in the polity depends upon public acknowledgment by the state or by other ethnies that a particular collective deserves a place of esteem. Esman (1994, 218) emphasizes that claims for such recognition are especially likely when members of an ethny believe its status has been denigrated by those in authority. The social reality of symbolic goods should never be in doubt.

Basic Processes: Some Illustrations

Timing and Sequence

Mobilization may be fitful, with many lulls and starts, involving changing sets of interests, issues, and active parties. Violent conflict can escalate from small nonviolent movements without there ever being a clear moment of transition. Original aims and grievances can disappear or move into the background as collective boundaries become rigid and the violence itself becomes self-sustaining, as happened in the protracted "Troubles" in Northern Ireland from 1968 into and beyond the 1990s (Stevenson 1996–97, chaps. 1–3).

Studies of protracted intrastate conflicts have shown the difficulty of understanding such events through analyses of the static attributes of states, societies, ethnies, and other collective actors. Recognition of this difficulty has led to calls for greater attention to timing and sequencing of actions (Williams 1994)—that is, to analysis of conflicts as processes (Moore 1995), especially as sequences of strategic interactions (Sutter 1995). Although the importance of sequence and timing thus has often been noted, at least in passing, the problem only rarely has been subjected to detailed analysis. Gurr (1993b, 94) has commented, "When tracing minorities over time, we have repeatedly observed that violent political action follows a period of nonviolent activity that was either ignored or dealt with repressively." Gurr further notes that of seventy-nine cases of collectivities engaged in civil wars and rebellions, forty-three conflicts had escalated from earlier protests and twenty-eight had escalated from lower levels of violence. The mean interval between first reported protests and later violence was about thirteen years—a period presumably long enough to permit diagnosis of grievances and possible remedial action. Not surprisingly, the levels of political mobilization in one period correlate strongly with mobilization in a following period. Presumably the indicators of mobilization reflect the cumulative effects of past disadvantages, and grievances and their sources (Gurr 1993b, 182–83).

A common view of ethnic conflict is to suppose that strong ethnic identity is a necessary, although not a sufficient, condition for the development of conflict. But the reverse sequence also occurs: conflict renders ethnic differences more salient, intensifies a sense of identity, creates shared grievances, and thereby increases the likelihood of further ethnic differences. Once under way, ethnic conflict and ethnic identity thus interact in a reciprocal feedback sequence.

Processes of mobilization obviously are highly path-dependent, in the sense that events at any one time are shaped by prior events, so that one observes branching sequences that have the appearance of a decision-tree with outcomes linked to choice-points along a time line. An important aspect of this path-dependence in the dynamics of collective interactions is the interplay of tactical moves by one party and responses by the other. Because excluded or challenging groups often have few resources to offer as inducements, they are likely to resort to disruptive tactics, which in turn will be met by counter-tactics on the part of target groups. The outcomes of such tactical innovations and counter-moves depend upon the communicative and organizational structures of challengers, and the political opportunity structures available to them (Gamson 1975; McAdam 1983, 736–37). Given potent infrastructures and some minimal political openings, the actual course of claims, protests, and insurgent activities will be governed to a substantial degree by the interactions of tactical innovations and adversaries' tactical resistance. Thus skill and timing become realistic factors in social struggles.

McAdam's (1983) detailed analysis of Black protests and demonstrations before and during the civil rights movement of the 1960s showed a sequence of specific protest tactics: bus boycotts, sit-ins and jail-ins, freedom rides, total community campaigns, and urban uprisings and "riots." After initial shocks, the opposing segregationists devised control measures—harassment and violence, legalistic obstruction, economic intimidation, closure of facilities, new laws, negotiations, reutilization of arrests, and, finally, massive police and military interventions to use force to put down civil disorders (riots). The later counter-insurgent tactics showed increased sophistication in evasion and absorption of protests, as well as more coordinated and calculated use of force. Sophistication eventually bred counter-sophistication.

Attention paid to change and timing becomes especially necessary as rapid communication and transportation increase the likelihood of contagion and diffusion of ethnic ideologies and strategies of action across political boundaries and over large geographic distances. So it is, for example, that in an age of rapid and cheap mass communication, the material of ethnic hatreds can be quickly disseminated through international networks—travel by advocates, sales of magazines and recordings, appearances by skinhead rock bands, and the use of Internet and electronic bulletin board services. A result is that "hate groups" in any one country have multiple linkages with similar groups worldwide (cf. *The Skinhead International* 1995, Anti-Defamation League). Dispersed networks of terrorist organizations can coordinate actions around the world, with increasing sophistication in tactics and in the use of advanced technologies of death and destruction.

Mass communication and international organizations link some ethnies together across state lines, most notably for militant Islamic groups and indigenous peoples. Indirect "demonstration effects" appear to be increasingly important as information about social movements and state actions create possible models, strategies, and tactics. External aid and support often contribute powerfully to ethnic cohesion and mobilization. And the basic substructures of ethnicity, kinship networks and their symbolic extensions, are no respecters of the state boundaries that have been drawn on maps: as noted in Chapter 5, nearly two-thirds of the communal groups included in Gurr's world survey (1993a, 175) have kindred in one or more adjacent countries.

Students of ethnic behavior today are increasingly noting the part played by intergroup and interstate communication via modern technology in shaping ethnic identities, issues, and modes of collective action. Thus Gurr (1993a, 164) observes, "By the 1960s there was a standard repertoire of anticolonial strategies and tactics, known to virtually all leaders of colonial people throughout the world and used, then and now, by many communal nationalists. By the 1980s a comparable repertoire of strategies had emerged for taking action against discrimination and repression in plural societies."

Disaffected and rebellious ethnies are increasingly able to emulate the tactics and strategies of similar collectivities across state boundaries. With rapid communication and transportation, when ethnic populations spread across two or more state lines, support and coordination become easier. And the dense networks of communication can strengthen ethnic loyalties, raise hopes of successful protest or rebellion, and spread awareness of relevant events elsewhere (cf. Stack 1981).

In the future, ethnicity is likely to be less closely linked with territory or physical proximity of individuals than in the past. The widespread and increasing availability of relatively inexpensive means of communication already has linked together dispersed populations. Newer technologies facilitate targeted or "addressable" communication through satellites with many channels, e-mail, Internet, World Wide Web, and other emerging devices. Thus possibilities exist for reinforcing separate cultures and languages across existing political boundaries, and for reconstituting or even creating new ethnic identities (Elkins 1997). "Possibility," of course, need not mean actuality; the technology is permissive, not directive, and nonethnic uses may dominate or unforeseen restrictions may develop. Certainly, however, expanded opportunities exist for diffusion and contagion of ethnic movements and appeals.

Change and Mobilization

Numerous historical cases make it clear that *chronic* grievances by themselves are not sufficient to evoke ethnic mobilization. Instead, mobilization is best predicted when there is a serious immediate threat to shared vital interests, coupled with the perception of new opportunities and the development of expanded resources. Stable misery contrasts with hopeful aspiration; relative deprivation and hope are more potent than absolute deprivation and despair. Although not yet subjected to rigorous analysis, the influence of *speed of change* can be seen in many cases. Grievances of ethnonationalists and indigenous peoples rise with the rapidity of state expansion. The sudden relaxation of state repression in the former Soviet Union was followed by an "explosion" of violent interethnic conflicts and violent attempted secessions. Abrupt imposition of new state controls arouses separatist movements (e.g., Sri Lanka's government policies toward Tamils). *Rapid* transition from autocracy to democracy is dangerous. Lost autonomy is a potent source of independence movements. Rapid immigration tends to increase anti-foreign and nationalistic political activity. Recent violence, as compared with earlier violence, is a better predictor of subsequent violence. In these instances and in many others, the rapidity of change appears to have strong effects, over and above those to be expected from cross-sectional correlations of presumed causes and posited outcomes. Rapid change unsettles expectations and relationships among ethnies, and sharpens perceptions of cultural differences and group positions, thus increasing the likelihood of mobilizations.

Other basic processes affecting the possibilities of mobilization involve the roles of elites in inciting ethnic conflicts or in reducing them. Just as ethnic politicians and other leaders can help to bring about the mobilization of their own supporters, so can such leaders act to demobilize their opponents and potential opponents. The leader who wants to use the ethnic issue to maintain or gain power needs to radicalize his potential supporters and to render ineffective the moderate, accommodative portions of the politically relevant populace. Analysis of the events in Yugoslavia that led up to civil war show that Milošević and his cadres succeeded in silencing and dispersing protests by "pro-democracy" elements within Serbia (Gagnon 1994/1995). And while ethnic manipulation by political entrepreneurs seeking to hold or gain power can accentuate cleavages and incite collective violence, in contrast, other kinds of leaders can help to reduce and restrain tensions. Thus elites in the North Caucasus and in Dagestan made strong efforts to suppress potential inter-ethny violence in the wake of civil war in Chechnya (Garb 1996). Always one needs to closely trace the *intra*-ethnic processes that affect interethnic relations. Similarly, the possibilities of ethnic mobilization directed toward states often hinge upon changes in state policies. Particularly striking are changes in state coercion.

The effects of state coercion of restive ethnies are likely to vary not only with the extent and intensity (severity) of repressive measures, but also with timing and sequencing, and with the character of the social movement generated within the ethny. Maximum short-term suppression of dissent, it would seem, would be effected if coercion were sharply applied early in the development of protest and then followed by continuous surveillance and punishment—that is, the classic scenario of "state terror." On the other hand, vacillating and apparently capricious coercion applied to a full-blown protest movement appears likely to provoke backlash and escalation—perhaps especially so if the repressive measures are perceived, as is likely, as indiscriminate and wholly disproportionate to the level of protest. A third hypothetical pattern would be sporadic and/or localized sanctions of greatly varying intensity that are imposed at irregular intervals all along the developing course of ethnic mobilization. This pattern seems a reasonably close approximation to that followed by southern U.S. states against the African-American civil rights movement, and by Israeli authorities in the early phases of the Palestinian Intifada.

Severe repression of a disaffected ethny whose disadvantages have been imposed by force typically will increase grievances and reinforce a shared sense of identity and group position at the same time that it reduces the immediate possibilities of successful protest. Yet it is too simple to assume that severe repression uniformly affects dissent and protest. Especially when there are strong commitments, and dense and diverse networks that had been formed prior to pervasive repression, new and drastic repression can actually incite mobilization. In response to "disappearances," torture, and killings, the bereaved and their relatives and friends may conclude that only high-risk opposition is an acceptable course of action (cf. Loveman 1998 on the emergence of human rights movements under military dictatorships in Latin America).

Two useful reminders have been emphasized by White and White (1995): (1) *all* states are repressive in greater or lesser degrees (including democratic/liberal states), and (2) official, high-level state repression often differs from and may be less than repression by individual low-level/local agents and those they incite or encourage by example. State troops and police who are physically threatened often overreact; militias, paramilitary groups, and death squads often engage in unrestrained violence. Accordingly, domestic violence can escalate beyond the bounds of formal state policy, sometimes becoming essentially uncontrollable, as in Colombia's *la violencia*, in the civil war in Rwanda, in some instances of ethnic warfare in Bosnia-Hercegovina, and in many cases of failed and collapsed states.

In severely repressive centralized states, once central control loosens but grievances remain high, there are grounds for protests and the opportunity to mount public displays. The typical result is a volatile mixture of partial repression and uneasy turmoil (see Taagepera 1993, 160–61).

Opportunities and Constraints: State Actions and Interstate Influences

The world-system of national states has created incentives and pressures for nationalistic ethnic mobilization, since the state is the primary means for making claims and resisting domination in the international arena. Within states, furthermore, laws, judicial actions, and administrative policies define ethnic boundaries and shape interethnic relations. In particular, when ethnies are concentrated in different geographic regions of a territorial state, even non-ethnic centralized decisions are likely to have differing impacts on ethnic interests, thus increasing the likelihood of the framing of mobilization in ethnic terms (cf. Nielsen 1985, 143).

The sheer complexity of such ethnoregional cases has been displayed for us in a real-world laboratory of peaceful secession in a modern state. Immediately after the 1989 collapse of Communism in Czechoslovakia, tensions between Slovaks and Czechs began to threaten political stability, and were primary factors in the later breakup of the state. Other ethnic tensions involving Moravians, Hungarians, Gypsies, and Ukrainians/Ruthenians also emerged. Although collective violence did not occur, leaders of the main ethnic collectivities strongly disagreed on power sharing, economic policies, and many other concrete issues. Initially, Slovakia was far less "modern" than the Czech regions, although the inequalities had been greatly reduced under Communism. But increased levels of urbanization, education, and industrialization not only did not reduce Slovak dissatisfaction, they rather provided potential resources for social mobilization when the transition to a market economy proved especially painful to Slovakia. Under the pervasive uncertainty of the transition from Communism, mass dissatisfaction was then channeled by nationalistic leaders, who in a post-1989 era had new freedom of action. Mobilization by ethnonationalistic appeals helps to explain this otherwise anomalous case of secession.

Most of the social science literature on mobilization focuses on actions by partisans—ethnies and their leaders. This is mobilization "from the bottom up." But it is clear that there also can be mobilization from the top down when authorities actively endorse, encourage, agitate, finance, and organize ethnic-based movements against substate ethnies. State instigation, guidance, and support have been evident in a long series of violent events—pogroms against Jews in Czarist Russia, campaigns against ethnic separatists in Aceh and East Timor in Indonesia, ethnic expulsion and democide in Bosnia and Kosovo, and in Rwanda. Just as there can be state-activated mobilization, there can be state-imposed demobilization when protest movements are harassed, blocked, fragmented, and silenced by state actions. Actions include censorship and closure of media, closing schools, imprisoning leaders, spreading rumors, bribing dissidents, increasing surveillance through informers and secret police, firing employees, and so on through a familiar list.

Ethnic mobilization often has been analyzed as if it were wholly explicable as a process internal to a particular state-society. But in fact many ethnic mobilizations are conflicts that have been strongly affected by interstate influences, ranging from encouragement to material aid to intervention. Further, there is international mobilization—as in the cases of Kurds,

Cypriots, Tamil Eelam, and many others—in which a struggle-group seeks outside aid, or a diaspora supports co-ethnics across national borders. As the case of the Tamil separatist movement shows, "the extension of ethnic conflicts beyond national boundaries is not merely due to instrumental factors [interests] ... or affective factors such as kinship bonds" (Pinnawala 1992, 14). Such extension also represents purposive organization and concentrated influence by ethnic representatives abroad.

As we have seen, structures of open political opportunity increase the likelihood that disaffected ethnies will choose nonviolent strategies over collective violence, if only because of the prospects of gains within the system. But the other side of the matter is that open political opportunities are the prerogatives of strong states—those with the ability to permeate the society, to collect taxes, and to hold the allegiance of military and police forces. Accordingly, such states are able to offer rewarding political allegiance and are not highly vulnerable to an ethnic attempt at secession or rebellion. At the same time, a disaffected minority faces exceedingly high costs if it relies primarily on violence. Thus in democratic systems both potential rewards and potential costs point in the direction of nonviolent protests and negotiated change.

Transitions to and from autocratic and democratic political systems typically arouse opposing claims, uncertainties, and fears. The breakdown of nascent democratic arrangements, often through a military coup d'état as in the 1994 Nigerian case, with the consequent rule by junta or one-party dominance, usually means suppression of dissent and exclusion of defeated ethnies from voice or access. Even what might be expected to be a benign transition from autocracy (often, ethnocracy) to a more responsible and accessible democratic regime is fraught with possible conflicts. In well-established democracies having protection of minority rights, the payoffs are promising for ethnic contenders willing to use nonviolent advocacy, protest, and negotiation. In contrast, the democratization of an authoritarian polity opens numerous opportunities for ambitious groups and their ethnic entrepreneurs to mobilize for both protest and rebellion. As mobilization develops and issues become defined, communal groups are likely to meet increasing resistance from the state or other ethnies. In this escalatory phase, there is a built-in tendency to increase the intensity and/or scope of demands and claims. To the extent that hard bargaining continues—or even just the continuation of a commitment to a particular oppositional strategy—"self-sustaining conflict dynamics tend to develop: fighting groups and their opponents get locked into action-reaction sequences from which it is difficult to escape" (Gurr 1993a, 189).

If this is true, why is it so? Escalation can develop not only from the interaction of the engaged collective opponents, but also—and often primarily—from the internal dynamics of each of the adversaries. To retain credibility with their constituencies, ethnic leaders must not appear to be "too soft," to be making excessive concessions. Challengers to current leaders typically bring charges of selling out, of weakness or gullibility. An oft-observed result is a gladiatorial contest in which the more moderate leaders lose to those who espouse more extreme demands. Studies of social movements have long pointed to the self-sustaining process of conflict and conflict escalation. Ongoing conflict is a vortex into which are drawn desires for revenge and a variety of opportunistic motives for economic, sexual, and political gains. Into the vortex of mobilization and violence are also drawn ideological commitments, the "sunk capital" of ethnic killers (e.g., suspected war criminals), continuing in-group pressures, and closure of opportunities for peaceful careers. Thus Esman (1994, 31) observes, "Mobilization seldom occurs spontaneously: once underway, however, it may activate and radicalize impatient, violence-prone, even criminal elements whose actions cannot be controlled or disciplined by the leaders of the community or of its factions and for whom violence may become a form of self-justifying behavior, even a way of life." In various ways, these processes of escalating violent mobilization have been prominent in the cases of the Islamic Jihad, Hamas, and Hezbollah in the Middle East; in Rwanda and Burundi; in Kashmir; among Tamil rebels in Sri Lanka; in the south of Sudan; and, much earlier, in *la violencia* in Colombia. At the extreme, self-perpetuating violence produces state collapse, war-lordism, banditry, and factional fighting—thus, "chaos." The original aims of mobilization can be lost in these processes.

Major Interpretations and Theories of Mobilization

One of the most complete general schemes for describing mobilization has been given by Gurr (1993b). It outlines predisposing conditions, including a strong sense of collective identity and substantial group cohesion, collective disadvantages (economic, political, cultural), and opportunity versus repressive control by the state. Prior cultural differences along with rivalry or conflict with other culturally distinct groupings tend to strengthen group identity. Disadvantages, discrimination, and past repressive controls create both persisting and active grievances. Strong identity and shared grievances tend to lead to the emergence of leaders and of initial core activists. Given some minimal political opportunities, either within a democratic regime or in a situation of relaxation of prior control, the likelihood of mobilization increases. Violent protest often is an early response to a sudden collapse of severe repression, but in "open" regimes nonviolent means are more likely. When an autocratic state attempts severe repression against a highly mobilized collectivity, ethnic or not, the odds increase for violent conflict—which may, in turn, lead to stalemate, victory of one side, succession, autonomy, or revolution (cf. Gurr and Harff 1994).

The background factors of disadvantage and grievances have their strongest influence in the early stages of mobilization, as a nascent social movement struggles with the start-up problem. Once mobilization has passed some phase of critical mass, the course of events will become increasingly shaped by state responses; by external aid to one party or another; by diffusion and contagion from other external movements; and by leadership, organization, and the interplay of strategies and tactics between the mobilized ethny and its opponents.

On the whole, institutionalized democracies that follow accommodative policies will have many protests but few violent conflicts, whereas autocratic regimes that suddenly lose central control or abruptly "democratize" are likely to encounter collective violence—a pattern repeatedly experienced in the former Soviet Union. Analysis (Beissinger 1991) of 2,347 nonviolent protest demonstrations and 329 violent collective actions in the USSR from 1965 to 1989 revealed striking differences in mobilization and outcomes. Nonviolent protests were less frequent in situations of open opportunity *and* in rigidly controlled conditions, but violent actions were relatively independent of the extent of political opportunities. Collective violence was most frequent among people with little or no experience in a democratic state, who had strong grievances but could command few organizational resources. In these circumstances, "picking up the gun" may be a readier option than prolonged protests and negotiations. In a later analysis, Beissinger (2002) shows that nonviolent protests, primarily nationalistic or ethnic, rose rapidly in the years preceding and during the effective collapse of central Soviet authority (1987–91) and then declined. Such protests were frequent in the Baltic States (Estonia, Latvia, Lithuania), in the Ukraine, and in other parts of Eastern Europe. In contrast, violent protests erupted in 1991 and 1992 as the Soviet Union disintegrated, and centered upon questions of territorial control among the former republics.

The low correlation found by Beissinger between nonviolent and violent protests is consistent with Gurr's report (1993a, 178) that "communal protest" and "rebellion" are only very slightly correlated ($r = .136$). A recurrent sequence is that violence follows a long period of nonviolent activities that were repressed or disregarded.

An important line of theory-building has focused upon macro-structural conditions—the level of "high politics." Among the main concepts in this approach is the idea of political opportunity structure. Components of political opportunity structure include the following: openness or closure of the polity (voice, exit), repressive capabilities of state actors, elite dissent, presence of allies or supporters, and the stability of political alignments (Tarrow 1988, 429). Thus, for example, a recurrent hypothesis is that non-institutional protest is rarely a visible strategy in extremely closed systems, whereas protest in fully open systems is unnecessary. Accordingly, protest is most likely at intermediate levels of accessibility and responsiveness, where the polity is relatively flexible and vulnerable to the demands of excluded groupings (Eisinger 1973, 28).

State structures, policies, and political parties constitute a major part—sometimes nearly all—of the political opportunity structures that repress, permit, encourage, or divert and co-opt social movements. Variations in protest movements across national states are, therefore, directly linked to the social spaces created by such opportunity structures (Jenkins and Klandermans 1995). Opportunities or the lack of them are most important in the early formation of protest movements, becoming less so as the organization and its strategies and tactics develop (McAdam, McCarthy, and Zald 1996).

In addition to states and parties, there are the constraining or facilitating actions of transnational ethnies, of other national states, and of international bodies. Less evident, however, is the additional scope afforded to intrastate ethnic movements by declines in state nationalism, especially in Europe and North America. To the extent that state sovereignty is being eroded by international agencies such as the European Union, United Nations, World Trade Organization, and by economic globalization, the way is cleared for new claims by both indigenous and political counter-movements. The increasing permeability of states to external influences that are linked to ethnic issues—from boycotts and other economic sanctions (South Africa, Burma) to peace-enforcing UN intervention—means that opportunity can no longer be thought of as restricted to intrastate conditions.

Still other outstanding conceptualizations of macro-conditions affecting mobilization include the modernization scenarios or models of ethnic change that gained wide currency in the mid-twentieth century. These schemes visualized ethnicity as being eroded or diluted by marketization, industrialization, and urbanization. The result was thought to be increased geographic and social mobility, increased cross-ethnic interaction, and greater economic interdependence—all leading to nation building and the diminution of ethnic exclusiveness. In contract, a reactive or "internal colonialism" model conceived of ethnic persistence in "developed" societies as the outcome of a cultural division of labor, most clearly seen in the dominance of a center over peripheral regions (Hechter 1975). This model's distinctiveness rested on the insight that more than common economic interest was needed for political mobilization. The alternative "ethnic competition" scheme posits that *lack* of separate economic niches results in *individual* competition (e.g., for jobs), which in an unexplained fashion becomes *group* competition (Leifer 1981). Neither approach dealt adequately with the prior question: why are there ethnic collectivities in the first place?

Similarly, there are two major contrasting explanations of ethnic resurgence in industrialized societies (Nielsen 1985, 133–34). The *reactive-ethnicity* model singles out ethnic solidarity as a reaction of a disadvantaged, culturally distinctive periphery against a dominant center. On the other hand, the *competition* model looks to the breakdown of formerly separate ethnic niches, so that individuals still carrying ethnic markers compete for the same scarce values of jobs, markets, resources, political power, prestige, and other rewards. Both approaches evidently have varying explanatory power in different times and settings. Neither has dealt with the overarching framework of state authority, particularly with the resurgence of ethnic cleavages and violent conflict when central state authority so drastically weakens that it can no longer be relied upon for protection and security. Indeed, the geopolitical processes that have produced many failed and collapsed states were background causes for prominent oppositional movements, as in the former Soviet Union, the former Yugoslavia, South Asia, and sub-Saharan Africa. Not just discontent nor resource mobilization, but state weakness has been a primary condition for successful anti-state movements (Waller 1992, 43–44).

Underlying the relatively concrete formulations thus far reviewed are certain more abstract generalizing concepts and schemata.[1] One whole family of this kind consists of "evolutionary" theories that look back, as it were, to sociobiological bases of ethnicity. In the present context, these theories would predict behaviors that give priority to kin-based survival and reciprocal altruism. Interpretations from this perspective emphasize the importance of dense interaction and kin-linked symbolism in ethnic mobilization, and readily grant the importance of rivalry for power and scarce resources, as implied by evolutionary strategies of inclusive fitness (van den Berghe 1987).

A second type of conceptualization may be called "institutional." Interpretations in this mode emphasize values and norms, as emergents of ongoing interaction, which in turn have selective and directive influences on future behavior. In terms of mobilization theories, this approach pays special attention to vested interests and to contrasting principles of allocation and authority. It is alert to processes of relative deprivation and changes in group position.

---

[1] I am indebted to James March for the basic idea here of three broad types of social theories.

A third group of theories are "instrumental." These look forward to the consequences of action, and are most clearly seen in what is now known as the rational choice approach. This family of theories actually is quite diverse in the assumptions that are accepted, such as to what extent and how ethnic collective action is rational; what the sources are of actors' preferences, beliefs, values, and norms; and how ethnic boundaries are constructed and maintained. In the most austere or simplified form, actors are assumed to act rationally to maximize or "satisfice" their individual interests; accordingly, "private" or special incentives have to be supplied to induce participation in collective actions (Olson 1965). In later and more complex versions, attention is paid to shared preferences, including group identification, and to the development of social norms (Hardin 1995; Lichbach 1995).

Whatever their basic assumptions, however, all theories of mobilization have to cope with two great explanatory problems: (1) the question of how it is possible to initiate collective mobilization in spite of its costs and risks to individuals, that is, the *start-up problem,* and (2) the dilemma of collective action, otherwise known as the *free rider problem.*

The start-up problem, as well as the free rider problem, are unsolvable in a hypothetical world of self-interested, rational individuals acting to maximize their immediate rewards. Neither problem, however, exists in that extreme form in a real world of socialized persons who are embedded in long-term relationships within continuing social groups of interdependence and mutual identifications and solidarities. These conditions exist in many kinship groups, stable local communities, religious orders, military units, and ethnic collectivities. The virtue of game-theory analysis—analyses of strategic interactions of individual actors—is that they bring out clearly the sheer logic of rational, utility-maximizing (or optimizing) interactions.

The Start-Up Problem

The mobilizations we are here considering are collective actions that produce public goods, such as official recognition of a language, which, once attained, are accessible to an entire population—individuals cannot be excluded because they did not contribute. A second defining feature of public goods is jointness of supply: the average costs decrease as the number of "consumers" (participants) increases. These two features signify that initial participants bear heavy costs and that the threat of free riding is always present (Heckathorn 1996). All mobilization efforts face the start-up problem. How can individuals be induced to take risks and make sacrifices to initiate collective action? Mobilization has costs—often very high costs for the vanguard volunteers in social movements. Those who bear those costs in the interest of collective gains may find that nonparticipants share the rewards as free riders. If individual short-term rationality prevails, how can contributors to collective action be elicited without selective incentives (side payments)? These problems seemed unsolvable within the framework of private rational choice theory. But there are several routes of escape from the two dilemmas: early vanguard commitments, social networks, group identifications, and momentum from early success.

A first clue is the well-observed fact that social movements typically start with very small clusters of individuals who show strong commitments to a cause—commitments that can arise from a great variety of motives: one observes idealists, adventurers, persons traumatized by persecution and bereavement, those imbued with a passion for revenge, and early activists recruited through personal loyalties. These committed cadres can become the vanguard of a movement. Uniformity of motivations is not a requirement. What *is* necessary?

A second insight has been the recognition that mobilization, or more generally any collective action, depends not just on the strength of collective interests, but on "the network of social ties that channel the necessary chain reactions" (Macy 1991, 735). Certainly it is well known that preexisting social ties facilitate recruitment into religious groups, interest groups, and a variety of social movements, and that linkages across localized clusters of interaction facilitate coordination in the pursuit of collective goals. Macy's simulations demonstrate that serial actions—in which each potential participant looks at what others are doing—differ greatly from parallel actions by independent actors (1991, 1993). Indeed, serial actions can create the coordination needed to escape from a noncooperative equilibrium, whereas separate decisions by rational actors can cause failures of collective action.

Individuals are not moved to participate in protest activity or collective rebellion simply as separate individuals who are making egocentric calculations. They "decide," whether deliberately or not, as committed members of groups and as parties in social relationships (Goldstone 1998, 840–41). Their actions are embedded in networks and have consequences for other persons as well as for the self. (Even the suicide bomber must know that his/her actions may bring glory or great harm to family and friends.) The early contributors to social movements take risks and make sacrifices when success is uncertain. Typically they are not isolated individuals, but members of small, densely connected networks. (Later followers will be more loosely interconnected.) The tight network allows stable interactions among activists—which in turn enhance commitment and sense of identity. At the same time, the network insulates the activists from the nonparticipants (the "defectors"). This "ideological envelope" permits the intensification of militancy and the diffusion of activism to ambient populations (Kim and Bearman 1997, 84–85).

Within the early vanguard, commitment and loyalty have been established by self-selection and selective recruitment. As the number of participants grows, the average cost of involvement goes down because the "sunk costs" have already been paid—the costs of creating the initial organization, assembling resources, and absorbing deprivations and assaults. As intragroup norms develop, as they will, the social rewards of participation increase, and negative sanctions by fellow participants increase the costs to individuals of their own slack performance and outright defection. In this way continuing collective efforts provide tests of membership, helping to eliminate or reclaim the free riders and disloyals—the "summer soldiers and the sunshine patriots."

Also important is the oft-unnoticed phenomenon of the second-order choice of rewarding or punishing the first-level cooperators and defectors. Here, as Heckathorn (1996) has demonstrated, conformity to group norms may be enforced not only by the full cooperators, but also by the hypocritical cooperators, who have not themselves contributed to the attainment of any collective goals but who are motivated to sanction others for noncooperation.

Of course, it must be emphasized that the effects of network density differ greatly in different contexts of interest, resources, centrality, and power. For example, increased density of linkages may blur distinctions between cooperators and defectors (Macy 1991) and increase the influence of peripheral actors (Gould 1993). Nevertheless, in those settings in which committed and central actors initiate action ("privileged" and "rebellious" regimes), dense networks of activists are required to create the conditions for successful collective action (Kim and Bearman 1997, 90–91). All else being equal, an ethny's capability for mobilization is greater the more extensive, dense, and strong is its network of organizations and personal ties. As one of many examples, in the 1960s the struggle for civil rights by African Americans, a major asset was the overlapping of dense networks of religious groupings and other supportive organizations (Morris 1984; Jaynes and Williams 1989). Again, small-group solidarity, coordinated by local organizations, formed an essential basis for the Parisian revolt in the 1871 Commune. An earlier uprising had been primarily class-based, but in the 1871 Commune mixed-class neighborhoods showed strong solidarity among near-dwellers who had a common history of opposition to the central government (Gould 1995).

In summary, dense networks with strong ties of kinship, friendship, local religious group membership, or durable neighborhood relationships form supportive and conformity-inducing social settings for collective action. Such networks can also insulate their members from external influences and can provide secrecy for dangerous enterprises. Mutual monitoring of individuals' behavior helps to ensure trust and accountability; deceptive or wavering commitment is easily detected, as are informers and agents of external adversaries.

Yet if such strongly connected localized networks lack connections to larger organizations and extended networks, they can be immobilized and overwhelmed by pervasive and severe state repression. For insulation can also mean isolation—that is, lack of access to funds, information, public support, national and international political influence, and other resources. Clusters of solidarity in resistance to state impositions or threats from other political actors are highly vulnerable unless they are linked to larger social entities, such as religious organizations, political parties, labor unions, or international governmental and nongovernmental organizations concerned with human rights. These external agencies can supply essential resources and some degree of security to social movements that challenge incumbent power holders in repressive regimes (Loveman 1998, 484–55). In some instances, as in the reactions to the "dirty war" repression in Argentina in the 1970s, international publicity for demonstrations by families of victims dramatized the tortures and disappearances of regime opponents. Heightened international exposure, together with the activities of "watchdog" nongovernmental organizations and prominent individuals, created an umbrella of protection for the protesters as the governmental regime became more sensitive to external opinion (cf. Perruzotti 1996). Over time, the protests undermined the legitimacy of the repressive regime and helped to create popular demands for accountability of state agents and for a constitutional state, bound by the rule of law.

Aside from suppression by pervasive intimidation and force, an initially promising critical mass may fail to gain a sufficient following because of its isolation. In general, the potential for mobilization will be greater the more a disaffected social formation has positive ties with other groupings that can be brought into alliances against a common adversary (Barkey 1991).

The Free Rider Problem

Network structures and vanguard formations by themselves, however, still do not solve the free rider dilemma, the problem of individuals and subgroups benefiting from the collective effort without sharing the burdens. The attempted solution of offering selective benefits to active participants is limited because the larger the proportion of free riders, the greater the collective costs to those offering the special benefits. Since ethnic mobilizations seek to create public goods such as collective respect and prestige or cultural autonomy, private incentives are inadequate tools that cannot be decisive for sustaining large-scale mobilization.

We have seen that the start-up problem can be surmounted by the identification and organization of a critical mass of committed volunteers—committed to the movement either because of selective incentives (whatever the source) or of dedication to collective values and goals. Such a vanguard's initial successes can induce a cascade of further recruitments of the less committed by increasing the rewards and spreading the shared costs. The second main solution to the problem of collective action is implicit in the "vanguard" approach. Generalized to a larger mass, the indispensable condition is *group identification*, such that individuals derive a sense of efficacy and psychological reward from successful *collective* action in the attainment of *group* objectives (see Marwell and Oliver 1993).

But this formulation begs the question of how these "psychological rewards" can be generated. Part of the answer lies in the intrinsic gratifications of social participation, of approval, of esteem, of a sense of personal worth, of a conviction of a duty fulfilled. But how could these incentives be maintained if there is no likelihood that the endeavor will ever be sustained? True, some individuals may so value the public good that they will participate even if nonparticipants will gain a cost-free benefit. And, to be sure, if a critical mass of such volunteers can be mobilized, their initial efforts may make the collective enterprise increasingly attractive to the laggards, as costs to individuals are reduced and the odds of success go up (Marwell and Oliver 1993).

A basic problem remains in this scenario: participation is still dependent upon individuals deciding that *their own* efforts and sacrifices will make a worthwhile increase in the likelihood of attainment of the collective goal. But since individual contributions go into a common pool, they lose a specific identity, and in any case, in large-scale movements the individual contribution will be small and difficult to appraise. A key to a more complete explanation for successful mobilization is Macy's (1994, 664) observation that volunteers who are primarily interested in the public good rather than in private credit will base their crucial sense of efficacy upon the *success of the collective action itself.* Thus it can happen that small and resource-poor ethnic movements can mobilize and successfully challenge powerful opponents by the chain-reaction impact of the initial successes of a devoted cadre upon potential supporters, and can maintain the movement by group identifications and the increasing net rewards created by the internal dynamics of the collective enterprise.

This chapter has surveyed how ethnies mobilize. In the next chapter we ask how in some places and at some times mobilization leads to violent conflict, whereas in other settings it leads to nonviolent outcomes.

CHAPTER SEVEN

From Mobilization to Violent Conflict

Mobilization does not necessarily lead to conflict. The most likely immediate action for a mobilized ethny in a relatively permissive political environment is to voice its claims through nonviolent means of petition, lobbying, negotiations, voting, demonstrations, marches, and numerous other forms of peaceful political action (see Sharp 1973 for the many varieties of nonviolent political action). Even if mobilization does lead to obstructive and punitive actions, the outcome need not be deadly; aggressive actions may consist of damaging property, defacing symbols, obstructing movement of people and goods, denying access to public buildings, or occupying factories and other workplaces. Such collective actions always run the risk of becoming more deadly and of instigating violence from opponents; however, in societies with institutionalized channels for protest and with strong legal and customary norms against physical aggression, there is a definite barrier between relatively peaceful encounters and mass killings. When that barrier is crossed, a new dynamic is unleashed as the former normative order is breached (cf. Horowitz 2001, 539). As noted in Chapter 5, nonviolent protests and violent rebellions in fact are only very weakly correlated. Violent collective conflicts involve the ultimate stakes for individuals of killing or being killed. There is a radical difference between situations where dominant social norms forbid, and provide sanctions against, killing, as over against a situation in which the killing of individuals in an opposing collectivity is categorically accepted (and often regarded as obligatory). Not individual motives but collective processes are at issue.

A crucial question is how the restraints and understandings of ordinary social life are breached. The pathways are many and complex by which ethnies may move from political inaction to mobilization and then to protests and then, in some crucial cases, to collective violent conflict. The following propositions outline some of the main interacting processes in that long sequence.

1. First, *ethnic identity* must become prominent and consequential for the ethny's members. It ceases to be merely one of many identities; it comes to stand out against the background. Such ethnic salience will be greater the more the ethny's members are subjected to negative stereotyping and discrimination; especially important will be the imposition by a ruling state of a categorical definition of membership, and of accompanying discriminatory practices that create important disadvantages. More generally, external threats from the state or from other ethnies strongly increase ethnic salience. Short of the more drastic threats, economic competitions and political rivalry enhance awareness of identity and of its consequences.

2. Yet salience alone does not signify ethnic solidarity, arising from a shared sense of membership and a common fate and increasing mutual defense and mutual aid. *Ethnic solidarity* will be increased, all other conditions being equal, by the following conditions: territorial concentration and ethnic segregation; high importance of kinship ties within the ethnic population; concentration of fellow ethnies in distinctive occupations and economic niches; high intragroup density of social interaction, ranging from workplace associations and neighborhood visiting to intragroup marriages; low rates of interaction with other ethnies; and high levels of cultural homogeneity. All these factors work in the direction of in-group closure and out-group distancing and exclusion.

3. In its turn, *ethnic mobilization* will be more likely: the greater the salience and solidarity, the more intense and widely shared the grievances, the more extensive and available the infrastructure of communication and transportation, the higher the level of collective aspirations, and the more that the ethny has experienced loss of prior autonomy.

4. *The political opportunity structure* is expected to have the following effects: (a) the greater the degree of democracy, the less likely civil wars or other mass violence, but the more frequent nonviolent protests; (b) the greater unilateral foreign aid to the state and to its ethnic challengers, the longer the conflict and the greater the casualties; (c) short of massive, "overwhelming," and sustained use of force by the state against ethnic insurgents, the greater will be violent resistance to violent state suppression; (d) both protests and violent insurgency will be most likely in periods of rapid sociopolitical transitions. In such periods, violent collective insurgency will be favored by state weakness and vacillating

policies in the context of a high level of collective grievances felt by solidarity ethnies, especially when efforts are made by the state to impose new severe suppression; (e) peaceful ethnic efforts to secure protection and advantages are most likely in relatively open political systems that have leaders who are experienced in negotiation and compromise.

The very idea of an "ethnic nation" in the setting of newly created multiethnic states may well be seen as a "permanent provocation" for war (Ayoob 1996, 45); however, multiple ethnies within a territorial state obviously can live together without fighting. And even when violent ethnic conflicts do occur, they do not invariably lead to separatist movements. Whether ethnic cleavages will lead to violent secessionist struggles—as in Sudan, Nigeria, Sri Lanka, and Eritrea in Ethiopia—depends upon a confluence of such factors as prior colonial policies, efforts of new states to erase ethnic diversity, presence of strong ethnoreligious regimes, and a regional environment of support or opposition (Mayall and Simpson 1992, 9–10). Mobilization that otherwise might have led simply to peaceable political claims and negotiated settlements can be turned into violent conflicts by misguided state action.

Types of Conflictual Outcomes

As earlier chapters have emphasized, ethnic-based conflicts vary greatly all the way from local and sporadic vandalism, brawling, and episodic attacks over to riots, pogroms, and mass communal violence, and then may move to highly organized rebellion, civil war, and finally to democide and genocide. In all this motley profusion, several major types of ethnically based structural conflicts can be distinguished, according to the different collective actors that confront one another: states versus ethnies, ethnies versus states, and ethnies versus ethnies. First are the cases (Type 1) in which a state controlled by a dominant ethny engages in severe repression of another ethny, such as prohibiting language use or religious observances, imposing drastic political and economic discrimination, or expelling and massacring the people. Prominent recent examples include the Sinhalese government's treatment of the Tamil minority, the Islamic/Arab state's treatment of the southern Sudanese, and the Yugoslavian/Serbian violence in Bosnia and Kosovo. Second, there are "communal" conflicts (Type 2) in direct confrontations between ethnies (and their armed groups), as in mass violence between Muslims and Hindus in India at the time of partition and at many later times, or in the protracted conflicts in the collapsed states of Liberia and Zaire. In such situations, violence ranges from sporadic and diffuse rioting, through organized pogroms, to all-out civil warfare. A third type (Type 3) is that of ethnic rebellion against a state that claims authority to rule over the ethnic challenger. The typical cases are autonomy-seeking or secessionist movements that challenge an encompassing territorial state. Almost all recent instances arose in reaction to the state impositions of Type 1, such as the attempted secession of Biafra from Nigeria, of Tamil Eelam from Sri Lanka, of Kosovo from Yugoslavia, and of Chechnya from the Russian Federation.

From extensive case studies, Horowitz (1985) reported that "backward" (disadvantaged) groupings in disadvantaged (poor, peripheral) regions frequently tend to be early secessionists. Cases include Karens in Myanmar, Nagas in India, Moros in the Philippines, Hmong (Meo) of Laos, and Dayaks of Borneo. Conquests and state building have left many ethnies with little hope of advancement within the state and little commitment to it on ethnic grounds. Given some prospect of viable separate existence, such ethnies often seek "exit." In contrast, most recent secessions in Europe, and many in the former Soviet Union, were relatively "advanced" nationalities seeking escape from a burdensome state of which they had been a reluctant part. Ethnic cohesion and past autonomy reduce the importance of economic differentials or discrimination as a factor in inducing separatism (Heraclides 1991, 19). The single best predictor of separatist movements is former autonomy or independence that has been lost, especially in the recent past (Gurr 2000, 71). Autonomy or separation is most likely to succeed in very strong or very weak states (Gurr 2000, 82). Because states typically resist secession, separatist movements often are a potent source of intrastate violence.

The range of types of collective conflicts can be usefully illustrated further by a brief review of three other examples: ethnic ("communal") riots (from Type 2, above), coups d'état (limited violence), and guerrilla warfare (Type 3).

Ethnic-based Coups d'État

A distinctive form of intrastate conflict is the military coup—the "irregular transfer of a state's chief executive by the regular armed forces or internal security forces through the use (or threat) of force" (Jenkins and Kposowa 1990, 861). Such events are frequent: from 1900 to 1976, some 81 states experienced one or more coups (counting 20 percent that were nonmilitary) and from 1946 to 1970, 174 coups were reported in 59 states (Zimmerman 1980). Most coups involve little violence, primarily because they represent small numbers of persons and are brief. Coups do not necessarily require mass discontent—indeed, they typically are the work of small elites or factional groupings, often within particular military units or officer cliques. These "irregular" transfers of power are quite different from diffuse communal violence or from large-scale rebellions or secessionist movements (Jenkins and Kposowa 1990, 872). But in many cases the outcomes are so unstable that a rapid succession of see-saw coups may lead to ethnic dominance in a one-party regime. These coup-prone states are highly concentrated in particular countries and world regions; ethnic coups are especially prominent in the Middle East and in sub-Saharan Africa. Thus of 45 independent Black African states, between 1960 and 1982, nearly 90 percent experienced a military coup, an attempted coup, or a plot. As a result, in the late 1980s in 35 of those states, the central executive power was in military hands, and in most of the others the military forces were politically powerful (see summary in Williams 1994, 70).

What can account for the striking repetitions of these sudden shifts in control? In the case of Africa, a detailed analysis found little support for the "modernization" hypothesis that invoked the combination of weak states with increased political awareness and mobilization. Nor was there decisive evidence to support the idea that economic dependency upon "advanced" wealthier states was a major cause. What did predict the likelihood of coup-susceptibility was the combination of military centrality and intense rivalry among a few large ethnic grouping (Jenkins and Kposowa 1990). Especially potent was competition for control between the two largest ethnies within a multi-ethnic but strongly centralized state. As Horowitz (1985) has suggested, electoral contests in such situations between ethnic-based parties are likely to trigger a strong sense of threat among the members of an ethny facing electoral defeat. The fear, often realistic, is that the winning ethny will then force the loser into permanent subordination and exclusion.

Ethnic Riots

Communal ethnic riots represent a distinct type of violent ethnic conflict. They are sudden mass outbreaks by civilians—not by police or military forces—who attack the property and persons of others who are victimized solely on the basis of their ethnic membership (Horowitz 2001). The assaults typically are directed to a specific group or category of persons, and the violence is localized. Such outbreaks usually follow a precipitating incident, real or imagined, in which members of the out-group are said to have inflicted outrageous injury upon the in-group—rape, torture, killing, destruction of sacred symbols, and so on. Rumors of such violence spread rapidly. The subsequent attacks often give the appearance of mass frenzy—houses and cars are burned, victims are beaten and slashed; sexual mutilations are frequent.

Behavior in western urban riots has well illustrated major features of conflict dynamics. For example, studies of riots in Britain found two distinct types of participants—"rioters" and "looters." The rioters lived closer to the center of the disturbances, were older, more often Black, were more often those arrested for confronting the police. There was a core population of persons committed to protest and resistance, and a peripheral aggregate of individuals engaged in opportunistic actions under conditions of collective disorder (Keith 1993). Studies of riots ("civil disorders") in American cities find that the people involved engage in riot behavior in areas close to where they live—the issues may be translocal but such riots are locality-based. Interethnic ("interracial") clashes are especially likely in areas of residential succession where prior occupancy by one ethny is being displaced by the incursion of large numbers of a different ethny. In the case of the massive 1992 Los Angeles riots, the more rapid the immigration of a foreign-born population into areas previously largely inhabited by Black Americans, the more likely were fatalities (Bergesen and Herman 1998, 48). In that case the background was one of great ethnic inequality, severe poverty, large numbers of unemployed young males, a history of discrimination, and a succession of provocative incidents (Baldassare 1994). A consistent pattern in civil disturbances of this kind is that violence is set off by police raids or arrests, involving what are widely perceived as undue force, false arrests or harassment, and failure to protect ethnic minority persons and property. Although participants clearly act on the basis of numerous diverse motives and beliefs, a central focus is a sense that authorities are unfair and discriminatory. Police forces, as the front line in the state's attempted monopoly of legitimated violence, are a salient symbol of systems of differential privilege, opportunity, and dominance.

In many of these ferocious events, members of an ostensibly weaker ethny attack the stronger grouping—a curious fact, contrary to common sense. Close studies of such cases reveal several possible bases for the apparently anomalous behavior. The attacks may represent a continuation of traditional hostilities that periodically erupt in violence, including instances in which a politically and economically subordinate ethny seeks to establish an intimidating aggressive reputation. Not infrequently the contenders are allied with the different adversaries in an interstate war, or one or both receive support from co-ethnies in a neighboring state. Finally, a common pattern since World War II has been that the disadvantaged attack the advantaged as a way of building psychological strength and collective mobilization. As "redemption through violence," this phenomenon has been a prominent part of anti-colonial movements.

Of course, events that are called "riots" are not always what they appear to be, that is, spontaneous, unplanned, diffuse outbursts. Events wearing this surface visage may be, indeed, instigated and organized by governments or by translocal organizations, such as networks of militias or small cells of militants, linked by electronic mail, fax, telephone, and other means of rapid communication. So what may appear to be a localized event can have complex connections with states, political parties, and ethnoreligious movements. In a striking case, hundreds of militant Hindu partisans in December 1992 destroyed the mosque known as the Babri Masjid in Ayodhya, India. This highly organized public vandalism was followed by widespread violence, which briefly attracted worldwide attention. The event was often characterized as a manifestation of Hindu "fundamentalists" who wished to change India from a pluralistic democracy to a Hindu Raj—a polity defined by assertive religious rule, excluding Muslims and other non-Hindus (Bayly 1993). This interpretation was sharply challenged by Dirks (2001), and earlier had been placed in context by Larson (1995, 266–76), who described in detail the complex historical background of the so-called Ayodhya crises.

The controversy over the site of the Babri Masjid—whether a mosque or a Hindu temple—apparently was well developed by the eighteenth century, and armed conflict between Muslims and Hindus had occurred in the mid-nineteenth century. There was no resolution under the British rule, and after the partition of India and Pakistan a political and legal stalemate prevailed until the 1980s. At that point several conservative Hindu political groupings, including the Bharatiya Janata Party (BJP), were treating the simmering controversy as a live issue. In the complex political struggles from 1986 into the 1990s, the BJP rapidly gained influence. A national campaign was launched to collect bricks from persons all over India for building a temple on the site of the mosque. Some of the BJP's adherents, along with other Hindu nationalists, encouraged the mass assault that physically destroyed the Babri Masjid in 1992. Mass violence followed in many areas of India (Larson 1995).

This episode well illustrates how ethnoreligious issues and symbols can both engender and be used in political contestation in which mobilization is initiated "from the top down." It also shows that a so-called riot can reflect the many diverse cultural influences and shifting political alignments among politicized fractions of a large-scale ethnoreligious movement.

Guerrilla Warfare

In contrast to the focalized and limited character of coups d'état and to the communal confrontations of riots, guerrilla warfare of ethnies against one another or against the ruling state often are long-lived, persisting for decades. Once under way, widespread guerrilla movements supported by a favorable public and operating in familiar surroundings can frustrate much larger forces of a state that attempts to repress them. Few are quickly and decisively defeated.

Preceding chapters have described the deadly consequences of such

protracted conflict. Here we focus on the movement from limited and localized struggles to the larger and more lethal conflicts. What are the dynamics of this transformation?

Dynamics of Conflict

How can the great divide be crossed, from limited struggle to mass
slaughter? A short answer is that no one fully understands that fateful step.
Some reasonable inferences, however, can be made. First, we must discount the most evident possible factor: the availability of the means of destruction. It seems obvious to common sense that the worldwide flood
today of cheap and highly lethal weaponry would permit and encourage
mass killings. To repeat, over most of the globe, it is relatively easy to acquire assault rifles, mortars, machine guns, grenades and grenade launchers, shoulder-fired missiles, land mines, and (increasingly) materials for
producing chemical and biological weapons. Recycled weapons from prior
violence add to the abundance created by arms sales and transfers by states
and private dealers.

No doubt easy access to the World Arms Bazaar increases killing power.
But it surely cannot be a primary factor in the leap to ethnic carnage. Although the Hutu death groups in Rwanda had light arms, much of the
butchery was accomplished with knives, garden machetes, axes, and clubs.
In Liberia, Bosnia, Sudan, Sierra Leone, or with the Lord's Resistance
Army in Uganda, or with Hindu militants at Ayodhya—in case after case,
advanced technology has not been necessary.

Grievances

A much more significant factor is the character of the grievances that
impel ethnies into collective action. As Chapter 4 suggested in passing,
genuine grievances of the kind that favor collective protest or rebellion are
not merely deprivations or dissatisfactions. Rather, they always involve
some sense of violation of norms, some wrongfulness, some illegitimacy,
some breach of rules of proper conduct, some essential injustice. Indeed,
many people over long periods endure deprivations and frustrations without protest; some substantial level of chronic discontent probably can be
expected in any collective arrangement. What is crucial is that poverty or
inequality or social exclusion come to be seen by a whole collectivity as
wrong, and that a shared ideology develops in which the wrongfulness is
seen as being categorically imposed. Violent ethnic conflicts occur when a
cohesive grouping infused with such a systematic view encounters resistance that seems to preclude peaceful resolution. Protesters and rebels in

these circumstances believe that they are fighting for things that they deserve.

Elite Manipulation

A second enabling condition for deadly clashes is implicit in all of our preceding review: violence often is incited and organized by agents of states as a result of deliberate policies of ethnic dominance and the use of ethnic expulsions and massacres. We have said that these elite-managed campaigns are not possible without an initial base of widely accepted stereotypes and hostile presuppositions; equally, however, the cultural base often remains inert without state-led selection of targets and provocation for mass violence. Social movements on behalf of ethnic interests have been stimulated and organized in country after country by ambitious ethnic entrepreneurs and intelligentsia—teachers, civil servants, political ideologues, clergy, journalists, writers, lawyers, professors, media "personalities." With great regularity, newly resurgent or ethnogenic groupings turn out to be activated and led by aspiring elites—usually urbanized and relatively well educated—who feel themselves to be excluded from economic opportunities and political power or subject to unjustified discrimination and inequalities. Such elites formulate grievances as *communal-ethnic* rather than *class-based* or *individualized.* These aspiring leaders and cadres then often become catalysts in further ethnic mobilization (Fishman 1981).

Even as political manipulation of ethnic identities is evident in many violent conflicts, this cannot simply mean that gullible masses are duped into bloody internecine warfare on sheerly "imaginary" issues. There must be some minimal initial ethnic identities for manipulation to succeed. For the case of the former Yugoslavia:

> The seeds of ethnic cleansing did not mutate into reality in our own time. Its roots lie in the work of generations of nationalist ideologues, intellectuals, politicians, and clergy. . . . In Croatia, Serbia, and Slovenia, the "born again" nationalists among the communist leaders as well as in the academies, the universities, and the media all routinely declared that their people were threatened with cultural and even biological eradication (Job 1993, 53 and 60).

Nor, of course, are states alone in the mobilization for deadly conflict. Ethnic leaders at all levels from local to international always are tempted by, and many times use, all the devices of demonization to characterize ethnic opponents. As we have noted before, a frequent primary theme is that of the threat of being permanently subjugated, with all the deep resonances thereby invoked. Adversaries are depicted as terrorists, bandits, thugs, rapists, arsonists, murderers, demons, beasts; they are rats, lice, cockroaches, pigs, snakes—in all, not human and fearfully menacing. When effective, inflammatory propaganda both creates anxious insecurity and identifies a hateful and vulnerable target.

Over and over again one finds that militant ethnic movements gain much of their early impetus from intellectuals. Evidence for this initial importance of the intelligentsia comes from diverse settings around the world—in the independence movement in Canada (Québec), France (Brittany), Spain (Basques, Catalonia), Trinidad, Yugoslavia (Serbia, Kosovo), Nigeria, Sudan (militant Islam). A typical diagnosis: "The rise of a radical Islamist movement in Sudan was strictly an elite phenomenon, building slowly among university students and the professional and political class in Khartoom before and after independence" (Finnegan 1999, 67; see Deng 1995).

In Sri Lanka, the Buddhist monks and allied historians continually emphasized the superior value of Sinhalese civilization and advocated a theocratic state; it certainly is plausible that over the long run, they encouraged the intransigence of the state against Tamil demands for autonomy and, later, for independence (c.f. Tambiah 1986; de Silva and May 1991; Holsti 1996, 113).

Thus, many massive ethnic conflicts are preceded by the work of those who create ideological justifications for ethnic claims and further incite hostilities by advocating supremacy, claiming priorities and reiterating historicized wrongs and atrocities, pointing to past glories and dehumanizing ethnic opponents. Thus Hutu historians in Rwanda declared that Tutsis were a malignant cancer that must be destroyed (Chege 1996–97). Similar pronouncements preceded the civil wars in Yugoslavia, notably from the Serbian Academy of Sciences. In Sri Lanka, an ideology of Sinhalese superiority and priority of place was repeatedly promulgated in advance of the anti-Tamil discrimination and mob violence. Doctrines of separatism in Québec were formulated and widely advocated by teachers, publicists, and other intellectuals for years before major political actions.

And when words and images by themselves appear to be insufficient to activate and focus the desired antipathy, the tactics may turn to the provocateurs, such as arson and killings in Bosnian Muslim villages by Serbs dressed as Croats, or the employment of double agents within the organizations of an opposing ethny.

Newly militant nationalisms around the world are led by political entrepreneurs, who articulate grievances and aspirations and claims, and who incite fears and hatreds. There is little doubt that preexisting hostilities of Serbs toward "Muslims" and "Albanians" made it easy for Slobodan Milošević to lead his followers into civil wars, pogroms, and mass killings. But the ethnic cleavages could well have remained politically manageable in the absence of elite-inspired propaganda and organized provocation. The role of the "ethnic philosopher"—the spokesperson and formulator—typically is to invoke a glorious past, to elaborate doctrines of group virtue, and to identify external sources of opposition and threat (cf. Manuel 1992).

In short, the ethnic intellectuals formulate and focus diffuse and varied materials, but by themselves they only prepare the way for the agitators and organizers who use the receptive culture for their own purposes.

In the domestic struggle for power, elites cannot rely just on threats of punishment or material rewards to gain long-term support. They need legitimacy and authority, which rest in part on religion, ethnicity, and other cultural beliefs and values. The appeal of the state is not only to economic and security interests, but also to the protection and advancement of common beliefs and values. But beliefs and values are typically contested, and elites when threatened need a legitimating ideology to justify the state and their control within it. Thus elites may try to control the initial political agenda, to control what options will be considered. One way to do this is to identify the state with the existing structure of power, and the latter, in turn, with an ethnic community. Then the state is pictured as under crucial threat from another ethny or ethnic state. Violent conflict with "The Outside" may be initiated so that external threat outweighs any other domestic interests. In this strategy, the elites define the situation in terms of commonality of *culture* (*ethnicity*) rather than commonality of *interests* (Gagnon 1994–95).

Despots who rise to power through appealing to or instigating ethnic hostilities belong to the broader grouping of "ideological tyrants," described by Chirot (1994). Although the modern dictators espouse different ideologies—communism, fascism, nationalism, racism—their most effective message is to people in economic adversity who feel victimized and who readily focus upon ethnic scapegoats.

With reference to the former Yugoslavia, Job (1993, 69) has contended that "old resentments [although present] did not have to lead to savagery. . . . Violent eruptions of unrestrained butchery do not take place unless sanctioned by high authorities, whether of the state, ethnic or religious groups, or nationalist political movements." Although this generalization does not hold under all circumstances, it does fit a wide range of cases. So the next immediate question is why such "high authorities" instigate and support such ethnic violence. A quick shorthand answer, often given, is "threat to elites" or "elite insecurity." It follows that violent conflict along ethnic lines may arise from processes within the ethny rather than, or in addition to, relationships with other ethnies. As Gagnon has concluded (1995, 88–89):

In certain cases, in the face of threats to their own positions, elites may be willing to undertake policies that have very high costs for individual members of the ethnic group but which bring great benefits to themselves. . . . The use of violence, which inevitably provokes retaliatory violence against members of the group, has a particularly striking effect in that it solidifies the ethnic cleavage, "proves" that commonality of interests run only along that cleavage, thus reifying the image of the "ethnic group" as a real unit with real objective interest vis-à-vis other ethnic groups in the same way that the international system has done for states. It imposes this ethnicized reality as something natural, thereby further limiting political options in the future, redirecting them away from internal conflict toward this external focus.

Importantly also, such polarization can have the effect of silencing potential opponents of the elite policies, because the ethnic definition renders other issues irrelevant or harmful.

It seems clear enough that in severely divided societies, political elites confronted with imminent danger of losing power will be tempted to resort to ethnic agitation as a means of averting the threat to their position. We have reviewed how this scenario has been acted out in the 1980s and 1990s in the cases of Rwanda, Sri Lanka, and the former Yugoslavia, among others. But there is no compelling reason why there would have to be any extraordinary insecurity to induce such elites to make inflammatory appeals, invoking ethnic threat as means of solidifying support. Ordinary ambition and greed, along with minimal scruples, favor tactics of ethnic mobilization when prior cleavages provide leverage. It follows that ethnic entrepreneurs among political elites will always be present in situations where a mobilizable ethnic constituency presents an appealing means of gaining or maintaining political power and its accompanying rewards. This anticipation does not imply, however, that attempted ethnic manipulations will be successful, or, even if successful in gaining support, will alone be sufficient to turn peaceful rivalry or other opposition into violent collective conflict.

When violent ethnic conflict does arise, however, it is stimulated and organized by state elites and party officials who treat opposition as coming from ethnies *as units*—rather than from class interests or ideological opposition. And in situations of deprivation and insecurity where prior ethnic cleavages are present, what initially seem to be minor affronts or threats can become the basis for the emergence of small but highly militant groupings. Often it requires little more than the violence of those groups to start the cycle of conflict. After all, the deadly conflicts on the ground usually are the work of such militants—the suicide bombers, the assassins, the militias, and others paramilitary bodies—who form initially secretive, elusive networks of partially hidden partisans, which then can develop into public groupings that avidly seek publicity for their bombing and other acts of violence.

Other Processes

Very small differences and apparently trivial issues can rapidly escalate in ethnic leaders' confrontations. Harmonious coexistence can collapse into ferocious conflict. As Keyfitz (1995, 212–13) vividly puts it: "Enmities can be created out of nothing. . . .Once the blows and counter blows start to accumulate, each episode furnishing a grievance to one side or perhaps both, it is the fact of communication among those who share a common language and common set of meanings that places the cleavage line between the groups within which hostile sentiment is gathering."

Furthermore, violent ethnic conflicts, if protracted, usually become internationalized. Ethnic conflicts within states elicit external aid and other interventions, in the first place through direct contagion, such as when fellow ethnies in a neighboring state supply funds and arms, and provide safe homes and press their government to give partisan support. In its turn, the spreading involvement arouses fears among other states of dangerous political instability in a region. A third source of internationalization—of great and increasing worldwide importance—is the massive flows of refugees (displaced persons) from civil warfare. Vast numbers of people fleeing from persecution and atrocities task the resources of receiving countries for humanitarian aid; the influx may increase ethnic tensions and political insecurity in the host state; responses to refugee crises may quickly alter relationships among states.

In addition, the inescapable presence of atrocities—mass murder of unarmed civilians, rape, arson, torture—rendered vivid by the mass media may so influence public opinion as to bring unilateral or collective intervention by other states. Large-scale violations of human rights increasingly are seen as legitimate grounds for intervention by third parties.

All ethnies contain internal subdivisions; all ethnic mobilizations eventually develop cleavages based on ideological disagreements, personal ambitions and rivalries (note the chronic factional fighting among Kurdish leaders in Iraq, or ethnic leaders in Afghanistan), class interests, regional claims, or sub-ethnic kinship and local loyalties. It follows that conflicts between ethnies and the state and among different ethnies themselves can be strongly affected by intra-ethnic ("in-group") processes. Militant subgroupings often attempt to keep reluctant fractions of an ethnic rebellion in line by sanctioning those regarded as moderates or collaborators with adversaries. Kidnappings, torture, and killings of such deviants are not uncommon: contemporary large-scale cases include the rebellion in Sierra

Leone, the Tamil insurgency in Sri Lanka, the anti-apartheid movement in South Africa, the civil war in Liberia, the Lord's Resistance Army in Uganda, and the Palestinian uprising in Israel. Even short of these extreme sanctions, in-group "policing" can be a major source of in-group cohesion vis-à-vis adversaries—and thereby a source of intergroup polarization. Where ethnic political parties vie for control of the state, these dual processes are well nigh universal.

As politicized groupings engage in increasingly polarized confrontations, each will become less receptive to the other's views and more preoccupied with reinforcing intragroup messages. The intragroup flow of communications thus begins to occur within a social echo chamber. Each of the contending collectives creates its own reality, its own history, its own set of "facts," its distinctive "explanations" of events. It ignores, transforms, or rejects alternative beliefs and interpretations. At the extreme, each fighting collectivity develops a self-contained, systematic ideology, tending toward a rigid, closed, paranoid-like image of the world. Up to some limit, the longer a sequence of violent interactions, the more likely it is that the total process will acquire an autonomous self-generative character.

Whatever it is that starts collective violence may be very different from that which maintains it once under way. Typically, so a vast amount of experience suggests, it is easier to incite violence than to stop it. Once collective violence becomes widespread in a society, a whole set of powerful processes are set in motion to perpetuate it. Most conspicuous, perhaps, is sheer opportunism—mass violence opens up possibilities for rape, looting, seizure of land and other resources, laying claim to military and political advantages. Second, violence brings injury, loss, and death—arousing grief, rage, and desires for revenge on the part of the affected survivors. Revenge is a basic and extremely strong human motive—often ignored or underestimated by external observers, from journalists to academic social scientists. And, of course, revenge stimulates counter-revenge, as exemplified in the countless historical records of feuds, vendettas, "blood revenge," protracted guerrilla and civil wars, and tribal conflicts.

As these two self-sustaining processes continue over time, something else happens—a complex, multifaceted process of normalization of violence. At the psychological level, mechanisms of denial ("numbing") and distancing and compartmentalization come into play. Violence becomes an environing fact of life: "that is the way things are," *c'est la guerre*. Shock and horror merge into a numbed, affectless acknowledgment. Possession, display, and use of weapons become routine—"don't forget to take your pistol to the office."

A fourth, easily observable, process is the development of vested interests in the continuation of the violence. Leaders of politicized ethnies and other warring collectivities see their personal destinies directly linked to victory or defeat, not to peaceful resolution. Both material gain and valued identity become dependent on prevailing in violent struggle. Peace may bring retribution to members of death squads, to prison guards, to leaders who can be identified as war criminals or persons who have committed crimes against humanity. Those who wore masks to kill their neighbors fear a probable unmasking.

When the mobilization of a fighting collectivity decreases, or when a peace agreement seems near or has been accepted by the leadership, there is always a high risk that disaffected subgroups will engage in renewed violence in the effort to destroy or radically change the imminent peace. This pattern has appeared in Northern Ireland, repeatedly among Israelis and Palestinians, with the Liberation Tigers in Sri Lanka, and in the insurgency in Kosovo.

The intertwined processes of sustained ethnic conflicts show why permanent settlements are so rare and difficult to attain. Social change inevitably has differential effects on ethnies, on their relations to states, and on interethnic relations. Some groupings prosper, others languish or suffer economic loss. Political coalitions wax and wane. Interstate alignments have changing impacts on domestic ethnic affairs. Ethnic bargains, agreements, and understandings that last for a full generation without any major change are exceedingly rare.

Conclusion

This survey of the pathways from peaceful mobilization to violent collective conflict leaves us with a picture of some important empirical findings.

1. Mobilization does not necessarily lead to violence. The outbreak of major and sustained violence may come from many small changes, but the transition itself is a radical phase change.
2. Mobilization involves the continually interacting processes that create ethnic salience, solidarity, grievances, and opportunities. There are numerous feedbacks, interruptions, and shifts in tactics and strategies.
3. Conflicts themselves are diverse, and the several main types arise under different conditions and follow different pathways. Accordingly, each type calls for a specific analysis.
4. Ethnic/religious movements readily become politicized and open to manipulation by leaders and other elites. The development of exclusionary and hostile definitions of ethnic others is a central process that

is facilitated by and contributes to collective readiness for violent confrontations.

Although the world of ethnic mobilizations contains many examples of the role of state regimes, special attention must be given to the most deadly outcomes—the attempted destruction of whole ethnic peoples. The phenomenon of genocide is the focus of Chapter 8 to follow.

CHAPTER EIGHT

From Identity to Genocide

The Problem of Understanding

Democides and Genocides

Genocide differs so radically from ordinary political oppositions and rivalries as to render suspect many of the conventional economic and political explanations (Monroe 1995, 216). Ethnic competition for scarce valuables, for example, often occurs without overt conflict. Ethnic rivalry for the collective goods of recognition, respect, and prestige does not invariably lead to mass violence. The wholesale killings that go under the names of democides and genocides represent a disjunction—a phase change, a radical discontinuity—between peaceful competition, rivalry, protest (and ordinary political opposition), and the slaughter of whole populations on the basis of *categorical* ethnic distinctions—Armenians, Jews, Tutsis, Bosnian Muslims, Kosovars, Slavs, Roma.

How does "ordinary" ethnic rivalry and restrained conflict turn into what appear to be vast orgies of slaughter of helpless people?[1] What are we to make of democides and genocides? We are dealing here with the politics of fear and fury.

Persisting problems of definition have hampered clarity in efforts to understand the mass killings by governments of social categories of "their own" populations. The most inclusive term, *democide*, refers to such killings directed against people solely or primarily because of their membership in a social category, whatever the basis of classification may be. *Politicide* con-

[1] For unforgettable photographs of the world's savage civil wars and massacres, see James Nachtwey, *Inferno* (New York: Phaidon, 1999). There are 428 searing pages.

sists of government-sponsored or accepted murders of political dissidents or "class enemies," or others who are killed for political purposes. Finally, *genocide* is that form of democide in which the victims are chosen because of their national, religious, or ethnic membership (on all this, see Grimshaw 1999; Smith 2000). The definition of genocide in Article II of the United Nation's Convention is itself problematic both because of gaps in its coverage and because of ambiguity; for example, "destruction in whole or in part" and the concept of destroying a group "as such" (Grimshaw 1999). The relevant UN text reads as follows:

> Genocide means any of the following acts committed with intent to destroy, in whole or in part, a national, ethnical, racial or religious group as such: (a) killing members of the group; (b) causing serious bodily or mental harm to the group; (c) deliberately inflicting upon the group conditions of life calculated to bring about its physical destruction in whole or in part; (d) imposing measures intended to prevent births within the group; (e) forcibly transferring children of the group to another group. (Two of these conditions that will terminate the existence of a society are (1) the biological extinction or dispersion of the numbers and (2) the absorption of the society into another society.)

The many difficulties with this definition have led to later detailed revisions and specification. The original definition does not include politicides—the mass killings of political opponents who are not members of the specified ethnic categories—nor local riots, pogroms, and other attacks that are not intended to destroy a group "as such." It does not refer to public health or educational measures that may reduce ethnic membership but are intended to promote welfare. Genuine genocide itself is not really difficult to recognize—it involves actual intentional killing, whether active or passive (as in induced famines and the withholding of aid)—but many varieties of mass deaths do not qualify (see Grimshaw 1999, at length).

So although definitions of genocide are thus varied, and often controversial, the core meaning is "the intentional killing by government of people because of their race, ethnicity, or other indelible group membership" (Rummel 1995a, 3). In its strict application, the term refers to the actual or attempted intentional annihilation of whole peoples, not just selected individuals (Lemkin 1944).

Democides have been defined as the mass killings of people "without arms in their hands" by states, quasi-states, and stateless groups; the primary murderous regimes, however, have been state regimes. Democides include executions and deaths in massacres, in forced labor, prisons and camps, in assassinations, in purposive famines, deportations and expulsions, and in murder by quotas as in death squads and "disappearances" (cf. Rummel 1995a, 1994). Whole populations may be forced into starvation, even when external aid is readily available, as in Sudan, Somalia and Eritrea (Kuper 1992, 760). State-organized mass killings from 1945 to 1989 are estimated to have claimed more lives than were lost in all wars and natural disasters during the same period (Smith 2000, 1066). Although it is clear from abundant evidence that states are the greatest killers of civilian populations, it must be emphasized also that many millions have been killed in communal violence (as in the Indian-Muslim violence in 1947), in settlers' encroachments on indigenous peoples, and in the chaos of collapsed states.

Origins of Genocides

The Holocaust (and later genocides and democides) are twentieth-century horrors that often have been seen as both unprecedented and as inexplicable aberrations in "modern" societies. But the willful destruction of entire peoples actually was present as early as the advent of agriculture and large empires (ca. 10,000 B.C.E.), although it may have become more common in later centuries. These early genocides appear to have been primarily instrumental, to gain land or other wealth, to ward off threats, to terrorize resisting peoples and to build states. By the twentieth century, however, the great *ideological* genocides became dominant (Smith 2001; Jonassohn, with Björnson 1998).

Much of the foundation for the modern slaughter of ethnic and religious minorities had been laid before World War I. The mechanization of war and the idea of total war had appeared in the American Civil War with railway transport, mass industrial production, and General Sherman's doctrine of utter destruction of an adversary's capabilities. With the Great War of 1914–18 came industrial mobilization, new lethal technology, and total war against both military forces and civilian populations.

By World War II, all these trends were enormously amplified. The impersonalized killings in the struggles of massed armies, in submarine warfare, and in bombings of cities reached new levels of destruction. In the case of Nazi Germany's systematic death camps, the militarized extermination was joined with racism—the Holocaust was self-defined as the destruction of eugenic defectives or as a matter of a "racial cleansing." More generally, the well-known examples of distancing, dehumanization, and routinization of mass killing in modern wars may well have created dispositions favorable to all genocidal forces (Bartov 1996). In the Holocaust, an additional precedent was in the doctrines of eugenics and racial inferiority, justifying, first, compulsory sterilization of individuals judged to be biologically "unfit" or handicapped, and then extended to systematic killing (Friedlander 1995; Proctor 1999). The program of bureaucratic, centralized extermination of Jews and Gypsies (and Slavs) surely drew upon beliefs and attitudes from these sources. However, neither the acceptance of indiscriminate killing in war nor of doctrines of racial inferiority fully account for the specific definition and selection of Jews as categorical victims. Before the Final Solution there had been a long history in Germany of active political anti-Semitism, widely promulgated and widely accepted. Although this ideology was not universal, its persistent and pervasive influence helps to explain why so many "ordinary" German people voluntarily aided and participated in the imprisonment and killing of millions of Jews (Goldhagen 1996; Browning 1992).

Levels of Explanation

Well over 200 "explanations" have been offered for the decline and fall of the Roman Empire, and in time a similar proliferation may come to develop in efforts to account for twentieth-century genocides and democides. In the scholarly accounts (Grimshaw 1999), the following types of explanations are found: (1) biological/ethnic or sociobiological; (2) psychological processes and personality structures; (3) cultural patterns, including political, ethnic, and religious ideologies; (4) social structural factors, e.g., class opposition, types of political systems and states; (5) social processes, ranging from conformity to group interactions to "rational choice"; and (6) specific situational contexts, especially economic distress and political instability, war, and revolution. From the welter of ideas, can some synthesis be found? The phenomena to be explained obviously are multivariate and multilevel, but some combinations of factors surely are of more causal weight than others. The range of explanations are diverse not only because the phenomena to be explained are complex; the complexity certainly is there, but this does not necessarily preclude unified and simplifying interpretations.

The diversity of explanatory accounts of ethnic conflicts that we have reviewed emerged in substantive part from different levels of analysis that themselves partially correspond to empirical "levels" in the observed events. At the level of individuals and localized groups, some of the necessary but not sufficient ingredients are found in psychological processes of identification and stereotyping, in personality structures (authoritarianism, self-righteousness), and in social processes of indoctrination and conformity. At the next level of corporate kinship groupings, village communities, ethnies, and castes there are intergroup processes of exchange and accommodation, along with collective rivalry and conflict. At the macro-level and in state-societies, an array of new structures and processes emerge: regional clusterings, political parties and coalitions, legislatures, interest groups, military formations, judicial and administrative organizations, and decision-making elites. And beyond individual states and interstate alliances and coalitions are trans-state organizations, from multinational corporations to the UN to militant ethnic networks that repeatedly have shaped ethnic relations within states and substate structures.

These are levels of social structure. At each there are specific "micro" factors to be taken into account. In the case of genocidal behavior, much can be learned in terms of *psychological* processes of "dehumanization" that involve learned stereotypes, distancing mechanisms, and in-group conformity ("docility"). Something more, however, is required to account for the selection of specific affinities and targets, or to say why conflict emerges at one time and place rather that at others. Here we find *studies of collective phenomena*—of ethnic networks and boundaries, of interdependencies and oppositions, of group symbols and myths, of ethnic public goods, of relative standing and vested positions. The ascending search for causes may have to go still further into *processes of political sovereignty, state-building, interstate wars and agreements.* Sometimes remote in time and far removed from local societies, these super-structural events can create conditions that have effects upon apparently separate localized ethnic conflicts, as when the 1878 Berlin conference divided Africa among the Great Powers in ways that have enormous consequences upon the conflicts of today.

On the level of mass behavior, it thus appears that genocidal attacks require much more than ethnic distinctions and competitive relationships. The major historical genocides have been preceded by mass distress by reason of economic depression, political instability, and defeat in war; the targeted populations have been ethnically salient and accessible—in short, visible and vulnerable. All these conditions, however, are not sufficient to predict to genocidal massacres; something more is needed.

In psychological terms the "something more" includes processes of distancing from persons who are to be the objects of assault—"critical cognitive perception of one's neighbors as 'the other.' This initial psychological distancing from former friends and neighbors facilitates an eventual process of dehumanization of 'the other'" (Monroe 1995, 216). Individuals in the out-group cease to be seen as persons: they become utterly evil. They are animals (rats, lice, pigs, snakes), vermin; they are infidels, barbarous savages, subhuman. The dehumanization and demonization of the target population typically goes along with the exaltation of the in-group as superior and virtuous. In the end, the virtuous killers can slaughter the now-nonhuman others with little sign of compunction or remorse.

Thus, we have to conclude that no single antecedent condition has been shown to account for genocides; rather, a convergence of several major factors increases the probability. Facilitative conditions include: strong ethnic cleavages and past discrimination, economic distress, war and revolution, political threat to ruling groups, rapid change in political alignments, and ideologies of group superiority and group threat. When all of these circumstances prevail, the opportunity opens for elite manipulation of mass fears, for opportunistic greed, for desires for revenge, for lust for domination, and for diffuse hostility that can be directed against a collective scapegoat. It then appears that genocidal states have little difficulty in recruiting willing killers.

The multilevel approach we are sketching can be applied as an aid to understanding in the contrasting examples of collapsed states, as over against the organized slaughter brought on by centralized states.

Collapsed States

Consider first the situations in collapsed states such as Liberia, Zaire, or Sierra Leone in the last decades of the last century.

In all societies, a central concern of everyone must be security—security of life, limb, and the means to maintain a continuing life. A compelling reason for ordinary people to accept state authority is the state's capability and willingness to protect against enemies from abroad and from force, fraud, and violence from domestic predators. Always under the surface of peaceful everyday life is the latent fear of disorder and violence. When the courts and the police no longer can be relied upon for impartial protection, when central administrations fail to maintain essential services—in short, when states collapse—a life and death question is "Who will safeguard us?" The terror behind that question should not be underestimated; it creates the basis for ethnic entrepreneurs and warlords to set formerly peaceable co-dwellers at one another's throats.

Failed and collapsed states as they erode and disintegrate create the classic Inherent Security Dilemma (of interstate anarchy) on the domestic scene. If the overarching authority of the state no longer protects, the result will be a Hobbesian world to the extent that trust breaks down between and among individuals and subgroups. Any prior fault lines of distrust among collectivities become activated. Faced with the increasing uncertainty of safety and support elsewhere, individuals tend to turn to kin and locality groupings. If local community solidarities then are threatened by ethnic divisions, the only remaining security-collectivity beyond immediate family and kin typically turns out to be the ethny. But if each family thus turns inward to co-ethnics for protection, the whole society eventually becomes ethnically segmented into mutually suspicious and fearful segments.

Fear is omnipresent in ethnic conflicts, and the more so the higher the stakes and, especially, the perceived imminence of violence. Accordingly, ethnic entrepreneurs who wish to mobilize a constituency or to silence intragroup dissent often will seek to dehumanize and demonize an opposing ethny. They do this by numerous and diverse tactics: dramatizing historical wrongs, stressing contradictory religious beliefs, spreading allegations of atrocities (rapes, torture, killing of infants, mutilations, etc.), asserting inherent evil in the other (cf. Keen 1988). They also may use the propaganda of the deed: using provocateurs, unleashing the terrorist squads to burn and kill. The devices are legion, the aim to intimidate and polarize.

As described in Chapter 7, ethnic leaders often play a key role in inciting violence; we are now asking why they are able to do this in the extreme. When leaders of ethnic or ideological movements seize control of central states through protracted violence—in civil war or in successive coups—they usually have been able to capitalize upon deep resentments and extreme polarization. Their political support is likely to be impassioned, dogmatic, intolerant, autocratic. The resulting regime is likely to claim absolute certitude and to demand total conformity. The combination of ethnicized resentment, dogmatism, and the demand for unity is a recipe for unchecked power of the dominant elite. This is the groundwork for tyranny, for unchecked power that can cause enormous abuse, suffering, and deaths without compensatory justifications (Chirot 1994).

Whatever its sources, extreme ethnic polarization creates intense insecurities and a volatile and precarious set of stand-offs between the mutually hostile and suspicious contenders. In such situations, for example, pogroms and mass riots may require no more than elites' agitation and use of provocateurs. And the roots of "ethnic cleansing" are to be found in the combination of pervasive ethnic identities, failure of transethnic authority, elite manipulation, and escalating threats.

States as Destroyers

In contrast to the turmoil of collapsed states, where interethnic factions and warlords dominate, genocidal states promote, incite, and organize the systematic killing of whole ethnic peoples. In a stark example, the 1994 genocide in Rwanda was not the outcome of a collapsed state. On the contrary, the state was centrally organized, with extensive and meticulous administrative procedures (Gourevitch 1998). The mass killings were planned—and announced—well in advance, were overtly sponsored by the incumbent government, and were carried out by highly organized militias (e.g., with lists of intended victims). The mobilized population had an earlier reputation of orderliness and obedience to authority. Rwanda had appeared to foreign observers as a well-organized society with good roads, improving education and public health measures, and high rates of participation in churches. There had been, indeed, long-standing economic and political inequality, and episodes of violent attacks by Hutus upon Tutsis, but not the overwhelming organized mass ferocity of the 1990s (cf. Prunier 1995).

As in Rwanda, confronted with threats to their control of the state, governing groups elsewhere have repeatedly used irregular militias and other paramilitary forces to intimidate and destroy insurgents. A conspicuous instance was the role of the Indonesian military in mobilization of militias against the pro-independence population in the 1999 referendum in East Timor. After a protracted insurgency in which an estimated 200,000 people died (one-fourth of the total population), the Indonesian political leaders had agreed to abide by the results of a referendum in which voters chose between autonomy within Indonesia or independence. Attempts by the militias to terrorize voters failed to stop participation in the referendum—which resulted in overwhelming support for independence. The sequel was mass violence, incited and organized by anti-independence forces, that continued, after being ignored abroad, until it was finally halted by the UN and other external interventions.

In autocratic states, governing under cover of plebiscites, ethnic nationalism provides historical heroes, origin myths, visions of unity, and security of identity (Ignatieff 1994). Concepts of glory, honor, and a prominent place in history enter into the decision making of leaders and elites. To explain the behavior of governing regimes in dictatorial or autocratic states we need to understand the interests, preferences, and visions of key decision making. In the 1990s in Iraq, Saddam Hussein seemed to think of himself as a present-day successor to Saladin and Nebuchadnezzar. Hitler had a vision of a glorious conquering state that would endure for a thousand years—the Tausendjärig Reich. Napoleon sought an empire, and his memory is still revered by many French citizens. In attempted explanations of such historical cases, narrow theories of "interests" give too little attention to the high value people can place upon personal honor, national glory, ethnic pride, or religious convictions. In a more comprehensive perspective, these nonmaterial values can be seen as powerful motivators for both the leaders and the followers of vast collectivities. Napoleon and Hitler understood this well.

The Cultural Frames for Genocide

The very definition of the identity of groupings that are contending for power can be a substantial factor in extreme ethnonational conflicts. The concrete context for genocidal massacres in the former Yugoslavia was shaped in part by the varying definitions imposed upon the collective actors by international agencies, Western states, and nongovernmental observers and interveners. So the Bosnians were, in effect, denied national standing by being designated merely as Muslims, but the Christian Orthodox in Serbia (and Bosnia) were called Serbs, and the Catholics were not labeled as Catholic but as Croats. From the beginning, Serbia and Croatia were treated as state-like entities while Bosnia-Herzegovina was defined in religio-ethnic terms and thus easily characterized by the Serbian state as successors to the hated Ottoman Muslims (cf. Cushman and Meštrović 1996). Such definitions are part of the larger cultural context that shapes conceptions of ethnic enemies. The particular cultural frame can be crucial, as shown by the influence of ideologies of group superiority and inferiority. Under the Nazi regime, there was a preoccupation with the purity of the *Volk*—the Master Race—associated with an expressed fear of contamination by disease, pollutants, and alien and undesirable people (Proctor 1999). Thousands of mentally or physically handicapped persons were killed and more thousands of the "undesirables" were sterilized—the retarded, mentally ill, homosexuals, and the others thought to be genetically inferior. From the obsessive concern with "racial" purity, it was one more step to the policies that led to the mass murder of Gypsies, Jews, Slavs, and other people regarded as impure or subhuman (Sofsky 1997; Caplan 1992).

Doctrines that claim "racial" superiority are not confined to any one country or culture. In what might seem to be a far-removed instance, among Hutu refugees (from ethnonational conflict in Burundi) in camps directed by Tanzanian authorities, there soon developed an ideology of moral superiority—a "mythicohistory." The Hutus claimed original possession of the land, as over against the ruling Tutsis, depicted as invaders from the north. The attempt to thus claim moral superiority was joined with racist stereotyping of Tutsis to create a reified ethnicity (Malkki 1995). Such a conception of essential ethnic differences easily lends itself, as it had in Rwanda in 1992–94, to attempted genocide.

The very phrase "ethnic cleansing" echoes the repeated themes of purity and pollution that appear both in caste societies and in modern genocides. "Cleansing" implies that there is something noxious, dirty, polluting that must be cleansed away. One cleans away dirt, lice, soiled things, bacteria, viruses, pests (cf. Keen 1988). When ethnic cleansing is invoked, as in Hitlerian Germany or in Serbian onslaughts in Bosnia and Kosovo, the ethnic others are defined as no longer human beings, but as alien defilements to be swept away, expelled, or exterminated. The theme of purity versus defilement is one part of the larger process of dehumanization in which the ethnic adversary is demonized, depicted as monstrous, and reduced to dangerous and despicable animals (Keen 1988).

States and ethnic collectivities themselves can thus indoctrinate aversion, fear, and hatred. But from state policies to the killing fields, connections are made by a long chain of preparations and organization. In this sequence, the extensive descriptions we have of the behavior of those who actually carried out mass killings show the central importance of *group conformity* and *obedience to authority*. Democides and genocides always involve "Special Forces" of one kind or another (order battalions, death squads, militias, paramilitary groups, special police, and so on). These men (almost all are men) do the "dirty work" of physical assault and killing. Their action is no battle frenzy, no running amok with rage and fear, but rather the methodical, planned murders of helpless victims. Within the social units that carry out the killings, training and indoctrination emphasize obeying orders, no matter how repulsive. The "hardening" of new recruits often involve injuring or destroying victims under the watchful eyes of veterans. Once the recruit is involved in slaughter, any failure to kill is seen as weakness, as disloyalty to comrades, or as a criticism of one's fellows. Defection from the deadly activity exposes the offender to ridicule, contempt, ostracism, and other sanctions (Monroe 1995, 237, reviewing Browning 1992). This is not the "banality of evil" but rather the evil of banality.

Recapitulation: The Pathways from Ethnicity
to the Destruction of Peoples

Running through the scholarly analyses of violent social conflicts, both ethnic and non-ethnic, is a recurrent debate over the importance to be assigned to deep discontent as over against expansive ambition. Overlapping this controversy is the question of the respective roles of mass attitudes versus the actions of leaders, officials, entrepreneurs, and elites. A detailed review of hundreds of studies provides ample evidence to support each of these interpretations in particular instances. The specific findings are highly context-dependent—varying according to historical period, basic social structures, and the many variables we have noted in preceding chapters. Nevertheless, amidst all the detailed variations there are strong regularities. The available evidence does not permit precise quantitative estimates, but the broad patterns can be reasonably well identified. What are the more important of such regularities?

First, among the background factors is the *ethnic salience*. In general, salience of a particular ethny will be the greater:

- the more the external threats;
- the more the rivalry with other ethnies;
- the more there is state-imposed categorization;
- the greater the initial cultural distinctions;

- the more developed are intra-ethnic institutions, e.g., religious, educational, political.

These conditions create perceptually outstanding markers, identifying an entity that stands out against a background. But they do not yet predict to a second major characteristic: *ethnic solidarity* or *cohesion*.

Ethnic solidarity, in its turn, will likely be enhanced by the following circumstances:

- high salience;
- central importance of kinship ties among members of the ethny;
- territorial concentration; spatial segregation;
- intra-ethny cultural homogeneity;
- occupational concentration;
- lack of intra-ethny oppositions, based on class or regional or rural-urban divisions;
- positive economic interdependence;
- high density of social interactions.

Given high salience and solidarity, we then will observe a clearly bounded entity, internally crisscrossed with dense and positively charged interactions. But there can be strong solidarity without extensive mobilization to undertake collective action in the service of group interests and objectives. So a third question has to do with the main conditions we can posit as conducive to *mobilization*.

Original identity and the processes producing solidarity interact with one another. Then, given a solidarity ethny, mobilization will be most likely if the members share a strong sense of grievances—either in the negative sense of deprivations and inflicted wrongs (e.g., lost political autonomy) or in the sense of frustrated aspirations and expectations. Especially potent are the frustrations of ambitious, upwardly mobile members whose rising hopes and claims are being thwarted by ethnic discrimination. Such individuals regularly form a "vanguard" or elite cadre to articulate and focus the grievances of other members. All may still come to naught unless the ethny has or can develop resources for mobilization—funds from members' contributions and from external allies, a network of communication and transportation, media linkages and outlets, and an action-oriented organization. The forms of organization will vary greatly—from loose decentralized linkages among segmented parts or secretive "cells," to centralized organizations with an authoritative leadership structure. Likewise, the relevant resources will range from a subset of local organizations (churches, mosques, unions), to indigenous "expertise" (lawyers, publicists), to material goods (safe houses, weaponry, communicative devices).

So mobilization is more likely if there is:

- solidarity;
- grievances and aspirations;
- available infrastructure and internal resources;
- external aid and support.

What then? The beginnings of mobilization may be destroyed by suppression and cooptation; abortive movements are legion. It follows that the course of mobilization, all else being equal, will depend on the opportunity structure the movement encounters. At one extreme, mobilization confronts a centralized and militarized ethnocracy of unchecked power, with its ubiquitous secret police, informers, and paramilitary squads. At the most benign pole, the mobilized ethny can make its claims to a resource-rich parliamentary democracy, functioning with a non-ethnic party system and a regime of law. Under the more open political systems, mobilization often leads to accommodations and compromises, although it is sometimes accompanied by mild to moderate conflicts. The greater the responsiveness of the state to claims of mobilized ethnies, the more frequent will be protests but the less drastic the tactics—provided that ethnic demands are not so great as to produce reactive, backlash responses from social formations that feel thereby threatened.

Opportunities for mobilization are not limited, of course, to intrastate circumstances. External conditions include not only various forms of assistance from fellow ethnies across state boundaries and not only unilateral support from other states, but also the activities of nongovernmental organizations and interstate agencies.

In short, whether mobilization will succeed in attaining particular objectives rests upon the possibilities of effective intrastate political voice and influence, and the extent and kind of external support (including benign non-interference). In particular, as already noted, unilateral foreign aid to states or to their restive and rebellious ethnies often supports protracted and deadly civil warfare when neither of the parties can win or will agree to a settlement. In still other cases, the external support enables a central state to crush an ethnic mobilization.

In short, mobilization can be the route to the redress of grievances and to the mutual accommodation of interests. But it tends to lead to collective violence in autocratic but weak states, and is especially likely to have that result in periods of major sociopolitical change.

There is not a neat unilinear sequence from mobilization to conflicts; indeed, the two interact, as when mobilization on one side stimulates countermobilization. The fateful tipping point comes when mobilization of the other is seen as a threat of violent conflict. The trigger for this perception can be attacks on ethnic symbols—cemeteries, churches, mosques, temples, flags, monuments, leaders—or vandalization of property, or intimidation and attacks by small guerrilla groups or death squads who commit atrocities. Many of the provocations are encouraged or directly organized by political elites. Cycles of assault and revenge often are thus initiated by shadowy groups of what may be called either "armed psychopaths"—or committed militants.

Studies of social movements have long pointed to the self-sustaining processes of conflict and conflict escalation. Ongoing conflict is a vortex into which pour desires for revenge and a variety of opportunistic motives for economic, sexual, and political gains. Into the vortex of mobilization and violence are also drawn ideological commitments, the "sunk capital" of ethnic killers (e.g., suspected war criminals), continuing in-group pressures, and closure of opportunities for peaceful careers. Thus Esman (1994, 31) observes: "Mobilization seldom occurs spontaneously; once underway, however, it may activate and radicalize impatient, violence-prone, even criminal elements whose actions cannot be controlled or disciplined by the leaders of the community or of its factions and for whom violence may become a form of self-justifying behavior, even a way of life."

In various ways, these processes have been prominent in the cases of Hamas, Islamic Jihad, Hizbollah, and other militant groups in the Middle East; in Rwanda and Burundi; among Tamil rebels in Sri Lanka; in the south of Sudan; and much earlier, in *la violencia* in Colombia. At the extreme, self-perpetuating violence produces state collapse, war-lordism, banditry, factional fighting—thus chaos, exemplified in Sierra Leone and Liberia.

Warfare that is publicly defined as ethnic struggle in the beginning typically comes to cover looting, confiscation, extortion, and illegal trade—as warlords and their violent followers profit from the victims. Both states and rebels can continue the fighting when arms and supplies can be obtained in profusion from sales of narcotics, gold, diamonds, oil, and so on.

When political leaders, avid for power and wealth, use threats and fear to create carnage where previously interethnic peace had prevailed, campaigns of mass killings, rape, and torture become the justification for the slaughter that originally "lacked all reason." That is, the very existence of the killings creates the mutual hatreds that now make sense of what initially was senseless.

Conclusions

Let us now put together a network of key conclusions that can be gleaned from the available research and commentary on democide and genocide.

The resources of these conclusions are in studies that wear the labels of history, biology, sociology, psychology, anthropology, and several other disciplines.

1. Humans are capable of a wide range of aggressive behaviors, but collective lethal violence is highly dependent upon social contexts.
2. There is an important distinction between expressive and instrumental aggression; the first is "hot," emotional, impulsive; the second is a means to other ends and it may be cold, calculating, impersonal. Although longstanding hatred and chronic resentment often are present, such structural animosities are not necessary conditions. Both "class enemies" (Stalinist Soviet Union; Cambodia) and inhuman ethnic threats ("Muslims," "Albanians" in former Yugoslavia) can be newly created.
3. There is an important difference between individualized aggression and collective (group) aggression. The latter features powerful forces of conformity, leadership, and authority. When political and religious authorities endorse or actively promote definitions of an ethnic target as wholly alien and evil, they can set in motion processes of dehumanization or desensitization that have two genocidal effects: widespread acceptance of or apathy toward categorical killing, and activation of systematic slaughter by special groups.
4. Group identities set boundaries for attachment and commitment; it is within such boundaries that cohesion and conformity can have their strongest influences.
5. In organized violence between large collectivities the killers typically are a small proportion of the ambient population.
6. Democides and genocides can develop because of the acquiescence or acceptance by the mass of people of the deadly acts of the few.
7. Genocides require substantial levels of planning, indoctrination, and purposive organization. Genocides do not occur without extensive and detailed organization.
8. States—or more directly, the incumbent governing bodies—are the great perpetrators of mass killings of their own peoples. All the great genocides of the last century were sponsored and organized by agents of centralized states—special police, death squads, militias, and the like.
9. War, revolution, drastic political change, and severe economic distress—all these create conditions favorable to genocide. None is a sufficient cause, but each contributes to the uncertainties and dislocations that create receptivity to group violence.
10. Struggles for power among insecure elites in centralized states increase incentives for violent actions aimed at keeping power and elim-

inating threats. Vulnerable and salient ethnies provide tempting targets.

11. Initial violence by a dominant ethny against a victimized other can rapidly escalate as violence comes to be perceived as justified and as it attracts opportunistic perpetrators who hope to gain material and social rewards. In these ways, collective actions once regarded as unthinkable can be routinized.

12. Finally, the cultural setting of beliefs and values has provided self-justification for genocidal regimes. Of special importance has been the idea of absolute sovereignty of a nation-state, combined with ideologies of racial/ethnic purity and pollution.

PART IV

WHAT CAN BE DONE

CHAPTER NINE

Avoiding the Gathering Storm

The Array of Preventive Actions

> What if they gave a war and nobody came?
>
> Slogan from the anti-war movements of the 1960s

The hope of preventing violent conflicts springs eternal, as the rhetorical question suggests, but wishing that no one would participate ignores historical experience. What experience does show, however, is that some conflicts can be anticipated and then averted by purposive action. The record shows an array of potentially useful preventive policies and practices.

The Problem of Prevention

We say "potentially," for it is difficult to demonstrate the effectiveness of the actions that have been described by diplomats, journalists, scholars, and "peace practitioners." How does one explain the non-occurrence of an event? Thus, preventive diplomacy may be employed, and peace is maintained: did the diplomacy forestall conflict, or would peace have prevailed in its absence? Or, preventive diplomacy is invoked, but civil war erupts nevertheless: was the diplomacy at fault, or was the conflict unavoidable? In appraising efforts to avoid violent, ethnic-based conflicts, definitive proof seldom will be attainable; reasonable plausibility on the basis of careful empirical study will be the best available outcome.

A sustained concentration of attention upon the prevalence and destructiveness of ethnic conflicts and of civil warfare more generally can create pessimism about the prospects for preventing such occurrences. Conditions that favor violent conflict are numerous, widespread, persistent, deep-seated, and, of course, complex. An easy conclusion is that essentially nothing can be done, that hope of prevention is illusory. Yet the historical record leaves open the possibility of effective policies and actions that prevent collective violence and favor mutual acceptance. So, after this lengthy review of conflict, it is important to remind ourselves that most of the world's ethnies are *not* fighting each other or the states within which they reside. Of the some 1,600 major cultural groupings, fewer than 300 have recently mobilized in politicized protest or rebellion, and only some 30–40 wars are ongoing in a particular year. This is an impressive record of peaceful coexistence, of mutual accommodation, and even of active cooperation. Once we know that relatively harmonious relations actually do occur, we can realistically begin to search for the favoring conditions. But that search needs to be informed by awareness of limitations, ambiguities, and paradoxes, and unexpected pitfalls.

To what extent, if at all, is it possible to avoid the most undesirable kinds of ethnic conflict?

Even in extreme circumstances what appear to be fixed positions and non-negotiable demands will not be entrenched for all time. Certainly there are instances in which impending conflicts may be averted, and many other cases in which ongoing conflicts may be reduced, mitigated, contained, regulated, or actually resolved. Our present attention is directed toward those situations in which needless misery could be reduced by properly chosen preventive measures.

A necessary consideration immediately arises: to what degree do we have the knowledge and procedures technically required to engage in effective prevention? Given the immense complexity of ethnic phenomena and the many diverse approaches that actually have been used in preventive attempts, is it realistic to suppose that knowledge adequate to guide effective prevention actually exists? The answer has to be a highly qualified yes.

The answer is affirmative because the storehouse of recorded historical experiences provides information about which methods have been successful and which have not in specified types of situations. An affirmative appraisal is justified also by the substantial inventory of empirical generalizations connecting prior conditions—including intentional actions—with systemic outcomes of cooperation, accommodation, peaceful protest, or collective violence. Many testable hypotheses are likewise present in what we may call the informed folklore of experienced practitioners, from international diplomats to neighborhood workers. Finally, important clues as to effective action are to be found in formal analyses of strategic interactions, known as game theory.

But the "highly qualified" nature of this affirmative appraisal must be emphasized. Ethnic conflicts represent stunning dynamic complexity, including many near-chaotic processes and novel emergents. Our sturdiest generalizations are conditional and probabilistic—holding only with an estimated likelihood under partly specified conditions. In particular cases, therefore, there will always be a need for detailed local knowledge.

A second qualification is that the feasibility of procedures depends upon "who" (or "what") the relevant actors are. What is feasible for a head of state cannot be done by the executive of a local business firm. What *you* can do depends upon who "you" are—upon what resources, abilities, social relations, and political connections are available to a given actor. A local human relations commission, established by a city council, has capabilities and constraints different from those of a federal court or state legislature, or a warlord. Although this point seems obvious, it is often overlooked or ignored in evaluations of programs intended to influence ethnic relations.

Limitations and Cautions: Conflict Reduction as Difficult but Not Impossible

> Condemned to try to control a future they cannot predict by reacting to a past that will not be repeated, policy makers are nonetheless faced with an imperative need to act that cannot be ignored as a practical or political matter. (Lie 1995, 311)

As experience in every part of the world shows us, it is relatively easy to describe policies and practices that are likely to reduce conflict, but it is very difficult to find the occasions that will induce governments or ethnic leaders to follow what outside observers regard as wise counsel. Over and over again one hears the plaintive refrain: what is lacking is the political will to do what needs to be done.

As one reviews the numerous articles and books that attempt to propose policies and actions for avoiding or reducing conflict, a discouraging initial impression may be that so many of the recommendations seem vacuous, amounting to saying that people should be nice. Religious groups should be more understanding and tolerant of differing faiths. States should be less repressive, more democratic, more willing to seek compromises. Ethnic protesters should be more reasonable, less fanatical. And so on.

These generalized injunctions share two major defects. First, they contain no clue as to how one gets from here to there, no hint of the necessary means and pathways to desired goals. Second, these bland admonitions have no specified address; they seem directed to whomever it may concern. An appeal of this kind may fail to have an appreciable effect upon any actors potentially able to make a difference.

None of the "political engineering" proposals for preventing or mitigating intrastate conflicts is without its disadvantages—as demonstrated by clear cases of failure. The establishment of elections and political parties is not enough to avoid conflict in societies with strong ethnic, regional, and class cleavages and antagonisms. Federalism, devolution of decision making, multiplication of substates to cross-cut regional-ethnic divisions—all hold promise, but all have failed in some cases to avoid secessionism and violence.

Power sharing has been hailed by influential thinkers (Lijphart 1990; Horowitz 1985, 1991) as a promising solution in ethnically divided societies. Power sharing involves three main policies, established in constitutional guarantees: (1) decision making in the central government is inclusive, that is, all major groupings are represented among the political elites; (2) decision making at the national level is consensual, requiring agreement of all leaders or ethnies—each has veto power when vital interests of its constituency are at issue; and (3) ethnic autonomy in important respects is assured, such as language use, religious practice, or regional government. Switzerland usually is cited as the prototype of successful power sharing, but India, Malaysia, and Spain also are sometimes claimed as other "successes." In contrast, power sharing has failed to prevent secessionist attempts, communal conflict, or civil war in Burma (Myanmar), Chad, Cyprus, Ethiopia, Guyana, Iraq, Lebanon, Nigeria (1960–66 and 1976–83), the Philippines, Sri Lanka, and Sudan. The negative outcomes greatly outnumber the positive cases 12–4, or, arguably, 14–2 (Roeder 1999).

If warfare within territorial states arises from the weakness of these states—their failure to win legitimate authority and to create an inclusive state-community—the obvious remedy is to strengthen the vulnerable states (Holsti 1996, chap. 9). But how is this to be done? All the standard proposed solutions that may be useful in some circumstances have severe limitations, and unwanted side effects under some other conditions. Thus, institutionalized political parties and regular elections hold promise but often are subverted in societies with deep ethnic, regional, and class divisions. Similarly, federalism and regional devolution—proven valuable in conflict management in Western democracies—have not prevented civil wars in societies as diverse as Nigeria, Zaire, and Yugoslavia. Consociational political systems—basically consisting of elite bargaining with vetoes available on vital ethnic issues—have helped to maintain accommodative policies in Switzerland and, less successfully, in Belgium and a few other cases. But the conditions necessary for such arrangements to work well are rare; for example, demographic stability, segmented ethnies, and rewarding economic and political interdependence.

Sometimes all earlier claims by a restive minority for economic and political equity and cultural expression and autonomy can be met, but peaceful accommodation can still be wrecked by non-negotiable insistence upon symbolic issues, such as language dominance. The case of Québec comes close to being prototypical, but there are many others (cf. Sri Lanka) (Gurr 1993b, 162).

No line of action will be cost-free—there always are trade-offs. One may get peaceful accommodation among ethnies at the price of frozen inequalities. A particular ethny may gain control of the central state apparatus, but with the high costs of continuing suppressive and chronic conflict. Interethnic violence may be ended for a time by power-sharing bargains that immobilize the system so that crucial needed changes are not made. A policy of seeking societal integration through amnesty and truth and reconciliation devices may secure confessions of wrong-doing at the price of retributive justice. For a minority ethny, the price of continuing access to economic opportunities may be a loss of political power.

Finally, there is an important difference between conflict management and conflict resolution (Azar 1990): "management" may take place without dealing at all with the basic causes of conflict, as in deterrence or mediation; "resolution" implies a search for ways of bringing about a mutual convergence of interests and a reconciliation of the parties as members of a shared community. Managed conflicts may reignite if there is even a minimal shift in perceptions. Genuine resolutions involve meeting the fundamental needs of the parties, the establishment of mutual trust, and the growth of consensus on shared goals and the rules of the game. Such resolutions are at once difficult, rare, highly rewarding.

The Range of Alternatives—and Visions of the Good Society

Decades ago, Zolberg (1968, 87) pointed to the problem of the containment of conflict as a central problem of the social sciences, and advocated "the institutionalization at the cultural level of a belief that conflict is a potentially manageable aspect of society, rather than the persistence of wishful thinking about its permanent disappearance expressed in the form of ideological or scientific theories."

As preceding chapters have shown, violent ethnic conflicts are not inevitable. Most ethnies at any given time are not fighting one another or the state that encompasses them. Clearly, then, ethnic warfare is preventable. This is true, in part, because the *necessary* conditions for severe conflicts are not *sufficient* conditions. Without definite ethnic identities, there is no basis for collective conflict. Without group rivalries for scarce valuables or resources—jobs, land, credit, educational opportunities, religious rights, language rights, governmental contracts and subsidies, and so on—the likelihood of violent conflict approaches zero. Even with strong ethnic rivalry, conflict often is avoided by regulation and mediation by a well-functioning democratic state. The absence of provocative intervention by ethnic diaspora or by other states reduces risk. Even in new states containing a great many ethnies, peaceful relations can be maintained in complex political rivalries and shifting coalitions, as in the remarkable case of Tanzania (see Gurr 1990).

Earlier chapters noted evidence that the structural conditions associated with peaceful interethnic relations included at least moderate economic security and positive interdependence, absence of extreme ethnic inequalities (relatively equitable distribution of opportunities and rewards), non-ethnic political parties, a political system relatively open to voice and access, and lack of imposed segregation and discrimination. Even in such societies relative deprivation exists, and ethnies often have substantial grievances but do not engage in collective violence. We found that a basic factor was group weakness: lack of resources, internal dissension and social fragmentation, lack of a committed elite, small size, and geographic dispersion. In addition, violent protest and rebellion may be inhibited by fear of provoking retaliatory responses from other ethnies or the state, and by lack of third-party support.

For basic causes of grievances, reduction of risk depends upon such factors as economic growth, reduction in extreme economic inequalities, establishment of democratic regimes (where feasible), and access and voice for ethnic minorities (including protection). These are enormously complex, macro-level conditions that are not easily changed in the short run. For present purposes, their significance is as predictive indicators of likely conflicts ahead. For the long run, they can be the object of policies and actions by states and other major collective actors. Indeed, many plausible policy suggestions already exist (see, e.g., Van Evera 1994).

Severe ethnic conflicts have appeared most often in those situations in which ethnic identity has become the primary basis for individuals' total life chances. To reduce the likelihood of violence, some ways must be found to give people a basis other than ethnic membership for their physical security, psychosocial support, and economic and political opportunities.

A strong state, governed by reasonably secure elites, can be a key player in maintaining ethnic peace by means of mediation and arbitration of disputes and opposing demands. By clarifying the preferences and claims of ethnic organizations and providing accurate information to all parties, benign states can reduce misunderstandings and unrealistic fears. Similarly, a trustworthy state regime provides crucial third-party assurance that agreements will be fulfilled and that lethal aggression will not be tolerated. Such assurance is a prime requirement in multi-ethnic societies for avoiding the Intrinsic Security Dilemma and for rendering commitments reliable and enforceable. The particular institutional arrangements that provide realistic assurances include power sharing through electoral rules and mutual veto powers, as well as ethnic balance in judicial, police, and military agencies. Whatever the particulars, the essential requirements are that no ethny is excluded from effective voice and that there are credible safeguards against ethnic domination and violence (cf. Lake and Rothchild 1996).

Strategies for preventing collective violence may be coercive or noncoercive. The most obvious and time-honored recourse of states for dealing with ethnic unrest is coercive suppression. In the modern world such coercive actions have a mixed record, and only rarely have kept the peace for long periods. Often the result has been increased resentment and rebellious uprisings. The complex consequences are shown in time series data (1960–80) for some twenty-four countries (Gupta, Singh, and Sprague 1993). Not surprisingly, evidence suggests that governmental coercion exerted against dissident activities (ranging from protest demonstrations to coups d'état) has different effects depending upon the type of regime and the type of dissidence. In democratic regimes, state sanctions are followed by increased protest demonstrations. But in nondemocratic regimes, severe sanctions bring a decrease in political deaths. Apparently if state repression is used, its effectiveness in reducing lethal conflict—in the short run—is greatest when it is sudden and severe. But the long-run sequences that have appeared repeatedly are recurrent protests and protracted conflicts—in Israel, South Africa, Guatemala, Sudan, Kashmir, Sri Lanka, the Philippines, Burma (Myanmar), Lebanon, Iraq, Yugoslavia, and Russia (Chechnya). In general, repressive dominance in recent experience has seldom been stable.

Yet coercive means are widely used, as in the attempts by states and state-sponsored organizations to *eliminate* an unwanted ethnic people, through forced emigration, violent ethnic cleansing, forcible population transfer between states or regions, and, at the ultimate extreme, massacres and genocide. Also coercive are policies and practices of *domination* and forcible suppression that silence protests and claims of ethnic challenges. A final type of imposed control is actual *partition* of a multi-ethnic state into two or more political entities.

Among the noncoercive approaches are those that may be called *pluralistic accommodations,* having the common feature of some kind of ethnic autonomy. These include measures to develop or protect cultural pluralism in language, religion, family and kinship norms, and the like. The state may develop various forms of devolution of political authority, as in federalism and in regional autonomy; the common feature here is decentralization of power. A different road to ethnic accommodation consists of some form of sharing of political power in the central state, as for example in proportional ethnic representation in elective offices, in reserved seats or administrative offices, in military forces, or in rotation of key decision-making posts. A special form of power sharing is consociationalism.

A third main approach is the establishment of *electoral systems* designed to reduce ethnic polarization and to encourage compromises and consensus. The essential characteristic is that politicians must win the support of multi-ethnic constituents to be elected. The intent is to harness self-interest to political moderation.

In a different dimension are those state policies that seek to reduce ethnic conflict through *group preferences,* as in diverse forms of affirmative action.

Next are policies and procedures aimed at ensuring *voice and access* in major institutions, such as equal access to political participation, employment, educational opportunities, and public facilities and services. Under this rubric are anti-segregation and anti-discrimination laws and regulations, and provisions for their enforcement. More generally, provision is made for equal access to the courts and for legal remedies against misuse of state power, as in cases of police brutality or discrimination in the penal system. In recent decades, an important addition to these measures is the acceptance in national constitutions and laws and court decisions of internationally recognized human rights. These acknowledged rights derive from treaties, from the United Nations Charter and subsequent declarations and resolutions, from regional conventions and other agreements, from international law and the rulings of international courts. Although often ignored by current governments, the doctrines of human rights surely will be significant in future ethnic policies.

This brief inventory is enough to show that efforts to avoid, reduce, manage, or ameliorate severe ethnic conflicts are both numerous and diverse. They may be undertaken before, during, or after the conflicts. They may use any or all of the major ways of influencing any human conduct—that is, inducement (reward, exchange), persuasion (information, appeal to values, example), coercion (effective threat), or the activation of commitments that define what is possible (treaties, laws, the claims of homeland constituents). They may operate at the macro level of "high politics" among the leaders of states and interstate agencies and international non-governmental organizations. At the same time or separately, the violence-mitigating efforts may take the micro form of intrastate and local activities, of people-to-people interaction, and the diffuse interpersonal flows of information and other attempts to persuade.

It is not surprising, therefore, that no simple formula emerges from all this variety, or that appraisals of effective procedures and policies are difficult to make and frequently are inconclusive. There is no universal solution, no panacea, no silver bullet. Instead, a diverse array of possible means must be fitted to similarly diverse ethnies, states, political alignments and environing social structures, and differing trajectories of past conflict and cooperation. Some of these possibilities we will now examine.

Arms Control and Deterrence

Some of the major policies or methods that may be used by states, ethnic formations, and other interested parties to avert or forestall violent intrastate ethnic conflict mirror those employed in the interstate arena.

A major approach to avoidance or restriction of conflict between states is arms control, repeatedly and extensively attempted in many diverse forms. Well-informed evaluations of its effectiveness differ radically, and the resulting perennial controversies often have been inconclusive. Our present concern, however, is in the relevance of arms limitations to intrastate ethnic conflicts. To the extent that interstate arms control agreements actually do reduce states' stocks of weaponry, there may be a reduction in incentives for violent repression of ethnic challengers, but clear evidence of such effects is lacking. A similar appraisal applies to the many efforts to restrict the worldwide flood of light arms—AK-47s, Uzis, M-16s, shoulder-fired missiles, land mines, light machine guns, grenades and grenade launchers, and so on and on—not forgetting knives, pistols, and machetes shipped in boxes labeled "agricultural implements." The difficulty of restricting the highly profitable trade in light arms is formidable. The weaponry is cheap, easily transported and concealed, and obtainable from a large number of suppliers that are linked in elaborate networks of sophisticated dealers. Nevertheless, citizens' movements, nongovernmental organizations, international organizations, and individual states will continue efforts to restrict and modify the trade. Any resulting control will somewhat reduce killing power and may reduce the sense of threat among the contesting parties.

Of more immediate urgency are efforts, both successful and unsuccessful, to reduce interethnic violence or to forestall its escalation through disarmament of the opposing forces. Full implementation of peace accords sometimes is wrecked by refusal of one party to surrender its arms, as in Northern Ireland around the turn of the twenty-first century. Disarmament, however, was accomplished in several civil wars, including Guatemala and Mozambique. NATO intervention brought about a negotiated disarmament of Albanian rebels in Macedonia in 2001. So this form of arms control does hold substantial promise.

A second and highly important approach to prevention or limitation of ethnic violent conflict is deterrence, the credible threat by an external party to use force or other negative sanctions against a party that is believed to be intending to use or already using violence. The target of deterrence may be a state that is threatening an ethnic minority or that is engaged in armed repression, expulsions, and mass killings. Or the object of deterrence may be an ethnic political party or social movement that is inciting violence or advocating expulsion and killing of ethnic "Others." Negative sanctions by another state may be threatened against those who attempt to exclude members of a rival ethny from political voice, as in the case of external sanctions against some indigenous Fijian leaders who in 2000 mounted a forcible coup to displace persons of Indian descent from any political power. The party attempting to deter the undesired actions may be another state acting unilaterally, or a coalition or a regional organization (e.g., the Organization of American States or the Economic Community of West African States), or the United Nations, or (conceivably) a major nongovernmental organization.

Deterrence has had a decidedly mixed record in interstate affairs. At its worst, military deterrence leads to arms races, as in the years preceding World War I. At its best, it is most likely to be effective either in a nuclear stand-off between rivals in a bipolar world or in limited bargaining in relatively low-stakes confrontations. It needs well-organized collective actors, able to make reliable commitments, and it deals best with clearly defined issues.

None of the conditions most favorable for effective deterrence is likely to be found in ethnic-based civil wars or other forms of collective intrastate violence. Effective bargaining and reliable agreements are rendered difficult by reason of the familiar characteristics of ethnic struggles—multiple parties, factionalism, rapidly shifting coalitions, multiple poorly defined issues, intense emotional involvements, and complex "symbolic politics." Factional leaders of violent movements may not fear sanctions that are threatened against the larger society of which they are a militant part. And dictatorial heads of repressive ethnocracies may wholly discount those sanctions that injure the population but leave the ruling clique in power.

How likely is it, then, that internal warfare and democide can be deterred by the threat of military intervention? The short answer is that it is possible, but likely only in exceptional cases. As Holsti (1996, 193) specifies: "Uprisings of resistance, secessionist wars, and communal strife are not likely to be deterred by the armed forces of an international organization even if such forces are deployed prior to the outbreak of armed violence—a rare event." The chief use, thus far, of preventive military intervention has been either to support one party or to attempt peace-enforcing, as in the former Yugoslavia or in Sierra Leone in 2000.

Yet military threat or action is not the only means for deterrence; a wide assortment of economic and political sanctions may be used, such as embargoes, withdrawal of aid, or international legal actions.

One possibly useful mode of deterrence is preventive deployment: that is, the deployment of small multinational military forces along one or both sides of a border between states or regional bodies when there is a severe threat of outbreak or escalation of conflict. Such forces presumably will be authorized by the Security Council of the UN and could be primarily drawn from regional organizations. In one of several conceivable versions, the positioned military forces would be lightly armed and too small to resist a major armed attack, but would serve as a "trip wire"; an attack would activate a larger and better-armed force able to mount effective resistance, taking action under the legal provisions of Chapter 7 of the UN Charter. Whatever the particular arrangements, however, preventive deployment will involve major problems of decision making, funding, timing, organization, and information gathering and analysis. Clearly it is a high-risk strategy and therefore unlikely to be used by the UN or other interstate organizations except in rare circumstances. Up to the beginning of the twenty-first century, the only clear case was the Security Council's approval and the actual deployment of a small force in the former Yugoslav Republic of Macedonia, intended to deter escalation of ongoing ethnic warfare in the region (see Evans 1993, 61–85).

In the absence of definitive evidence, deterrence must still be appraised on its merits in particular cases. Thus a dismissal of the possibilities of deterring intrastate ethnic violence or its spread across state boundaries would be premature. As we have noted, ethnic disagreements and political struggles do not inevitably lead to violence, nor are leaders of governments and ethnies immune to anticipations of costs from third-party sanctions and interventions. Just as the failure to extend aid can increase the likelihood of conflict, the threat of withdrawal may be of some use.

Preventive Diplomacy

Actions taken by third parties when conflict already is on the threshold of large-scale violence—"late prevention"—is not a promising strategy (Evans 1993). At that point mutual tensions will be high and preparations for armed confrontation will be under way. Intervention will be crucially dependent on detailed and accurate intelligence—and the information must be believed and carefully evaluated by decision makers. In the case of Rwanda, the notorious failure of the UN officials to respond to clear warning of imminent genocide illustrates the danger of an inadequate system for effective late prevention.

The alternative of early intervention evidently has many attractions for agencies committed to preventive policies. But if early action is so desirable, why is it not taken more often? Obvious objections are that the world continually contains numerous "trouble spots"; that interventions are costly and their outcomes uncertain; that states are reluctant to consent to, or support, preventive actions unless their national vital interests are at risk.

"Preventive diplomacy" should not be confused with the much broader concept of "conflict prevention." The latter term applies to a wide range of actions—from programs aimed at reduction in poverty or establishing a democratic state to mediation in specific territorial disputes. Basic structural or systemic problems call for long-range, complex, expensive, and highly controversial approaches. Preventive diplomacy, in contrast, consists of a more modest set of efforts to deal with situations in which states and substate actors are seen as likely to engage in coercive actions that may cause collective violence. A useful formulation says that preventive diplomacy consists of "actions, policies, and institutions that are taken deliberately to keep particular states or organized groups within them from threatening or using organized violence, armed force, or related forms of coercion . . . as the means to settle interstate or national political disputes" (Lund 1996a, 384–85). Preventive diplomacy is employed in unstable situations to forestall likely violence: by definition it ceases to exist once a full-blown crisis or overt violence erupts.

In a comprehensive survey and evaluation of preventive diplomacy, Lund (1996b) has identified five conditions associated with relative success: early and unified third-party pressures; multiple strategies of reward and warning to meet the varied sources of potential violence; active support by or tolerance from potential disruptive third parties (major powers or nearby countries); within the target society, strong state institutions and accommodative political leaders; and finally, well-organized disputing parties with effective control over their constituents. Preventive efforts have not been highly effective in societies with fragmented contestants, severe ethnic tensions and few shared institutions, and with autocratic political leaders. In sharply divided ethnic struggles, therefore, one might say that prevention is less likely where most needed.

Because early efforts are more effective than late ad hoc responses to crisis conditions, and serious conflicts usually are preceded by warning signs in the early stages, interested third parties—the UN, regional alliances, ad hoc coalitions, or individual states and nongovernmental organizations—need to continually monitor potentially troublesome situations, to establish early warning systems, and to have preventive services ("good offices," conciliation, mediation, general diplomacy) routinely available. So-called "lessons from international experience" are said to imply that such arrangements can help to clarify issues, broaden the options perceived by the contenders, call attention to common interests, identify possible compromises and new alternatives, and improve persuasive communication. All of these presumed virtues, of course, are traditional contributions of ordinary diplomacy. Preventive diplomacy focuses sharply on reducing the likelihood of mass violence.

But to have the desired positive effects, preventive diplomacy has to overcome several main difficulties (Jentleson 1996). First, there is the problem of obtaining effective warning of possible crisis through adequate quantity and quality of accurate information. Second, even if an accurate diagnosis has been developed, there is the chronic problem of activating the political will to act before the crisis occurs. The relevant national and international authorities may not be convinced that their vital interests are threatened or that intervention can be effective, and a decision to act may involve a lengthy process of mobilization that is too slow to meet the urgency on the ground. Third, there always are difficult tasks of establishing credibility and trust, and maintaining the will for long-term involvement. Fourth, there is the formidable barrier of the claims to state sovereignty; the traditional norm is likely to prevail unless countered by acceptable international legal claims. As new norms of justifiable intervention currently are being established, preventive diplomacy through the UN potentially can be a major resource to meet threats posed to international peace and security by internal strife. In actual cases, the UN's efforts often have been hastily improvised, slow-moving, and lacking in the funds, personnel, and other organizational resources needed for continuing and systematic actions. But observers of the conflicts we have reviewed in this work—diplomats, journalists, workers in nongovernmental organizations—repeatedly have argued that with greater support, and some needed reforms, the United Nations (and the Organization for Security and Cooperation in Europe) holds promise for important preventive actions: the ability to mediate conflicts, to monitor peace agreements and elections, to help negotiate agreements, to engage in early diplomacy, and to detect warning signs of impending conflicts, including the disintegration of peace accords (cf. Zimmermann 1996, 242–43).

State Structures and Major Policies: Proposed Political Solutions

The likelihood of maintaining peaceful ethnic relations depends upon the *interaction* of (1) basic social conditions, such as the nature of ethnic formations and economic deprivation or prosperity; (2) state structure—the organization of the polity; and (3) ongoing sociopolitical processes—voting, elections, collective mobilization, factionalism, and so on. Much scholarly controversy has dealt with the relative weight to be attributed to each set of factors and with the varying interactions among them. What is also apparent, however, is that state structures do nevertheless affect the policies of governing regimes, in particular regarding whether domination or accommodation is chosen.

In democratic states, strategies of accommodation helped to produce gains for ethnopolitical "minorities" in some twenty-three of twenty-four cases during the 1980s and 1990s (Gurr 1993b, chap. 10). The main policies include provision of political and civil rights for subordinated ethnoclasses, programs intended to reduce poverty, and recognition and support for minority cultures and languages. For regional nationalists and indigenous peoples, accommodation has meant granting measures of self-government and control of local resources, as well as some outright subsidies. Court decisions often have been important in implementing such policies.

"Relatively successful" states presumably include the more than twenty countries in the "peace zone" stretching from New Zealand and Japan to Finland and the Baltic states, but also India, Malaysia, Benin, Mauritius, Lesotho, Tunisia, several emerging Latin American democracies, and others (cf. Holsti 1996, 185). Political changes in Madagascar and economic development in Botswana also illustrate developments that can support stronger states and less conflict-ridden politics.

Many ethnies occupy particular, especially peripheral, regions in central states: East Timor and Aceh in Indonesia, the Delta in Nigeria, north and east in Sri Lanka, the south in Sudan. Where such ethnic concentrations exist, denial of the demands for autonomy that are likely to arise have led to separatism and conflict. Regional autonomy—on its face promising as a preventive measure—depends upon the willingness of governing regimes to accept this reorganization. State resistance often makes regional autonomy a source of conflict rather than accommodation.

Decision makers and other leaders of dominant ethnies that have substantial control of a state do have available to them a rich, although unsystematic, store of folk wisdom or common sense concerning ways of reducing ethnic conflict. Although this proverbial store may lack academic respectability—being judged as untested, banal, imprecise, platitudinous, and the like—much of it corresponds to the findings of more tightly controlled research. Here are a few illustrative precepts:

(1) Know the situation. Respect reliable information. Continually monitor changes in attitudes and behavior.
(2) Be alert to signs of increased tensions, fears, aspirations, claims. Pay attention.
(3) Maintain lines of communication. Listen. Negotiate continuously.
(4) Be moderate. Avoid provocation. Show respect.

224

(5) Do not overreact to protests. Do not make extreme threats.

(6) Do not break promises. Keep agreements.

(7) Provide access and voice across ethnic lines.

(8) Reward cooperative leaders.

(9) Be patient.

(10) In extremity, be open to claims for some types of ethnic autonomy.

More formally, certain broad policies appear to have contributed to maintaining relatively low levels of ethnic conflict in Western democracies. These include guarantees of political and civil rights, access to educational and economic opportunities, protections against extreme economic distress, recognition of and provision of resources for maintaining ethnic cultures, and—for indigenous peoples and regional nationalists—provision of special aids and limited autonomy.

It is a valuable truism that violent ethnic conflict is rendered less likely to the extent that coexisting ethnies can develop mutual trust. The likelihood of ethnic violence can be reduced when and if a state that is perceived by its minorities as representing the interests of a dominant ethny can make credible commitments to honor and safeguard the interests of these minorities. Commitments to protect minorities in their basic security and to ensure voice in vital political decisions will be more believable in democratic or consociational systems with constitutional (or other institutional) guarantees.

The less the fear of oppression and of violence by the Other, the less likely interethnic violence. Ethnic activists and entrepreneurs typically emphasize the sharpness of collective boundaries and impute hostile or aggressive intentions to rival ethnies. Preventive actions by states and nongovernmental organizations, accordingly, may include use of mass media and other modes of communication to disseminate credible countermessages that point to common interests and values, emphasize shared commitments to nonviolent political processes, and present personalized images of ethnic individuals. Anything that reduces a sense of future threat lessens the security dilemma and the polarization it incites. Anything that enhances mutual confidence in safety and in the protection of group status increases interethnic stability.

On the more positive side, interethnic relations will be more cooperative to the extent that mutual recognition and respect are shown. Public displays of admiration for achievements, celebrations of joint enterprises, acknowledgment of ethnic historical leaders and accomplishments—these illustrate the numerous ways in which respect and appreciation can be demonstrated. Mutual positive regard is increased whenever spokespersons of each ethny can truthfully say good things about the other.

Political leaders can help to reduce ethnic tensions by taking strong

225

stands against internal violence between ethnies, and by discouraging provocative propaganda, as well as by dramatizing interethnic cooperation and solidarity. Ruling elites can recognize a need for early alertness to signs of increasing friction (e.g., "hate" messages, street fights, increased sales of weapons) by maintaining systems for monitoring the ethnic climate. Similarly, state policies can encourage and support institutionalized arrangements for conciliation, mediation, and arbitration.

Taken in abstract form, the policies just sketched seem to bear the stigma of being pious platitudes. Taken seriously and applied in concrete social and political forms, however, such generalized prescriptions can represent realistic options in actual cases. Let us review some of the possibilities.

Electoral Systems and Strategies of Moderation

Constitutional provisions for minority protection can help to create over time a presumption that ethnic rivalry and ethnic dominance have limits, that struggles should be rule-governed. But constitutions can be treated as scraps of paper, not effective constraints, in severely divided societies. If there are sharp ethnic cleavages, deep antipathies, and intense rivalry for high stakes, what can support constitutional guarantees?

One major line of analysis answers this crucial question by looking to electoral mechanisms that harness politicians' self-interest in support of moderation over compromise. The basic formula is an electoral system that favors cross-ethnic voting, so that to be elected politicians must appeal to voters not of their own ethny. Moderation will be encouraged by multi-ethnic districts, by multi-ethnic parties, by multi-ethnic voting slates, by vote pooling, and by other specific devices. In contrast, the dynamics of a system of ethnic parties drives ethnic rivalry, so that extreme (militant) fractions compete to attract votes *within* each ethny. Moderating influences are structurally foreclosed. On the other hand, multi-ethnic political coalitions-of-commitment, once established for whatever reasons, provide incentives for inclusive cross-ethnic appeals, for moderated demands, and integrative policies (see the detailed arguments in Horowitz 1985, chaps. 7–10).

Where ethnic parties prevail and minorities do not have credible political protections, elections only show numerical predominance (Pavlowitch 1994, 222), and every election can be a threat. In much of Asia and Africa after the independence of former colonies, the new states contained a numerically dominant ethnic group that took power and excluded all others. Thus ethnic voting could lead to permanent exclusion of minorities. Single-party regimes, civil violence, and military coups were expectable consequences of such classic 60/40 percent, winner-take-all situations. Three main routes have been taken to deal with the dilemma: (1) a *rotating exec-*

utive (not very likely to succeed); (2) *"all-union national government"*—claimed by many one-party systems that actually are systems of ethnic dominance; and (3) rearranging the electoral system to encourage ethnic party *fragmentation*. Option 3 can have two outcomes: (a) Party A splits into two groups, neither with a majority and thus needing interethnic coalitions; or (b) splits occur in both Party A and Party B, producing more fluidity and the possibility of several interethnic coalitions (Horowitz 1985, 629–30).

Negotiation and Ethnic Recognition

When ethnic representatives do seek inclusion in the sociopolitical system rather than separation or rebellion, and the state is committed to nondiscrimination, many issues will be open to negotiated compromises (Esman 1994, 255). The very in-group policing that can support bellicosity in relations of ethnic conflict can reduce violence if initial conditions of interethnic cooperation exist such that in incidents of violence the perpetrators can be sanctioned by their co-ethnics in the interests of maintaining peaceful coexistence (Brubaker and Laitin 1998, 439–40).

The distinction between divisible/distributive and nondivisible/integral objects of contention affects the difficulty of negotiation. Money is a divisible stake; relative prestige or religious allegiance have a dominantly all-or-one, either-or character. The amount of territory controlled is divisible; whether a particular site is a mosque or a temple or a church is not. Contentions over objects to be shared are more easily resolved if the prizes can be subdivided, if need be, into many pieces. In principle, it is possible to arrive at a stable division that seems fair to all parties such that no one can be made better off by changing the shares.

In negotiated settlements, nondivisible stakes require side payments or trade-offs. The Golan Heights *as an entity* either is controlled by Syria or by Israel, not both, and a mutually acceptable bargain presumably would require some trade-offs. When only one issue is a stake and it is indivisible, the issue is non-negotiable and may lead to sheer power struggles (Rothchild 1986). Because relative standing in a stratification system always is zero-sum, it is difficult to negotiate *group status*. More open to agreements are *distributional* issues that lend themselves to exchange, as in allocations of educational opportunities, housing, or even power sharing. The search for trade-offs works best when confidence in the credibility and reliability of the adversary can be increased by step-by-step exchanges during negotiations.

Many claims that are presented as absolute or non-negotiable are actually subject to redefinition when their most important ("real") basis is a demand for recognition and acceptance of identity. When this is the case, the claims often can be satisfied in part by symbolic responses: the naming of streets, buildings, or cities; the right to display flags, monuments, insignia; acknowledgment of and apologies for past wrongs; and paying token compensation (Wedge 1986, 60).

Whereas state policies that aim to reduce ethnic distinctiveness and its political impact have stressed doctrines of "individualism"—individual citizenship, individual rights and duties—and have avoided any recognition of collective ethnic actors or group rights, in other cases states have adopted policies of pluralism. Instead of seeking assimilation, the state recognizes and promotes cultural distinctiveness, supporting multilingual education, or special laws and practices concerning different ethnic religious bodies, and in general encouraging retention of cultural traits and historical memories. When ethnies are strong, pluralism usually means preferential policies, such as the allocation of entitlements on the basis of ethnicity. Over time, pluralistic policies tend to strengthen ethnic parties and political interest groupings. In practice, then, avoidance of severe conflict depends upon continuous balancing and bargaining among ethnic organizations. A typical problem is that of political backlash, a countermobilization of the disaffected against the privileged groupings—which has been a prominent pattern in India and is evident also in several Western countries with new immigrant populations. In fully realized pluralism, the predictable tendencies will be to accentuate separate segments and to move toward some form of ethnic autonomy or power sharing.

Federalism, Devolution, and Ethnic Autonomy

Federalism and decentralization of political authority have been useful in reducing ethnic rivalry and conflict in countries as different from one another as Switzerland, India, and Papua New Guinea (Jalali and Lipset 1992–93, 601). On the other hand, federalism is successful only under special conditions, and has failed in such spectacular cases as Nigeria and Yugoslavia. These obvious generalizations are not helpful, except by calling attention to the need for identifying conditions that differ between successful and unsuccessful instances. The difficulties in the failures include, most prominently, strong ethnic cleavages among regions, great regional inequalities, and discriminatory and inflexible policies of the central state: in short, a "mosaic" society without well-developed mechanisms of economic and political interdependence. Federalism has prospered in societies in which different regions do not represent homelands for strongly bounded ethnies and in which the political system encourages moderation—in ways already suggested.

Closely related to federalism is the devolution of central authority by ceding some decision making to regions and localities, either in functional areas such as education, or in more general jurisdictions such as taxation.

When carried far enough, devolution merges into agreements for autonomy. Applied to ethnoregional claims, such autonomy may range from
limited rights to de facto self-determination. In fact, governmental leaders typically fear that devolution can encourage the appetite for independence, and they often seem to feel threatened by any move toward
reducing the sacredness of a state's territorial boundaries or invoking a
policy of ethnic self-determination. China has Tibet and the Muslim peoples of its western regions. Russia has Chechnya and the Central Asian ethnies. Many African countries are roiled by communal demands and
conflicts. Nevertheless, in the moderately long run there is adequate experience to show that secession rarely is a viable option and that well-de-
signed autonomy agreements often avoid the more costly and less stable
outcomes of suppression.

Power Sharing

Where ethnies are strong, there will be some societies in which some form
of power sharing will be the strategy of choice in the search for peaceful coexistence in deeply divided societies. This is so primarily because in societies
where ethnic allegiances are strong, majority rule is a recipe for ethnic dominance and subordination: whenever one ethny has a majority of voters,
there is no direct constraint upon its political rule, and minorities may feel
permanently excluded from voice and access. To avoid these conflict-
inducing possibilities, some form of power sharing is a prime remedy.

From the experience of power sharing in Switzerland, several generalizations have been drawn: (1) past violent conflict does not preclude later
power sharing, but a lengthy learning process is required to develop workable arrangements; (2) power sharing is most feasible when the various
ethnies have approximately equal economic status; (3) neutrality in foreign policy facilitates power sharing; (4) stability of power sharing may
require frequent use of referenda (Steiner 1990). In several respects
Switzerland is unique, but nevertheless its history suggests that a relatively
stable structure of communal identities and of demographic proportions
may be important elsewhere. The strong form of power sharing illustrated
there usually is labeled as consociationalism—basically an agreement
among elites to share power among ethnic segments of the society while
pursuing their own interests.

Strong criticisms of the consociational model have been made. A particularly comprehensive attack has been presented by Brass (1991, chap.
9), who argues that consociational theories make the unwarranted assumptions that ethnies are stable and nondivisible, that publics are inert
and deferential to elites, and that elites will make consensual bargains. He
further contends that consociational systems are anti-democratic and that

in practice they actually are highly subject to outbidding by communal militants, resulting either in breakdown (Lebanon), ethnic domination (Malaysia), or drastic modification (Belgium). On the other hand, competitive party systems in multicultural democracies have proven to be practicable in major instances, such as the United States, Great Britain, and, thus far, India.

In spite of sharply divergent appraisals, empirical evidence suggests that in one or another form power sharing will be attempted in many of the world's unstable multi-ethnic societies.

Partition

When all attempted political solutions and external interventions have failed to stop severe ethnic conflicts, and one or more of the adversaries calls for its own separate state, an initial reaction of external observers often is the question, "Why not partition the existing country? If they can't live together, let them live separately." But the seemingly simple solution, as is so often the case, is rarely simple. The peaceful separation of Slovakia from the Czech Republic and of Singapore from the Malaysian Federation (1965) are unusual events. In the partition of the island of Cyprus between Greek and Turkish sectors, the installation of international peacekeeping forces prevented further outbreaks of violence for a full generation. But basic issues were not resolved, so that estrangement was solidified. The resulting "frozen conflict" has proved intractable to repeated conventional methods of peacekeeping and negotiations.

Why is partition of the segments of an ethnically divided society rarely peaceful, and why does it rarely produce a stable accommodation of the contending parties? In the first place, states typically resist secession or partition by all the means at their disposal, including military force. Conspicuous recent examples are numerous, including Biafra in Nigeria, Bangladesh in Pakistan, and Kosovo in Yugoslavia. And even if partition has been accomplished, the resulting separate collectivities are unlikely to be ethnically homogenous: usually ethnies will be territorially intermingled, and the very act of partition is likely to bring into play hitherto weak or nonsalient ethnic distinctions within what was at first thought to be a single ethny. Also, the political energizing of a separatist people by a leadership seeking autonomy or secession frequently results in rival movements and factions that easily fall into fratricidal conflict, as in Sri Lanka (Tamils), Eritrea, Somalia, Iraq (Kurds), or southern Sudan.

For all these reasons, partition tends to collective violence. As Donald Horowitz puts it, "Partition . . . with rare exceptions, ought not to be the policy of choice, but of desperation" (1985, 582). Actual partitions involving religious and political differences have included India, Palestine, Ireland, and Cyprus. Other cases have developed directly from superpower rivalries, as in East and West Germany, North and South Korea, and North and South Vietnam. Warfare in such divided states since World War II has resulted in more than 12 million deaths. Yet there are occasions when partition, no matter how unattractive in the eyes of outside observers, will be chosen by the partisans as the lesser of the evils at hand.

Observers who favor partition, however, point to the actual frequency of deadly protracted conflicts. Often the "hurting stalemates" turn out to be bearable stalemates—the level of anguish is endurable, even if terrible. Long-continued civil wars (both ethnic and non-ethnic) always will have created widespread distrust, grief, hatred, and desires for restitution and revenge. At the same time, the breakdown of civic order and the massive destruction of productive assets and infrastructures will have created severe difficulties for the revival of positive societal interdependence. Under these conditions, separation of the mutually alienated peoples may be the least costly situation.

Basic Social Integration and Assimilation

Since states and ethnies are the great central collective actors in the conflicts we have examined, the whimsical formula for ethnic peace would be to abolish ethnies, or states, or both. Since neither erasure is at all feasible, are there other ways in which the central collective actors in ethnic conflicts—states and ethnies—could be rendered less menacing? One route is to seek ways to reduce the strength and salience of ethnicity. Another is to reduce the destructive role of the state. Indeed, some observers, seeing the enormity of mass killings by states, hope for the near-abolition of centralized states as we know them. Short of doing away with the state, indeed, one conceivable solution for ethnic conflicts is the simple and drastic proposal: "Denationalize the state" (van den Berghe 1996, 65). The rationale for this approach is straightforward: if the attempted fusion of ethnicity and statehood encourages, facilitates, or results in nationalistic wars, ethnic cleansing, persecution, massacres, and genocide, then the remedy would be to reduce the politicization of ethnicity—to separate ethnicity entirely from the state and to relegate all ethnic affiliations to private life. The argument draws strength from contemporary movements for devolution of authority, regional autonomy, linguistic pluralism, and non-ethnic bases for citizenship; at the same time, interstate organizations and regulations reduce the autonomy of the state, and thereby its nationalistic claims. A further basis for breaking the linkages between state and ethnicity is a system of strictly individual rights, with no place for recognition of group rights (van den Berghe 1996, 67).

How far ethnicity can be made to fade away in the political world obviously is problematic, and certainly the prospects are highly variable across regions and states. Since the institutional emphasis on ethnicity is a matter of degree, however, deemphasizing ethnicity in public policies is one pragmatic route to reducing conflict.

Where the state remains strong, the most obvious alternatives are ethnic assimilation or some form of pluralism. In short, there is an important fork in the road toward workable political policies and practices concerning ethnic diversity: one road leads through pluralism and power sharing, the other moves from initial tolerance and interdependence to mutual accommodation, and thence to substantial assimilation into a common culture. The first route can be followed quickly, but political stability over the longer run requires continuous and difficult balancing of opposing interests and incompatible claims. On the other hand, the move toward the second is complex, uncertain, and has its main positive effects only after a considerable time: the costs come early, the benefits later. Yet policies facilitating assimilation have led to some of the most durable arrangements for maintaining ethnic peace.

Success in securing mutual acceptance among ethnic peoples depends not only upon the large-scale processes just reviewed, but also upon the everyday experiences of individuals in small groups and localized networks that generate much of the content of ethnic identities and interethnic evaluations and stereotypes. A substantial inventory of social, psychological, anthropological, and sociological research has documented the relevant processes (Williams 1947, 1977, 1994). So, for example, there is much evidence that nonstereotypic and friendly interethnic relationships are favored when interactions are frequently repeated, are of equal status, and result in the joint accomplishment of valued objectives. Together with a history of past cooperation and the mutual expectation that the relationships will continue into an indefinite future, these are major conditions favoring an "evolution of cooperation" (Axelrod 1984).

The reduction of categorical ethnic distinctions is another avenue for mutual accommodation and acceptance. Its importance derives from the basic character of ethnicity itself: any marked categorization of persons creates expectations of cooperation and trust or the reverse, even in the absence of actual interaction with the individuals so categorized or of direct knowledge of which persons are in the "in-group" category. Just the sheer awareness of a shared category (smart students, foreigners) is sufficient to induce a differentiation of in-group and out-group and to evoke preferential behavior. Such differentiation appears to be universal across known cultures, and it typically leads to some degree of in-group favoritism—although it does not uniformly result in hostile out-group discrimination (Brewer 1999; Williams 1964). This unavoidable segmentation of social ties suggests once again the many-sided question of how social integration can be attained in large multi-ethnic societies. We have just reviewed what might be called political engineering approaches to this problem. Are there other important roads toward prevention or amelioration of ethnic conflicts?

We proposed in Chapter 2 that religion as a sociocultural phenomenon is a special case of ethnic attachment and cleavage. Given the strength of these attachments, if leaders and officials of a religiously divided multi-ethnic state wish to preserve internal peace, they are unlikely to do so by the imposition of laws and practices that directly threaten followers of one faith-grouping and signal the dominance of another. A striking case is the 1983 action of the Northern Islamic regime in the Sudan to impose Islamic law, *sharia*, breaking the peace accords that had been negotiated in 1972. In a magisterial study, *War of Visions: Conflict of Identities in the Sudan* (1995), Francis M. Deng has shown how protracted deadly conflict grew out of the attempt of the central government to exert dominance and to impose an Arabic-Islamic identity—racial, cultural, linguistic, and religious—upon the animistic and Christian ethnic peoples of the South. The religio-political polarization thus induced interacted with other complex regional and ethnic divisions and with rival claims to resources to destroy previously conceivable arrangements for a peaceable federalized society. Another case in point is the dynamic interplay of ethnic, regional, and religious identities (Islamic and Christian) in Nigeria, where the attempted secession of Ibos into the projected state of Biafra was put down in a civil war in which a million people died. In the same society, by the year 2000 new lethal conflicts developed in the Islamic Northern provinces as eight of them adopted *sharia*, leading to the exodus of many Christians from "mixed" regions. Similar conflicts have occurred in Indonesia, notably in peripheral regions, and in other countries where political control becomes defined as a central "religious" issue.

Some separation of religion and state—some toleration of religious/ethnic diversity—has been necessary for peaceful coexistence in societies as different as the Ottoman Empire and the United States. Strong convictions and opportunistic interests may lead to rejection of this historical "lesson," but that is another story.

What is the place of consensus upon beliefs, values, and norms in the functioning of societies containing ethnic/religious/cultural diversity and sharp differences in moral views? It appears that, by definition, such societies cannot ensure harmony or mutual accommodation by consensus upon norms (Berger 1998). Some accommodations can be developed through acceptance of shared rules and procedures, but some conflicts run too deep to be resolved by such rules of the road. If neither normative nor nonprocedural consensus is sufficient to maintain social order (or cohesion), what remains? One answer points to "mediating institutions" that act in effect as third parties in social conflicts. Although effective mediation is not always or necessarily provided by the institutionalized civic sphere of voluntary associations and other nongovernmental groupings, many potentially severe conflicts can be forestalled or reduced and controlled by the workings of markets and the relationships created by positive economic interdependence. Similarly, agents of the state sometimes can mediate conflicts that otherwise would spiral out of the control of the protagonists and of local institutions. And state intervention (which often is not perceived as such) is pervasive in the form of courts and the legal system—where in fact the great majority of small-scale disagreements are settled in the United States and other Western democracies.

State-centered proposals for reducing ethnic conflicts, useful as they may be, have severe limitations. Above all, (1) they tend to ignore the great importance of cultural presuppositions that define (or frame) the issues and set the agenda for political action, and (2) they minimize the influence of social movements (the civil rights movement in the United States, *Solidarnosc* in Poland, mobilization against racist groups in France and Germany). Lasting changes in ethnic relations are unlikely unless there is pervasive discussion at all levels of a society. As an experienced diplomat has insisted (Saunders 1999), sustained dialogues among the citizenry often will be a prerequisite for effective negotiations. Many conflicts are not ready for negotiation, and will only be tractable when leaders and their constituents have dealt with fears, conceptions of collective identity, and questions of injustice and historical grievances.

Because so much of ethnic rivalries and conflicts ensue from struggles over collective respect and dignity, an obvious means of reducing tension is public recognition of a group position of esteem (Esman 1994, 218). Recognition may be in the form of official holidays and commemorations (Martin Luther King Jr. Day), official apologies for past wrongs, appointment of individuals to honored positions, public monuments, and the like. Leaders in all fields of social life can show by words and deeds that cultural differences are accepted and respected, that public expressions of ethnic hatred and contempt are not permissible, that common values and interests reach across ethnic lines (if and when this is, in fact, the case).

In societies committed to civic patriotism, as distinct from ethnic nationalism, even if one ethny is politically dominant, other ethnic leaders can be accepted into the higher levels of the state, of economic organizations, the media, and education. Public policies can be designed to reduce or effectively eliminate involuntary segregation and ethnic discrimination. And an overarching sense of shared identity can be fostered by emphasis in the educational system and in public discourse on common national symbols, beliefs, and values. Rituals and ceremonies can dramatize inclusiveness and a common future.

In a society in which acceptance of ethnic diversity has become widespread, the development and promulgation of codes of public civility may help to maintain the accommodative order—without requiring a deeper consensus. To date, we have little systematic evidence on this proposition, but ordinary observation strongly suggests that norms of proper conduct can bridge over many difficulties and substantially reduce social friction.

In general, the conditions most conducive to ethnic peace parallel those that favor interstate peace—in capsule summary: *connection, complementarity, consensus.* Connection means continuing interaction, creating dense and rich communication. Complementarity means multiple ties of positive and complex interdependence in economic and political affairs. Consensus means the growth of similarities and compatibilities in culture, such as acceptance of democratic ideas. All these conditions and processes will be favored by the effective functioning of strong states embedded in developed civic social structures. Also, over some extended time, mutual accommodation may be facilitated by social learning from past experiences of futile and ruinous conflicts.

Finally, it must be said, none of the approaches here reviewed, nor any actual combination of them, guarantees that violent ethnic conflict can be entirely avoided. The likelihood of deadly outbreaks can be reduced and mutual accommodation can be fostered by careful and well-informed statecraft, based on a complex and flexible social structure. But there often will be some oppositions of beliefs and values, and some incompatible collective claims that cannot be resolved in the short run in particular times and places. The prospect is not for paradise, but a less savage world may be possible. This hope alone is enough to motivate sustained efforts to understand the wars within.

CHAPTER TEN

Terminations, Accommodations, and Resolutions

World Context—Again . . .

Just as ethnic conflicts can best be understood by placing them in their local, national, and international settings, so can the endings of conflicts.

In the early years of the twenty-first century, three great societal processes were transforming the world. Each is a complex set of sub-processes. The first is commonly called globalization—a vague term covering much diversity. In economic affairs, it includes worldwide financial markets in which stocks and bonds, currency, and other financial instruments totaling trillions of dollars can be bought and sold in a matter of hours. It includes direct foreign investments in business firms. It includes the intra-firm transnational dealings in which the various divisions of a single firm trade among themselves. Whatever the particular forms of economic globalization, however, the effect is that of heightened interdependence across the boundaries of nominally sovereign states. All major economies are linked together in a massive web of exchanges affecting interest rates, monetary supplies, prices, wages, and movements of information, services, and people.

Globalization also means rapid mass communication and transportation, extensive intercultural contacts, and growth of some forms of shared culture. At the same time there is an array of other less-welcome worldwide forms of "globalization": the international reach of well-financed and well-organized networks of violent terrorism; the extensive impact of local and regional warfare; and the spread of diseases, pests, and air and water pollution.

The second set of macroprocesses is the rapid growth of international and transnational organizations, both intergovernmental (IGOs) and nongovernmental (NGOs). There is the United Nations, and its many important specialized agencies and subsidiary organizations. There are the several major political regional organizations—including the Organization of American States, the Organization of African Unity, the North Atlantic Treaty Organization, and the Arab League. There are the regional arrangements for trade and economic cooperation, ranging from the North American Free Trade Agreement to the Economic Community of West African States. And there is the European Union, the comprehensive economic and political organization that has grown out of earlier, more limited, arrangements for economic cooperation and that has begun to exercise extensive regulation and control over many of the policies and activities of member states. Meanwhile, a dense network of many hundreds of nongovernmental organizations set technical standards, deliver medical care and other humanitarian aid, facilitate professional and scientific communication and cooperation, create linkages among religious organizations, spread social movements, monitor human rights, and increasingly influence the behavior of governments.

Third, transnational flows of people—of economic migrants, business personnel, tourists, and displaced persons and refugees—create new relationships and challenge conventional boundaries. More and more persons have homes in two countries, speak two or more languages, and have continuous personal contacts across state boundaries. Large trans-state ethnic communities link immigrant groups in industrialized countries to the sending countries and hometowns. Dual citizenship is only the tip of this iceberg (Portes, Guarnizo, and Landolt 1999); numerous diaspora link together the sending and the receiving countries through remittances, frequent communication and back-and-forth visitations and migrations, and political influences.

These three master processes are restricting and redefining state sovereignty in multiple ways, eroding the Westphalian doctrines of non-interference and territorial integrity of sovereign states. Increasingly, multilateral interventions are justified in cases of massive violations of human rights, or of widespread humanitarian crises. Increasingly, states find it difficult to carry out unilateral economic policies or to violate international environmental norms without incurring important penalties or disadvantages.

Even as state sovereignty is being thus attenuated and reshaped, substate entities increasingly are resisting centralized state controls. Successful movements for substantial regional autonomy or "devolution" have arisen in the historical European home of the national state: Basque country and Catalonia in Spain, Brittany in France, and Scotland and Wales in the United Kingdom. Actual secession occurred peaceably as Slovakia separated from the Czech Republic. Pressures for ethnic/religious cultural autonomy have emerged on every continent. And no further repetition is needed here to highlight the numerous violent ethnopolitical encounters that have been the main objects of our own analysis.

The three Master Processes continually interact. The weakening of absolute state sovereignty and the growth of interstate organizations provide political space for autonomy claims within states. The growth of interstate authority encourages dissenting collectivities within states to seek legitimation and support from outside in their efforts to gain increased voice and control. Economic globalization reduces the state's claim to an exclusive role as protector, adjudicator, and dispenser of benefits. Intergovernmental and international NGOs become increasingly important as actors in dealing with economic distress, collective violence, and state impositions. While the world becomes more closely linked and interdependent, the differential impact of interstate processes upon different parts of state-societies recurrently produces "backlash" in the form of militant ethnocentric and nationalistic political movements. Demands for protectionism and the restriction of immigration grow. Workers who lose jobs, small businesses now unable to compete, managers subject to corporate "downsizing," communities faced with plant closings—all such losers may come to blame immigrants, the UN, the IMF, the World Bank, the EU, NAFTA, the World Trade Organization, or all "foreign" influences.

We have seen how ethnic conflicts in this increasingly interconnected world can be ignited and prolonged by translocal influences. Are similar processes at work when such conflicts end?

Every War Must End is the evocative title of a well-known book by Fred Iklé (1971)—a title that may appear to be a truism. But the endings of wars and other collective conflicts may be a very long time in coming: there was the Thirty Years War and the Hundred Years War; there are run-on civil wars that last for decades; feuds and "clan" or "tribal" warfare can go on intermittently for centuries. Not only is it the case that peace can be long deferred, as in regimes of "stable war" (Boulding 1985), but many conflicts can cease without resolution or settlement of basic issues that derive from enduring conditions and that almost guarantee recurrence of violent struggle. *The Guns of August* (Tuchman 1962) fell silent in 1918, but sounded again with renewed ferocity a short generation later.

Definitive resolutions of large-scale ethnic conflicts are rare (cf. Esman 1994). Some of the reasons are not too difficult to find. Short of massive and comprehensive assimilation, the continuity of familial and kinship ties means that ethnic boundaries tend to persist over generations. Given that these ethnic identities endure, it is inevitable that social changes will differentially alter collective status and opportunities. This means that stable interethnic political accommodations will be likely only if there is demographic stability, economic well-being, and low levels of threat. Change rarely will have the same impacts across ethnies. When advantaged collectivities see their position eroding, they are likely to feel that what is rightfully theirs is in hazard. When the disadvantaged groupings gain enough to hope for more, rising aspirations may outrun the willingness of political dominants to make concessions. All this is familiar ground, and so is the phenomenon of intractable ethnic conflicts.

Previous chapters of our review have noted many long-lasting ethnic conflicts. Thus, major protracted ethnopolitical warfare has included the more than thirty years of the Eritrean rebellion in Ethiopia (Ottaway 1991)—an insurgency joined in the later years by the Tigrean People's Liberation Front, the Oromo Liberation Front, and several other collective movements—and the Sudanese civil wars from 1956 to 1972 and from 1983 into the twenty-first century. The civil war in El Salvador (both a class conflict and an ethnic struggle) lasted over a decade. The violent conflict between the Tamil insurgents and the Sinhalese state in Sri Lanka has been carried on with great ferocity since 1983. Since 1975 a complex civil war, with ethnoregional cleavages, has devastated Angola (Rothchild and Hartzell 1991). Separatist ethnic conflicts have been endemic in Burma (Myanmar) over more than a half century. The chronic low-level conflict in Northern Ireland began in 1969 and an uneasy peace was only partially in place at the beginning of the twenty-first century. The ethnoclass civil war in Guatemala lasted from 1960 to 1996. The ethnoregional conflict in Mindanao in the Philippines has resisted resolution since 1974. The roll call goes on: West Africa has been the scene of multiple violent conflicts that have combined ethnic cleavages with political struggles for control of valuable resources as in Nigeria, Angola, Sierra Leone, and Liberia—conflicts frequently leading to state failures and continuing warlordism. Indonesia's ethnoregional conflicts have included Irian Jaya (1963), Aceh, and East Timor (1975–99). The lists could be extended, and in many cases lulls in the fighting occur only to be followed by new outbreaks.

Why so many of these conflicts last so long is an unhappy and puzzling question, as we have seen. Yet even the most violent collective conflicts end. How does this ending occur?

How Do Violent Conflicts Ever End?

For wars between states the record is mixed, but termination by military force is a dominant pattern. Quincy Wright's magisterial studies (1965) arrived at complex answers, but in his set of 311 substantial wars (1480–1970) less than one half were terminated by treaties of peace. Holsti's sam-

ple of 77 international conflicts, from 1919 to 1965, had just over one half
ending in forcible settlements or continuing standoffs. In a different sample, 1940 to 1990, negotiated settlements were found in 55 percent of the
cases (cited by Walter 1997). Even when a negotiated peace is the outcome, military force shapes the terms of settlement.

Civil wars are even more likely than interstate wars to end in the military
victory of one side. Of the terminated civil wars studied by Licklider (1995,
684), 76 percent ended by the victory of one side, and of 100 internal wars
(1900–1962) studied by Modelski (1964), 78 had ended in complete defeat for either the rebels or the incumbent government. In Gurr's sample
of 28 ethnonational wars of independence between 1944 and 1991, only
12 had ended in independence or some measure of autonomy (1993b,
296–97). So it is true that most civil wars are terminated by the expulsion,
extermination, or total surrender of one side.

Yet civil wars, too, must end, and do, although often some residual violence continues. Over half of the civil wars studied by Licklider (1995)
ended within five years and two-thirds within ten years—but since World
War II some thirty ethnonationalist groupings have fought protracted
wars for independence or for unification with co-ethnies elsewhere (Gurr
1993a). Examples include the Kurds in Turkey and Iraq, the Tamils in
Sri Lanka, the southerners in Sudan, the Kachins and Shan in Myanmar
(Burma),and the Sikhs in India; these continuing conflicts have averaged
about twenty-five years in duration. Estimates of the proportion of civil
wars that have been settled by negotiations vary from 15 percent to one-third
(Stedman 1991; Pillar 1983), depending upon definitions and sources of
data, but the overall picture is that civil wars are more difficult to settle than
interstate wars. This conclusion is supported also by Walter's (1997) finding that negotiations in civil wars typically succeeded only when an external third party agreed to provide security guarantees.

Most contemporary civil wars are primarily fought over issues of ethnic/
religious identity: 69 percent of the 91 civil wars analyzed by Licklider
(1995). In comparison with *political-economic* wars, the *identity* conflicts,
contrary to expectations, did not last longer, had similar casualties, and
were about equally likely to end by negotiations. On the other hand, negotiated endings of identity wars were less likely to be stable, and military
victories in identity wars were more likely than negotiated settlements to
be followed by genocide (all these findings are from Licklider 1995).

The evidence from history, then, is that military victories are more
decisive in bringing an end to identity wars than negotiated settlements—
partly because the latter leave in place vested interests that can be remo-
bilized to resume warfare, whereas military victories destroy the ability of
the defeated to renew the fighting. But the apparent decisiveness may have

a high price in the increased likelihood of mass killings in the aftermath of victory.

Licklider's finding that identity wars "are not clearly more intense than nonidentity ones" (1995, 686) contradicts the plausible expectation that ethnoreligious wars would be especially ferocious. But the finding may be partly explicable in terms of the common dynamics of collective violence: whatever the original issues may have been, civil war feeds on itself as it raises the stakes of victory or defeat, inflicts terrible injuries, and incites fearful hostility and desires for revenge. And in both types of civil wars, the contenders face the difficult prospect of coexistence when the killing has ceased. Nevertheless, the fact that in identity wars negotiated settlements are clearly less likely to be stable than the outcomes of military victories may be due not only to residual "veto power" after negotiation, but also to the resurfacing of ethnic antagonisms. In any case, when negotiated peace does occur it is generally acknowledged to be preferable in human terms to the more destructive endings. Hence, understanding the negotiation processes is a difficult but vital task.

Basic Conditions for Negotiation

Negotiated settlements are not absent for lack of trying, for in nearly half of civil wars between 1940 and 1990, some formal negotiations were attempted. Second, viable peace agreements have been reached in important instances. Hard-won but reasonably effective agreements have been attained in Zimbabwe (formerly Rhodesia), El Salvador, the Sudan (peace for ten years), Namibia, South Africa, Nicaragua (the 1988 accord with the Miskitos), and India (several "tribal" peoples). There have been accommodations with Berbers in the states of the Maghreb, between Muslims and Coptic Christians in Egypt, with the Chittagong hill peoples in Bangladesh, and with (some) Moros in the Philippines (cf. Gurr 1995). Few of the "successes" can be seen as total or permanent, but at least they stop the killing for a time. Of course, sometimes all earlier claims by a restive minority for economic and political equity and cultural expression and autonomy can be met, but then peaceful accommodation still is threatened by nonnegotiable insistence upon "symbolic" issues, such as language dominance or the control of religious sites. The cases of Israel and the Palestinians and of Québec (for a time) come close to being prototypical (Esman 1994), but there are many others (cf. Sri Lanka or Kashmir).

An unusual example of negotiated peace (even if temporary) in a civil war with strong secessionist overtones was the 1972 Addis Ababa agreement that halted hostilities in Sudan. By then the sixteen-year civil war between the "Arab" (Muslim) north and the "African" (Christian and animistic) south had caused an estimated 500,000 deaths in the south. Differences in religion, ethnicity, regional economic states, and political history and structures formed the background, and foreign aid helped to maintain the guerrilla war. A temporary negotiated peace was achieved through a complex protracted process, including the informal interventions of nongovernmental organizations (see the comprehensive account in Deng 1995). The agreement was revoked in 1983 by the government of Sudan in response to the political demands of military Islamic groupings. But the 1972 accord was an example of what can be achieved by persistent efforts of nongovernmental organizations, even in extremely complex and difficult circumstances.

The constraints upon, as well as the opportunities for, conflict management or resolution are shaped in complex and important ways by the symmetrical or asymmetrical structure of the relationship between the parties (Mitchell 1991). In the first place, intrastate conflicts typically involve contending parties that differ in their social structures and internal dynamics—as evident in the very characterizations of the parties, as, for example, states, ethnoclasses, ethnonationalists, indigenous peoples, ethnoreligious groupings, or regional collectivities. The primary conflicts are, indeed, asymmetric in the qualities or attributes of the respective collectivities. Also, the parties may be different and unequal in their legal status; thus, states have obvious advantages over challengers in their legal rights to tax, to use military force, and so on. The agents of the state claim legitimate authority and define insurgents as rebels, traitors, terrorists, or bandits. Also, for the insurgents the goal of access, or autonomy, or independence is likely to be of central importance, whereas an incumbent government may have many other concerns of equal or greater salience. Similarly, one party or both may define the conflict as one of survival, may see the threat as cultural obliteration or genocide. There are other asymmetries: for example, the degree of unity (cohesion, coordination, consensus) within each of the parties, with the challengers usually more disunited or fragmented than the state authorities. Finally, one contender may be able to secure aid from external allies or patrons while its adversary lacks such support. As a special form of cohesion or disunity, the leadership of each contender may be secure or insecure. Conflicts in which the main leaders are threatened by militants within their own constituency (challengers who interpret any move toward compromise as a betrayal) will be especially difficult to terminate. Although asymmetrical conflict therefore seems to render resolution especially difficult, there are cases in which seemingly intractable issues can be redefined through intensive discussions and negotiations that involve strong and resourceful third parties (see the detailed analysis in Mitchell 1991, 30–89).

Intuitively plausible is the notion of a "hurting stalemate" (Zartman 1991) as a condition facilitating negotiations or other processes that lead toward mitigation or resolution of violent collective conflicts. After all, if the parties in a protracted conflict have reached a point at which future gains appear unlikely and future damage is certain, continued conflict at the same time verges upon a minus-sum game. And if both (all) sides are severely suffering, why not have mutual calls to leash the dogs of war? But—there is always a "but" in these matters—things are rarely so simple or transparent. In the first place, the kind and degree of injury ("hurt") are seldom symmetrical: the discomfort or agony of one party is greater than that of the other. So, Party A may fight on in the expectation that Party B soon will give way. Hurt is seldom evenly balanced. The long deadly civil war in Sri Lanka, dating from 1983, had by the turn of the twenty-first century inflicted more than 60,000 deaths, had utterly devastated the Tamil territory in the north, and had severely injured the economy. But militant forces in the Sinhalese government blocked any feasible compromise, while the Sinhalese population suffered far less than the Tamils. The embittered Tamil leaders continued to strike back, and their suicide fighters destroyed a substantial part of the Sinhalese air fleet in 2001. And so the killing and destruction continues. Second, who or what is hurting? If negative feedback comes primarily to politically inarticulate and weak members of the polity, whereas elites continue to enjoy power and other rewards, the conflict may be pursued in the face of massive deprivations of a cowed or ideologically captured populace. Widespread deaths and injuries are not effective deterrents for entrenched ethnocracies or other dictatorial regimes—not for the Khmer Rouge in Cambodia, Hussein's Iraqi government, Syria's Al-Assad, the murderous ruling groups in Rwanda and Burundi, Idi Amin in Uganda, or Milošević in Serbia. Third, the investment of lives and treasure in the conflict may be perceived as so great that a negotiated settlement will be seen as betrayal. Fourth, and closely related, the cumulative effects of fear, grief, rage, moral revulsion, and desires for revenge may be so strong and prevalent on all sides as to preclude for the time a prudent appraisal of consequences.

Even so, a hurting stalemate does sometimes become so burdensome that negotiations can be initiated, although this by itself obviously does not foretell a settlement. Indeed, for "hurt"—negative feedback—to decisively affect decision-making, the disagreeable and unwanted consequences of continuation of the conflict must impinge upon leaders who make binding decisions for the respective collectivities. Large numbers of Iraqis suffer from an embargo that nevertheless leaves a Saddam Hussein and his entourage firmly in control of the central government. Many Serbs have suffered from civil war and economic chaos, but this did not stop a Milošević from pursuing belligerent policies. Only when the hurts directly affect the leadership (e.g., by threatening their safety, power, or achievement of primary objectives) does a hurting stalemate open the way for possible resolutions.

The specific character of the military stalemate itself is more important than the mere fact of an impasse. Thus, hurting stalemates are not necessarily situations in which military power is approximately equal between the warring parties—indeed, such "balance" always holds the temptation for one or another party to believe that additional combat will bring victory. The asymmetrical stalemate, in contrast, is the common situation, in which one side has a preponderance of force but the other has a capability to indefinitely deny the dominant grouping a decisive victory. For example, this was the situation in the late years of the civil war in El Salvador that finally led to a negotiated settlement.

On the other hand, some ethnopolitical conflicts, including rebellions and civil wars, never do attain a stalemate that is sufficiently agonizing to bring about a negotiated settlement. Instead the parties become locked into a mutually tolerated stalemate, with the dominant state unable to decisively defeat the insurgents and the communal rebels unable to force their demands. Such deadlocked conflicts can then become encapsulated or "contained" (Darby 1987), or remain "run-on" struggles. Violence continues at chronic but relatively low levels—assassinations, arson, car bombings, sabotage—but with the effects "tolerable" because violence is confined to limited geographic areas, to isolated incidents, or to politically subordinated social strata (Mitchell 1991, 35; Darby 1987).

In Zartman's formulation the conditions favorable for a settlement or resolution of conflict include not only a hurting stalemate but also an "impending catastrophe" and a "formula for a way out" (Zartman 1991, 11). In this view, the task is to make multilateral outcomes more attractive then unilateral ones. A major observation is that the parties in conflict typically seek to impose their own solution and thus find the conventional notion of negotiation to be unappealing. For "the usual concept of negotiation, as a process of exchanging concessions or reaching below the bottom line, makes negotiation sound like half a defeat and does not provide guidelines for making multilateral outcomes enticing" (Zartman 1991, 13). The alternative approach is to find a common definition of the problem (a formula) and some principles or rules that can set the outlines for a mutually beneficial accord.

For negotiated settlements to succeed in civil wars, a hurting stalemate and the prospect of severe future costs for all parties can encourage willingness to negotiate but cannot guarantee agreement or, even less, the implementation of peace accords. The parties must be able to make credible commitments to refrain from resuming violence, and this they typically cannot do without credible third-party guarantees. Even so, durable peace requires that the parties themselves favor it and that detailed power-sharing arrangements are in place (Walter 1997).

Two contrasting hypotheses have been advanced concerning the effectiveness of alternative strategies for negotiating peace agreements. One formulation predicts that best outcomes will result from negotiations that proceed from general principles or basic assumptions to later consideration of particular issues (Zartman 1984, 1989); that is, first, seek agreement on a master formula or set of principles (e.g., "land for peace"; spheres of influence) and then make successive efforts to reach detailed agreements. The partly contradictory hypothesis holds that satisfactory agreements are most likely when small, discrete items are considered first—leaving aside general principles, larger issues, or comprehensive packages until agreements on details have been reached—or even eschewing any effort at all to reach agreements in principle. A related dictum is to begin with those issues upon which agreement is most likely, putting aside the more difficult problems for later consideration. Experienced and well-informed negotiators have given accounts of success from a strategy of "fractionating the issues," and equally persuasive cases of the approach from general formula to particular details.

The bold approach that goes from "basic" principles to a master formula and then to details appears to be a high-risk, high-gain strategy. It implies a belief on the part of a third-party intervener that the protagonists indeed can accept a central formula as a framework for negotiations and that such agreement actually will facilitate convergence or compromise on specific issues. Proponents of the graduated or incremental approach, on the other hand, base their case on the possibility that early successes and continuing interaction will promote the growth of trust and will provide intermediate rewards, encouraging a deepening and broadening of the initial bargains.

There are similarities between the incremental scheme and the model of graduated reciprocity in interstate relations, elaborated in Osgood's GRIT proposal (graduated reciprocal initiatives in tension reduction), in which one state makes a relatively cheap unilateral concession, hoping for reciprocity that will lead to a series of cooperative moves. A similar contention is found in studies of the reduction of intrastate warfare. The hypothesis is that small, that is, less risky or less costly, reductions in conflictful behavior repeated over several consecutive occasions are likely to be more effective in moving toward conflict resolution than a more dramatic single breakthrough. This supposition is supported by limited evidence from single-country case studies in which repeated gestures are found to be more effective than one-shot initiatives. A suggestive instance is the termination of the combined intrastate/interstate war in Rhodesia (Zimbabwe), which was preceded by a series of events in which the conflicting parties did monitor and reciprocate one another's conflictful or accommodative behavior. A pattern of reciprocity gradually opened the way for third-party mediation and a graduated reduction in collective violence (Moore 1995, 163–64). In this case the European-origin Rhodesians and the African nationalists reciprocated both one another's particular behavior and its deviations from expectations. Both parties also showed what can be called policy inertia by persisting for a time in an immediately preceding policy. Thus a single effort to reduce the level of violence was not likely to be immediately reciprocated, but repeated signals did result in overcoming the inertia or "lag" in responses. Eventually there were peace agreements that halted a war that had cost at least 13,000 deaths (Moore 1995, 137).

Failures to attempt negotiations, or to reach agreements, or to implement accords that have been reached, have been attributed to several different but important factors. Most easily noted is the extent and kind of resources available to the parties, especially support and aid from external sources of funds, arms, political support, and various forms of encouragement and reassurance. Then there is the question of the scope and intensity of the grievances and the importance of the stakes of the struggle. A third set of explanatory conditions has to do with the organization of the fighting and the sociopolitical structure of the adversaries. The fourth condition is the basic security dilemma of the contenders. Finally there is a complex set of conditions affecting the strategies of negotiation and mediation.

A great deal of what is usually seen as conventional wisdom had been distilled from examination of putative mistakes and successful actions in negotiations and mediation in ethnic warfare. Many lists of proposed rules of thumb have been formulated, incorporating reflections upon what has seemed to move conflicting parties toward peace agreements. So, for example,

- A third party seeking to mediate between the combatants must be able to offer incentives for agreements, assurances, and guarantees for the security of the parties. The mediator should facilitate but not dominate the negotiation, should use threats sparingly or not at all, should not urge overly rapid decisions, should be sensitive to different styles of negotiations and be prepared to accommodate them, should have a detailed knowledge of the history of the parties and their relationships, should recognize and take into account the limitations and constraints of each party (Stein and Lewis 1996, 463–73).
- The third party must give credible evidence of a willingness to stay committed to the peace process over a substantial period.

- Successful mediation depends upon choosing a time when the parties see continued conflict as dangerous and self-defeating—when future prospects are for loss rather than gain.
- In third-party mediation, concerted action by regional organizations or neighboring states is helpful, and often necessary. Early involvement of respected regional leaders is an important positive factor (Spencer and Spencer 1995, 192–93).
- Pre-negotiations usually will be needed over a considerable period to develop trust in mediators and to increase understanding between the conflicting parties.
- The timing of interventions is crucial, and the type of intervention that is appropriate depends upon the changing conditions of the conflict over time. (When both sides are confident of military victory, mediation will fail.)
- The likelihood of a durable peace agreement is increased when the conflicting parties have reached a hurting stalemate, can foresee a worsening future or an impending catastrophe, have reliable and valid spokespersons, and can visualize an acceptable way out (Zartman 1991).

    In many conflicts, none of these conditions is present—both or all parties still expect victory or an improved outcome through continued fighting, leadership is fragmented and ambiguous, and no viable compromise is envisioned. A representative example was the protracted Eritrea-Ethiopia conflict (Ottaway 1991). And in the case of Sri Lanka, the difficulties included a multiplicity of parties, fragmented insurgent movements and divided authorities in the state, extremist factions on both sides, and interstate intervention perceived as partisan (de Silva and Samarsinghe 1993, 14).
- A common recipe for constructive negotiations is incremental bargaining in which the parties begin by dealing with those partial issues that appear to be most easily resolved. This procedure may require that large, comprehensive problems be broken down in sub-issues; the hope is that by fractionating the conflict, additional possibilities will be opened for trade-offs and compromises. The stakes in early negotiations may thus be lowered, and the successive settlements reached may increase confidence between the parties.

    Nevertheless, there are hazards in this approach: partial solutions may reduce incentives for more complete agreements, or the negotiation process itself may bring to the front basic unresolved issues (cf. Zviagelskaia 1991, on the Arab-Israeli case). The result can be a "frozen conflict," in which the parties prefer a continuing confrontational relationship to any other outcome.
- All major political actors must be involved in peace negotiations, if sta-

ble agreements are to be achieved. So, to ignore or reject the participation of those defined as extremists increases the hazard of later renewal of conflict.

Obstacles and Social Traps

Two main conditions have been cited in the research literature as crucial for the proverbial difficulty of ending civil wars: (1) the extremely high stakes—such as control of the state and social and physical survival, and (2) the absence of a trustworthy authority to guarantee a peace agreement. If the conflicting parties are to live together in the same territory, some way must be found to create a political arrangement that can guard against a resumption of mass violence. For this reason, negotiated settlements appear to be one attractive possibility. Yet as noted above the possibility is realized in only a small minority of cases—ranging from one-third (Pillar 1983) to about 15 percent (Stedman 1991), depending upon definitions.

Among the formidable obstacles in the way of negotiated settlements is the perceived magnitude of what is at stake in the struggle, including the intensity and extent of grievances: thus a central characteristic of civil wars once under way is the rapidity with which sheer survival becomes salient for the parties. The very processes of conflict themselves create fears of extinction, desires for revenge, and deep distrust of any negotiated agreement. For this reason, the initial issues that were the occasion for violence often do not predict well the nature of its ending.

The likelihood of effective regulation or resolution of a conflict is diminished when any of the parties regards the encounter as a single, non-repeatable occasion in which defeat will be total and irreversible. Many of the ethnic conflicts reviewed by Esman (1994), Gurr (1993b), and Horowitz (1985) develop genocidal fury because one party believes that another seeks total and irreversible domination: "they will enslave our children and our children's children," or "they intend to kill us all." Beliefs about what the future holds are weighty influences. A collectivity already heavily engaged in conflict is not likely to reduce or terminate its effects so long as either continuation promises high gains or cessation holds heavy losses. A winning side must be convinced that maximum advantage already has been achieved. A losing side must be convinced that further struggle will worsen the situation, or at the least that deescalation or termination will not bring in catastrophic results. (If an opponent is seen as wholly implacable and merciless, one may continue to "fight to the last man.")

Lack of clear signals from an adversary in violent conflict tends to produce escalation, for no hint of possible deescalation is contained in the continuing diffuse violence. Indiscriminate terrorism, for example, gives a signal of merciless and arbitrary hostility.

Thus, a central difficulty of resolving protracted ethnic conflicts is that the fighting parties are being asked to render themselves vulnerable in the face of perceived deadly threat. Such conflicts are radically different from the oppositions that are manageable under peaceable political processes. The violent protracted conflicts are characterized by being "'identity-driven' . . . the result of an underlying fear of extinction that grows out of the experience of being a vulnerable ethnic group living with memories of persecution and massacre" (Crighton and MacIver 1991, 127). Even politically dominant ethnies can be permeated by fears of annihilation—as manifested by Protestants in Northern Ireland, Maronite Christians in Lebanon, even the Sinhalese in Sri Lanka and Serbs, Croats, and Bosnians in Yugoslavia. A typical response is to resist any loss of political dominance.

In general, the more intense and prevalent the sense of victimization among aggrieved peoples, the more difficult it is to arrive at a peaceable settlement of an ethnic conflict. Typically the imposition of collective violence will be perceived by the injured as unjust and undeserved, and all the more so when past violence implies a continuing or future threat (see Montville 1990, 535–41). *All* parties in severe ethnic conflicts are likely to claim victimhood (and *all* typically will have suffered).

In peace negotiations in civil wars an especially difficult issue is the disposition of military forces. Rebels typically want to retain their weapons and control over territory until they have been included in a new government. Governments typically insist that rebels disarm prior to elections and before any transfer of power or incorporation of rebel forces into the state's army. In successful settlements it appears that rebel forces usually were demobilized before elections were held (Shugart 1992, 129). For such demobilization to be acceptable to the rebels, the existing government probably must hold out realistic possibilities of political participation and institutional reforms. Such incentives to be believable usually require third-party monitoring and security guarantees. But even if third-party intervention may be possible, a further obstacle to meaningful negotiations may be the lack of valid and reliable negotiating partners. One of the criteria proposed by Zartman (1991, 78) for judging when a conflict may be amenable to resolution is the presence of valid spokespersons. A major difficulty for third-party intervention in ethnic disputes is posed by the fragmented and ambiguous character of representation and authority within the contending parties. Crucial questions often include the following: With whom should one negotiate? Among what grouping should mediation be attempted? Major conflicts among large ethnies very frequently reveal sub-ethnies and rival conflict organizations within each of the contenders, namely, multiple armed groups in Afghanistan, Tamils in Sri Lanka, southerners in the Sudan, Eritreans in Ethiopia, and Palestinians in Israel. In general, the less definite and enduring the decision-making structures within the conflicting collectivities, the less likely a negotiated settlement and the less reliable any agreements that have been elicited through third-party efforts.

These familiar features of ethnic insurgency do have important implications for conflict settlement. In the first place, the internal divisions render negotiations for peace especially difficult. Will a negotiated agreement be repudiated by dissenting subgroups? Second, once a negotiated agreement has been reached and the rebels hold some significant political power, will the internal dynamics of the now-institutionalized ethny lead to autocratic and coercive outcomes that diverge radically from the initial settlement? And will the ethnic solidarity that was built by united efforts against adversaries be eroded by latent oppositions of interests and values? An ever present possibility is the resurgence of violent conflicts and newly fragmented rebel movements and newly activated ethnic forces. The result can be a chaos of contending militias (Lebanon, Liberia) or total breakdown into warlordism and banditry.

In the protracted ethnic wars, extending over decades, not only are the issues typically complex and rapidly changing, but the leadership of one or more contenders is frequently fractionated and unstable. At the extreme, there may be no responsible leaders who can make binding commitments. The collapse of a central state, as in Liberia or Somalia, is likely to be followed by a chaos of multiple armed contenders for power, of numerous bandit gangs, of deadly riots, of assorted terrorists, of corrupt officials and criminal networks, and of vengeful killings and assaults. For the aspiring peacemaker, the first question becomes: With whom can you negotiate? And often there is no clear or ready answer.

Even after substantial compromises have been made and major agreements have been reached on important issues (such as territorial concessions or power sharing), violent conflict may return at the hands of militant "spoilers" within the more inclusive ethnies. So it was in the late 1990s in Northern Ireland, when splinter factions from both the Protestant paramilitary groups and the Irish Republican Army continued the chronic cycle of killings. Year after year in the long, painful so-called peace process in Israel, various pro-Palestinian forces (e.g., Hamas, Islamic Jihad, Hizbollah) have engaged in bombings and other armed attacks on both Israeli military personnel and civilians, ensuring retaliation and stalling or wrecking moves toward peace. And Israeli hard-liners have resisted any concessions, have mounted armed incursions, and have engaged in provocative actions. Whatever may be the aims or the motives of the extreme factions, the effect is to intensify antagonism, to harden distrust, to polarize attitudes—in short, to "spoil" the prospects for ending the conflict. No matter how deadly and hurtful the slaughter, there will always be some people who really do not want peace.

The conditions just reviewed are parts of a generic problem—the proverbial "inherent security dilemma."

The Inherent Security Dilemma

As noted in earlier chapters, in interstate relations under a general state of anarchy in which there is no overarching authority and in which, therefore, each state has to look out for its own military security, there is an inherent security dilemma. It is defined by the fact that when any state in its search for safety begins to increase its armaments, the arms build-up is likely to appear to other states as preparation for aggression. Accordingly, the dilemma is that each move to defend one state's security may create the very insecurity it sought to remedy.

This classic societal trap is found in an acute form in civil wars. The combatants are intensely distrustful of one another; each has suffered losses; if there is a peace agreement, they must continue to live together in the same society under the same political order; during the fighting they will have done their best to mislead the other as to their arms through secrecy and misinformation. In the path toward a peace agreement, therefore, a main barrier is that the warring parties in such internal conflicts are highly vulnerable to attack if they disarm; each fears the other and distrusts any uninsured peace agreement: "Why would they want to keep their weapons if they don't intend to use them?"

Between civil war and peace is a period of transition when two tasks have to be accomplished: first, some credible guarantee of survival and against cheating and renewed killing; second, credible commitments for sharing of power after a cease-fire has been established. The parties typically cannot by themselves create these conditions. The high costs of continued conflict and a hurting stalemate do encourage negotiations, but a successful peace agreement almost always requires a third-party security guarantee. The external party has to make believable commitments to use force, if necessary, and to remain involved until a stable postwar order has been established.

There are instances in which negotiations reach agreements but warfare still returns—in about one half of the cases studied between 1940 and 1990 (Walter 1999). Common explanations for failures have pointed to the severity of the opposition of interests or to disagreements about sharing the rewards of the settlement, but these accounts seem unconvincing in view of the fact that the parties actually had been resolving the issues in the prior agreement. The decisive factor appears to be the lack of credible and enforceable guarantees of physical safety and for the implementation of the peace accords. True, it is possible that the opponents could attempt to surmount the security dilemma by (1) unilateral increases in defense, or by (2) step-by-step disarmament, or by (3) presenting clear evidence of peaceable intent by such measures as conspicuous disarmament. Each of these actions is likely to be either unsustainable or subject to misperception ("defenses") or vulnerable to exploitation (disarmament). It follows that the processes of establishing peace typically need the intervention of a trusted third party that can offer credible guarantees for carrying out the crucial transitions and reestablishing a new common political and social structure (see the detailed analysis in Walter 1999, 127–43).

Note that these conclusions apply to the cases in which none of the parties has won overwhelming armed victory or has expelled or destroyed the opposing population. Each still has retained a significant capability to harm the other, but each has given signs of a willingness to seek an end to the killing. These are the conditions that favor third-party intervention, a topic to which we now turn.

Intervention

Interventions into the internal affairs of sovereign states are neither new or rare. Historically, a preferred form, of course, has been military incursions and conquests, numbering in the thousands, by the forces of individual states and alliances. Over several centuries modern states in their worldwide conquests and colonial wars rearranged boundaries, destroyed states and created new ones, and massively altered ethnic identities and relationships. Treaties and other agreements among major powers and the development of interstate organizations have long since been the basis for deep interventions into ethnic and religious affairs within individual countries (Lake and Rothchild 1999, 315–21).

But these are not the interventions under consideration here. Our present focus rather is upon interventions aimed at promoting a negotiated agreement between the contenders to end the violence and to create the basis for peaceful coexistence within the same society in the future. Such efforts by outside parties—individuals, ad hoc groups, NGOs, individual states, coalitions, or interstate organizations—perhaps are best characterized as risky, difficult, costly, and highly needed for enduring settlements. But some cautions are evident in the experiences recorded thus far.

First, there is no guarantee of immediate success or of long-term stabilization of mutually acceptable arrangements. As we have reiterated, warfare does not typically "burn itself out," as a popular formulation would have it, and a large-scale war may be officially ended while violent conflict continues. Many civil wars drag on for years or decades and may end—

more or less—as a "frozen" conflict, never fully resolved but continued at a relatively low level of intermittent and limited violence.

The experience of the late twentieth century suggests still another cautionary note. As between rebels, including secessionists, and state regimes, no settlement is likely so long as the government elite is solely interested in maintaining itself in power. Neither a military dictator nor a populist autocrat can be easily dislodged by mere threats or embargoes or limited military incursions, particularly when the incumbent leader controls the central military and paramilitary forces (the usual cases) and can count on external partisan support in diplomatic, economic, and material military aid. When a coalition of states seeks to contain or defeat such elites, time typically will be on the side of the beleaguered autocrat, for ad hoc coalitions are notoriously unstable over a long pull and the initial advantages of democratic opponents rapidly decline in protracted warfare.

The experience of the twentieth century, on the whole, was that the so-called international community rarely attempted to intervene in any major way to stop intensive intrastate violence. The examples are numerous. No state tried to mobilize collective action to halt the Biafran civil war in Nigeria; none of the 126 members of the United Nations at that time proposed UN action. No member proposed UN action to end the Khmer Rouge massacres in Cambodia that cost about 1.7 million lives. None attempted to stop the killings in separatist Bangladesh—until India unilaterally used major military force. There were several missed opportunities for the United States to lead efforts (e.g., through a boycott of coffee exports) to check the killings of Tutsis in Rwanda by Hutus in 1959 and 1963 and of Hutus by Tutsis in Burundi in 1972. In these and many other instances, international bodies refused to intervene in the face of dangers, costs, and the decision of member states that their vital interests were not at stake or that intervention would set a precedent that could threaten their own sovereignty at a later time.

Matters are very different, however, when major powers do believe that vital strategic interests are at issue. Then unilateral interventions can tip the balances—or else intensify and prolong the fighting. Thus, it is usual for contenders in civil wars to seek external aid; during the Cold War the opposing sides frequently received assistance from the Soviet Union and the United States, and in some cases combat was halted only when the superpowers disengaged. In an analysis of the complex and protracted negotiations in Angola between the two local parties and the four external actors (the United States, USSR, Cuba, and South Africa), Rothchild and Hartzell (1991, 55) found that the latter powers shifted from interventions supporting the fighting to disengagement behavior between 1975 and 1988. The shift appeared to be due primarily to major changes in the incentives motivating the external parties, as the Soviets reduced their commitments to rivalry with the United States. The temporarily successful outcomes of the Angola-Namibia negotiations in 1991 depended heavily upon the positive incentives offered and the pressures exerted by the two superpowers upon their clients.

Unilateral peacekeeping missions by a single state seem destined to be regarded as partisan by one or all of the fighting groups. An outstanding case is the Indian peacekeeping force sent into Sri Lanka (by intergovernmental agreement) to stop the civil war between the Tamil insurgents and the Sri Lanka (Sinhalese) government. The initial contingent of troops, in 1987, became engaged within a few months in warfare with the Tamil forces. Intensive but inconclusive fighting for two years, resulting in increased hostility and in the escalation of violence, led to the withdrawal of the Indian troops. The initial force of some 8,000 lightly armed troops had increased to nearly 100,000 by the time of withdrawal. The end result was intensified and more complex warfare (Ganguly and Taras 1998, chap. 7).

To effectively contain or terminate civil wars and democides, the UN and/or multistate coalitions have had to violate or radically reinterpret the rule of non-interferences in the "domestic" affairs of territorial states. Otherwise mass murders and genocides continue to recur unchecked. The UN charter, adopted in 1945, prohibited UN actions on matters that fall "within the domestic jurisdiction" of states (Article 2, Paragraph 7), but actual practice in recent years has repeatedly violated this Westphalian norm under the legal cover of Chapter 6 of the charter, which permits intervention when there is a "threat to the peace."

"Peacekeeping" is a misnomer for third-party interventions while warfare continues. As the case of Bosnia shows, humanitarian aid becomes hostage to the fighting on the ground. If humanitarian aid workers or traditional peacekeepers themselves attempt to use force, they lose any vestige of impartiality. Yet in the role of impartial peacekeepers they will be forced to stand by helplessly while civilians are massacred, as at Srebrenica in 1995. In the chaos and savagery of state-supported democide or communal civil war, peacekeeping is impossible and peace enforcing requires the stern use of military power—an intervention that always will be seen as partisan (witness the regional peacekeeping effort in Liberia). So peacekeeping occurs only when there actually is a peace to keep. Otherwise there is peacemaking, to stop the killing; peace enforcing, to ensure that hostilities do not immediately resume; and peace building, to reestablish workable societal arrangements for the longer term.

Third-party intervention may involve one or more of these: another national state, a regional organization or coalition, an interstate organization (usually the UN), a nongovernmental organization, an informal, off-the-record ad hoc group ("Track II diplomacy"), or a prominent and respected individual. Whatever the particular case, an essential outcome is an effective guarantee that no social segment will be excluded from future decision making affecting its vital interests. In practice, what this usually has meant is that the peace settlement includes continuing arrangements for protecting the terms of settlement, such as permanent electoral boards to provide independent monitoring, and reorganization and retraining of police forces (on all this see, again, Licklider 1995). After peace accords comes the problem of coping with widespread corruption, economic and physical destruction, institutional breakdown, and continuing political-military threats. No wonder that continuing external monitoring and assistance remain crucial in the implementation of peace agreements. Nominal guarantees are unlikely to be believable unless there are clear commitments from the intervener to remain engaged until a secure peace and civic order are in place and to use force to ensure that outcome. As the case of Bosnia reminded us, a lack of these conditions probably implies that peacekeeping will turn into peace enforcing, and peace enforcing likely means the use of military force in ways that will be perceived as favoring one side over others.

The very first deployment of UN peacekeeping personnel was in 1948, when unarmed military observers were sent to supervise a truce between the new state of Israel and its Arab opponents, followed by the establishment a few months later of a similar operation in Kashmir. The next major development was the deployment of an armed peacekeeping force in Egypt after warfare between Egypt and combined forces of Israel, France, and Great Britain in 1956. A spectacular intervention was undertaken during the years 1960–64, in the Congo; it began as peacekeeping but ended as a military operation to stop the secession of a rebellious province. By the 1980s some thirteen UN operations had been activated, and a set of peacekeeping rules or principles had been generally accepted on the basis of the accumulated experiences. There were five such major dicta. First, the operations were authorized by and under the authority of the UN and paid for as a collective obligation of the member states. Second, the peacekeepers were to be deployed only with the consent of the conflicting parties. Third, the peacekeepers were to maintain strict impartiality, even under provocation. Fourth, the peacekeeping forces were to be multinational, provided on a voluntary basis by member states; for many years there was an implicit understanding that troops from the superpowers would not be used. Fifth, peacekeepers would use minimal force and only in self-defense (as variously defined in practice).

The early UN operations thus had involved what is now called traditional *peacekeeping*. It attempted to avoid confrontations with the belligerents and to maintain a posture of impartiality. Accordingly it could be effective only in situations in which the parties wished to end the fighting or to maintain a truce or cease-fire. By the late 1980s it had become clear that other types of operations were being called for. These included the use of armed forces to protect the delivery of humanitarian services and the insertion of combined civilian-military organizations to aid in reestablishing a functioning society. *Peace enforcing* (or peacemaking) may require extensive use of force, and peace building involves added tasks and responsibilities. Peacemaking, peace enforcing, and *peace building* overlap and merge in actual field operations. Thus when military force has stopped the internal warfare and a peace settlement of some kind has been reached, as in the Dayton peace agreement for the former Yugoslavia, there always will remain a complex set of peace-building tasks. These may include disarming and demobilizing the combat forces, administering humanitarian aid, supervising exchange of war prisoners, organizing and monitoring the return of refugees, rebuilding infrastructures, selecting and training police, establishing and monitoring elections, and in general helping to reestablish peacetime social institutions.

How successful are UN peace operations? Much discussion and acrimonious debate continue to center upon this vague and difficult but vital question. Often left unanswered is the central problem of defining "success." The effort to deliver and protect humanitarian aid to famine-stricken Somalia ended in the humiliating withdrawal of U.S.-led forces, in reaction to the deaths of eighteen soldiers trapped in a failed effort to seize a local war leader. Commonly labeled by the mass media as an enormous failure, the operation nevertheless can be credited with saving several hundred thousand persons from starvation. Peacemaking and peace-building efforts in Namibia, El Salvador, and Mozambique have been judged by most expert observers to have been successful; the several intertwined operations in Cambodia have received mixed verdicts—whereas the efforts in Angola have been seen as an unambiguous failure.

Clearly these diverse evaluations reflect multiple criteria. Has a ceasefire been achieved and maintained? Have the armed forces been demobilized and disarmed? Have the opposing forces been integrated into a new national military? Have "free and fair" elections been held, with a new constitutional order agreed upon, mutually acceptable arrangements for return of refugees and release and exchange of war prisoners, and an integrated and reformed police and judiciary? To what extent have basic human services—medical care, schools, communication and transportation facilities, and so on—been reestablished? A comprehensive scorecard obviously would have to extend and further specify these items.

So it is not at all surprising that different observers with their divergent interests and ideologies emphasize different criteria and may arrive at contradictory judgments. What is certain is that any major peace operation will be complex, representing multiple trade-offs of costs and benefits across a range of possible policies and actions. A minimal objective may be defined simply as stopping the killing for some substantial period. A maximal objective may be to reconstruct an entire society. In between lie an impressive array of concrete actions and their consequences.

Recognition of the problems of administration in the UN Secretariat led in the 1990s to the creation of a new Department of Peacekeeping Operations and to large increases in the number of persons employed in UN Headquarters. Other innovations have included an expanded role in the peace operations for the special representative of the secretary-general and steps taken toward forming a standby force at UN Headquarters (Morrison 2000, 84). Whatever the many specific problems of this complex and cross-pressured organization, in the decades of its peacekeeping operations the United Nations has established itself as the center and "natural frame of references for any international action to prevent or defuse a crisis" (Morrison 2000, 83).

Actual and Possible Outcomes

Major types of outcomes of civil wars are broadly applicable to the special class of ethnic-based warfare. The roster includes these outcomes:

1. Military victory by one side, with the dominant result of a military or one-party government. Forced expulsions, democides, and genocides are not unusual.
2. Stalemate or partial victory, sometimes followed by partition or de facto secession.
3. Negotiated autonomy; federalism.
4. Cultural pluralism vs. forced assimilation.
5. Power sharing; consociationalism.
6. Induced assimilation.

Let us examine some of these possibilities.

As we have seen, the most obvious ending of civil war by military dominance is also the most frequent. The typical result is either military government or one-party rule with substantial military influence. Such coercive regimes can endure for long periods but this condition does not preclude social unrest or political upheavals (coups d'état, local insurrections, mass protests). Militarized states in Latin America, Southeast Asia, the Middle East, and Africa provide numerous examples. Conspicuous is the case of Nigeria, where there have been successive military governments for about two-thirds of its history since independence. Since the destructive civil war that resulted in the total defeat of the rebellious Ibo ethny seeking an independent state (Biafra), the country has had high levels of inequality and of unrest, partly fueled by ethnoregional divisions. The central government has attempted to deal with ethnic divisions by creating more and more subunits (provinces)—from four in 1960 to nineteen by 1976, and thirty by 1991—and some six hundred local governments by 1993. Although federalism and devolution are favorite political arrangements to cross-cut ethnic allegiances and to reduce pressure on the center, the multiplication of units has not solved regional and ethnic cleavages (see Welch 1995).

A harsh reality is that reconciliation is impossible—perhaps one can even say unthinkable—during some protracted civil wars in which armed struggles by multiple groupings for control of lucrative resources have not reached a decisive termination. Consider the extremely destructive warfare in Angola that began as an anti-colonial struggle against Portugal in 1961. By the time independence had been attained, in 1975, there was full-fledged warfare among three ethnonationalist groupings: the MPLA, which drew support from the Mbundu ethny and from the partially assimilated bourgeoisie; the FNLA, based on the Bakongo in the rural northern areas; and UNITA, mainly based on the large ethny, Ovimbundu. The MPLA, with Soviet support and Cuban troops, won an early victory over the FNLA. This left UNITA with its South African and U.S. aid to continue the civil war, which went through five major cycles from 1974 to 2000. Thirty-plus years of incessant fighting produced more that a half million deaths, created over two million internal refugees, wrecked the economy, and destroyed most of the infrastructure, including educational and health services. The protracted warfare depended upon rival interventions and partisan support from the Soviet Union, Cuba, South Africa, and the United States (see Knudsen 1995). Both superpowers supplied funding and military equipment to their clients. Traditional financing to support the protracted warfare came to the central government from large oil revenues, while the rebel UNITA forces have relied upon the diamond trade from the areas they controlled and upon convert aid allegedly received from the United States during the Cold War.

After the two superpowers withdrew their support and the Cuban forces followed suit, a preliminary peace accord was signed in 1991. At that point the prospects appeared favorable for a negotiated resolution of the war, but in elections held in 1992, UNITA refused to accept its loss and the fighting resumed (Rothchild and Hartzell 1991; Knudsen 1995). A UN peace observer mission, having only a limited mandate and sparse funding from the Security Council, ended in failure. All peace efforts were blocked by a combination of external partisan intervention, high stakes, ethnoregional divisions, divisive material interests, and intransigent leadership. Experienced observers regard the Angolan experience as an object lesson for the failure of peace operations. None of the requirements for successful mediation and negotiated settlement were present—valid representatives, a hurting stalemate sufficient to create a conviction that further combat would be futile, a mutual acceptable way out after elections, or an expectation of reciprocity in concessions.

A peace accord is only the first step toward a stable settlement. In many situations, an agreement is not even a first step. Cease-fires are notoriously unreliable, and more comprehensive agreements may mean little in countries in which the state has collapsed and rebel armed forces are fragmented. Clan warfare in Somalia in the 1990s was an extreme example. In the civil war in Sierra Leone, the rebel group Revolutionary United Front (RUF) signed a peace agreement in 1996 but promptly resumed the killing and the systematic mutilations of civilians; in 1999 after the rebels had invaded the capital city, killing over 5,000 people, another peace agreement promised amnesty for the rebels in return for disarmament, but again the RUF resumed warfare, including attacks on UN peacekeepers. At stake was the lucrative trade in illegal diamonds—an attractive incentive for intervention by leaders in Liberia and Burkina Faso in support of the rebels. Multilateral armed peace enforcement by other states in such cases may be the only feasible route to a decisive termination.

The empirical record is that relatively stable settlements of civil wars (e.g., lasting for five years or more) usually depend upon two basic conditions: (1) a military standoff in which neither party foresees further combat as decisive, and (2) reliable peace-seeking intervention by a third party acceptable to all sides.

Because deeply divided societies that have experienced high levels of violence differ among themselves in important respects, different countries have followed very different paths in terminating the warfare. We have repeatedly pointed to instances of forced expulsions (so-called ethnic cleansing) and democides. Short of these deadly policies, the parties may decide that sharing a common territory is not feasible and that territorial partition is necessary to avoid continuing conflict. The historical record of the years since World War II, however, is that partition of an ethnically divided society often is itself a source of conflict and that it rarely produces a stable accommodation. National states typically resist secession and are willing to use force to prevent it.

Partition itself is likely to bring into play hitherto weak or nonsalient distinctions within what at first was thought to be a single entity. And the political energizing of the newly self-conscious population by a leadership cadre that in its turn seeks autonomy or separation within the separatist population can lead to rival movements and factions that easily fall into fratricidal conflict. A study of thirteen major partitions that have occurred since 1920 concluded that partitions are, indeed, drastic outcomes of intrastate conflicts (Schaeffer 1990). None of the cases studied provided a promising model for dealing with later conflicts. The experience of the 1990s, as movements for self-determination and democratization increased, showed that different partitions had radically different outcomes: from the frozen standoff in Cyprus, to wars of independence in Ethiopia, and to the disintegrations of the Soviet Union and Yugoslavia. The undesired outcomes of historical partitions are prominent and well known. Even so, it remains true that some form of partition or secession may be accepted as the "lesser evil" in a few highly important instances of large-scale intrastate conflict, as argued by Young (1995).

Less extreme measures to end conflict include agreements for some form of autonomy within the state. Between the 1950s and the late 1980s some seven cases of ethnopolitical conflict led to regional autonomy agreements: these concerned the Basques in Spain, the Miskitos in Nicaragua, the Chittagong hill people in Bangladesh, the Moros in the Philippines, the Afars in Ethiopia, and the Nagas and Tripuras in India. Partial autonomy has been achieved in several other instances and certainly would be possible in future negotiations in other protracted ethnic conflicts. In general, some measure of autonomy for regionally concentrated ethnies seems to be a relatively feasible way to reduce severe ethnopolitical conflicts (see Gurr 1995, 294–305).

When autonomy agreements have been reached, as in the Addis Ababa agreement between the rebels and the government of Sudan in 1972, but then are not fully carried out or are abrogated, the predictable result is the escalation of ethnonationalism into armed rebellion. This sequence was clear in the Sudan, in Baluchistan (Pakistan), and in Sri Lanka. On the other hand, sustained agreements that provide limited autonomy can reduce the cohesion of separatist movements because concessions by the state gain acceptance by substantial portions of the restive ethny. What is seen as fragmentation or factionalism from the viewpoint of hardcore militants may then be regarded by the more moderate elements of the original movement as the basis for attractive compromises or other means of peaceful resolution. Thus although divisions within an ethnonationalist movement usually are likely to reduce bargaining leverage against the state, exceptions do occur when "moderates" are able to use the implicit threat posed by the more radical factions to extract concessions from the dominant authorities.

Common to the various forms of ethnic accommodation—in federalism, in devolution of central political authority to regions and municipalities, and in both regional and cultural autonomy—is the acceptance of some substantial degree of cultural pluralism. All these arrangements reject the contrasting policies of ethnic dominance and forced homogeneity.

In societies with strong ethnic segmentation, another important possibility for peaceful ending of ethnic warfare, as well as for conflict prevention (Chapter 10), is power sharing. Systems of power sharing exist in several versions but the common characteristic is that each major ethny shares in central political decision making and public administration. Power sharing is most likely where a few large and cohesive ethnies, each with important economic and political resources, find themselves—for whatever historical reasons—within a common polity. They face the choice of separation or coexistence. They can share the advantage of belonging to a shared state or the potential benefits and costs of separation. When the advantages of coexistence are great and ethnic conflict is likely to be severely damaging, power sharing becomes an attractive option. It can then be regarded as a "viable process of mutual deterrence" (Esman 1994, 258), but it is also a partnership of convenience in which the players share the rewards of joint participation in a single political unit.

A hallmark of many post-conflict settlements is the provision for elections and the establishment of an electoral system intended to be permanent. For obvious reasons, initial elections are likely to be problematic, entailing risks of fraud, intimidation, and violence, and the unwillingness of defeated parties to accept the results. Third-party monitoring and supervision may be necessary to ensure acceptable procedures. A moot question always is whether elections should be held only after demobilization and disarming of armed forces: the conventional wisdom has been to insist upon advance disarmament, but there are important exceptions in actual practice, such as Nicaragua (Sereseres 1996). For an enduring electoral system, once the initial hurdles have been passed, a prime requirement is avoidance of arrangements that reward ethnic militants by encouraging ethnic bloc voting. Although the most divisive effects of a system of ethnic parties can be reduced by coalitions, the risks of further violence can be lessened more reliably by non-ethnic parties, multi-ethnic electoral districts, and other devices that require politicians to appeal to voters across ethnic lines (Horowitz 1990a, 1990b; Esman 1994, 258).

Conclusion

In the setting of the interdependent world of today, ethnopolitical civil warfare challenges our knowledge and often baffles statecraft. We have reviewed how destructive and persistent are many of these conflicts, and how forceful domination is the most frequent outcome. But we found that negotiated settlements do occur, and we saw how crucial for successful peace settlement is the continuing support and oversight of responsible third parties. We surveyed an impressive array of conditions and practices that favor negotiated accords among contending ethnies. Among the actual outcomes of intrastate conflict, we found that there is much promise in various forms of federalism, devolution of authority, provision of substantial sociocultural autonomy, and in voluntary assimilation. Negotiation and flexible state policies contrast sharply with coercive rigidity and imposed ethnic uniformity. There is much wisdom in the chastened experience of interventions in ethnic conflict. Peaceful settlements are difficult, possible, and urgently needed.

CHAPTER ELEVEN

Peace at Last?

Reflections on Paths toward Reconciliation and Reconstruction

After the Shooting Stops—What Then?

This chapter differs from most of the preceding. It does not review systematic research or explanatory theories. Rather, it reports a series of reflections on the contemporary record of the efforts that have been made to establish durable peace after the traumas of intrastate warfare. Although much of the material to be reviewed is anecdotal or episodic, the lessons to be learned will be relevant for many years into a turbulent future.

Termination of communal fighting and civil wars, aside from the decisive victory of one side, involves the high-level politics of third-party interventions, negotiations, peace agreements, and interim arrangements for governance. These macro-processes occur in capital cities, in military encampments, or in far-away conference centers. But in the meantime, life goes on "out there" in the day-to-day interactions of people who are coping with the compelling and urgent sequels of conflict. And in those thousands and millions of intensely local interactions, much of the long-term outcomes and consequences of the initial terminations will be determined.

"Conflict resolution" is not the appropriate term for settlements that leave intact a state that is ineffective, repressive, exclusionist, and predatory. Rather, such settlements are more likely to be temporary accords, accepted as expedient by the weaker parties, but leaving unresolved the structural conditions that continually re-create grievances. Of course, the crucial task of stopping the killing (Licklider 1995) is a primary objective in third-party efforts to end intrastate wars and communal slaughter. Yet the termination of violence alone does not constitute a stable peace settlement or the resolution of basic issues. What else can be done?

We visualize post-conflict societal responses as a series of complex processes: remembering and forgetting, revenge, restitution, reparations, retribution, historical clarification, apologies, forgiveness, reconciliation, and reconstruction. These are the names we give to exceedingly diverse sets of actions, policies, and processes that may involve ambiguous and ambivalent feelings, contradictory beliefs, and incompatible values. What happens at the national level may differ greatly from the events that unfold in regions and localities. Small wonder, then, that attempts by governments, interstate organizations, and NGOs, to deal with the legacies of collective violence, have taken so many different forms. No surprise either that victims and oppressors, now intermingled, cannot quickly or easily find common ground for life in a reconstituted society.

To understand what conditions will exist at the end of protracted collective violence, one needs to know the modalities of repression and control that have been attempted by government and rebels. For example, as in Guatemala, the military, paramilitary, and police forces of the state typically take violent selective actions against leaders of communities and social organizations thought to be helping the insurgents. Rebel leaders disappear, are tortured, are killed; often there is public display of mutilated corpses. Families are threatened and raided; homes are burned; and equipment, crops, and farm animals are destroyed or stolen. There are mass expulsions, and the forced concentration of people in military-controlled areas and camps. Over and over there are the unpredictable disappearances of individuals and the denial by authorities of any knowledge of the cases. There often is the forced participation of individuals, under threat of death, in the repression of others. There are massacres. In all this, the agents and leaders of the repressive governments typically deny the realities and disavow any responsibility for wrongdoing, and they systematically blame the victims, who are said to have brought it on themselves.

The result of such violent measures is to create a pervasive climate of fear and suspicion, intended to intimidate, demoralize, and fragment the society upon which resistance must depend. Counter-actions by insurgents are likely to include similar tactics of intimidation directed to those who support the government or are believed to be in other ways a danger to the rebel cause (e.g., recurrent suicide bombings in Sri Lanka). Many unfortunates will be caught between the incompatible demands of the belligerents, subject to violence from all sides.

Thus, massive and prolonged civil warfare leaves the dreadful but familiar consequences of the destruction of property and productive resources—ruined homes and businesses, destroyed crops and animals, wrecked infrastructures. It also leaves polarized communities and disrupted structures of local leadership and authority. There will have been a widespread disruption of the rituals and routines of daily life, from work patterns to family life to religious observances. The bare necessities of life may be lacking or in short supply: food, clean water, housing, clothing, medical aid, transportation, electricity, and fuel. Needless to say, the political structure will be in disarray.

What of the effects directly upon the people who have lived through the storm? Many will have been injured, some severely crippled, many will have untreated illness. Epidemics are common.

But there is more: the emotional and other sociopsychological consequences. The most commonly noted are feelings of sorrow, loss, grief, and rage, often with admixtures of shame and humiliation, as well as remorse and guilt. Incomplete and disrupted processes of grieving retard a sense of closure or resignation. The experiences of being dominated and persecuted without any effective recourse will have left strong unresolved feelings of powerlessness. Looming over the whole is the sense of having experienced great injustice. Not universal, but frequent and intense, is the desire for vengeance.

These are not all of the many aspects of the immediate post-conflict society that will be faced by those who seek to clear the way for reconciliation and the reconstruction of social order. For example, there is likely to be extensive crime, and many opportunistic accusations made in revenge. But the tasks in any cases are challenging enough.

In short, the ending of large-scale collective violence leaves the people of a riven society with the consequences of economic dislocation, displaced people, physical destruction of resources and infrastructure, and disruption of institutions and social relationships. And there is a residue of grief, desires for revenge and restitution, a sense of grievance among people who have experienced injury, deprivation, unjust treatment, and the death of loved ones. If the conflict is to be resolved, rather than merely terminated for the time being, the basic political and economic problems must be ameliorated. But these alone will not heal the sociopsychological wounds.

Revenge and Retaliation

A major barrier to full resolution of violent intrastate conflicts is the desire for vengeance. The strength of revenge as a motive is great—and apparently under-appreciated in much of the scholarly literature on conflict resolution. When survivors know the perpetrators of the murders and torture inflicted upon family members and friends, the grief and rage they feel often crystallizes into an enduring desire for vengeance. The hurt must be balanced by punishment of the offenders. And if specific persons cannot be identified as the particular killers and torturers, the blame can be focused on the ethny to which the perpetrators belong.

The difficulty of forgiveness must not be underestimated. In Rwanda, Tutsis live among Hutus known to have been killers in the 1994 genocide. How can they accept the daily reminders of how these people now go free after having raped, mutilated, stabbed, and hacked to death their fathers, mothers, sisters, and brothers? In Kosovo, how can Albanian Kosovars willingly refrain from retaliation against the Serbs who participated in the ethnic massacres and evictions? In South Africa, how can the victimized families forgive the smirking police who casually admit their killings? (See Ignatieff 1997b.)

It is not hard to understand how infuriating it can be when perpetrators of grievous wrongs refuse to admit that the acts in question did occur. Sheer denial that actual events happened adds insult to injury. To deny that the Nazi-inflicted Holocaust occurred is to heap contempt upon victimization. To say that known genocide was a mere incident of war is to the victimized an effort to trivialize the actual events, and an attempted imposition of humiliation in addition to the horror of mass murder. Similarly, bafflement and resentment are aroused when the perpetrators or their complicit bystanders deny responsibility: we were only following the orders of legitimate authorities; we did not understand what was being done; there was nothing we could do. Denial of wrongdoing and unwillingness to apologize to those most closely affiliated with victims can leave long-lasting residues of unresolved grief and hostility.

Care is needed, however, in generalizing from the most extreme cases of collective conflict in which rigid ethnic categorization has identified the contenders, and systematic genocide or undiscriminating killing has prevailed. When allegiances are not to states or ethnies but to families, clans, villages, regional militias, and other localized groupings, patterns of vengeance take the selective forms of feuds and vendettas. Thus, in contrast to the conventional interpretation of kin vendetta as based on revenge as an undifferentiated collective action against a target group as a whole (rather than a specific individual), there is evidence, from a detailed study of Corsican vendettas, that revenge attacks can be highly selective in targeting the persons who aided perpetrators as well as the actual assailants (Gould 2000, 691). In that case, group membership alone was not sufficient to make individuals potential objects of revenge, but support for an offender (e.g., by aid after the fact) did constitute ground for reprisal. The selective principle presumably discouraged a continuing cycle of violence of one solidary group against another—a "war of each against all" at the group level. Rather than total collectivism (in which any attack on a group member would elicit retaliation against any member of the assailant's group), the revenge pattern appears to have had a definite strategic logic:

266

collective reprisal was limited to cases of collaborative action by aggressors (Gould 2000, 701).

This example is a useful reminder of the general principle that *individualized* and *collective* patterns of retaliation and revenge have very different sources and consequences. A crucial difference is that categorical polarization of whole populations—whether ethnic or ideological—encourages wholesale reprisals and hinders the closure of a cycle of violence that could be achieved by selective identification and the just treatment of wrongdoers.

Restitution

Once the guns have been silenced and some peace agreements have been accepted, what then? When one side has won a decisive military victory, its most likely course is to establish political and economic domination over the losers—and some of its people will seek revenge. For the time being here, we leave aside this dismal but recurrent outcome. A wider field of prospects is open when each of the former belligerents still has important resources and must be taken seriously as a party to the future construction of a shared society. What then are the most important societal choices?

A central dilemma immediately is apparent in the processes of (selective) remembering and forgetting (Minow 1998, chap. 6). The common advice of naïve peace seekers—to forget and forgive—is utterly unrealistic for people who have witnessed genocide, democide, torture, and all the other varieties of inhumanity and degradation. An alternative response is the "surgeons' creed" for dealing with grave medical errors by a colleague: forgive but remember. One mistake may be forgiven; a pattern of disasters must be remembered. But this posture also will be unacceptable to many of the victims of collective violence. Something else will be called for, to deal with both the memory and the present consequences of the past.

Here again we find a range of actual policies and behaviors for coping with the residues of deadly conflict. Always there will be for the victims the emotional legacy of felt injustices. Some of the victims will themselves have been victimizers. What is to be done?

One possibility that often is attractive and sometimes embraced is the route of restitution—a giving back of something of value to those who suffered as a total or partial restoration of a former condition. In the case of loss of property, for example, there can be literal restoration or indemnification. More likely will be partial compensation for loss, damage, or injury—often this will mean token or "symbolic" reparations such as the long-delayed monetary awards to Japanese Americans who suffered incarceration during World War II or the much belated and small awards to victims of Nazi persecution and expropriation.

The effects of material reparations are problematic. Is a monetary payment for past wrongs an apology or an insult? To some, perhaps many, victims such compensation is grotesquely inappropriate—trivializing the damage and agony suffered by seeking a cheap way to gain public absolution for wrongs. On the other hand, even token restitution can be accepted as a genuine acknowledgment of injustice and acceptance of responsibility. It can be taken to signify that "someone cares," that our grievances are publicly accepted as legitimate, that our voices are being heard, that the victims are not forgotten. Further, the processes of getting to reparations—the statements of grievances and claims, the legal actions, the public debates, the surfacing of hitherto obscured facts—can serve to clarify what happened in the past and to dignify the victimized.

Clearly, therefore, restitutive attempts can be either clarifying and integrative or incitements to resentment and desires for revenge. Much depends upon the specific sociocultural context and the particular characteristics of the proferred restitutions. Numerous questions arise. What are the meanings attributed to reparations: are they primarily intended to punish those responsible for the injuries? Are they intended to restore the property or the health or social respect of the victims? Are they a political ploy by leaders to placate a critical constituency? Are they simply a response to international criticism and potential sanctions? Does the effort appear to be reluctant, forthcoming only under some form of public pressure or duress? Are any material awards accompanied by clear and (convincingly) sincere expressions of regret or remorse and apology? Are the feelings of the aggrieved treated with insight and respect? Do the victims have a decisive voice in whether to accept and acknowledge or to reject the offer? Are the reparations too little and too late? (Long delayed responses are likely to be perceived as both reluctant and insulting.) In short, no automatic therapy or cleansing can be guaranteed, but careful and nuanced efforts that convey messages of empathy and regret do seem to reduce the weight of a painful past. Even given the lack of hard evidence as to the effects of reparations, this possibility remains open.

Retribution: The Search for Justice

Retribution differs from retaliation and from revenge. Retaliation signifies an act of returning injury, evil for evil—a striking back in kind for harm inflicted. Revenge carries the further connotation of anger, hostility, or vindictiveness—the desire to inflict hurt upon the author of a wrong, to cause suffering of the offender or her/his collectivity that somehow matches the distress of the victim. Although retribution likewise is punishment of an offender, the concept conveys a sense of justified punishment imposed by an actor other than the victim. Retribution can be ordered by a court of law or other higher authority (cf. *Webster's New Dictionary of Synonyms* 1968, 692–93).

In the case of the former East Germany, both the criminalization of actions of party and state officials and the work of commissions on vindication and rehabilitation were part of the processes of establishing retributive justice (Borneman 1997, 1999). Commissions, in effect, staged ceremonial events that aimed to restore victims' dignity and to prosecute offenders. Whether these rituals of purification had the putative effects, however, remains unclear. Retributive justice may be one way of taming revenge, to the extent that the process of judgment and punishment can fix responsibility, reaffirm moral norms, and establish the moral standing and social dignity of the victims. On the other hand, many scholars and legal experts doubt that these desirable ends can be served in practice: over time the general public loses commitment, interest diminishes, perpetrators evade punishment, "compassion fatigue" grows, and many people come to feel that past events should be put aside. The empirical evidence is scanty and mixed. Borneman's studies (1997, 1999) of the establishment in Germany of a program to use criminal law to deal with East Germany's past showed thousands of investigations, hundreds of indictments, but only a few convictions. Nevertheless there were public proceedings at which issues were brought forward, evidence was presented, and victims were heard. It can be argued therefore that the process itself emphasized individual accountability and the role of the state as a moral agent in fixing responsibility.

The beginning of the twenty-first century brought increased calls for legal prosecution of suspected perpetrators of crimes against humanity (e.g., torturers, mass killers) and of war crimes. For example, Amnesty International in 2000 called upon the UN to establish a process of adjudication for Sierra Leone: "specifically the establishment of a judicial mechanism . . . to try suspected perpetrators of crimes against humanity and war crimes" (editorial, *Amnesty Now*, Fall 2000, p. 1). In another case, regarded as surprising at the time, officials in Mexico in 2001 agreed to extradite to Spain for trial an Argentinean officer accused of crimes against humanity, torture, and genocide during the "dirty war" of the 1970s and 1980s against opponents of the then-ruling military government in Argentina. This unprecedented action was taken in accordance with a treaty with Spain and with the emerging principle of international law that claims universal jurisdiction over such crimes. Advocates of this principle could point to the example of the nineteenth-century international acceptance of universal jurisdiction against piracy on the high seas. In essence, the supposition is that some crimes are so heinous that state sovereignty cannot block pursuit and retribution.

There are three main grounds for prosecution under international law. The first is that of alleged crimes against the peace, such as the flagrant breaking of treaties of non-aggression or the initiation of wars of aggression; although important, these crimes do not directly enter into the cases with which we are here concerned. The second category is that of war crimes, that is, actions performed during warfare in violation of law: wanton destruction, mistreatment of prisoners of war, plunder, killing of hostages, and massacres of civilians. The third class of offenses are crimes against humanity—primarily against civilian populations in torture, rape, enslavement, persecution, deportation, and mass murders.

To deal with these violations, there are several international courts, including the International Court of Justice at the Hague, commonly known as the World Court; the European Court of Human Rights (Strasbourg); and the European Court of Justice. In addition, there are the special war crimes tribunals established to deal with the aftermath of the genocidal acts in Bosnia and in Rwanda. The great inherent difficulties of the ad hoc tribunals have been widely recognized and have led to the proposed establishment of a permanent international criminal court that would have dependable resources and enhanced legitimacy.

A treaty establishing the International Criminal Court was approved in Rome on July 17, 1998, by a vote of 120 states to 7 (with 21 abstentions). (The court is to become operational in The Hague once 60 states have ratified the treaty.) Meanwhile, the indictment and trial of accused war criminals in the former Yugoslavia was in the hands of the International War Crimes Tribunal for the Former Yugoslavia—a specific and temporary agency. Plans for a court to try officials of the Khmer Revenge for mass killings in Cambodia in the 1970s were still being negotiated in year 2000—two decades after the events. An agreement in the same year by the UN Security Council to establish a war crimes tribunal in Sierra Leone was delayed in implementation by disputes over how authority should be shared between national and international representatives.

Whatever the specific mechanisms for legal retribution against war criminals and those charged with crimes against humanity, the tribunals have been extensively criticized. An obvious point of contention is that in actual practice, it will not be feasible to identify and punish all the perpetrators; indeed, it is predictable that high officials and other leaders who have incited and organized mass atrocities are especially likely to escape penalties. Many examples already are at hand of dictators and military leaders of murderous regimes who have never been prosecuted for war crimes or crimes against humanity. The military dictator, General Stroessner, who was accused of many atrocities during his thirty-five years of rule in Paraguay, was given a reputedly luxurious refuge in Brazil. Idi Amin, under whose rule in Uganda mass murders and ethnic expulsions were carried out, found a comfortable exile in Saudi Arabia. Haiti's Jean-Claude Duvalier escaped with a fortune and went to live in France. The well-known top political and military authors of massacres and ethnic expulsions in the former Yugoslavia long continued to openly defy international charges. General Augusto Pinochet escaped extradition and trial by European states, ultimately being released by Great Britain and returned to Chile, where he was welcomed by his hard-line supporters. The list goes on.

Rarely are officials in charge of military forces subject to retribution for war crimes and crimes against humanity committed under their rule. In the village of El Mozote and its environs in El Salvador, the governmental military forces in 1981 massacred more than 800 men, women, and children—an event denied by Salvadoran and American officials. In funeral ceremonies in December 2000, the exhumed remains of 141 people were reburied. One survivor said, "There is no justice. There is no recognition of what we faced. The government has done nothing" (*New York Times*, December 11, 2000, p. A3). A report by a United Nations Truth Commission attributed 85 percent of the fatal civil war atrocities to the military and its allies. None of the high officials involved had been convicted or punished (in different cases, the Supreme Court in El Salvador and a federal court in Florida absolved officials of responsibility). The powerful seldom pay.

Many high political leaders who have presided over democides and genocides but have escaped any retribution have found protection in the customary doctrine of the immunity of heads of states. Current rulers are understandably reluctant to abolish a rule under which they themselves are protected. Failure to prosecute or to charge former authoritarian leaders of violent ethnic repression often stems from the fear that retributive efforts would result in a violent reaction of "loyal" military forces and the destruction of democratic successor regimes. Political expediency both within the afflicted country and externally by third parties (states or international organizations) regularly has blocked legal retribution (for genocides, see Kuper 1985).

In contrast to this record, the national war crimes tribunal in Rwanda did convict and punish some of the leaders of the Hutu-dominated government that organized genocidal assaults against Tutsis and had instigated mass killings of moderate Hutu opponents of the government. And of course the Nuremberg trials after World War II resulted in convictions and execution or imprisonment of Nazi leaders. In both instances, however, the verdicts were criticized as impositions by military victors upon the vanquished.

Anything like "total" retributive justice clearly is not feasible in the cases of extreme collective violence, as in massive forced ethnic expulsions and attempted genocide. The sheer number of perpetrators and their collaborators and their presence throughout a whole society make incarceration, trial, and punishment unfeasible, if only because of limited time and resources. The prototype perhaps is Rwanda, where thousands of perpetrators inflicted as many as 800,000 deaths in the 1994 genocide. As of the beginning of the twenty-first century, Rwanda jails contained thousands of suspected Hutu *genocidaires*, and there probably were several hundred thousand more among the returnees and in organized refugee camps in Zaire (Congo), where militant leaders were awaiting opportunities for further killings of Tutsis and "moderate" Hutus. Leaders of the new Rwanda government publicly despaired of being able to bring to justice more than a few of the offenders.

Nevertheless, advocates of international tribunals continue to insist upon their value as concrete mechanisms for the establishment of the rule of law in the deadly anarchy of unrestrained power. Courts, and related enforcement resources, are seen as the most effective mechanisms thus far available to reduce cycles of atrocities and vengeance by means of legal procedures to fix responsibility, to extract some (even if limited) retribution, and to dramatize the moral issues (cf. Bass 2000). Not all who are guilty will be punished. The legitimacy of the courts will be challenged, and contradictions of norms and principles will be debated and negotiated, but the movement toward new international judicial institutions appears likely to continue. Evidence of the increasing role of war crimes tribunals is the 2001 conviction and sentencing to long prison terms of military leaders of Serbian forces that massacred Bosnian civilians at Srebrenica in 1995.

We have repeatedly noted the near impossibility that the parties to violent conflict can by themselves arrive at a consensual settlement. Third parties usually are essential. In a similar way, the cycle of collective injury-revenge-retaliation is likely to continue indefinitely unless an agent external to the parties can assume responsibility for crafting an alternative narrative—a truth account—that can be a basis for retributive justice. The third party does not have to present the one and only objective truth; indeed, this is an impossibility. What can be done is the introduction of a partial (or "perspectival") truth between the conflicting parties, together with a social mechanism for public and accountable retribution for misdeeds. To the extent that these two intertwined processes can be carried out, the felt needs of ethnic agents for revenge can be reduced or even obviated. For optimal effectiveness, the processes of truth seeking and truth telling must continue and permeate the society at all levels. Indeed, Borneman had argued that an enduring reconciliation is possible "only through a continuous truth-telling about the everyday, through witnessing and double rebuilding on the basis of trust: between neighbors, and between citizens and the state" (Borneman 2000, 14).

"Truth and Reconciliation"

Bringing into public discourse the hitherto silenced or unheard accounts of victims has been increasingly advocated as a first essential step in moving toward reconciliation in violence-torn societies. This assumption is a basis for the formation in several important cases of official bodies charged with the tasks of establishing through investigation a factual account of atrocities, to publicly disseminating the findings, and providing a public platform for the victims to be heard. Such public disclosures and the consequential public discussion and debate are intended as an essential step toward restoring the credibility and dignity of those who have been victimized. These procedures are intended to promote the development of shared conceptions of "truth"—the specific reality of what was done and by whom to those who have suffered loss and felt injustice. To have this effect, the testimony of the victimized and of the perpetrators must be widely heard through public fora and in mass media. For victims to know that their accounts have been publicly acknowledged and disseminated has the potential (not always realized) for some measure of restoration of dignity, some cleansing of deep feelings of unacknowledged humiliation and shame (Scheff 1994). For the offenders—when their confessions are not merely a cynical exchange for amnesty—the public disclosure conceivably may bring some closure on the past, even if not genuine regret or a reduction in a sense of guilt.

These are some of the "positive" or "good" consequences that have been claimed for public truth telling. It is clear, however, that there is simultaneous potential for the reinforcement of victims' feelings of grief, moral outrage, frustration over unpunished wrongdoing, and of their desires for revenge. Among the perpetrators, the public investigations and hearings may be condemned as biased and illegitimate—as shown by the reactions in South Africa and in Guatemala. Thus in Guatemala, the commission had reports on more than 42,000 alleged violations of human rights during the thirty-five years of civil war, in which most of the estimated 200,000 deaths were inflicted on civilians. The commission reported that 93 percent of the deaths were inflicted by government forces, centered upon people in areas thought to be supportive of rebellion. These findings were repudiated by governmental and military spokespersons. Experience therefore shows that the wider societal effects may conclude a sharpening of incompatible views of the past, a focus on culpability, and a general polarization of attitudes.

And the public testimony is not likely to have significant efficacy in reconciliation unless the telling is matched by active listening—a social process of *witnessing* that results in widespread and continuous debate, reinterpretation and reevaluation of present relationships. The existence of truth and reconciliation commissions presumably is intended to emphasize and to help to create a public affirmation of the value of truth and truth telling. Where the process is open and credible, it may help to bring some sense of closure to the violent past and some increased likelihood of establishing at least minimal social trust.

Borneman has insisted that reconciliation depends upon a decisive break with the past—a "sense of ending" (2000, 17). But the openness to a new set of relationships is unlikely to be established unless "the truth" is followed by evidence that wrongdoers are accountable for their actions. It follows that some form of regularized retributive justice, following legal forms and procedures, is necessary to affirm the responsibility of offenders and the value of the victimized. The putative value of legal prosecution, then, lies in the symbolic purification it can represent and thus its therapeutic effect upon desire for revenge (Borneman 2000, 19).

The work of truth and reconciliation commissions is likely to be tedious, extremely detailed, and lengthy. In South Africa, the Truth and Reconciliation Commission in 1998 published a 3,500-page report, based on the testimony of about 21,000 witnesses in public hearings held in 61 towns and cities. The commission had offered amnesty to alleged offenders in return for full confessions of human rights violations that had been committed for political purposes. By the time of the report, the commission had refused to accept applications for amnesty in about 4,600 cases, had accepted 7,060 applications, and had granted amnesty to 125 individuals. Charges of bias arose when amnesty was granted to some 24 leaders of the African National Congress, allegedly without investigation of accusations against them, while amnesty was refused to some white military and police leaders. A 1998 public opinion poll reported that 60 percent of the whites surveyed said that the commission had not been fair and that it had damaged interracial relations; Black respondents held opposite views on both counts (*Christian Science Monitor*, October 28, 1998). Although systematic data are lacking, available reports suggest that the work of the commission had forced greater public recognition of past abuses while evoking sharp disagreements; it apparently has brought considerable resentment but also wider acceptance than hitherto among whites of a need for reconciliation.

The example of South Africa shows that it is possible for the parties to long-continued intrastate conflict to establish, on their own, organizations and procedures for investigation and juridical action of alleged abuses. But in the aftermath of other cases of protracted collective violence, local efforts to investigate human rights violations have lacked credibility and feasibility. In such instances, as in El Salvador, international agencies and external commissions sometimes have been accepted by the former antagonists as necessary to move toward developing shared institutions (see Hampson 1996, 546–47).

Not at all surprising is the mixed record of efforts to establish a credible public record of the actual events of the past in the face of inherent complexity, differing perceptions, bias, secrecy, deliberate deception, strong vested interests, contradictory witnessing, faulty memories, and ambiguous behaviors. Nevertheless, the experiences in several countries (Germany, South Africa, El Salvador, possibly Guatemala) have shown that authoritative commissions and other publicly accountable investigatory bodies can reduce misinformation and denial. This reality-testing function can generate over time enough consensus for further problem-solving steps toward accommodation of former adversaries.

To set at rest the memories of collective sufferings and injustice often appears to be impossible without the first step of acknowledgment of what actually happened. This obviously is no simple or easy matter, for the reality is often a shifting and ambiguous cloud of images and selective perceptions of the various actors. Even the most massive instances of mass murder have been denied, or defined away (e.g., as unavoidable by-products of legitimized war). Endless ingenuity is evident in apologists' explanations as to why genocide was not genocide, why victims were really culprits and criminals, and the like. When sheer denial of the events cannot be plausible, the recourses can be deliberate silence—a persistent refusal to admit the putative realities.

In an age of genocide—and of demands for protection of human rights—the mass murders instigated and organized by repressive governments are usually kept as secret as possible, as in Guatemala or South Africa or for a time in Serbia, but they may be flagrantly displayed as in Rwanda or Cambodia. In either case, the victimized people and concerned external observers urgently express the need for investigation and establishing the truth(s) in the case. Indeed, amnesty may be offered in exchange for confession and testimony because so much that has happened had been carefully concealed. In the South African public hearings, truth seems to have been regarded by some as a kind of justice (see the report by Ignatieff 1997b).

And yet, when all complexities have been recognized and all criticisms taken into account, it remains true that little reconciliation is to be expected until there is some acceptance by the interested parties of the minimal Facts of the Case. So, we note that in Guatemala, the investigatory body was known as the Commission for Historical Clarification, as if by the name itself to emphasize the priority of establishing a verified factual record. Concealment of the past, denials, deceptions, and distortions—all these are commonplace, and they will prevail unless there is a public validation of what is real. If nothing is real, nothing can be done.

Programs of amnesty and "truth and reconciliation," useful as they may be, do not necessarily provide grounds for genuine reconciliation among

275

all who have suffered. By what means can further reintegration of peoples be supported?

Acknowledgment, Apology, and Forgiveness

Beyond truth commissions, searching for historical clarification, and verification of responsibility, there are national and international courts and ad hoc tribunals that attempt to assign guilt and mete out retribution for past wrongs. Beyond these organizations, laws, and procedures lies the uncharted territory in which the perpetrators and victims of collective violence can attempt to reach toward some new state of resignation, acceptance, or reconciliation—some measure of psychological peace and social equilibrium.

If revenge is ruled out as morally unacceptable and the forgetting of past wrongs is seen as practically impossible, what acceptable goals can be defined for post-conflict measures intended to restore some viable social order? We have reviewed truth finding, restitution, and retributive justice. For the establishment of an enduring peace, institutional reforms and long-term economic and societal development are obvious desiderata. But all these may still be insufficient for genuine reconciliation. What else may be possible?

Forgiveness is sometimes held out as a prime objective, but no matter how desirable forgiveness may be from some points of view, there are many situations in which individuals find it to be impossible. The wrongs were too awful, the hurt too deep, the perpetrators too evil—the victims simply and literally cannot bring themselves to forgive. So, if reconciliation depended entirely upon forgiveness it would be least likely in the situations where most needed, as in the aftermath of the multiple agonies of civil wars. Rather, reconciliation at the macro level of ethnies and states may entail, at best, mutual acceptance of a truth account—a credible narrative of the past events—as a basis for a shared belief in a common future (Dwyer 1999). Such a "consensual reality" may not signify that justice has been achieved and it may not and usually will not mean that victims accept or like their former oppressors or that hostilities will fade away. What may be possible nevertheless is the gradual growth of mutual toleration and practical accommodation.

A prominent theme in analyses of conflict resolution is the proposal that sociopsychological factors are crucial in the processes of reconciliation. In particular, the sense of having been victimized—often mutual among peoples emerging from violent ethnic conflict—is both a barrier to conflict resolution and a condition that must be ameliorated before the parties can establish a secure relationship for the future. The very difficult but essential processes are that "the victimizers accept responsibility for their acts or those of their predecessor governments and people, recognize the injustice done, and in some way ask forgiveness of the victims. In many cases the contrition may have to be mutual where victimizers have themselves been victims" (Montville 1990, 538). What may be needed is a kind of mourning process in which all parties can grieve for the violent acts. This is a process that third parties may be able to encourage and facilitate by informal means.

As formulated by Scheff (1994, 127–31), the basic emotional reactions of victims include "humiliated fury" and "unacknowledged shame and rage." Other feelings of grief, fear, and anxiety typically occur. A plausible case can be made that such feelings if suppressed or otherwise unacknowledged can lead to interminable conflict. As we saw earlier, public acknowledgment and judicial proceedings are sometimes used, essentially as rituals of collective purification (Scheff 1994, 131). But how—if at all—can forgiveness be made possible? To grant forgiveness is an extraordinary act. It is plain that to admit guilt for one's participation in or acquiescence in collective wrongdoing is very difficult, and to actually ask for forgiveness is even harder. In large-scale events in which responsibilities are widely diffused—and the possibly extenuating circumstances are many and diverse—denial is an easy and favored tactic. Further, even if reconciliation is seen as both desirable and dependent upon apology and forgiveness, it is a costly burden to be borne in the present primarily for the benefit of other people in the future. And the longer the apologies are deferred, the more the grievous events recede into the past, until the realities fade and a sense of personal responsibility attenuates. At some point, expressions of regret and remorse can be made to seem absurd.

Yet it is an impressive fact that many collective apologies are made. This phenomenon warrants serious analysis. For apologies are much more that sheer acknowledgments. They do require, indeed, an acknowledgment of fact as a first ingredient: "Yes, this is actually what was done." The death squads did exist; the killing fields and the concentration camps were real; the police did torture prisoners and conceal murders; the soldiers did rape, kill, and sack the cities. A second requisite, then, is acceptance of responsibility: yes, we did it, we are the authors of the actions; what we did was not an accident or an unintended side effect. A third characteristic of an apology is an expression of regret or remorse: we are sorry that we did it. And for a full-fledged apology that invites acceptance, a fourth component is believable signs of empathy, of fellow feeling, of some understanding of the emotional meaning of the events. Often the credibility of apologies is more effectively conveyed in deeds rather than merely in words: in actual restitution and reform, but also in presence at memorializing ceremonies, a wreath on a grave, an embrace, or political support in crises. There is anecdotal evidence that some collective apologies with these characteristics do have dramatic positive effects—although others are ignored or dismissed as insufficient, self-serving, or hypocritical. When accepted as genuine, however, apologies constituted one more step toward reduction in the emotional traumas of shame, grief, and rage (Scheff 1994, 139).

In a detailed and insightful analysis, Tavuchis (1991) has described four distinct kinds of apology: of the one to the one, of the one to the many, of the many to the one, and of the many to the many. The last type refers to a collective, public action looking toward some measure of reconciliation between states or ethnies or religious bodies or any other major collectivities. Such apologies typically are offered by acknowledged leaders, such as heads of states, who are understood to speak for a whole collectivity.

The act of public apology for past behavior may be strongly resisted. Leaders of the People's Republic of China have repeatedly called for explicit apologies from the government of Japan for atrocities by Japanese military forces in the invasion and occupation of Chinese territory. The Japanese government's formal statement of regret has not satisfied this demand. In 2001, President Clinton refused to apologize for an alleged massacre by American troops in the early phases of the 1950s war in Korea. There are other cases of such refusal or minimal response. Evidently, apology can be regarded as a costly and difficult concession. All the more impressive, accordingly, is the frequency of apologies on behalf of collectivities.

Official acts of apology and regret for past actions grew in number and variety in the closing years of the twentieth century and continued into the new century. Examples include the following:

- President Clinton apologized for the earlier unethical Tuskegee medical experiments performed on Black men.
- The U.S government apologized and paid token reparations to Japanese Americans for the mass incarcerations during World War II.
- In August 1995, on the fiftieth anniversary of the end of World War II, Japanese officials, expressing "deep remorse," apologized for the "damage and suffering" caused by Japanese forces in World War II (China, however, demanded a formal apology, which Japan refused).
- In 1995, the government of Switzerland apologized to world Jewry for policies and acts that aided Nazi Germany's extermination of Jews.
- Officials of both the United States and the UN made trips to Rwanda to express regret and contrition for failure to intervene to prevent the mass slaughter of Tutsis and moderate Hutus in 1994.
- In 1999, the secretary-general of the United Nations apologized for the UN's failure to stop the mass killings by Serbs in Bosnia.

- In early 2000, the U.S. secretary of state apologized, in effect, for the past behavior of the United States toward Iran.
- In September 1999, the prime minister of Denmark apologized for the action of past national regimes in forcing Inuit people in Greenland from their homes when a United States airbase was expanding in 1953; the apology was offered shortly after a Copenhagen court had ruled that the eviction was a "serious infringement" of the rights of the indigenous people.
- In 1997, Prime Minster Tony Blair apologized for England's role in the nineteenth-century famine in Ireland.
- In March 2000, Pope John Paul II, speaking at the Yad Vashem Holocaust memorial in Israel, expressed sadness over hatred and displays of anti-Semitism by Christians.

The list could be greatly extended to characterize what has been called an age of public apology.

We do not have definitive evidence concerning the effects of such apologies. It is plausible, however, to suppose that the long-range and cumulative effects will facilitate mutual accommodations and reconciliation. And if public apologies are genuine—both asserted and sincere—they are low-cost actions that can carry great benefits. When moral conviction and enlightened self-interest do coincide, collective apology may recommend itself as a feasible action by those leaders who seek reconciliation.

Rebuilding Shattered Societies

The violence has ended. In some instances a rebellious ethny has won a military victory, has established a separate polity, and has achieved international recognition as an independent state. In other cases, multilateral intervention has imposed a cease-fire, or a more comprehensive third-party military occupation and development of a civilian regime. An inter-state war may have enabled partition into two states (Bangladesh). There even is the unlikely outcome of peaceful partition (Slovakia from the Czech Republic). Most likely of all, one of the contending parties has won the war and is in control of the state apparatus. Finally, a negotiated settlement has been achieved and the former belligerents have formed a more or less integrated political system (El Salvador, Mozambique). Whatever the other outcomes, the guns are silent and the killing has stopped. In some societies, prospects for long-term peace have been enhanced by continuing processes of restitution, justice, and reconciliation. In these most hopeful cases what remains is the reconstruction of a workable society.

For some intrastate conflicts, ethnic and non-ethnic, there simply are no solutions that will guarantee societal reintegration and reconstruction. Historical experiences show many cases, some repeatedly noted in this work, in which the conflicting peoples could neither resolve their differences nor learn to live with unresolved claims, nor make their needs and claims mutually intelligible even when disagreement continues. Outside intervention there may fail, or actually hinder or defer necessary accommodations that may have to be reached through painful social learning. A requisite "moment of truth" may not occur until a massive and dramatic event forces the antagonists to accept coexistence. And such acceptance may be unfeasible if the parties seek full consensus; rather they will have to settle for an agreement that makes their needs and claims mutually intelligible even when disagreement continues.

Obviously (but it needs to be said), what is desirable in societal reconstruction may not be possible. Some shattered societies will not become both peaceful and well integrated in the short term; some may remain violent and chaotic for generations. Third-party interventions may not be feasible, by reason of extremely high costs and lack of political will, and some attempted interventions will fail because of logistical difficulties, poverty of resources, divergences of interest among donors, and the depth of vested interests and systematic hostilities within the weakened society.

An ideal agenda for post-conflict rebuilding can recognize the difficulties but still formulate goals and norms to serve as criteria for collective action or public policy. Thus Crocker (1999) has inventoried a set of goals that can variously be regarded as acceptable, or desirable, or obligatory. Heading the list are truth accounts and retributive justice—designed to restore the dignity of victims and to hold perpetrators accountable. Desirable also is the establishment or re-imposition of the rule of law: to help develop organizations and procedures to ensure "due process" (procedural fairness), open proceedings (transparency), and impartiality. Provisions should be made, it is claimed, for reparations or, more generally, compensation and restitution for losses and injuries. Throughout a necessarily prolonged period, sustained efforts are needed to bring about institutional reform (e.g., fair elections, a reasonably impartial judiciary, professionalized and accountable military and police forces). In all the varied efforts, wide public participation and dialogue will be needed if popular consent and substantial political consensus is to develop. These formulations suggest possible normative frameworks within which the affected populations can try to work out their own conceptions of realities and their versions of a good society. The commonsense dictum is that at the end of the day, the people themselves must rebuild their society.

For the particular case of ethnic conflicts, a large body of research and practical experience has developed numerous specific recommendations for reduction and management of tensions and oppositions—a total inventory much too large to be reviewed here. (Works with useful bibliographies, cited in this book, include Zartman 1995; Esman 1994; Gurr 2000, 1993b; Horowitz 2001, 1990b, 1985; Montville 1990; and Williams 1977.) Substantial knowledge does exist.

In the broadest and long-term perspective, however, the multi-ethnic societies most likely to be both stable and peaceful will be those that are able to reduce the *salience* and *exclusiveness* of ethnic identities. This does not mean "the abolition of ethnicity," but it does imply public policies that deemphasize ethnic distinctiveness and that encourage participation in a shared civic culture. To the oft-posed question, "How do you rebuild a violence-torn society?" a ready reply is that it is an unanswerable question. No sensible answer can be given until we know who or what "you" is. Is "you" a newly victorious ethnic-based armed movement (Rwanda), an international peacekeeping force, a regional coalition, a nongovernmental humanitarian organization, a trusted individual mediator—or any concerned person anywhere? To answer the question, we need to know the actor, the resources, the detailed connections, and so on.

A more reasonable query is: What can be done? This question opens the possibility of considering a wide range of options, each of which can then be appraised in terms of specified settings. Whatever may be the particulars, however, it is clear that what is called peace building or societal reconstruction is a lengthy process—a matter not of weeks or months but of years, of decades, or of generations. It is prolonged because it is always delicate, precarious, complex, difficult, and costly. It always involves multiple relationships among diverse groupings with differing interests, beliefs, and values. Quick "solutions" do not exist; peace builders must be prepared for sustained efforts and many unavoidable frustrations.

A basic observation from many protracted conflicts is that peace depends most of all upon mutual security. For reconstruction to begin the first necessity is the reestablishment of physical, political, and social security for all major groupings. In the great majority of cases third-party guarantees and credible commitments for enforcement are necessary.

Some lessons can be seen in one of the greatest feats of the reintegration of warring states into an international system: the post–World War II treatment of Germany and Japan. Rebuilding these shattered societies was possible because the military expansionism of the two had been rendered impossible. The provision of military security by the victorious allies paved the way for the growth of economic and political integration. The second step in Europe was to link the financial aid of the Marshall Plan to acceptance by the recipients of the norms and obligations of interstate institutions for economic cooperation. Thus military security arrangements were followed both by the provision of strong incentives for cooperation, and by new organizations and normative regimes to facilitate participation and coordination among states and their subsidiary organizations (Snyder 1990). Does this experience have any applicability to the problems of intrastate post-conflict situations? Of course the obvious differences are great, but useful similarities also are present.

In societies that have just emerged from civil warfare, the tasks involved in peace building constitute a long and open-ended roster. There are the "material" problems of destroyed infrastructures and environmental damage (land mines, unexploded bombs, polluted water supplies, poisoned landscapes). Returning refugees bring multiple dilemmas. There are debts to be renegotiated. There are urgent needs to reestablish identities through validation procedures, from birth certifications to documents of ownership. Immunization programs must be activated if epidemics of disease are to be forestalled. Health care systems need medicines, equipment, rebuilt hospitals and clinics, and renewed training of personnel. Educational systems may have been wrecked.

All these problems clamor for attention even while urgent questions of justice press forward, from programs of amnesty to war crimes tribunals. Yet practical steps can be taken. A third-party with sufficient authority can require that ethnic symbols be minimized (e.g., flags, even slogans on automobile license plates), that a common currency be used, that freedom of the press be maintained, that hate crimes be prosecuted, that partisan police be restrained or replaced (all these were illustrated in the NATO-enforced regimes in Bosnia).

After peace agreements have been reached, a first requirement is that they not be made "orphans"—that third parties do not withdraw their support too soon after the signing of an accord. As Hampson (1996) has contended, the parties that have helped to bring about an agreement typically will be needed in the peace-building process, both to ensure implementation of the accord and to lay the basis for longer-term settlements. There will always be "spoilers," who for their own reasons will try to undermine the agreement; there will be unresolved issues and unexpected problems. In the early phases the interveners may be called upon to provide humanitarian aid, to monitor cease-fires, to supervise and monitor elections, and to mediate disputes over interpretation and implementation of the initial agreements. Continuing help will be needed to rebuild infrastructures and to establish stable political arrangements.

All this means that the external peace facilitator will need the will and the resources to stay engaged, often for quite lengthy periods. Quick exits increase the odds that conflict will reignite. The prospects for long-term ethnic peace will be enhanced if and when regional interstate organizations (and related ad hoc groupings, such as meetings of presidents of Central American states) promulgate codes of rights and provisions for protections of ethnies, and then hold out rewards for compliance and sanctions for violations. Conformity can be made a precondition for foreign aid, market access, or financial investment. What is possible in specific cases cannot be prescribed in advance, but discussions and negotiations conceivably can move in the direction of creating new trans-state institutions for preventing and moderating ethnic frictions.

The great majority of proposals for post-conflict peace building focus upon military, economic, and political arrangements intended to create security, to redistribute power and authority, and to reconstruct laws and norms for resolving oppositions of interests. These approaches have seemed to have self-evident priority. Yet some experienced observers and practitioners have argued that these conventional means of conflict management often have failed because they really do not meet the deeper needs of the people for secure identity and group recognition, for protection of valued relationships, and for control of the immediate environment (for example, see Azar 1990; Azar and Burton 1986). To remedy the putative deficiencies, scholars who regard *needs* as "not for trading" advocate a process of problem solving in which, it is hoped, new and mutually acceptable options can be found. The desirability of such problem solving may be generally acknowledged, but the necessary processes of dialogue are difficult to establish on a scale adequate to reach the hoped-for outcomes. Definitive evaluation of such proposed mechanisms, accordingly, still must await stronger empirical evidence.

In the most general terms, the requirements for societal reconstruction over the long term will be the same as those for the viability of already well functioning societies. These most general bases for social integration may be summarized as the three C's: connectedness, complementarity, and commonality. The first, connectedness, refers to the proposition that integration is favored by high density of interactions among individuals and collectivities that expect an indefinitely long series of future interactions. Thus, the "others," whoever or whatever they may be, will not just go away. They must be taken into account for the foreseeable future. But connectedness alone is not enough. A second favoring condition, "complementarity," is that the parties formerly in conflict can now be increasingly involved in relationships of positive and rewarding interdependence in economic activities, in providing essential services and amenities (infrastructure, roads, schools, health services, and so on), in protecting against external threats, and in maintaining some degree of public safety. The third ingredient, "commonality," refers to shared values, beliefs, and norms; it is in short supply in post-conflict situations. Nevertheless, it can be encouraged by public education, including the behavior of authoritative leaders who condemn "hate acts" and violence, who praise and reward cooperators, and who set out achievable norms of public behavior and civility. Whatever civic loyalties and shared culture that have survived the violence can be emphasized and dramatized in many ways.

Interdependence itself, over time, can further the growth of consensual solidarity. In the political realm, the reappearance of dangerous polarization can be guarded against through varying combinations of the institutional arrangements already reviewed in Chapters 10 and 11. Policies of nondiscrimination and the provision for wide availability of opportunities for upward social mobility of individuals have been important in several large-scale societies. Positive interdependence grows out of social and economic reciprocities—first in direct dealings between individuals and small groups in bounded communities, and then in indirect exchanges and generalized reciprocities. Extended systems of interdependence depend upon basic security—which means social trust. Trust creates and is created by networks of generalized reciprocities.

At the level of ordinary small-scale interactions, a multitude of practices, too familiar to be notable, help to reduce potential conflicts, both interpersonal and intergroup. Ordinary civility reduces uncertainties, smoothes over tensions, and allows for correction of misunderstandings and for the redress of minor offenses. Routine greetings acknowledge another's presence and imply legitimacy. Taking turns avoids confrontations. Little courtesies and acts of helpfulness are low-cost lubricants of daily social life. Standardized hypocrisies and formalities help to permit peaceful interchanges in tense relationships.

In economic transactions, for example, oppositions of interests are never far from the surface. Stylized bargaining, in many cultures, can reduce personal animosities. The impersonal devices of one-price systems, cash registers, receipts, and the like serve similar functions in modern societies. Civility in seller-customer relations in retail trade—so often a source of ethnic hostilities—can be facilitated by the use of ethnic "fronts," such as a Black manager in a Korean-owned store (J. Lee 2001, 89). Friction can be lowered when trading develops into long-term relationships in which familiarity and reliability bridge over ethnic cleavages.

Even something as simple as lining up for tickets of admission or for services avoids the conflictful crowding that otherwise would be likely. Interethnic fights for access to scarce bus transportation were dramatically reduced in wartime Detroit by just such queuing arrangements. Physical devices and layouts can serve as impersonal "traffic regulators." The devices are varied and numerous, but the cumulative effects can be substantial.

These elementary generalizations point toward the most fundamental of the processes that underlie cooperation and conflict, consensus and cleavage, peace and war. Societal integration depends upon successful coping with at least four universal and inevitable "problems" or exigencies that every society has (cf. Williams 1982, 352–82).

Highly relevant to ethnic conflict is, first, the classic Problem of Order, identified by Thomas Hobbes as the war of each against all in which the "life of man is solitary, poor, nasty, brutish, and short." This so-called "state of nature" is predicted because and insofar as individuals seek only to maximize their short-term self-interest and are not united by mutual identifications, shared norms, or collective aims. In this hypothetical world, each actor will find that power over others is the most direct means to his or her private ends. But if in this zero- or minus-sum arena each actor (individual or other sub-unit) acts to maximize power, the struggle moves to sheer coercion and thus to the universal "war." This is a radically individualistic scenario. In ethnic conflicts the magnitude of power struggles is greatly expanded, for the opponents are collective actors that seek control over others.

The postulate of rationality leads directly also to the second universal: the Tragedy of the Commons. If there is a valuable scarce exhaustible resource (a village pasture, fishing grounds) to which all have access, it is to each actor's advantage to take as much as possible. But if everyone thus acts as a rational maximizer, eventually the resource is destroyed—the pasture is overgrazed, the fishing stock extinct, the rich soil eroded, the woodlands gone. Each actor was rational; the collective outcome is that all suffer. The Tragedy of the Commons can be generalized to include all cumulative social costs, negative externalities, or undesirable side effects. Unwanted results range from traffic congestion and air pollution to arm races, civil warfare, depletion of the ozone layer, or global warming. The world is filled with hundreds of dilemmas occasioned by the undesired and undesirable side effects of such uncoordinated, short-run rational actions of social units. And if this kind of individual myopic rationality was what got us into the Tragedy of the Commons or into a world of disorder in the first place, how can individual self-interested actions get us out of the entailed disasters? The short answer is that they cannot. The problem requires collective action.

If collective action is needed, how can it be achieved? Prominent in ethnic mobilization is the central issue of the free rider problem (see Chapter 6). If participation in collective solutions involves costs—deprivations, sacrifices, and foregone opportunities—how can actors be stopped from free riding? To conserve oil supplies and reduce air pollution, we may be urged to carpool and to ride a bicycle to work. As a dutiful citizen, I may do these things only to note that *you* ride alone in a higher-powered gas-guzzler. Thus you enjoy a double benefit: you expend no effort and make no sacrifice of time or comfort, while at the same time you benefit from the cleaner air and lower oil prices brought about by the actions of others. Again, as a member of an oppressed ethny, I may be urged by my fellows to contribute funds and risk imprisonment and other ills in the collective effort to end discrimination. I do so—and then see that others benefit while making no contribution. Without some ethnic solidarity, I and others like me may then decide in turn to free ride, throwing the whole system back into the original dilemma. Nevertheless, as we saw in Chapters 6 and 7, ethnic mobilizations do occur, and individuals do aid others. An overly narrow rational-choice model ignores the possibility that there may be evolutionarily adaptive dispositions for reciprocity and solidarity that are effective under specifiable conditions (see Nielsen 1994). But let us grant that even if such basic propensities exist (as strong evidence indicates they do), they often will fail in large-scale complex societies. The social solidarity of small, relatively self-contained social groupings is unlikely to prevail in the globalized world where social control no longer grows out of multi-bonded relations of indefinite future duration (see Axelrod 1984; Axelrod and Dion 1988). How the minimal "bargains" that are required for essential functioning can be established is neither simple nor automatic.

As we have seen, collective actions are required if the basic dilemmas are to be mitigated. And collective decisions in turn require some kind and degree of consensus. "Solutions" such as power sharing, regulation, taxation, social censure, or legal penalties entail enactment, monitoring, and enforcement. How may such measures be obtained? Short of Hobbes's Leviathan, the generic answer has to be the development of some minimal consensus. The Problem of Consensus, especially acute in ethnically divided societies, is how diverse individuals and other social units with different beliefs, values, and interests can be brought to agreement upon rules, procedures, limits, and goals. Obviously, there are many failures to attain consensus; a great many groups and whole societies have collapsed and disappeared. The old cliché, of course, is that what we learn from History is that people do not learn from History. Needed consensus, certainly, is not easily achieved, but without it any society is trapped in the dilemma of collective actions.

Other alternatives for dealing with these intractable problems can be developed through social learning, including the procedures and findings of the social sciences. The four great problems call for increased knowledge; for persuasion, negotiation, and legislation; for the development of new normative regimes and organizations. Thus, some collective solutions have emerged from consensus based on persuasion. A striking case is the reduction in adult cigarette smoking in the United States in one short generation. No new legislation forced anyone to stop a two-pack-a-day smoking habit, but the cumulative impact of public action and medical evidence caused millions of individuals to make a major change in behavior. Clearly this is a special case, but the point is that massive changes in behavior can be achieved through persuasion.

Aside from persuasion—essential, but limited—consensus develops from diverse sources and through varied channels. For in our view, "consensus" does not imply a sentimental or utopian notion of undifferentiated and spontaneous agreement. Rather, the consensus that is feasible refers to complex agreements, including tacit understandings, often attained only through prolonged and arduous processes. Indeed, such agreement often emerges only through reiterated and painful conflicts. It can grow out of negotiated resolutions of conflicts, from informal consent in debates, from the development of various kinds of checks and balances, from the reluctant recognition of the prudence of an agreement to disagree. Many such processes of strategic interaction do exist and are open to close observation and analysis.

A final comment, then, is that there are definable ways in which ancient and intractable social conflicts and dilemmas can be mitigated. Of course, we all face ontological scarcity—we all will die; there is only so much time in our world. And, of course, we always face trade-offs.

But recognition of constraints and limits can in itself free us to undertake what can be done in the here and now.

Epilogue

This book has not attempted to find timeless and universal generalizations—our aspirations do not match those of the great Thucydides, who said in effect that he wrote not for a day or a year but for all time. All our findings come from particular contexts, although some of them do appear to have wide applicability—such as the combination of conditions most conducive to ethnic conflict, or the dangers of violent repression of ethnic political movements. More broadly, however, we have focused upon one relatively short span of human history that might be called a century of global transition. The great wave of intrastate conflicts extending from the mid-twentieth century into the twenty-first century were phenomena of an enormous series of transitions: *from* imperialism/colonialism and the worldwide rivalries of nationalism based on a system of sovereign Westphalian states, *to* the multiple processes of globalization, *to* the sweeping collapse of nineteenth-century colonialism and *to* the multiplication of new and weak and repressive states that often experienced failure or collapse, *to* the emergence and reactivation of ethnopolitical formations, and *to* endemic intrastate collective violence. The result has been a world of greatly increased interdependence at all levels, and the simultaneous and dialectical growth of separatism, reactive religious and ethnic movements, and a great variety of other cultural and social particularisms.

This particular historical confluence, of course, will pass away in its turn, and rivalries and conflicts will take on new forms. But collective conflicts will not disappear. They will continue because they are rooted in basic human propensities to form both small social groups and extended collectivities, to assert claims to scarce desirables, to resist encroachment from the demands of other social actors, to develop vested interests, to hold and defend differing values and beliefs. Contradictions and disagreements are inevitable, as are the resulting necessities for choice. When accommodations among individuals or collectivities fail, as some always will, conflicts will occur, bringing their toll of human tragedies.

Within the limits of these unavoidable realities are the numerous possibilities for preventing, limiting, and resolving the more severe conflicts. There are the clear possibilities for the growth of positive, rewarding interdependence among groups and societies. Evident also are the possibilities for further development of worldwide sets of institutions that promote and enforce norms by cooperation, negotiation, and peaceful management of some formerly lethal rivalries.

It is said that Dag Hammarskjöld, the former secretary-general of the United Nations, once said that the organization's task was not to bring mankind to Heaven but to save it from Hell. This combination of realism and hope may well serve as a proverb to remind us that the Perfect is often the enemy of the Good. At the same time we are always in need of hope and of visions of a more livable world.

References

Aho, J. A. 1994. *This thing of darkness: A sociology of the enemy*. Seattle: University of Washington Press.

Alba, R. D. 1990. *Ethnic identity: The transformation of White America*. New Haven: Yale University Press.

———. 1992. Ethnicity. In *Encyclopedia of Sociology*, vol. 2, ed. E. F. Borgatta and M. L. Borgatta, 575–84. New York: Macmillan.

Altemeyer, B. 1988. *Enemies of freedom: Understanding right-wing authoritarianism*. San Francisco: Jossey-Bass.

Amalrik, A. 1969. *Will the Soviet Union survive until 1984?* Amsterdam: Herzen.

Anderson, W. K. 1990. Multiethnic conflict and peacemaking: The case of Assam. In *Conflict and peacemaking in multiethnic societies*, ed. J. V. Montville, 327–29. Lexington, Mass.: D.C. Heath.

Armstrong, J .A. 1976. Mobilized and proletarian diasporas. *American Political Science Review* 70 (2): 393–408.

———. 1982. *Nations before nationalism*. Chapel Hill: University of North Carolina Press.

Ashworth, G., ed. 1980. *World minorities in the eighties*, vol. 3. Sunbury, U.K.: Quartermaine House.

Axelrod, R. 1984. *The evolution of cooperation*. New York: Basic Books.

Axelrod, R., and D. Dion. 1988. The further evolution of cooperation. *Science* 242: 1385–90.

Ayoob, M. 1996. State making, state breaking, and state failure. In *Managing global chaos: Sources of and responses to international conflict*, ed. C. A. Crocker and F. O. Hampson, with P. Aall, 37–51. Washington, D.C.: United States Institute of Peace Press.

Azar, E. E. 1990. *The management of protracted social conflict: Theory and cases*. Aldershot, Hampshire: Dartmouth.

Azar, E. E., and J. W. Burton, eds. 1986. *International conflict resolution: Theory and practice*. Brighton, Sussex: Wheatsheaf Books.

Baldassare, M., ed. 1994. *The Los Angeles riots: Lessons for the urban future.* Boulder, Colo.: Westview Press.

Bales, R. F. 1999. *Social interaction systems: Theory and measurement.* New Brunswick, N.J.: Transaction Publishers.

Balibar, E. 1990. The nation-form: History and ideology. *Review* (Binghamton University) 13 (3) 329–61.

Banac, I. 1992. The fearful asymmetry of war: The causes and consequences of Yugoslavia's demise. *Daedalus* 121 (2): 141–74.

Barkey, K. 1991. Rebellious alliances: The state and peasant unrest in early seventeenth-century France and the Ottoman empire. *American Sociological Review* 56: 699–715.

Bartlett, R. 1993. *The making of Europe: Conquest, colonization, and cultural change, 950–1350.* Princeton: Princeton University Press.

Bartov, O. 1996. *Murder in our midst: The Holocaust, industrial killing, and representation.* New York: Oxford University Press.

Bass, G. J. 2000. *Stay the hand of vengeance: The politics of war crimes tribunals.* Princeton: Princeton University Press.

Basu, A. 1995. Why local riots are not simply local: Collective violence and the state in Bijnor, India, 1988–1993. *Theory and Society* 24 (7): 35–78.

Bayly, S. 1993. History and the Fundamentalists: India after the Ayodhya crisis. *Bulletin—American Academy of Arts and Sciences* 46 (7): 7–26.

Beissinger, M. R. 1991. Protest mobilization among Soviet nationalities. Presented at the eighty-sixth annual meeting of the American Sociological Association, Cincinnati.

———. 2002. *Nationalist mobilization and the collapse of the Soviet state.* Cambridge: Cambridge University Press.

Bélanger, S., and M. Pinard. 1991. Ethnic movements and the competition model: Some missing links. *American Sociological Review* 56 (4): 446–57.

Benedict, K. 1999. International relations in the global village. In *Violent conflict in the 21st century: Causes, instruments and mitigation,* ed. C. Hermann, H. K. Jacobson, and A. S. Moffat, 111–28. Chicago: American Academy of Arts and Sciences, Midwest Center.

Berdal, M., and D. M. Malone. 2000. *Greed and grievance: Economic agendas in civil wars.* Boulder, Colo.: L. Rienner.

Bergesen, A., and M. Herman. 1998. Immigration, race, and riot: The 1992 Los Angeles uprising. *American Sociological Review* 63: 39–54.

Berger, P. L., ed. 1998. *The limits of social cohesion: Conflict and mediation in pluralist societies. A report of the Bertelsman Foundation to the Club of Rome.* Boulder, Colo.: Westview Press.

Bertelsen, J. S., ed. 1977. *Nonstate nations in international politics: Comparative system analyses.* New York: Praeger.

Bilder, R. B., S. Korman, and D. Kennedy. 1997. The right of conquest: The acquisition of territory by force in international law and practice. *American Journal of International Law* 91 (4): 745.

Bobo, L., and V. L. Hutchings. 1996. Perceptions of racial group competition: Extending Blumer's theory of group position to a multiracial social context. *American Sociological Review* 61 (6): 951–72.

Bobo, L., and C. Zubrinksy. 1995. Prismatic metropolis: Race and residential segregation in the City of Angels. *Working Papers* #78: 53 pp. New York: Russell Sage Foundation.

Bogdanor, V. 1997. Forms of autonomy and the protection of minorities. *Daedalus* 126 (2): 65–87.

Borneman, J. 1997. *Settling accounts: Violence, justice, and accountability in postsocialist Europe*. Princeton: Princeton University Press.

———. 1999. Can apologies contribute to peace? An argument for retribution. *Anthropology of East Europe Review* 17 (1): 7–20.

———. 2000. Reconciliation after ethnic cleansing: Listening, retribution, and affiliation. Department of Anthropology, Cornell University.

Boulding, K. E. 1978. *Stable peace*. Austin: University of Texas Press.

———. 1985. *The world as a total system*. Beverly Hills, Calif.: Sage.

Bourgois, P. I. 1989. *Ethnicity at work: Divided labor on a Central American banana plantation*. Baltimore: Johns Hopkins University Press.

Boyarin, J. 1991. An inquiry into inquiries and a representation of representations. *Sociological Forum* 6 (2): 387–95.

Brass, P. R., ed. 1985. *Ethnic groups and the state*. London: Croom Helm.

———. 1991. *Ethnicity and nationalism: Theory and comparison*. New Delhi: Sage Publications India Pvt. Ltd.

———. 1996. *Riots and pogroms*. New York: New York University Press.

Brecher, M., J. Wilkenfeld, and S. Moser. 1998. *Crises in the twentieth century*. Vol. 2, *Handbook of foreign policy crises*. New York: Pergamon.

Bremer, S. 1993. Democracy and militarized interstate conflict, 1816–1965. *International Interactions* 18 (3): 231–49.

Brewer, M. 1999. Social identity, group loyalty, and intergroup conflict. In *Violent conflict in the 21st century: Causes, instruments, and mitigation*, ed. C. Hermon, H. K. Jacobson, and A. S. Moffat, 67–88. Chicago: American Academy of Arts and Sciences, Midwest Center.

Brogan, P. 1990. *The fighting never stopped: A comprehensive guide to world conflict*. New York: Vintage.

Browning, C. 1992. *Ordinary men: Reserve Police Battalion 101 and the Final Solution in Poland*. New York: HarperCollins.

Brubaker, R. 1994. Rethinking nationhood: Nation as institutional form, practical category, contingent event. *Contention: Debate in Society, Culture, and Science* 4 (1): 3–14.

———. 1995. National minorities, nationalizing states, and external homelands in the new Europe. *Daedalus* 124 (2): 107–32.

———. 1999. *Nationalism reframed: nationhood and the national question in the new Europe*. New York: Cambridge University Press.

Brubaker, R., and D. D. Laitin. 1998. Ethnic and nationalist violence. *Annual Review of Sociology* 24: 423–52.

Caplan, A. L., ed. 1992. *When medicine went mad: Bioethics and the Holocaust*. Totowa, N.J.: Humana Press.

Carmet, D. W., and P. James. 1995. Internal constraints and interstate ethnic conflict: Toward a crisis-based assessment of irredentism. *Journal of Conflict Resolution* 39 (1): 85–100.

———, eds. 1998. *Peace in the midst of wars: Preventing and managing international ethnic conflicts*. Columbia: University of South Carolina Press.

References

Carneiro, R. L. 1970. A theory of the origin of the state. *Science* 169: 733–38.
———. 1988. The evolution of complexity in human societies and its mathematical expression. *International Journal of Comparative Sociology* 28: 111–28.
Carrère d'Encausse, H. 1979. *Decline of an empire: The Soviet Socialist Republics in revolt.* New York: Newsweek Books.
Chase-Dunn, C. 1992. The comparative study of world-systems. *Review* 15 (3): 313–33.
Chazan, N. 1986. Ethnicity in economic crisis: Development strategies and patterns of ethnicity in Africa. In *Ethnicity, politics, and development,* ed. D. L. Thompson and D. Ronen, 137–58. Boulder, Colo.: L. Rienner.
Chege, M. 1996–97. Africa's murderous professors. *National Interest* 46: 32–40.
Chipman, J. 1993. Managing the politics of particularism. In *Ethnic conflict and international security,* ed. M. E. Brown, 237–64. Princeton: Princeton University Press.
Chirot, D. 1994. *Modern tyrants: The power and prevalence of evil in our age.* New York: Free Press.
Church, R., and W. Outram. 1998. *Strikes and solidarity: Coalfield conflict in Britain.* New York: Cambridge University Press.
Clark, S. 1998. International competition and the treatment of minorities: Seventeenth-century cases and general propositions. *American Journal of Sociology* 103 (5): 1267–1309.
Clark, T. N., and V. Hoffmann-Martinot. 1998. *The new political culture.* Boulder, Colo.: Westview Press.
Cohen, Y., B. R. Brown, and A. F. K. Organski. 1981. The paradoxical nature of state making: The violent creation of order. *American Political Science Review* 75: 901–10.
Collier, P. 2001. Economic causes of civil conflict and their implications for policy. In *Turbulent peace: The challenges of managing international conflict,* ed. C. A. Crocker, F. O. Hampson, and P. Aall, 143–62. Washington, D.C.: United States Institute of Peace.
Collier, R. B. 1982. *Regimes in tropical Africa: Changing forms of supremacy, 1945–1975.* Berkeley: University of California Press.
Collins, R. 1994. Review essay of *The handbook of economic sociology,* ed. N. J. Smelser and R. Swedberg. *Contemporary Sociology* 24 (3): 300–304.
Connor, W. 1981. Nationalism and political illegitimacy. *Canadian Review of Studies in Nationalism* 8: 201–28.
———. 1992. The nation and its myth. In *Ethnicity and nationalism,* ed. A. D. Smith, 48–57. Leiden: E. J. Brill.
Constable, N., ed. 1996. *Guest people: Hakka identity in China and abroad.* Seattle: University of Washington Press.
Coomaraswamy, R. 1994. Linkages between methodology, research and theory in race and ethnic studies: A case study of Sri Lanka. In *"Race," ethnicity, and nation: International perspectives on social conflict,* ed. P. Ratcliffe, 134–50. London: UCL Press.
Cooney, M. 1997. From warre to tyranny: Lethal conflict and the state. *American Sociological Review* 62 (2): 316–38.
———. 1998. *Warriors and peacemakers: How third parties shape violence.* New York: New York University Press.
Corr, E. G. 1995. Societal transformation for peace in El Salvador. *The Annals, AAPSS* 541: 144–56.

Crighton, E., and M. A. MacIver. 1991. The evolution of protracted ethnic conflict: Group dominance and political underdevelopment in Northern Ireland and Lebanon. *Comparative Politics* 12 (2): 127–42.

Crocker, D. A. 1999. Reckoning with past wrongs: A normative framework. *Ethics and International Affairs* 13: 43–64.

Cushman, T., and S. G. Meštrović, eds. 1996. *This time we knew: Western responses to genocide in Bosnia.* New York: New York University Press.

Daedalus. 1992. Issue on *The exit from communism.* Vol. 121 (2).

Darby, J. 1987. *Intimidation and the control of conflict in Northern Ireland.* Syracuse, N.Y.: Syracuse University Press.

Darnell, A. T., and S. Parikh. 1988. Religion, ethnicity, and the role of the state in explaining conflict in Assam. *Ethnic and Racial Studies* 11: 263–81.

Demerath, N. J. III. 2002. A sinner among the saints: Confessions of a sociologist of culture and religion. *Sociological Forum* 17 (1): 1–19.

Deng, F. M. 1995. *War of visions: Conflict of identities in the Sudan.* Washington, D.C.: Brookings Institution.

De Silva, K., and R. May, eds. 1991. *Internationalization of ethnic conflict.* New York: St. Martin's Press.

De Silva, K. M., and S. W. R. de A. Samarsinghe, eds. 1993. *Peace accords and ethnic conflict.* New York: St. Martin's Press.

Diamond, J. M. 1992. *The third chimpanzee: The evolution and future of the human animal.* New York: HarperCollins.

Dirks, N. B. 2001. *Castes of mind: Colonialism and the making of modern India.* Princeton: Princeton University Press.

Douglas, W. A. 1988. A critique of recent trends in the analysis of ethnonationalism. *Ethnic and Racial Studies* 11: 192–206.

Dutter, L. E. 1990. Theoretical perspectives on ethnic political behavior in the Soviet Union. *Journal of Conflict Resolution* 34: 311–34.

Dwyer, S. 1999. Reconciliation for realists. *Ethics and International Affairs* 13: 81–98.

Eisinger, P. K. 1973. Support for urban control-sharing at the mass level. *American Journal of Political Science* 17 (4): 669–94.

Elkins, D. J. 1997. Globalization, telecommunication, and virtual ethnic communities. *International Political Science Review* 18 (2): 139–52.

Eller, J. D. 1999. *From culture to ethnicity to conflict: An anthropological perspective on international ethnic conflict.* Ann Arbor: University of Michigan Press.

Ember, C. R., and M. Ember. 1994. War, socialization, and interpersonal violence: A cross-cultural study. *Journal of Conflict Resolution* 38 (4): 620–46.

Ember, C. R., M. Ember, and B. M. Russett. 1992. Peace between participatory polities: A cross-cultural test of the "Democracies rarely fight each other" hypothesis. *World Politics* 44 (4): 573–99.

Enloe, C. H. 1980. *Ethnic soldiers: State security in divided societies.* Athens: University of Georgia Press.

Enzensberger, M. 1994. *Civil wars: From L.A. to Bosnia.* New York: New Press.

Esman, M. 1990. Ethnic pluralism and international relations. *Canadian Review of Studies in Nationalism* 17 (1–2): 83–93.

———. 1994. *Ethnic politics.* Ithaca, N.Y.: Cornell University Press.

Evans, G. 1993. *Cooperating for peace: The global agenda for the 1990's and beyond.* St. Leonards, NSW: Allen and Unwin.

Evans, P. 1995. *Embedded autonomy: States and industrial transformation.* Princeton: Princeton University Press.

Exum, W. H. 1985. *Paradoxes of protest: Black student activism in a White university.* Philadelphia: Temple University Press.

Falk, R. A. 1968. Conflict of laws. In *International encyclopedia of the social sciences,* vol. 3, ed. D. L. Sills, 246–53. New York: Macmillan.

Fein, H. 1979. *Accounting for genocide: National responses and Jewish victimization during the Holocaust.* New York: Free Press.

———. 1993. *Genocide: A sociological perspective.* London: Sage.

Finnegan, W. 1999. The invisible war. *New Yorker,* January 25: 50–73.

Fishman, J. A. 1981. Language maintenance and ethnicity. *Canadian Review of Studies in Nationalism* 8: 229–47.

———. 1989. *Language and ethnicity in minority sociolinguistic perspective.* Philadelphia: Multilingual Matters.

Fleissner, E. 1999. Race and the human gene. *Hastings Center Report* 29 (4): 40–42.

Forbes, H. D. 1997. *Ethnic conflict: Commerce, culture, and the contact hypothesis.* New Haven: Yale University Press.

Francis, E. K. 1976. *Interethnic Relations: An essay in sociological theory.* New York: Elsevier.

Francisco, R. A. 1995. The relationship between coercion and protest: An empirical evaluation in three coercive states. *Journal of Conflict Resolution* 39: 263–82.

Frankland, E. G., and T. Noble. 1996. A case of national liberation with feminist undertones: The secession of Eritrea. *Small Wars and Insurgencies* 7 (3): 401–24.

Friedland, N. 1992. Becoming a terrorist: Social and individual antecedents. In *Terrorism: Roots, impact, responses,* ed. L. Howard, 81–93. New York: Praeger.

Friedland, R., and R. Hecht. 1996. *To rule Jerusalem.* Cambridge: Cambridge University Press.

Friedlander, H. 1995. *The origins of Nazi genocide: From euthanasia to the Final Solution.* Chapel Hill: University of North Carolina Press.

Frey, R. S., T. Dietz, and L. Kalof. 1997. Characteristics of successful American protest groups: Another look at Gamson's *Strategy of social protest. American Journal of Sociology* 98 (2): 368–87.

Frye, T. M. 1992. Ethnicity, sovereignty and transitions from non-democratic rule. *Journal of International Affairs* 45: 599–623.

Fugita, S. S., and D. J. O'Brien. 1991. *Japanese American ethnicity: The persistence of community.* Seattle: University of Washington Press.

Gagnon, V. P., Jr. 1994/95. Ethnic nationalism and international conflict: The case of Serbia. *International Security* 19 (3): 130–66.

———. 1995. Ethnic conflict as an intra-group phenomenon: A preliminary framework. *Revija za sociologija* 26 (1–2): 81–90.

Gamson, W. A. 1975. *The strategy of social protest.* Belmont, Calif.: Wadsworth.

———. 1990. *The strategy of social protest.* 2nd ed. Belmont, Calif.: Wadsworth.

Ganguly, R., and R. Taras. 1998. *Understanding ethnic conflict: The international dimension.* New York: Longman/Addison-Wesley Educational Publishers.

Gans, H. J. 1979. Symbolic ethnicity: The future of ethnic groups and cultures in America. In *On the making of Americans: Essays in honor of David Riesman,* ed. H. J. Gans, N. Glazer, J. R. Gusfield, and C. Jencks, 193–200. Philadelphia: University of Pennsylvania Press.

Garb, P. 1996. Ethnic alliance building and the limited spread of ethnic conflict in the Caucasus. Paper prepared for the University of California Institute on Global Conflict and Cooperation Project, March 11.

Giddens, A. 1995. *Beyond left and right: The future of radical politics.* Stanford: Stanford University Press.

Giugni, M. G. 1998. Was it worth the effort? The outcomes and consequences of social movements. In *Annual Review of Sociology*, ed. J. Hagan and K. S. Cook, 371–93. Palo Alto, Calif.: Annual Reviews.

Gochman, C. S. 1996/97. Correspondence: Democracy and peace—Henry S. Farber and Joanne Gowa. *International Security* 21 (3): 177–87.

Goetz, D. 1996. Evolution and the origins of ethnic identity. Paper prepared for annual meeting of the Western Political Science Association, San Francisco, Calif., March 14–16.

Goldhagen, D. J. 1996. *Hitler's willing executioners: Ordinary Germans and the Holocaust.* New York: Knopf.

Goldstone, J. A. 1998. Initial conditions, general laws, path dependence, and explanations in historical sociology. *American Journal of Sociology* 104 (3): 829–45.

Goldstone, J. A., and B. Useem. 1999. Prison riots as microrevolutions: An extension of state-centered theories of revolution. *American Journal of Sociology* 104 (4): 985–1029.

Goodwin, J. 1993. Why insurgencies persist, or the perversity of indiscriminate state violence. Revision of paper presented at the seventeenth International Congress, Latin American Studies Association, September 1992, Los Angeles.

Gordon, M. M. 1981. Models of pluralism: The new American dilemma. *The Annals, AAPSS* 454: 178–88.

Gordy, E. D. 1999. *The culture of power in Serbia: Nationalism and the destruction of alternatives.* University Park: Pennsylvania State University Press.

Gould, R. V. 1991. Multiple networks and mobilization in the Paris Commune, 1871. *American Sociological Review* 56 (6): 716–29.

———. 1993. Collective action and network structures. *American Sociological Review* 58 (2): 182–96.

———. 1995. *Insurgent identities: Class, community, and protest in Paris from 1848 to the Commune.* Chicago: University of Chicago Press.

———. 1996. Patron-client ties, state centralization, and the Whiskey Rebellion. *American Journal of Sociology* 102 (2): 400–429.

———. 1999. Collective violence and group solidarity: Evidence from a feuding society. *American Sociological Review* 64 (3): 356–80.

———. 2000. Revenge as sanction and solidarity display: An analysis of vendettas in nineteenth-century Corsica. *American Sociological Review* 65 (5): 682–704.

Gourevitch, P. 1998. *We wish to inform you that tomorrow we will be killed with our families: Stories from Rwanda.* New York: Farrar, Straus, and Giroux.

———. 2000. A reporter at large: Forsaken. *New Yorker*, September 25: 52–67.

Gowa, J. 1999. *Ballots and bullets: The elusive democratic peace.* Princeton: Princeton University Press.

Green, D. P., D. A. Strolovitch, and J. S. Wong. 1998. Defended neighborhoods, integration, and racially motivated crime. *American Journal of Sociology* 104 (2): 372–403.

Greenfield, L. 1993. Transcending the nation's worth. *Daedalus* 122 (3): 47–62.

Grimes, B. F. 1988. *Ethnologue: Languages of the world.* Dallas: Summer Institute of Linguistics.

References

Grimshaw, A. D. 1999. Genocide and democide. In *Encyclopedia of violence, peace, and conflict*, ed. L. Kurt and J. Turpin, 53–74. San Diego: Academic Press.

Grofman, B., and R. Stockwell. 2001. Institutional design in plural societies: Mitigating ethnic conflict and fostering stable democracy. Center for the Study of Democracy, School of Social Sciences, University of California, Irvine.

Gupta, D. K., H. Singh, and T. Sprague. 1993. Government coercion of dissidents: Deterrence or provocation? *Journal of Conflict Resolution* 37: 301–39.

Gurdon, C. 1989. Instability and the state: Sudan. In *The state and instability in the South*, ed. C. Thomas and P. Saravanamuttu, 61–80. New York: St. Martin's Press.

Gurr, T. R., ed. 1980. *Handbook of political conflict: Theory and research*. New York: Free Press.

———. 1990. Ethnic warfare and the changing priorities of global security. *Mediterranean Quarterly* 1: 82–98.

———. 1993a. Why minorities rebel: A global analysis of communal mobilization and conflict since 1945. *International Political Science Review* 14 (2): 161–201.

———. 1993b. *Minorities at risk: A global view of ethnopolitical conflicts*. Washington, D.C.: United States Institute of Peace.

———. 1994. Peoples against states: Ethnopolitical conflict and the changing world system. Presidential address, International Studies Association annual meeting, Washington, D.C., April 1.

———. 1995. Transforming ethnopolitical conflicts: Exit, autonomy or access. In *Conflict transformation*, ed. K. Rupesinghe, 1–36. New York: St. Martin's Press.

———. 2000. *Peoples versus states: Minorities at risk in the new century*. Washington, D.C.: United States Institute of Peace.

Gurr, T. R., and B. Harff. 1994. *Ethnic conflict in world politics*. Boulder, Colo.: Westview Press.

Habermas, J. 1984, 1987. *The theory of communicative action*, vols. 1–2. Trans. T. McCarthy. Boston: Beacon.

Hadden, J. K. 1992. Religious fundamentalism. In *Encyclopedia of Sociology*, vol. 3, ed. E. F. Borgatta and M. L. Borgatta, 1637–42. New York: Macmillan.

Hadjipavlau-Trigeorgis, M., and L. Trigeorgis. 1993. Cyprus: An evolutionary approach to conflict resolution. *Journal of Conflict Resolution* 37: 340–60.

Hall, J. A. 1993. Nationalisms: Classified and explained. *Daedalus* 122 (3): 1–23.

Hammond, P. E., and K. Warner. 1993. Religion and ethnicity in late twentieth-century America. *The Annals, AAPSS* 527: 55–66.

Hampson, F. O. 1996. Why orphaned peace settlements are more prone to failure. In *Managing global chaos: Sources of and responses to international conflict*, ed. C. A. Crocker and F. O. Hampson, with P. Aall, 533–50. Washington, D.C.: United States Institute of Peace Press.

Hardin, R. 1995. *One for all: The logic of group conflict*. Princeton: Princeton University Press.

Harff, B. 1987. The etiology of genocide. In *The age of genocide*, ed. M. N. Dobkowski and I. Walliman, 41–59. Newport, Conn.: Greenwood Press.

Hartzell, C. A. 1999. Explaining the stability of negotiated settlements to intrastate wars. *Journal of Conflict Resolution* 43 (1): 3–22.

Heberer, T. 1989. *China and its national minorities: Autonomy or assimilation*. Armonk, N.Y.: M. E. Sharpe.

Hechter, M. 1975. *Internal colonialism: The Celtic fringe in British national development, 1536–1966*. Berkeley: University of California Press.

298

Heckathorn, D. D. 1996. The dynamics and dilemmas of collective action. *American Sociological Review* 61 (2): 250–77.

Heisler, M. O. 1990. Ethnicity and ethnic relations in the modern West. In *Conflict and peacemaking in multiethnic societies*, ed. J. V. Montville, 21–52. Lexington, Mass.: D. C. Heath.

Heraclides. A. 1991. *The self-determination of minorities in international politics.* London: Frank Cass.

Higham, J. 1999. Cultural responses to immigration. In *Diversity and its discontents: Cultural conflict and common ground in contemporary American society*, ed. N. J. Smelser and J. C. Alexander, 39–61. Princeton: Princeton University Press.

Hintzen, P. C. 1989. *The costs of regime survival: Racial mobilization, elite domination, and control of the state in Guyana and Trinidad.* Cambridge: Cambridge University Press.

Hirschman, C. 1992. How to measure ethnicity: An immodest proposal. Paper presented at the Joint Canada–United States Conference on the Measurement of Ethnicity, Ottawa, April 1–3.

Hoffman, B. 1992. Low-intensity conflict: Terrorism and guerrilla warfare in the coming decades. In *Terrorism: Roots, impact, responses*, ed. L. Howard, 139–54. New York: Praeger.

Holsti, K. J. 1996. *The state, war, and the state of war.* Cambridge: Cambridge University Press.

Horowitz, D. L. 1985. *Ethnic groups in conflict.* Berkeley: University of California Press.

———. 1990a. Making moderation pay: The comparative politics of ethnic conflict management. In *Conflict and peacemaking in multiethnic societies*, ed. J. V. Montville, 451–75. Lexington, Mass.: D. C. Heath.

———. 1990b. Ethnic conflict management for policymakers. In *Conflict and peacemaking in multiethnic societies*, ed. J. V. Montville, 115–16. Lexington, Mass.: D. C. Heath.

———. 1991. *A democratic South Africa? Constitutional engineering in a divided society.* Berkeley: University of California Press.

———. 1999. Group loyalty and ethnic violence. In *Violent conflict in the 21st century: Causes, instruments and mitigation*, ed. C. Hermann, H. K. Jacobson, and A. S. Moffat, 89–110. Chicago: American Academy of Arts and Sciences, Midwest Center.

———. 2001. *The deadly ethnic riot.* Berkeley: University of California Press.

Howard, L., ed. 1992. *Terrorism: Roots, impact, responses.* New York: Praeger.

Hudson, M. C. 1968. *The precarious republic; political modernization in Lebanon.* New York: Random House.

Huntington, S. P. 1996. *The clash of civilizations and the remaking of world order.* New York: Simon and Schuster.

Ignatieff, M. 1994. *Blood and belonging: Journeys into the new nationalism.* New York: Farrar, Straus, and Giroux.

———. 1997a. Unarmed warriors. *New Yorker*, March 24: 54–71.

———. 1997b. Digging up the dead. *New Yorker*, November 10: 84–88, 90–93.

Ignatiev, N. 1995. *How the Irish became white.* New York: Routledge.

Iklé, F. C. 1971. *Every war must end.* New York: Columbia University Press.

Iyob, R. 1995. *The Eritrean struggle for independence: Domination, resistance, nationalism, 1941–1993.* Cambridge: Cambridge University Press.

Jackman, R. W. 1978. The predictability of coups d'état: A model with African data. *American Political Science Review* 72: 1262–75.

Jackson, R. II, and C. G. Rosberg. 1982. Why Africa's weak states persist: The empirical and the juridical in statehood. *World Politics* 35 (1): 1–24.

Jackson, T., and K. Reeves. 1994. Stereotypes and segregation: Neighborhoods in the Detroit area. *American Journal of Sociology* 100 (3): 750–80.

Jalali, R., and S. M. Lipset. 1992–93. Racial and ethnic conflicts: A global perspective. *Political Science Quarterly* 107 (4): 585–606.

Janowitz, M., ed. 1977. *Military institutions and coercion in the developing nations.* Chicago: University of Chicago Press.

———, ed. 1981. *Civil-military relations: Regional perspectives.* Beverly Hills, Calif.: Sage.

Jasper, J. M. 1998. The emotions of protest: Affective and reactive emotions in and around social movements. *Sociological Forum* 13 (3): 397–424.

Jasper, J. M., and J. Goodwin. 1999. Trouble in paradigms. *Sociological Forum* 14 (1): 107–25.

Jaynes, G. D., and R. M. Williams Jr., eds. 1989. *A common destiny: Blacks and American society.* Washington, D.C.: National Academy Press.

Jenkins, J. C. 1982. Why do peasants rebel? Structural and historical theories of modern peasant rebellions. *American Journal of Sociology* 18: 161–85.

Jenkins, J. C., and C. M. Eckert. 1986. Channeling black insurgency: Elite patronage and professional social movement organizations in the development of the black movement. *American Sociological Review* 51: 812–29.

Jenkins, J. C., and B. Klandermans. 1995. *The politics of social protest: Comparative perspectives on states and social movements.* Minneapolis: University of Minnesota Press.

Jenkins, J. C., and A. J. Kposowa. 1990. Explaining military coups d'état: Black Africa, 1957–1984. *American Sociological Review* 55: 861–75.

Jenkins, J. C., and K. Schock. 1992. Global structures and political processes in the study of domestic political conflict. *Annual Review of Sociology* 18: 161–85.

Jentleson, B. W. 1996. Preventive diplomacy and ethnic conflict: Possible, difficult, necessary. *Policy Paper* no. 27. Institute on Global Conflict and Cooperation, University of California, Irvine.

Job, C. 1993. Yugoslavia's ethnic furies. *Foreign Policy* 92: 52–74.

Johnson, T. H., R. D. Slater, and P. McGowan. 1984. Explaining military coups d'état, 1900–1982. *American Political Science Review* 78: 622–40.

Johnston, H. 1991. *Tales of nationalism: Catalonia, 1939–1979.* New Brunswick, N.J.: Rutgers University Press.

Jonassohn, K., with K. S. Björnson. 1998. *Genocide and gross human rights violations in comparative perspective.* New Brunswick, N.J.: Transaction Publishers.

Jowitt, K. 1992. *New world disorder: The Leninist extinction.* Berkeley: University of California Press.

Jürgensmeyer, M. 1993. *The new Cold War? Religious nationalism confronts the secular state.* Berkeley: University of California Press.

Kapferer, B. 1988. *Legends of people, myths of state: Violence, intolerance, and political culture in Sri Lanka and Australia.* Washington, D.C.: Smithsonian Institution Press.

Kaplan, R. D. 1996. *The ends of the earth: A journey at the dawn of the 21st century.* New York: Random House.

Karpat, K. H. 1985. The ethnicity problem in a multi-ethnic national Islamic state:

Continuity and recasting of ethnic identity in the Ottoman state. In *Ethnic groups and the state*, ed. P. R. Brass, 94–114. London: Croom Helm.

Katzenstein, P. K. 1977. Ethnic political conflict in South Tyrol. In *Ethnic conflict in the Western World*, ed. M. J. Esman, 287–323. Ithaca, N.Y.: Cornell University Press.

Keen, S. 1988. *Faces of the enemy: Reflections of the hostile imagination.* New York: Harper and Row.

Kegley, C. W., Jr., and M. G. Hermann. 1995. Military intervention and the democratic peace. *International Interactions* 21 (1): 1–21.

Keith, M. 1993. *Race, riots and policing: Lore and disorder in a multi-racist society.* London: UCL Press.

Kelley, J., and M. D. R. Evans. 1995. Class and class conflict in six Western nations. *American Sociological Review* 60 (2): 157–78.

Kendirbaeva, G. 1997. Migrations in Kazakhstan: Past and present. *Nationalities Papers* 25 (4): 741–51.

Keyfitz, N. 1995. Subdividing national territories: The drive to live in a political community whose boundaries are congruent with the cultural community. *Geographical Analysis* 27 (3): 208–29.

Khalaf, S. 1987. *Lebanon's predicament.* New York: Columbia University Press.

Khawaja, M. 1993. Repression and popular collective action: Evidence from the West Bank. *Sociological Forum* 8 (1): 47–71.

Kidron, M., and R. Segal. 1995. *The state of the world atlas.* 5th ed.. New York: Penguin.

Killian, L. M. 1981. Black power and white reactions: The revitalization of race-thinking in the United States. *The Annals, AAPSS* 454: 42–54.

Kim, H., and P. S. Bearman. 1997. The structure and dynamics of movement participation. *American Sociological Review* 62 (1): 70–93.

Kirk-Green, A. H. M. 1980. "Damnosa Hereditas": Ethnic ranking and the martial races imperative in Africa. *Ethnic and Racial Studies* 3: 393–414.

Kiser, E., K. A. Drass, and W. Brustein. 1995. Ruler autonomy and war in early modern Western Europe. *International Studies Quarterly* 39 (1): 109–38.

Klandermans, B., H. Kriesi, and S. Tarrow, eds. 1986. *From structure to action: Comparing social movement research across cultures.* Greenwich, Conn.: JAI Press.

Klare, M. T. 1995. Stemming the lethal tide in small and light weapons. *Issues in Science and Technology* (fall): 52–58.

———. 2001. *Resource wars: The new landscape of global conflict.* New York: Metropolitan Books.

Knudson, C. M., with I. W. Zartman. 1995. The large small war in Angola. *The Annals, AAPSS* 541: 130–43.

Kober, S. 1994. Idealpolitik. In *Conflict after the Cold War: Arguments on causes of war and peace*, ed. R. K. Betts, 250–79. New York: Macmillan.

Kposowa, A. J., and K. C. Jenkins. 1993. The structural sources of military coups in postcolonial Africa. *American Journal of Sociology* 99 (1): 126–63.

Kroes, R. 1982. The small-town coup: The political intervention in Surinam. *Armed Forces and Society* 9: 115–34.

Kuper, K. 1985. *The prevention of genocide.* New Haven: Yale University Press.

———. 1992. Genocide. In *Encyclopedia of Sociology*, vol. 2, ed. E. F. Borgatta and M. L. Borgatta, 757–62. New York: Macmillan.

Kuropas, M. 1991. *The Ukrainian Americans: Roots and aspirations, 1884–1954.* Toronto: University of Toronto Press.

References

Laitin, D. D. 1998. *Identity in formation: The Russian-speaking populations in the near abroad.* Ithaca, N.Y.: Cornell University Press.

Lake, D. A., and D. Rothchild. 1996. Containing fear: The origins and management of ethnic conflict. *International Security* 21 (2): 41–75.

Lall, B. 1999. Constitutional engineering in post-camp Fiji. Paper presented at the Kellogg Institute Conference on "Constitutional Design 2000." University of Notre Dame, December 9–11.

Larson, G. J. 1995. *India's agony over religion.* Albany: State University of New York Press.

Lash, S., and J. Urry. 1994. *Economies of signs and space.* Thousand Oaks, Calif.: Sage.

Lawson, S. 1995. The politics of authenticity: Ethnonationalist conflict and the state. In *Conflict transformation,* ed. K. Rupesinghe, 116–42. New York: St. Martin's Press.

Lederach, J. P. 1995. Conflict transformation in protracted internal conflicts. In *Conflict transformation,* ed. K. Rupesinghe, 201–22. New York: St. Martin's Press.

Lee, J. 2002. From civil relations to racial conflict: Merchant–customer interactions in urban America. *American Sociological Review* 67 (1): 77–98.

Leifer, E. M. 1981. Competing models of political mobilization: The role of ethnic ties. *American Journal of Sociology* 87: 23–47.

Lemkin, R. 1944. *Axis rule in occupied Europe: Laws of occupation, analysis of government, proposals for redress.* Washington, D.C.: Carnegie Endowment for International Peace, Division of international law.

Lenski, G. 1994. Societal taxonomies: Mapping the social universe. *Annual Review of Sociology* 20: 1–26.

Levine, R. A., and D. T. Campbell. 1972. *Ethnocentrism: Theories of conflict, ethnic attitudes, and group behavior.* New York: Wiley.

Levinson, D., ed. 1991–1993. *Encyclopedia of world cultures,* vols. 1–4. Boston: Kittall.

Lichbach, M. I. 1987. Deterrence or escalation? The puzzle of aggregate studies of repression and dissent. *Journal of Conflict Resolution* 31 (3): 266–97.

———. 1995. *The rebel's dilemma.* Ann Arbor: University of Michigan Press.

Licklider, R., ed. 1993. *Stopping the killing: How civil wars end.* New York: New York University Press.

———. 1995. The consequences of negotiated settlements in civil wars, 1945–1993. *American Political Science Review* 89 (3): 681–90.

Lie, J. 1995. From international migration to transnational diaspora. *Contemporary Sociology* 24 (4): 303–11.

Lijphart, A. 1990. The power-sharing approach. In *Conflict and peacemaking in multiethnic societies,* ed. J. V. Montville, 491–509. Lexington, Mass.: D. C. Heath.

Loveman, M. 1998. High-risk collective action: Defending human rights in Chile, Uruguay, and Argentina. *American Journal of Sociology* 104 (2): 477–525.

Lund, M. S. 1996a. Early warning and preventive diplomacy. In *Managing global chaos: Sources of and responses to international conflict,* ed. C. A. Crocker and F. O. Hampson, with P. Aall, 379–402. Washington, D.C.: United States Institute of Peace Press.

———. 1996b. *Preventing violent conflicts: A strategy for preventive diplomacy.* Washington, D.C.: United States Institute of Peace Press.

Mack, R. W., and R. C. Snyder. 1957. The analysis of social conflict: Toward an overview and synthesis. *Journal of Conflict Resolution* 1: 212–48.

Macy, M. 1991. Chains of cooperation: Threshold effect in collective action. *American Sociological Review* 56 (6): 730–47.

———. 1993. Backward-looking social control. *American Sociological Review* 58 (6): 819–36.

———. 1994. Review of *The critical mass in collective action* by G. Marwell and P. Oliver. *Contemporary Sociology* 23 (5): 663–64.

Macy, M. W., and A. Flache. 1995. Beyond rationality in models of choice. *Annual Review of Sociology* 21: 73–91.

Magagna, V. U. 1991. *Communities of grain: Rural rebellion in comparative perspective.* Ithaca, N.Y.: Cornell University Press.

Malkki, L. H. 1995. *Purity and exile: Violence, memory, and national cosmology among Hutu refugees in Tanzania.* Chicago: University of Chicago Press.

Mandel, R. 1999. Deadly transfer, national hypocrisy, and global chaos. *Armed Forces and Society* 25 (2): 307–28.

Mandell, B. 1992. The Cyprus conflict: Explaining resistance to resolution. In *Cyprus: A regional conflict and its resolution,* ed. N. Salem, 201–26. New York: St. Martin's Press in association with the Canadian Institute for International Peace and Security, Ottawa.

Mann, M. 1993a. *The sources of social power.* Vol. 2, *The rise of classes and nation-states, 1760–1914.* New York: Cambridge University Press.

———. 1993b. Nation-states in Europe and other continents: Diversifying, developing, not dying. *Daedalus* 122 (3): 115–40.

Mansfield, E. D., and J. Snyder. 2001. Democratic transitions and war: From Napoleon to the millennium's end. In *Turbulent peace: The challenges of managing international conflict,* ed. C. A. Crocker, F. O. Hampson, and P. Aall, 113–26. Washington, D.C.: United States Institute of Peace.

Manuel, F. E. 1992. A requiem for Karl Marx. *Daedalus* 121 (2): 1–19.

Maoz, Z. 1997. The controversy over the domestic peace: Rearguard action or cracks in the wall? *International Security* 22 (1): 162–98.

Maoz, Z., and N. Abdolali. 1989. Regime types and international conflict. *Journal of Conflict Resolution* 33 (1): 3–35.

Maoz, Z., and B. Russett. 1992. Alliances, contiguity, wealth, and political stability: Is the lack of conflict between democracies a statistical artifact? *International Interactions* 17 (3): 245–67.

Markides, K. C. 1977. *The rise and fall of the Cyprus Republic.* New Haven: Yale University Press.

Markoff, J., and S. R. D. Baretta. 1986. What we don't know about the coups: Observations on recent South American politics. *Armed Forces and Society* 12: 207–35.

Marshall, M. G. 1993. States at risk: Ethnopolitics in the multinational states of Eastern Europe. In *Minorities at risk,* ed. T. R. Gurr, 173–216. Washington, D.C.: United States Institute for Peace.

Martin, D. 1997. *Does Christianity cause war?* Oxford: Clarendon Press.

Marwell, G., and P. Oliver. 1993. *The critical mass in collective action: A micro-social theory.* Cambridge: Cambridge University Press.

Mason, D., and D. Krane. 1989. The political economy of death squads: Towards a theory of impact of state sanctioned terror. *International Studies Quarterly* 33: 175–98.

Massey, D. S., with N. A. Denton. 1993. *American apartheid: Segregation and the making of the underclass.* Cambridge: Harvard University Press.

References

Massey, D. S., A. B. Gross, and M. L. Eggers. 1991. Segregation, the concentration of poverty, and the life chances of individuals. *Social Science Research* 20: 397–420.

Matlock, J. 1999. The one place NATO could turn for help. *New York Times,* April 20, p. 23.

Mayall, J., and M. Simpson. 1992. Ethnicity is not enough: Reflections on protracted secessionism in the Third World. *International Journal of Comparative Sociology* 33: 5–25.

McAdam, D. 1983. Tactical innovation and the pace of insurgency. *American Sociological Review* 48 (6): 735–54.

McAdam D., J. D. McCarthy, and M. N. Zald, eds. 1996. *Comparative perspectives on social movements: Political opportunities, mobilizing structures, and cultural framings.* New York: Cambridge University Press.

McCarthy, J. D., and M. N. Zald. 1977. Resource mobilization and social movements: A partial theory. *American Journal of Sociology* 82 (6): 1212–41.

McNeely, C. L. 1995. *Constructing the nation-state: International organization and prescriptive action.* Westport, Conn.: Greenwood Press.

Melson, R., and H. Wolpe. 1970. Modernization and the politics of communalism: A theoretical perspective. *American Political Science Review* 64 (4): 1112–30.

Merton, R. 1968. *Social theory and social structure.* Enlarged ed. New York: Free Press.

Meštrović, S. 1995. Review of H. M. Enzensberger, *Civil Wars from L.A. to Bosnia. Contemporary Sociology* 24 (6): 768–69.

Meštrović, S. G., with S. Letica and M. Goreta. 1993. *Habits of the Balkan heart: Social character and the fall of Communism.* College Station: Texas A&M University Press.

Midlarsky, M. I. 1995. Environmental influences on democracy: Aridity, warfare, and a reversal of the causal arrow. *Journal of Conflict Resolution* 39 (2): 224–62.

Minority Rights Group International. 1997. *World Directory of Minorities.* London: Minority Rights International.

Minow, M. 1998. *Between vengeance and forgiveness: Facing history after genocide and mass violence.* Boston: Beacon Press.

Mintz, A., and N. Geva. 1993. Why don't democracies fight each other? An experimental study. *Journal of Conflict Resolution* 37 (3): 484–503.

Mitchell, C. R. 1991. Classifying conflicts: Asymmetry and resolution. *The Annals, AAPSS* 518: 23–38.

Moberg, M. 1997. *Myths of ethnicity and nation: Immigration, work, and identity in the Belize banana industry.* Knoxville: University of Tennessee Press.

Modelski, G. 1964. International settlement of internal wars. In *International aspects of civil strife,* ed. J. N. Rosenau, 14–44. Princeton: Princeton University Press.

Monroe, K. R. 1995. Review essay: The psychology of genocide. *Ethics and International Affairs* 9: 215–39.

———. 1996. *The heart of altruism: Perceptions of a common humanity.* Princeton: Princeton University Press.

Montville, J. V., ed. 1990. *Conflict and peacemaking in multiethnic societies.* Lexington, Mass.: D. C. Heath.

Moodie, M. 1995. The Balkan tragedy. *The Annals, AAPSS* 541: 101–15.

Moore, W. H. 1995. Action-reaction or rational expectations? Reciprocity and the domestic-international conflict nexus during the "Rhodesia problem." *Journal of Conflict Resolution* 39 (1): 129–67.

Moran, R. F. Courts and the construction of racial and ethnic identity: Public law litigation in the Denver schools. *Bulletin — American Academy of Arts and Sciences* 2 (6): 19–39.

Morris, A. D. 1984. *The origins of the civil rights movement: Black communities organizing for change.* New York: Free Press.

Morrison, A. 2000. Disentangling disputes: Conflict in the international arena. In *Patterns of conflict: Paths to peace,* ed. L. J. Fisk and J. L. Schellenberg, 67–101. Peterborough, Ont.: Broadview Press.

Morrison, P. A., and I. S. Lowry. 1994. A riot of color: The demographic setting. In *The Los Angeles Riots: Lessons for the Urban Future,* ed. M. Baldassare, 19–46. Boulder, Colo.: Westview Press.

Muller, E. N. 1985. Income inequality, regime repressiveness, and political violence. *American Sociological Review* 50 (1): 47–61.

Nachtwey, J. 1999. *Inferno.* New York: Phaidon.

Nagel, J., and S. Olzak. 1982. Ethnic mobilization in new and old states: An extension of the competition model. *Social Problems* 30: 127–43.

Nanda, V. P. 1992. Ethnic conflicts in Fiji and human rights law. 25 *Cornell International Law Journal* 565: 570–71.

Neilsson, G. P. 1985. States and "nation groups," a global taxonomy. In *New nationalisms of the developed West: Toward explanation,* ed. E. A. Tiryakian and R. Rogowski, 27–56. Boston: Allen and Unwin.

Newbury, C. 1988. *The cohesion of oppression: Clientship and ethnicity in Rwanda, 1860–1960.* New York: Columbia University Press.

Newman, S. G. 1995. The arms trade, military assistance, and recent wars: Change and continuity. *The Annals, AAPSS* 541: 47–74.

Nielsen, F. 1985. Toward a theory of ethnic solidarity in modern societies. *American Sociological Review* 50 (2): 133–49.

———. 1994. Sociobiology and sociology. *Annual Review of Sociology* 20: 267–303.

Oberschall, A. 1973. *Social conflict and social movements.* Englewood Cliffs, N.J.: Prentice-Hall.

Olson, M. 1965. *The logic of collective action: Public goods and the theory of groups.* Cambridge: Harvard University Press.

Olzak, S. 1983. Contemporary ethnic mobilization. *Annual Review of Sociology* 9: 355–74.

———. 1992. *The dynamics of ethnic competition and conflict.* Stanford: Stanford University Press.

Orbell, J., L. Zeng, and M. Mulford. 1996. Individual experiences and the fragmentation of societies. *American Sociological Review* 61 (6): 1018–32.

Orlove, B. S. 1990. Rebels and Theorists: An examination of peasant uprising in southern Peru. In *Research in social movements, conflicts and change,* ed. L. Kriesberg, 139–87. Greenwich, Conn.: JAI Press.

Ottaway, M. 1991. Mediation in a transitional conflict: Eritrea. *The Annals, AAPSS* 518: 69–81.

Paige, J. 1975. *Agrarian revolution.* New York: Free Press.

Pavlowitch, S. K. 1994. Who is "Balkanizing" whom? The misunderstandings between the debris of Yugoslavia and an unprepared West. *Daedalus* 123 (2): 203–23.

Peach, C. 1986. A geographic perspective on the 1981 urban riots in England. *Ethnic and Racial Studies* 9: 396–411.

Perruzotti, E. 1996. The politics of rights in post-dictatorial Argentina: An evaluation. Paper presented to Peace Studies Program/Latin American Studies Program, October 17, Cornell University.

Petersen, R. 1998. Fear, hatred, resentment: Delineating paths to ethnic violence in Eastern Europe. Unpublished manuscript, Department of Political Science, Washington University, St. Louis, Mo.

Pettigrew, T. F. 1998. Reactions toward the new minorities of Western Europe. *Annual Review of Sociology* 24: 77–103.

Pfaff, W. 1992. The absence of empire. *New Yorker*, August 10: 59–69.

Pfaffenberger, B. 1994. The structure of protracted conflict: The case of Sri Lanka. *Humboldt Journal of Social Relations* 20 (2): 121–47.

Pieterse, J. N. 1997. Sociology of humanitarian intervention: Bosnia, Rwanda and Somalia compared. *International Political Science Review* 18 (1): 71–93.

Pillar, P. 1983. *Negotiating peace: War termination as a bargaining process.* Princeton: Princeton University Press.

Pinard, M., and R. Hamilton. 1986. Motivational dimensions in the Quebec independence movement: A test of a new model. In *Research in social movements, conflicts and change,* vol. 9, ed. K. Lang and G. E. Lang, 225–80. Greenwich, Conn.: JAI Press.

Pinnawala, S. K. 1992. Ethnic separatism in Sri Lanka: Some observations and comments on internationalization of ethnic conflict. Unpublished paper, Peace Studies Program, Cornell University.

Pi-Sunyer, O. 1985. Catalan nationalism: Some theoretical and historical considerations. In *New nationalisms of the developed West: Toward explanation,* ed. E. A. Tiryakian and R. Rogowski, 254–76. Boston: Allen and Unwin.

Pollis, A. 1994. The Greek concept of national identity. *ASEN Bulletin* (London School of Economics) (spring-summer): 11–14.

Portes, A. 1984. The rise of ethnicity: Determinants of ethnic perceptions among Cuban exiles in Miami. *American Sociological Review* 49: 383–97.

Portes, A., L. Guarnizo, and P. Landolt. 1999. The study of transnationalism: Pitfalls and promise of an emergent research field. *Ethnic and Racial Studies* 22 (2): 217–37.

Poulter, S. 1998. *Ethnicity, law and human rights: The English experience.* Oxford: Clarendon Press.

Prager, J. 1982. American racial ideology as collective representation. *Ethnic and Racial Studies* 5 (1): 99–119.

Proctor, R. N. 1999. *The Nazi war on cancer.* Princeton: Princeton University Press.

Prunier, G. 1995. *The Rwanda crisis, 1954–1994: History of a genocide.* London: Hurst.

Purcell, T. W., and K. Sawyer. 1993. Democracy and ethnic conflict: Blacks in Costa Rica. *Ethnic and Racial Studies* 16 (2): 298–322.

Quillian, L. 1995. Prejudice as a response to perceived group threat: Population composition and anti-immigrant and racial prejudice in Europe. *American Sociological Review* 60 (4): 586–611.

Ra'anan, U. 1990. The nation-state fallacy. In *Conflict and Peacemaking in Multiethnic Societies,* ed. J. V. Montville, 5–20. Lexington, Mass.: D. C. Heath.

Rao, A. 1999. The many sources of identity: An example of changing affiliations in rural Jammu and Kashmir. *Ethnic and Racial Studies* 22 (1): 56–91.

Ratcliffe, P., ed. 1994. *"Race," ethnicity and nation: International perspectives on social conflict.* London: UCL Press.

Ridgeway, C. L., E. H. Boyle, K. J. Kuipers, and D. T. Robinson. 1998. How do status beliefs develop? The role of resources and interactional experience. *American Sociological Review* 63 (3): 331–50.

Roeder, P. 1999. Ethnicity within the state. Lecture, University of California, Irvine. Global Peace and Conflict Studies Seminar, March 11.

Rose, P. I. 1993. "Of every hue and caste": Race, immigration, and perceptions of pluralism. *The Annals, AAPSS* 530: 187–202.

Ross, J. A. 1980. The mobilization of collective identity: An analytical overview. In *The mobilization of collective identity: Comparative perspectives*, ed. J. A. Ross and A. B. Cottrell, with R. St.-Syr and P. Rawkins, 1–30. Lanham, Md.: University Press of America.

Rothchild, D. 1986. Hegemonial exchange: An alternative model for managing conflict in Middle Africa. In *Ethnicity, politics, and development*, ed. D. L. Thompson and D. Ronen, 65–104. Boulder, Colo.: L. Rienner.

Rothchild, D., and C. Hartzell. 1991. Great- and medium-power mediations: Angola. *The Annals, AAPSS* 518: 39–57.

Roy, W. G. 1984. Class conflict and social change in historical perspective. *Annual Review of Sociology* 10: 483–506.

Rubin, E. 1998. Letter from Uganda: Our children are killing us. *New Yorker*, March 23: 56–64.

Rule, J. B. 1988. *Theories of civil violence.* Berkeley: University of California Press.

Rummel, R. J. 1994. *Death by government: Genocide and mass murder since 1900.* New Brunswick, N.J.: Transaction Publishers.

———. 1995a. Democracy, power, genocide, and mass murder. *Journal of Conflict Resolution* 39 (1): 3–26.

———. 1995b. Democracies ARE less warlike than other regimes. *European Journal of International Relations* 1 (4): 457–79.

———. 1996. *Lethal politics: Soviet genocide and mass murder since 1917.* New Brunswick, N.J.: Transaction Publishers.

Rupesinghe, K., ed. 1995. *Conflict transformation.* New York: St. Martin's Press.

Russett, B., and H. Starr. 1989. *World politics: The menu for choice.* 2nd ed. New York: Freeman.

Ruth, A. 1997. Postwar Europe: The capriciousness of universal values. *Daedalus* 126 (3): 241–76.

Ryan, S. 1990. Ethnic conflict and the United Nations. *Ethnic and Racial Studies* 13: 25–49.

———. 1995. Transforming violent intercommune conflict. In *Conflict transformation*, ed. K. Rupesinghe, 223–65. New York: St. Martin's Press.

Sahlins, P. 1989. *Boundaries: The making of France and Spain in the Pyrenees.* Berkeley: University of California Press.

Saine, A. S. M. 1996. The coup d'état in The Gambia, 1994: The end of the First Republic. *Armed Forces and Society* 23 (1): 97–11.

Saunders, H. H. 1999. *A public peace process: Sustained dialogue to transform racial and ethnic conflicts.* New York: St. Martin's Press.

Schaeffer, R. K. 1990. *Warpaths: The politics of partition.* New York: Hill and Wang.

Scheff, T. J. 1994. *Bloody revenge: Emotions, nationalism, and war.* Boulder, Colo.: Westview Press.

Schelling, T. 1960. *The strategy of conflict.* Cambridge: Harvard University Press.

References

Schermerhorn, R. A. 1970. *Comparative ethnic relations: A framework for theory and research.* New York: Random House.

Schermerhorn, R. A. 1978. *Ethnic plurality in India.* Tuscon: University of Arizona Press.

Schnapper, D. 1997. The European debate on citizenship. *Daedalus* 126 (3): 199–222.

———. 1998. *Community of citizens: On the modern idea of nationality.* Trans. S. Rosée. New Brunswick, N.J.: Transaction Publishers.

Schultz, R. H. 1995. State disintegration and ethnic conflict: A framework for analysis. *The Annals, AAPSS* 541: 75–88.

Sereseres, C. 1996. The regional peacekeeping role of the Organization of American States: Nicaragua, 1990–1993. In *Managing global chaos: Sources of and responses to international conflict,* ed. C. A. Crocker and F. O. Hampson, with P. Aall, 551–85. Washington, D.C.: United States Institute of Peace Press.

Seymore, B., II, ed. 1994. *The Access guide to ethnic conflicts in Europe and the Former Soviet Union.* Washington, D.C.: Access.

Shafir, G. 1995. *Immigrants and nationalists: Ethnic conflict and accommodation in Catalonia, the Basque country, Latvia, and Estonia.* Albany: State University of New York Press.

Sharp, G. 1973. *The politics of nonviolent action.* Boston: Porter Sargent.

Sheffer, G., ed. 1986. *Modern diasporas in international politics.* London: Croom Helm.

Shnirelman, V. 1995. The past as a strategy for ethnic confrontation. *HCA Quarterly.* Helsinki Citizens Assembly, no. 14: 20–22.

Shtromas, A. 1990. The future world order and the right of nations to self-determination and sovereignity. *International Journal on World Peace* 7 (1): 17–49.

Shugart, M. A. 1992. Guerrillas and elections: An internationalist perspective on the costs of conflict and cooperation. *International Studies Quarterly* 36: 121–52.

Shweder, R. A., H. R. Markus, M. L. Minow, and F. Kessel. 1997. The free exercise of culture: Ethnic customs, assimilation and American law. *Social Science Research Council Items* 51 (4), Part 1: 61–67.

Simon, H. 1990. A mechanism for social selection and successful altruism. *Science* 21: 1665–68.

Slocum, J. W. 1995. Disintegration and consolidation: National separatism and the evolution of center-periphery relations in the Russian Federation. *Occasional Paper #19.* 58 pp. Peace Studies Program, Cornell University.

Small, M., and J. D. Singer. 1982. *Resort to arms: International and civil wars, 1816–1980.* Beverly Hills, Calif.: Sage Publications.

Smith, A. D. 1981. *The ethnic revival.* Cambridge: Cambridge University Press.

———. 1984. National identity and myths of ethnic descent. In *Research in social movements, conflicts and change,* vol. 7, ed. L. Kriesberg, 95–130. Greenwich, Conn.: JAI Press.

———. 1986. Conflict and collective identity: Class, *ethnie* and nation. In *International conflict resolution: Theory and practice,* ed. E. E. Azar and J. W. Burton, 63–84. Brighton, Sussex: Wheatsheaf.

———. 1989. The origins of nations. *Ethnic and Racial Studies* 12: 340–67.

———. 1992. Chosen peoples: Why ethnic groups survive. *Ethnic and Racial Studies* 15: 436–56.

Smith, D., et al. 1997. *The state of war and peace atlas.* 3rd ed. New York: Penguin Reference.

Smith, D. N. 2000. Genocide. In *Encyclopedia of Sociology*, 2nd ed., vol. 2, ed. E. F. Borgatta and R. J. V. Montgomery, 1066–73. New York: Macmillan.

Snow, D. A., and S. E. Marshall. 1984. Cultural imperialism, social movements, and the Islamic revival. In *Research in social movements, conflicts and change*, vol. 7, ed. L. Kriesberg, 131–52. Greenwich, Conn.: JAI Press.

Snyder, J. L. 1990. Averting anarchy in the New Europe. *International Security* 14 (4): 5–41

Sofsky, W. 1997. *The order of terror: The concentration camp.* Trans. W. Templer. Princeton: Princeton University Press.

Spencer, D., and W. Spencer. 1995. Third-party mediation and conflict transformation: Experiences in Ethiopia, Sudan, and Liberia. In *Conflict transformation*, ed. K. Rupesinghe, 162–200. New York: St. Martin's Press.

Spencer, M. 1998. *Separatism: Democracy and disintegration.* Lanham, Md.: Rowman and Littlefield.

St. John, O. P. 1996. Algeria: A case study of insurgency in the New World Order. *Small wars and insurgencies* 7 (2): 196–219.

Stack, J. F. Jr., ed. 1981. *Ethnic identities in a transnational world.* Westport, Conn.: Greenwood Press.

Stedman, S. J. 1991. *Peacemaking in civil war: International mediation in Zimbabwe, 1974–1980.* Boulder, Colo.: L. Rienner.

Stein, K. W., and S. W. Lewis. 1996. Mediation in the Middle East. In *Managing global chaos: Sources of and responses to international conflict*, ed. C. A. Crocker and F. O. Hampson, with P. Aall, 463–73. Washington, D.C.: United States Institute of Peace Press.

Steiner, J. 1990. Power sharing: Another Swiss "export product"? In *Conflict and peacemaking in multiethnic societies*, ed. J. V. Montville, 107–14. Lexington, Mass.: Lexington Books.

Stevenson, J. 1996–97. Northern Ireland: Treating terrorists as statesmen. *Foreign Policy* 105: 125–40.

Strang, D. 1996. Review of *Constructing the nation-state: International organization and prescriptive action* by C. L. McNeely. *American Journal of Sociology* 102 (2): 601–2.

Sugrue, T. J. 1996. *The origins of the urban crisis: Race and inequality in postwar Detroit.* Princeton: Princeton University Press.

Suny, R. G. 1991. The Soviet South: Nationalism and the outside world. In *The rise of nations in the Soviet Union*, ed. M. Mandelbaum, 64–88. New York: Council on Foreign Relations.

Sutter, D. 1995. Settling old scores: Potholes along the transition from authoritarian rule. *Journal of Conflict Resolution* 39 (1): 110–28.

———. 1998. Calculation of self-interest and constitutional consensus: The role of ideology. *Constitutional Political Economy* 9 (4): 232–33.

Swartzman, K. C. 1998. Globalization and democracy. *Annual Review of Sociology* 24: 159–81.

Swingle, P. G. 1970. Preface. In *The structure of conflict*, ed. P. G. Swingle, ix. New York: Academic Press.

Szporluk, R. 1997. Ukraine: From an imperial periphery to a sovereign state. *Daedalus* 126 (3): 85–119.

Taagepera, R. 1993. *Estonia: Return to independence.* Boulder, Colo.: Westview Press.

Tajfel, C. 1970. Experiments in intergroup discrimination. *Science* 223 (11): 96–102.

References

Tamamoto, M. 1995. Reflections on Japan's postwar state. *Daedalus* 124 (2): 1–22.
Tambiah, S. J. 1986. *Sri Lanka: Ethnic fratricide and the dismantling of democracy.* Chicago: University of Chicago Press.
———. 1996. *Leveling crowds: Ethno-nationalist conflicts and collective violence in South Asia.* Berkeley: University of California Press.
———. 2000. Transnational movements, diaspora, and multiple modernities. *Daedalus* 129 (1): 163–94.
Tarrow, S. 1996. Social movements in contentious politics: A review article. *American Political Science Review* 90: 1–10.
———. 1998. *Power in movement: Social movements and contentious politics.* Cambridge: Cambridge University Press.
Tavuchis, N. 1991. *Mea culpa: A sociology of apology and reconciliation.* Stanford, Calif.: Stanford University Press.
Taylor, P. J. 1991. Political geography within world-system analysis. *Review* 14 (3): 387–402.
Thomas, G. M., and J. W. Meyer. 1984. The expansion of the state. *Annual Review of Sociology* 10: 461–82.
Thompson, J. L. P., and G. A. Quets. 1990. Genocide and social conflict: A partial theory and a comparison. In *Research in social movements, conflicts and change,* vol. 12, ed. L. Kriesberg, 256–66. Greenwich, Conn.: JAI Press.
Thompson, W. R. 1995. Principled rivalries. *Journal of Conflict Resolution* 39 (2): 195–223.
Thomson, J. E. 1994. *Mercenaries, pirates, and sovereigns: State-building and extraterritorial violence in early modern Europe.* Princeton: Princeton University Press.
Thórarinsdóttir, F. 1994. Nation, state, and language: An invented unity. *Working Paper No. 88.* New School for Social Research. 56 pp. New York: Center for Studies of Social Change.
Thucydides. *The Peloponnesian Wars.* 1963. Trans. B. Jowett, rev. and abridged with an introduction by P. A. Brunt. New York: Twayne Publishers (Washington Square Press).
Tilly, C. 1992. *Coercion, capital, and European states, A.D. 990–1992.* Cambridge, Mass.: Basil Blackwell.
———. 1993. State-initiated violence, 1900–1990. *Working Paper* no. 177. New School for Social Research. New York: Center for Studies of Social Change.
———. 1999. Durable inequality. In *A nation divided: Diversity, inequality, and community in American society,* ed. P. Moen, D. Dempster-McClain, and H. A. Walker, 15–33. Ithaca, N.Y.: Cornell University Press.
Tilly, C., L. Tilly, and R. Tilly. 1975. *The rebellious century, 1830–1930.* Cambridge: Harvard University Press.
Tiryakian, E. A. 1997. The wild cards of modernity. *Daedalus* 126 (2): 147–81.
Tiryakian, E. A., and R. Rogowski, eds. 1985. *New nationalisms of the developed West: Toward explanation.* Boston: Allen and Unwin.
Torpey, J. 2000. *The invention of the passport: Surveillance, citizenship, and the state.* Cambridge: Cambridge University Press.
Touraine, A. 1985. Sociological interventionism and the internal dynamics of the Occitanist movement. In *New nationalisms of the developed West: Toward explanation,* ed. E. A. Tiryakian and R. Rogowski, 157–75. Boston: Allen and Unwin.
Trivers, R. 1985. *Social evolution.* Menlo Park, Calif.: Benjamin/Cummings.

Tsebelis, G., and J. Sprague. 1989. Coercion and revolution: Variations on a preda-tor-prey model. *Mathematical and Computer Modeling* 12: 547–60.

Tuchman, B. W. 1962. *The Guns of August*. New York: Macmillan.

Turton, D. 1997. *War and ethnicity: Global connections and local violence*. Rochester, N.Y.: University of Rochester Press.

Ullman, R. H. 1991. *Securing Europe*. Princeton: Princeton University Press.

van den Berghe, P. L. 1981. *The ethnic phenomenon*. New York: Elsevier.

———. 1987. *The ethnic phenomenon*. New York: Praeger.

———, ed. 1990. *State violence and ethnicity*. Boulder, Colo.: Westview Press.

———. 1992. The modern state: Nation-builder or nation-killer? *International Journal of Group Tensions* 22 (3): 191–208.

———. 1993. Does race matter? Working paper, Department of Sociology, Uni-versity of Washington, Seattle.

———. 1996. Denationalizing the state. *Society* (January–February): 64–68.

Van Dyke, V. 1985. *Human rights, ethnicity, and discrimination*. Westport, Conn.: Greenwood Press.

Van Evera, S. 1994. Hypotheses on nationalism and war. *International Security* 18 (4): 5–39.

———. 1998. Offense, defense, and the causes of war. *International Security* 22 (4): 5–43.

Vanhanen, T. 1997. *Prospects of democracy: A study of 172 countries*. New York: Rout-ledge.

Van Zyl Slabbert, F., and D. Welsh. 1979. *South Africa's options: Strategies for sharing power*. New York: St. Martin's Press.

Verdery, K. 1993. Whither "nation" and "nationalism"? *Daedalus* 122 (3): 37–62.

Vogel, J. 1991. Culture, politics, and national identity in Cote d'Ivoire. *Social Re-search* 58: 439–56.

Wallensteen, P., and M. Sollenburg. 1999. Armed conflict, 1989–98. *Journal of Peace Research* 36 (5): 593–606.

Waller, D. V. 1992. Ethnic mobilization and geopolitics in the Soviet Union: To-ward a theoretical understanding. *Journal of Political and Military Sociology* 20: 37–62.

Walter, B. F. 1997. The critical barrier to civil war settlement. *International Organi-zation* 51: 335–64.

———. 1999. The critical barrier to civil war settlement. In *Civil wars, insecurity, and intervention*, ed. B. F. Walter and J. Snyder, 38–69. New York: Columbia Uni-versity Press.

Weaver, M. A. 1990. Balochistan. *New Yorker*, January 15: 82–101.

Weber, E. 1976. *Peasants into Frenchmen: The modernization of rural France, 1870–1914*. Stanford, Calif.: Stanford University Press.

Wedge, B. 1986. Psychology of the self in social conflict. In *International conflict res-olution: Theory and practice*, ed. E. E. Azar and J. W. Burton, 56–62. Brighton, Sus-sex: Wheatsheaf Books.

Weiner, M. 1997. *Japan's minorities: The illusion of homogeneity*. New York: Routledge.

Welch, C. E. Jr. 1986. Ethnic factors in African armies. *Ethnic and Racial Studies* 9: 321–33.

———. 1995. Civil-military agonies in Nigeria: Pains of an unaccomplished tran-sition. *Armed Forces and Society* 21 (4): 593–614.

References

White, R. W., and T. E. White. 1995. Repression and the liberal state: The case of Northern Ireland. *Journal of Conflict Resolution* 39 (2): 330–52.

Widner, J. A. 1995. States and statelessness in late twentieth-century Africa. *Daedalus* 124 (3): 129–53.

Williams, R. M. Jr. 1947. *The reduction of intergroup tensions: A survey of research on problems of ethnic, racial, and religious group relations.* Bulletin 57. New York: Social Science Research Council.

———. 1964. *Strangers next door: Ethnic relations in American communities.* Englewood Cliffs, N.J.: Prentice-Hall.

———. 1977. *Mutual accommodation: Ethnic conflict and cooperation.* Minneapolis: University of Minnesota Press.

———. 1978. Intergroup relations: Problems of conflict and accommodation. In *Sociocultural change since 1950*, ed. T. L. Smith and M. S. Das, 153–92. New Delhi: Vikas Publishing House.

———. 1982. Individual welfare and collective dilemmas: Problems without solutions? In *Social structure and behavior: Essays in honor of William Hamilton Sewell*, ed. R. M. Hauser, D. Mechanic, A. O. Haller, and T. S. Hauser, 351–82. New York: Academic Press.

———. 1994. The sociology of ethnic conflicts: Comparative international perspectives. *Annual Review of Sociology* 20: 49–79.

———. 1999. The reduction of intergroup tensions. In *A nation divided: Diversity, inequality, and community in American society*, ed. P. Moen, D. Dempster-McClain, and H. A. Walker, 277–95. Ithaca, N.Y.: Cornell University Press.

———. 2001. Ethnic conflicts. In *International encyclopedia of the social and behavioral sciences*, ed. N. J. Smelser and P. B. Baltes, 4806–10. New York: Elsevier.

Wilson, R. 1995. *Maya resurgence in Guatemala: Q'eqchi' experiences.* Norman: University of Oklahoma Press.

Wippman, D. 1995. Ethnic conflict, internal powersharing, and international law. School of Law, Cornell University.

Wright, Q. 1965. *A study of war.* Rev. ed. Chicago: University of Chicago Press.

Wright, R. 1994. *The moral animal: The new science of evolutionary psychology.* New York: Pantheon.

Yancey, W., E. P. Ericksen, and R. N. Juliani. 1976. Emergent ethnicity: A review and reformulation. *American Sociological Review* 41 (3): 391–403.

Young, C. 1976. *The politics of cultural pluralism.* Madison: University of Wisconsin Press.

———. 1985. Ethnicity and the colonial and post-colonial state in Africa. In *Ethnic groups and the state*, ed. P. Brass, 59–93. London: Croom Helm.

Young, R. A. 1995. *The secession of Quebec and the future of Canada.* Montreal: McGill–Queens University Press.

Yun, M. S. 1990. Ethnonationalism, ethnic nationalism, and mini-nationalism: A comparison of Connor, Smith and Snyder. *Ethnic and Racial Studies* 13: 527–41.

Zachary, G. P. 2000. Market forces add ammunition to civil wars. *Wall Street Journal*, June 12: A21.

Zartman, I. W. 1984. Negotiation: Theory and reality. In *National negotiation: Art and science*, ed. D. Bendahame and J. McDonald Jr., 1–8. Washington, D.C.: U.S. Department of State, Foreign Service Institute.

———. 1989. *Ripe for resolution: Conflict and intervention in Africa.* 2nd ed. New York: Oxford University Press.

————. 1991. Preface; Conflict and resolution: Contest, cost, and change. *The Annals, AAPSS* 518: 8–22.

————, ed. 1995. *Collapsed states: The disintegration and restoration of legitimate authority.* Boulder, Colo.: Westview Press.

Zaslavsky, V. 1992. Nationalism and democratic transition in postcommunist societies. *Daedalus* 121 (2): 97–121.

Zhao, D. 1998. Ecologies of student movements: Student mobilization during the 1989 prodemocracy movement in Beijing. *American Journal of Sociology* 103 (3): 1493–1529.

Zimmerman, E. 1980. Macro-comparative research on political protest. In *Handbook of political conflict: Theory and research,* ed. T. R. Gurr, 167–237. New York: Free Press.

Zimmermann, W. 1996. *Origins of a catastrophe: Yugoslavia and its destroyers — America's last ambassador tells what happened and why.* New York: Times Books/Random House.

Zolberg, A. 1968. The structure of political conflict in the new states of tropical Africa. *American Political Science Review* 62 (1): 70–87.

Zviagelskaia, J. D. 1991. Steps versus solutions in the Arab–Israeli conflict. *The Annals, AAPSS* 518: 109–17.

Index

Index